The Formative Period of Islamic Thought

The Formative Period of Islamic Thought

W
MONTGOMERY
WATT

at the University Press
Edinburgh

Edinburgh University Press
22 George Square, Edinburgh
ISBN 0 85224 245 X
North America
Aldine. Atherton, Inc.
529 South Wabash Avenue, Chicago
Library of Congress
Catalog Card Number 73-79266
Printed in Great Britain by
Western Printing Services Ltd.
Bristol

Preface

Since writing the doctoral thesis which appeared in 1949 as *Free Will and Predestination in Early Islam* I have continued to be interested in the Islamic sects and have written a number of articles on aspects of the subject. Through my own work in this field and that of other scholars I have become convinced that, before any attempt is made to describe the development of Islamic thought, there has to be a radical critique of the sources. The standard Muslim writers see theological doctrine as already given in the revelation and as unchanging; as Henri Laoust has put it, they are concerned not with 'the history of the sects' but with 'a normative classification of these sects in respect of their greater or lesser distance from Sunnism' (*Gibb Festschrift*, 386). Because of this these writers are unable to appreciate the possibility that a doctrine eventually found unsatisfactory and rejected may yet have made a positive contribution to the development. The modern scholar has therefore to be highly critical of the sources and to detect and make allowance for the assumptions implicit in them. The present book is based on a radical critique of this kind, the principles of which are set out in the Introduction, while the following chapters provide confirmatory evidence. On this basis I have tried to present a coherent picture of the way in which Islamic thought developed in the period up to about A.D. 950. The materials available and accessible are already vast and are constantly being added to, and consequently, especially in the later chapters, all that can be given is an outline of the history. Nevertheless, since the outline which emerges from a radical critique differs in a number of points from the commonly accepted views, it has seemed important at the present stage of scholarship to survey the whole period and to give as coherent a picture as possible.

When I commenced this book I had hoped to include all that I still regarded as valuable in *Free Will and Predestination*, but as I proceeded I realized that to do so would lead to imbalance in the treatment, and therefore some material was condensed or omitted altogether. Something similar applies to my articles. It may also be remarked that in respect of biographical notices and the like the references are far from being exhaustive.

The system of transliteration is that employed in the Islamic Surveys Series of Edinburgh University Press. Common geographical names are given the usual spelling. With regard to dates, where only the year was mentioned in the sources, the convention has been adopted of giving the Christian year in which the Islamic year began.

My special thanks are due to Professors Josef van Ess and Annemarie Schimmel for helping me with unpublished material, to many other friends who have sent me offprints, and to Miss Helen Pratt and Miss Irene Crawford for typing assistance.

W. Montgomery Watt

Contents

Introduction

While the title of this book is intended to give some idea of its contents, certain aspects require to be explained more precisely. The term 'Islamic thought', for example, may seem to have been restricted to theology; but the reply may be made that 'thought' rather than 'theology' is justified in the title, since during the period under consideration religious doctrine was at the centre of the intellectual life of the whole community, including its political life, and had not become an academic preserve for professional theologians. The term 'formative period' indicates that the book is concerned with development; and this indeed gives it its distinctive claim to the attention of scholars. It sets out to show the lines along which the history of the development of Islamic thought has to be rewritten after due weight has been given to a radical critique of the heresiographical tradition.

The outstanding work in the heresiographical tradition is the *Book of Sects and Parties* of ash-Shahrastānī (d. 1153). Muslim and European scholars alike have regarded it as the basic work in this field. It was preceded by the book of sects of (Abū-Manṣūr 'Abd-al-Qāhir) al-Baghdādī (d. 1037), entitled *Al-farq bayn al-firaq*, which appears to be the earliest work in which the tradition has taken shape. There were of course many previous works containing information about sectarian views. A unique place is occupied by the *Maqālāt al-islāmiyyīn* of al-Ash'arī (d. 935), and Hellmut Ritter has listed a dozen earlier writers who provide information about sects: al-Yamān ibn-Ribāb, Ja'far ibn-Ḥarb, Sulaymān ibn-Jarīr, al-Karābīsī, Abū-'Īsā al-Warrāq, al-Jāḥiẓ, Ibn-Qutayba, Ibn-ar-Rāwandī, al-Khayyāṭ, Zurqān, an-Nawbakhtī and al-Ka'bī.[1] Most of these will be mentioned in the course of this book. Several are quoted by al-Ash'arī, but they are chiefly polemical writers. An-Nawbakhtī's book of *The Sects of the Shīʿa* is extant and is both a heresiography and a piece of Shīʿite apologetic.[2]

The special feature which marks the mature form of the heresiographical tradition in al-Baghdādī is that the sects have become the centre of interest for their own sakes, or at least for purposes of refutation. In al-Ashʿarī, on the other hand, though at one or two points the doctrines of a sect are given as a whole, for the most part he arranges his material under topics, and under each heading gives the views of various sects and individual thinkers. The new conception of heresiography seen in al-Baghdādī and ash-Shahrastānī,[3] though it doubtless has roots in the ninth century, appears to be closely connected with the Traditions about seventy-three sects. According to the version placed by al-Baghdādī at the opening of his book Muḥammad said: 'the Jews are divided into seventy-one sects and the Christians into seventy-two, but my community will be divided into seventy-three sects'; other versions are also given.

Ignaz Goldziher appears to have been the first European scholar to appreciate the importance and the problematic character of this Tradition. He plausibly argues that it is derived from another Tradition in which Muḥammad said that 'faith has seventy-odd branches'.[4] One can understand a Muslim being proud of the virtues of his religious community, but the multiplicity of sects is hardly a matter for pride. How did the Tradition about seventy-three sects come to find acceptance among Muslims? Perhaps a group of extreme rigorists was happy to maintain that they belonged to the one 'saved sect' (*firqa nājiya*) while the other seventy-two sects would go to Hell. It would seem, however, that there was a close connection between this Tradition and the study of the sects. Muslim scholars have always been hesitant in studying and expounding the views of an opponent except in so far as was necessary in order to refute them. Of the books in the great pre-Islamic library at Alexandria the caliph ʿUmar is alleged to have said, 'If they are in accordance with the Qur'ān, they are superfluous, and if they are contrary to the Qur'ān, they are dangerous; and so in either case they may be destroyed.' It is thus remarkable to find some of the heresiographers giving full and more or less objective accounts of heretical sects. The study of sects, then, we conclude, must have served some interest in these men. Perhaps the chief point was that these false views, by presenting a contrast, made possible a more precise formulation of the true doctrines.

While such speculations are entertaining, it is more important to note that the heresiographers proceeded within a framework created by certain assumptions. These may be summarized as follows:

1) Islamic doctrine and dogma was expressed in the Qur'ān and was fully present from the first in the community of Muslims. There could be no development of doctrine. At most it might be admitted that a scholar like Aḥmad ibn-Ḥanbal, because of the contemporary situation, placed more emphasis on the doctrine of the uncreated Qur'ān than most of his predecessors; but it would also be asserted that the doctrine had always been held (at least implicitly?) by sound scholars.[5]

2) There were no serious cleavages of opinion within the main body of 'Sunnite' scholars, but all held the chief elements of what was later accepted as Sunnite teaching; there were no deviants apart from the relatively small number whose strange views have been recorded. In opposition to this assumption the occidental scholar will hold that many of the trends of thought to be studied in this book occurred *within* the supposedly monolithic main body, and that the heresiographers glossed over these differences. He will also hold that one cannot properly speak of Sunnism until the later ninth century.

3) The primary concern of the heresiographers is whether a particular view is true or false; they are never in a position to ask whether a certain sect has contributed to the general development of thought.

4) A common aim of the heresiographers is the classification or grouping together of sects according to family resemblances between the doctrines held. Sometimes this may roughly correspond to the organic or historical connections between sects, but in other cases it may be seriously misleading, as, for example, with the Zaydiyya.

In addition to the misrepresentations involved in these assumptions, there are also certain misleading procedures which should be noted so that allowance may be made for them.

1) Al-Baghdādī and ash-Shahrastānī adopted various tricks to ensure that the number of heretical sects was exactly seventy-two. Individual Mu'tazilites, because their views differed in points of detail, were treated as sects; and so al-Baghdādī, where al-Ash'arī had spoken of the individuals, speaks of sects of Iskāfiyya, Thumāmiyya, Jāḥiẓiyya, Shaḥḥāmiyya and the like. At certain points al-Baghdādī

reduced the number of sects by holding that the views of a group were so heretical that they were outside the community of Muslims.
2) Any writer, reporting the views of other people, tends to reformulate them in the terms in which he himself normally thinks. He may at the same time give a slight twist to the opposing view in order to make the refutation more obvious. Even when the reporting is honestly done the change of terminology may alter the view in subtle ways.
3) It was a common practice among Muslim scholars to claim that their views were derived from acknowledged authorities of previous generations. Even the rationalizing Abū-l-Hudhayl, according to his disciple Zurqān, claimed that he had received his Muʿtazilism ('what I hold of *'adl* and *tawḥīd*') from 'Uthmān aṭ-Ṭawīl, who had had it in succession from Wāṣil from Abū-Hāshim from his father Muḥammad ibn-al-Ḥanafiyya from his father 'Alī from the Messenger of God to whom it had been brought from God by Gabriel.[6] The heresiographers accepted some of these claims without question, even if they rejected the more extravagant. The modern scholar will scrutinize all such claims with care.
4) The heresiographers' treatment of the names of sects has also to be examined carefully. In origin many of these names were nicknames applied contemptuously by opponents; and we know from our own experience that political and religious nicknames are often applied loosely to disparage an opponent one dislikes, and are used in different senses by different people. In at least one modern state the ruling party regards 'liberal' and 'communist' as virtually identical, whereas elsewhere they may be diametrically opposed. In the Islamic world one finds the term 'Qadarite' used in the opposing senses of 'upholder of free will' and 'upholder of predestination' (see chapter 4, section 5 below). Ash-Shahrastānī, again, speaks of 'pure Jabriyya' who deny that man acts or has power to act and 'moderate Jabriyya' who hold that, though man has power to act, this is ineffective;[6] it is doubtful if any individuals ever held such views, but they are a useful foil to the Ashʿarite view of *kasb*, 'acquisition', and enable ash-Shahrastānī to maintain that the Ashʿarite view is a mean between those of the Jabriyya and Qadariyya. Thus the treatment of the Jabriyya seems to be largely influenced by an apologetic purpose. Because this heresiographical tradition is now widely accepted and in a sense 'standard', it is easy to treat it as objective and to forget

that originally it was the view of only a section even of the Sunnites. It suffers indeed from Muʿtazilite-Ashʿarite bias and requires to be corrected by reference to the Ḥanafite and Ḥanbalite traditions and also in some respects by the various Shīʿite traditions.

In the light of this critique of the main heresiographical tradition, of which there is abundant illustration in what follows, certain procedural rules may be set down to guide the student of early Islamic thought. These are rules which have in fact been followed in this book.

1) As far as possible the focus should be on particular individuals and their views. General statements about sects, like those about the Jabriyya just quoted, are of little value unless one can identify the individuals whom the writer has in mind. The more precise but still anonymous statements of Khushaysh about 'a group of...' will of course be given more weight than the general classificatory statements of ash-Shahrastānī.

2) One must realize that sect-names are not objective and must always ask *who* is applying this name to *whom*. We say little by giving a sect-label to a person, since this cannot be done in any absolute or objective fashion. For the most part it is best to avoid the sect-names. In what follows it has occasionally been found convenient to use a sect-name, but it is hoped that the precise usage adopted will always have been made clear.

3) Early material is generally to be preferred to later, since it is more likely to retain the original form of expression; but occasionally late sources may be found to contain early material in relatively unchanged form.

4) During the period studied in this book it is desirable to link up doctrinal statements with the contemporary political and historical situation, since often the apparently abstract theological assertions have a political relevance.

It is perhaps appropriate at this point to remark that the word 'orthodox' is out of place in an Islamic context. The strict meaning of the word is 'of sound or correct intellectual belief'; but, despite the Inquisition begun by al-Ma'mūn and apart from acceptance of the Shahāda or confession of faith, correctness of intellectual belief has never been a criterion to decide whether a man was a Muslim or not. Indeed Islam has had no machinery comparable to the Ecumenical Councils of the Christian Church which could say authoritatively what constitutes 'right doctrine'. Nevertheless by the typically Islamic process of *ijmāʿ* or consensus a wide area of agreement was eventually reached (after the year 1000), and to this the term 'orthodoxy' might be applied were it not for the fact that the agreement was concerned more with matters of practice than of doctrine in the strict sense; 'Sunnism' and 'Sunnite' are more accurate. Even at the death of al-Ashʿarī in 935, though Ḥanafites, Ḥanbalites and Ashʿarites were moving closer together doctrinally, they were not prepared to recognize one another as fellow-Sunnites.

The vast and ever-increasing amount of material available for this study has made rigorous selection essential, especially in the second half. The aim has been to present a balanced picture in which the main lines of development stood out clearly, and this has meant that many interesting matters adjudged peripheral have been left aside after a cursory reference. Despite the shortcomings in the execution of the plan, it is hoped that this sketch of the formative period of Islamic thought will prove sound in its main emphases.

Part One

THE BEGINNINGS

632–750

1

The Khārijites

1
The murder of 'Uthmān and its causes

The murder of the caliph 'Uthmān in his house at Medina in 656 is a convenient starting-point for a study of Islamic thought, and of the Khārijites in particular. The Khārijites claimed continuity with the revolutionary bodies responsible for the murder, though the precise nature or importance of the continuity is not obvious. Countless later thinkers, too, argued about the rights and wrongs of the different positions adopted by Muslims during the period from the rising against 'Uthmān until the death of 'Alī in 661. In consequence of these arguments this is probably the most obscure and controversial period in the whole of Islamic history. Nevertheless it becomes possible to discern the political groupings and alignments from which there emerged the 'religio-political' parties with which we are here concerned.[1]

In the spring of 656 groups of malcontents from Egypt, Basra and Kufa proceeded to Medina to complain about various matters.[2] From the few names of participants that have been recorded it would appear that each group represented only certain sections of the local garrison of Arabs, but there is no obvious economic or social difference between those who were dissatisfied with 'Uthmān and those who were prepared to tolerate him. Most of these men were from nomadic tribes, and it may be that tribal rivalries played a part in deciding which sections supported 'Uthmān and which took an active part in the movement against him. Distinct from the former nomads were the Quraysh of Mecca, and among them it appears that members of clans formerly in alliance with 'Uthmān's clan (Umayya) tended to support him, while men from the rival group associated with the clan of Makhzūm tended to oppose him. The Muslims who had the most genuine economic grievance were the Anṣār, the old inhabitants of Medina, since, despite their support of Muḥammad in the difficult years of his struggle with the Meccans, they were less well off than some of his leading Meccan opponents. Nevertheless they did not join the provincials in the movement against ʿUthmān. Though at one point they are said themselves to have made an attack on ʿUthmān, they mostly stood aloof, and neither assisted nor hindered the insurrectionaries.[3]

Among the grievances mentioned as leading to the movement was the fact that ʿUthmān had given certain persons grants of land in Iraq. To the ordinary Muslim this must have appeared a breach of the agreement by which conquered lands were not to be divided out among those participating in the conquest, but were to be held in trust for the Muslims and the rents paid into the treasury. Technically ʿUthmān was within his rights in the particular cases referred to, since the grants had been made from special classes of land which from the first had belonged to the caliph and not to the Muslims in general.[4] There was some appearance of unfairness, however, even though the grants may have been made to increase stability and security, which were in the interests of the Muslims as a whole. There are also hints in the sources of a general demand that all lands should be divided up. It is unlikely that any responsible leader supported such a demand; but it may well have expressed the feelings of the average Muslim from a nomadic background as he contemplated the methods by which the former Meccan merchants and their like were organizing the conquered provinces with a view to maximum 'business efficiency'.

Another particular grievance was that ʿUthmān had given some of the most important (and most lucrative) governorships to men of his own clan or somehow related to himself. This was partially the case,[5] but ʿUthmān had considerable justification. If he appointed relatives—but they had not all been appointed by him—it was because they combined administrative competence with reliability. He refused the importunate requests of inefficient relatives. Once again, however, though he may have been aiming at the welfare of all, his policy had an appearance of unfairness.

A grievance of another type is also mentioned. It was asserted that ʿUthmān had failed in certain cases to carry out penalties prescribed by the Qur'ān. One of the most serious cases was that of al-Walīd ibn-'Uqba, governor of Kufa, who was found drunk, but whom 'Uthmān refused to punish.[6] It may well be that such points were brought forward only at a somewhat later date when the question was officially discussed whether 'Uthmān had been unjustly or justly killed. It seems unlikely that it was prominent in the minds of the actual insurgents.

The particular grievances mentioned do not by themselves appear to be sufficient to account for the violence of the movement against 'Uthmān. Underlying the grievances, however, was the general factor briefly alluded to, namely, the complete change in the way of life for those who had formerly been nomads. The ancestors of these men, and they themselves in earlier years, had made a living by herding camels in the desert and now and then raiding other nomads and the neighbouring settled lands. Now by 656 they may be said to have become professional soldiers. The military expeditions to frontier districts resembled nomadic razzias, though they were on a larger scale; but after the expeditions the men returned not to the black tents, but to the comparatively luxurious life of camp-cities. In desert life, too, there was little formal discipline, though some order was kept by the pervasive influence of tribal tradition. The chief of a tribe was its formal head, with certain special responsibilities, but he could not give orders on all matters as he pleased. In the new Islamic system, however, because of the larger scale of operations and the greater numbers involved, there had to be stricter discipline and a more elaborate organization. From the freedom of the desert men had come to be under the control of a powerful bureaucracy; and many doubtless felt that they were caught up in the workings of a vast administrative machine, and that there was no escape.

If there was a grievance in all this, it was not one that could be put right by any conceivable measures of any available leader. The trouble was that men wanted the advantages of living in an organized state, but found some aspects of this life very irksome. Only a few were prepared to go back to the life of the nomad, though among the few we find a wife of the caliph Mu'āwiya, by name Maysūn, from whom a poem has been handed down beginning:

> A tent in which are flapping winds
> to me is dearer than lofty palace.[7]

Obviously, however, no leader could have suggested that all the Arabs should return to the desert. For many, then, who hankered after the old freedom and saw no means of attaining it, there must have been a deep sense of frustration. Others may have experienced rather a feeling of insecurity. Whatever the precise nature of the feeling, the root of the problem was the new economic, social and political structure in which they found themselves, but to which they were not yet adjusted. In these circumstances emotional tensions were bound to keep mounting until they reached bursting point. The murder of ʿUthmān may be seen as the first of a series of explosions. In the following pages it will be maintained that the original Khārijite and Shīʿite movements are other, only slightly less explosive, methods of dealing with the same tensions

2
The first Khārijites

a) *The happenings at Ṣiffīn, Ḥarūrā' and an-Nahrawān*

On the death of ʿUthmān the Muslims in Medina appointed ʿAlī caliph, but he was not universally recognized. ʿAlī, though he disapproved of the murder, had shown considerable sympathy with the insurgents—or 'regicides' as they are often called—and took no steps to punish those responsible for the shedding of blood. In this way he had compromised his position. It was probably chiefly from religious motives, then, that ʿAbd-Allāh ibn-ʿUmar and like-minded men avoided recognizing ʿAlī by leaving Medina. In Syria ʿUthmān's governor and kinsman Muʿāwiya remained in control and refused allegiance to ʿAlī; and when ʿAlī failed to punish the regicides he claimed that he was the *walī*, the next of kin with the duty of avenging the death. A third group, led by Muḥammad's widow ʿĀ'isha along with two rich Meccans, Ṭalḥa and az-Zubayr, openly revolted after some months, but were defeated at the so-called battle of the Camel near Basra in December 656. Though this group claimed to stand for the application of legal penalties to all wrongdoers impartially, they do not appear to have had a distinctive religious position, and were perhaps moved chiefly by self-interest.

After the battle of the Camel, in which Ṭalḥa and az-Zubayr lost their lives, ʿAlī was free to march against Muʿāwiya. The two armies spent most of June and July 657 confronting one another at Ṣiffīn, near Raqqa on the upper Euphrates. There was minor fighting, interspersed with a truce, though the losses have been greatly magnified in some sources. At last, after a night engagement and when it seemed that both armies would be fully committed, some religious-minded men in Mu'āwiya's army went out to the enemy with copies of the Qur'ān tied to their lances. This was understood as a way of summoning their opponents to let the dispute be settled by a judgement according to the Qur'ān; and religious-minded men in 'Alī's following forced him to accept arbitration. Some elements in this story are suspect. It is unlikely that many copies of the Qur'ān existed at this period, but one would be sufficient. Whatever the details, however, the armies certainly withdrew and arbitration took place.

Meanwhile differences of opinion appeared among those who supported 'Alī. While they were still at Ṣiffīn, but after the agreement with Mu'āwiya, some of them raised the cry 'No judgement but God's!' (*lā ḥukm illā li-llāh*), and asserted that it was sinful to submit the dispute to human judges. These persons were joined by others, and on the return to Kufa several thousands withdrew to a place in the neighbourhood called Ḥarūrā'. 'Alī managed to meet the leaders, however, and by offering provincial governorships and making other concessions persuaded them all to return to Kufa. Despite this reconciliation, however, there was a second withdrawal when it became clear that the arbitration was proceeding. This was to an-Nahrawān, and involved three or four thousand men. Meanwhile the two arbiters seem to have had two meetings, the first at Dūmat al-Jandal. Of the two men 'Amr ibn-al-'Āṣ was a whole-hearted supporter of Mu'āwiya, whereas Abū-Mūsā al-Ash'arī, though representing 'Alī, was not so whole-hearted in his support of him. The first question to be considered was apparently whether 'Uthmān had been justly or unjustly killed; and it is to be inferred that the arbiters decided that the acts with which he was charged were not breaches of divine law which would have justified putting him to death. This may have implied that Mu'āwiya was his *walī* or heir, not merely to exact vengeance for the death but also in other respects. At least it would seem that in April 658 Mu'āwiya was acclaimed as caliph by his followers. The question of a *right* to the caliphate was probably considered by the two arbiters at Adhruḥ in January 659, and 'Amr is said to have outwitted Abū-Mūsā; but this event has little relevance for the present study.

In July 658 'Alī, after managing to win back some of those who had gone to an-Nahrawān, attacked the remainder; and there followed what was less a battle than a massacre. The secessions to

Ḥarūrā' and an-Nahrawān may be regarded as the first phase of the Khārijite movement under 'Alī, but they were not its end.

b) *The basic doctrine*

The slogan of these early Khārijites must be further examined, since it must include or imply their basic doctrine. The words 'No judgement but God's!' (*lā ḥukm illā li-llāh*) are based on several Qur'ānic verses (esp. 6.57; 12.40, 67 etc.), though not taken exactly from these. The verb *ḥakkama* can mean among other things to repeat this slogan (as *kabbara* means to repeat the phrase *Allāhu akbar*), giving the verbal noun *taḥkīm* for the repetition of it and the participial noun *muḥakkima* collectively for those who repeat it. Those who first used the slogan were called 'the first Muḥakkima'.

The phrase is, of course, susceptible of different applications. The general interpretation must be that, where there is a clear prescription of the Qur'ān, men must simply follow this. To the Khārijites it was presumably 'obvious' that 'Uthmān had broken some clear prescriptions of the Qur'ān. It may be that they first objected to the arbitration when they realized that the rightness or wrongness of 'Uthmān's death was to be examined. It was also possible, however, to apply the principle to 'Alī's continuation of the struggle against Mu'āwiya. They relied on the following verse : 'If two parties of the believers fight, make peace between them; but if one still oppresses (or "uses force against") the other, fight the oppressive (or "violent") one until it returns to obedience to God' (49.9). They held that the oppressive or violent party was that of Mu'āwiya, and that 'Alī had broken this prescription in ceasing to fight him. ('Alī himself is said to have used this verse of his opponents at the battle of the Camel; but he may simply have adopted the opinion from some of his followers.) Several other verses might be quoted in support of the same position; notably 9.29 : 'fight those who do not believe in God and the Last Day, do not forbid what God and his messenger have forbidden, and do not live according to the religion of truth . . . until they pay the *jizya* (poll-tax)'.

Some occidental scholars have supposed that 'the judgement of God' was what Europeans might have called 'the arbitrament of war'. This line of thought may seem closer to the Islamic than in fact it is. To the European the question is an open one, and victory in war will show who was right. This is not the Islamic, or at least the Khārijite, idea. The Khārijite began from the premiss that his party was right, that their opponents were wrong, and that it was his duty to fight the latter. A verse (7.87/5) said 'be patient until God judges between us'; and this was taken to mean that they were patiently to continue to fight until God gave them victory, as he was bound to do in the end.[8] In all this there is no suggestion of a doubt or uncertainty being resolved by the outcome of a battle. To the Khārijites the judgement of God is clear and already known, and it only remains to carry it out, so far as this is work for human agents.

The interpretations just described help us to understand the transition from the slogan 'No judgement but God's!' to the other distinctive doctrines of the Khārijites. Implicit in the slogan, or at least in the practice associated with it, is the conception of a righteous community, which knows the divine law and practises it, and which opposes communities and individuals which either do not know or do not practise the law. The doctrine most often referred to, namely, that the grave sinner is excluded from the community, follows from the above statement, since the grave sinner is a man who does not forbid (in the sense of regarding as forbidden for himself) what God and his messenger have forbidden (cf. 9.29 above); because of this it becomes a duty to fight against him, and exclusion from the community is then presupposed.

c) *The meaning of the name 'Khārijites'*

'Khārijites' is an anglicized form representing the Arabic *Khawārij* or *Khārijiyya*, which may be described as a plural and a collective noun respectively; a single person is a *Khārijī*. These are derivatives of the verb *kharaja*, 'go out'. This word can be understood in various ways, however, of which four are relevant to the explanation of the name 'Khārijites'. These are as follows:[9]

1) The Khārijites are those who 'went out' or 'made a secession' from the camp of ʿAlī.

2) They are those who went out from among the unbelievers 'making the Hijra to God and his messenger' (4.100/1), that is, breaking all social ties with the unbelievers.

3) They are those who have 'gone out against' (*kharaja ʿalā*) ʿAlī in the sense of rebelling against him.

4) They are those who go out and take an active part in the *jihād*, in contrast to those who 'sit still'; the two groups, and the concepts of *khurūj*, 'going out', and *quʿūd*, 'sitting still', are contrasted in the Qur'ān (e.g. 9.83/4).

For all of these interpretations there is justification, in the sense that some persons employed them at some period. The problem is to know which persons and when. It seems clear that the fourth sense cannot have been dominant in the time of ʿAlī himself, since, apart from the short period when he accepted the arbitration, he was prepared to go out and fight Muʿāwiya. On the other hand, the fourth sense is prominent in the doctrines of Ibn-al-Azraq. Of the other senses, the first might be a neutral description, and could apply to the 'secessions' to Ḥarūrā' and an-Nahrawān. It also seems likely that something like the second sense may have been present in the minds of those who made these 'secessions'; they were trying to separate themselves from a body of people they regarded as unrighteous. Again, from the point of view of ʿAlī and the Umayyad caliphs, the sense of 'rebels' would be appropriate.

It is important, however, to consider not only the appropriateness of the various senses, but also the earliest actual applications of the term. This is specially necessary in view of the tendency of the heresiographers to create 'sects'. Unfortunately there is little early information that can be dated with certainty. It is therefore also necessary to look at the inferences to be drawn from the usage of slightly later writers.

The earliest source is probably the letter from Ibn-Ibāḍ to the caliph ʿAbd-al-Malik, which appears to be authentic.[10] According to this the caliph seems to have meant by the term 'Khawārij' all those groups actively engaged in risings against the government (and thus excluding the Ibāḍites), whereas to Ibn-Ibāḍ the term comprised all the dissidents from the time of the movement against ʿUthmān, including his own followers but excluding the Azraqites who were reckoned to be unbelievers. In other words, this early text represents the government as taking the third sense of 'Khawārij', namely, those who rebelled against the government, whereas Ibn-Ibāḍ is prepared to use the term of himself and his party, presumably in the fourth sense. The sense of 'dissident' or 'rebel' is supported by the use of *khārija* for 'rebel band' in a speech by ʿAlī reported by aṭ-Ṭabarī.[11]

From the heresiographers and other sources it is apparent—as will be seen later—that there was a considerable intellectual ferment in Basra from the closing years of the seventh century onwards. From this ferment three main groups (Ibāḍiyya, Bayhasiyya, Ṣufriyya) and some minor ones emerge, which are labelled as 'Khārijites'. The impression is given that these groups at first argued almost exclusively with one another. The differences between them have left few traces in the general theological thought of the period, where arguments tend to be against 'the Khārijites' as a whole. In an early reference to the Ibāḍiyya specifically they are said to have claimed that a scholar Jābir ibn-Zayd (d. 711 or 721) belonged to them, though he denied it.[12]

At a rather later period—probably from about 770 onwards—there appear a number of men who are called *mutakallimūn* or 'theologians' of the Khārijites. The most important was al-Yamān ibn-Ribāb, who wrote a book, quoted by al-Ash'arī and others, on the subdivisions of the Khārijites, and who is said to have been first a Tha'labī and then a Bayhasī.[13] His date is roughly indicated by the fact that he wrote a refutation of Ḥammād ibn-Abī-Ḥanīfa, who died in 781 or 792. Another similar person was Yaḥyā ibn-Abī-Kāmil (or ibn-Kāmil), an Ibāḍī, and an associate of Bishr al-Marīsī (d. 833), who also exchanged epistles with the Mu'tazilite Ja'far ibn-Ḥarb.[14] These Khārijite *mutakallimūn* were clearly taking part in the general discussions of Kalām at this period. To judge from the titles of their books, and on general grounds, they would appear to have opposed the Mu'tazilites, at least in their doctrine of human and divine activity.

In connection with this last matter one may look at the report of views attributed to the early Mu'tazilite Wāṣil by al-Khayyāṭ, writing in the second half of the ninth century. Wāṣil argues for the doctrine of 'the intermediate position' (*al-manzila bayn al-manzilatayn*) against the views that the grave sinner is an unbeliever (Khārijites), a believer (Murji'ites) or a hypocrite (al-Ḥasan). Although this material was not written down, so far as we know, until near the end of the ninth century, the attribution to Wāṣil (d. 748) specifically suggests that arguments of this kind were being used in or shortly after the lifetime of al-Ḥasan al-Baṣrī (d. 728). The point that is most important in the present context is that the Khārijites are here treated as a unity.

Some other small points may be noted. There are a number of references to *Khawārij* or *Khārijī* in Ibn-Sa'd (d. 845) in his biographies of men who transmitted material about Muḥammad (see Index). These seem to be mostly to insurgents of the time of Ibn-az-

Zubayr or earlier, apart from one reference to men who 'went out' against 'Umar ibn-'Abd-al-'Azīz.[15] The only mention of a subdivision of the Khārijites appears to be that of the Ibāḍiyya in connection with Jābir ibn-Zayd (as noted above). Once or twice Ibn-Sa'd uses the phrase 'held the views of the Khārijites'; and this may imply that the man in question was not an actual insurgent.[16] In the *Maqālāt* or heresiography of al-Ash'arī (d. 935) the section on the Khārijites (86–131) has many reports that appear to refer to the period when certain persons called 'Khārijites' were in touch with Mu'tazilite circles. A little earlier we find Ibn-Qutayba (d. 889) apparently contrasting certain 'Khārijites'—presumably from among the Traditionists since they argue from Traditions—with the *qā'id* or 'sitter still'.[17] This implies that the writer accepted *kharaja* in the fourth sense, namely, active participation in the *jihād*.

The conclusion to which all this evidence points is somewhat as follows. From at least 685 onwards, and perhaps earlier, government circles and other opponents of the Khārijites used the term *khawārij* to mean 'rebels' or 'bands of rebels'. At the same time, however, sympathizers could regard it as meaning something like 'activists'. It did not necessarily have a definite doctrinal content at this period. For a time the doctrinal aspect may rather have been indicated by the 'sect'-names Ḥarūriyya and Wahbiyya. The former of these is from Ḥarūrā', the site of the early secession, and was used until after 750;[18] the latter is possibly named after the leader of those killed at an-Nahrawān, 'Abd-Allāh ibn-Wahb ar-Rāsibī.[19]

So far as common doctrines are concerned, al-Ash'arī mentions only two: they held that Alī was an unbeliever for accepting the arbitration; and they held that every grave sinner was an unbeliever and excluded from the community.[20] The first point implies that—at least for a leader—to disobey a Qur'ānic prescription (like continuing to fight the enemies of God) is tantamount to unbelief (*kufr*); the second point may be understood as a generalization of this. It is to be noted, however, that the second point in its explicit form can hardly have been a doctrine of all Khārijites at an early period, except in respect of men in a position of leadership. One of the doctrinally important early Khārijites, Najda, who ruled an extensive territory in Arabia, soon realized that exclusion from the community (leading to death or exile) was not a punishment that could be inflicted for every crime. It would seem, then, that the characterization of a Khārijite as one who held that the grave sinner was an unbeliever was not based on observation of the phenomena of the movement as a whole up to, say, the time of Najda's death in 692. It probably came into being as a result of the theoretical discussions centring in al-Ḥasan al-Baṣrī in the early eighth century, and was further developed in the discussions between the Muʿtazilites and other *mutakallimūn* in the late eighth and early ninth centuries. Despite the early usages of *khawārij*, it seems likely that the conception of the Khārijites as a 'sect' was largely created by heresiographers from al-Yamān ibn-Ribāb on to serve as a mould for certain phenomena, though these phenomena do not altogether fit this mould.

This hypothesis is perhaps hardly justified by the evidence so far given; but it becomes much more probable when one also considers the clearer evidence (to be given below) for the 'creation' of 'sects' like the Murji'a and Jahmiyya.

3

Doctrinal developments among certain 'rebels'

a) *The risings against ʿAlī and Muʿāwiya*

The present study is concerned only with doctrinal developments, but it is nevertheless essential to bring the material derived from the heresiographers into association with that derived from the historians. The historical material by itself was carefully examined by Julius Wellhausen in *Die religiös-politischen Oppositionsparteien im alten Islam* (Göttingen, 1901), and for the caliphate of ʿAlī this has now been supplemented from Ibāḍī sources by Laura Veccia Vaglieri and her colleagues at Naples.

After the battle of an-Nahrawān five small risings are recorded against ʿAlī, each involving about 200 men; while between 661 and 680 sixteen leaders of risings against Muʿāwiya are named, though some seem to have continued with the followers of a previous leader who had been killed. Of the risings against Muʿāwiya some had from 300 to 500 men, others only between 30 and 70.[21] In the sources these people are identified as Khārijites, but virtually nothing is said about their beliefs. It may be assumed that no development of Khārijite doctrine took place among them. On the other hand, most of them probably accepted a doctrinal position similar to that of the men at Ḥarūrā' and an-Nahrawān; one small group is said to have shouted the slogan 'No judgement but God's!' in the mosque at

Kufa. A study of the names in the lists further makes it clear that there was some continuity of personnel.

The fact that there were Khārijite risings against ʿAlī as well as against Muʿāwiya shows that these were not movements specifically against the Umayyads, and tends to confirm the suggestion made above (section 1, *ad fin.*) that the Khārijites were protesting against the vastness of the organizational structure in which they were now caught up. All the leaders were former nomads and not townsmen. It is therefore all the more significant that in their risings they might be said to be restoring the life in small groups with which they had been familiar in the desert. After one of these groups of Khārijites had 'gone out' they presumably maintained themselves by raiding or by levying food from the countryside. Just as the members of a nomadic tribe regarded as potential enemies members of all other tribes, except where there was an alliance, so the Khārijite bodies tended to regard all outsiders, even Muslims of differing views, as enemies whose blood might be shed. This justified not merely raiding of the desert type, but also activities that were little better than brigandage. The Khārijites appear to have had a pride in their group, analogous to that of a nomad in his tribe; and, again like some of the desert tribes, they became noted for their mastery of the Arabic language in both poetry and oratory.

The Khārijite bands differed from desert clans, however, in that they had an Islamic basis. They were not much given to abstract general statements, and contented themselves with speaking of particular sins of particular leaders. Implicit in this, however, was the belief that the body politic should be based on Qur'ānic principles and prescriptions. Strange as it seems to the occidental observer, their brigandage was combined with a vigorous religious faith. It is indeed precisely at this point that the Khārijite movement made its great contribution to Islamic thought and life, namely, when it insisted that the body politic and the structure of society should be based on the Qur'ān. Also implicit in their practice was a conception of group solidarity. The later history of Khārijite thought shows how these implicit ideas were gradually made explicit.

b) *Ibn-al-Azraq and the Azraqites (or Azāriqa)*

The first doctrinal development beyond the position of the earliest Khārijites is generally ascribed to Ibn-al-Azraq (more fully Nāfiʿ ibn-al-Azraq) and his followers, the Azraqites or Azāriqa. Ibn-al-

Azraq was no academic or theoretical thinker, but was deeply involved in affairs as a political and military leader. From the detailed reports of the external course of events, the following picture is derived.[22] From 675 to 684 the governor of Basra, ʿUbayd-Allāh ibn-Ziyād, maintained order on the whole, despite the presence of turbulent Khārijite and Shīʿite factions, whose animosity against one another may have been intensified by tribal rivalries. On the death of the caliph Yazīd in 683 the strong measures of the governor ceased to be efficacious, and in 684 he was forced to withdraw.[23] Before long the people of Basra decided to support the cause of Ibn-az-Zubayr, at this time established in Mecca and claiming the caliphate.

To escape from the coercive measures of the governor a number of Khārijites had gone to Mecca to help Ibn-az-Zubayr. When affairs became confused in Basra they returned there; but it is not clear whether they were hoping to profit from the confusion, or had simply realized that Ibn-az-Zubayr was not in sympathy with their political ideals. The latter is more likely, since Ibn-az-Zubayr had no intention of allowing the structure of the empire to disintegrate. Among those who returned from Mecca was Ibn-al-Azraq. When Basra began to favour the cause of Ibn-az-Zubayr, some Khārijites, including Ibn-al-Azraq, opposed by force the entry of a Zubayrid governor. In the end they were defeated, but Ibn-al-Azraq refused to give up the fight and retired eastwards to the province of al-Ahwāz or Khuzistan with a large number of followers. A Zubayrid army pursued them and Ibn-al-Azraq was defeated and killed in 685, but the Azraqites continued under other leaders as a body of rebels and terrorists. Wherever they were strong enough and the opponents weak—and this happened several times in the region between Basra and al-Ahwāz, and also elsewhere—pillage, arson and massacre became the order of the day, and none were exempt except those who actively supported the Azraqites. Several Zubayrid armies were sent against them at intervals, and with the utmost difficulty checked them temporarily. The recovery of Iraq by the Umayyads in 690 brought little change until after 694, when al-Ḥajjāj, having pacified western Arabia, took up the governorship of Iraq. The remnant of the Azraqites were at last wiped out in a battle in Ṭabaristan in 698. The name is occasionally encountered later.[24]

The doctrinal position of Ibn-al-Azraq was very much influenced by the conception of group solidarity.[25] He accepted the slogan 'No judgement but God's!' with its implication that the body politic must be based on the Qur'ān. This was interpreted, however, to mean that those who 'sat still' and did not 'go out' or actively associate themselves with the group prosecuting the struggle against the unbelievers were themselves breaking a divine command and therefore unbelievers. (This is in accordance with the fourth sense of 'going out' as described above.) In effect this meant that the only true Muslims were the persons in the Azraqite camp. The corollary was that all other persons—with the exception of Jews, Christians, etc. who had officially received 'protection' (*dhimma*) from the Islamic community as a whole—might lawfully be robbed or killed. This was the religious justification of their terrorism. Moreover it applied also to the wives and children of non-Azraqite Muslims, since by their conception of group solidarity the families of unbelievers were also unbelievers. Because when they encountered other Muslims they questioned them about their beliefs, the word *istiʿrāḍ*, which properly means 'questioning', came to connote 'indiscriminate killing' of theological opponents. Before joining the Azraqites, too, a test (*miḥna*) was made; and this is said to have consisted in giving the candidate a prisoner to kill. If the man complied, he would be more closely bound to the Azraqite body, since, especially if the man killed was of his own tribe, he would have broken existing ties, and would be dependent on the Azraqites for 'protection'. This test, however, may have been an occasional rather than a regular practice.

Thus the Azraqites were attempting to form a small body which manifested solidarity in its observance of Qur'ānic principles, as interpreted by them, and was in a state of potential war with all other Muslims. They may have thought of themselves as creating a new community of 'believers' in much the same way as Muḥammad had done at Medina; at least they spoke of making the Hijra to their camp. Muḥammad's community at Medina, however, had the advantage of having Muḥammad to guide it with his personal wisdom and authority and with the fresh revelations which he received appropriate to novel circumstances which had arisen. The Azraqites, on the other hand, based their community on a fixed set of rigidly defined principles, which gave little flexibility for adaptation to changing circumstances. Ibn-al-Azraq and his followers may be said to have despaired of being able to live according to Qur'ānic principles under either Zubayrid or Umayyad rule, and to have decided that there would be at least a small group among whom the divinely-given law was properly observed.

c) *Najda and the Najdites or Najadāt*

During the period when Khārijite doctrine was receiving its most extreme expression from Ibn-al-Azraq and his followers, a more moderate expression was being given to it in parts of Arabia under the leadership of Najda ibn-ʿĀmir (or ibn-ʿĀṣim) al-Ḥanafī. Najda, accompanied by Khārijites from the district of al-Yamāma in central Arabia, seems to have been among those who gave support to Ibn-az-Zubayr at Mecca in 683. It is not clear whether he returned to Basra, from which he had come. He reappears in 686 as leader of a body of Khārijites in al-Yamāma, and became effective ruler of a large area, including Bahrein on the Persian Gulf and (for a time) Oman in the east, as well as parts of the Yemen and Hadramaut in the south. When he was at the height of his power, his sway was more extensive than that of Ibn-az-Zubayr. Quarrels with a doctrinal basis, however, broke out among his subordinate officers, and these led to Najda's deposition and death in 692. This did not put an end to the dissensions. A party which remained in Arabia was defeated by the Umayyads in 693 and ceased to exist. Others escaped across the Persian Gulf, but they also disappeared. The views of some of the Najdite leaders may have influenced the moderate Khārijites who continued to live in Basra.

The doctrinal views of Najda and his followers[26] were conditioned by the fact that they accepted the responsibility for maintaining order over a large area, and were not simply concerned for a small body of people in a 'camp'. In these circumstances it was impossible to make death or exile (which were implied by exclusion from the community) the punishment for every instance of theft or adultery. This matter led Najda to make a distinction between fundamentals and non-fundamentals in religion. The fundamentals for Najda were the knowledge of God and of his messengers, acceptance of the revealed scriptures, and acknowledgement that the life and property of every Muslim was sacrosanct; in these respects ignorance was not condoned. In all other points, however, ignorance was excused, especially when it referred to some action about which there was no clear prescription in the Qur'ān. One such action was the appropriation of captured women by the leaders of an expedition, after assigning a value to each, but before the booty as a whole was distributed. When complaints were made to Najda about this incident, he decided that the leaders had acted wrongly, but had done so in ignorance, and were therefore to be excused. Because of this Najda and his followers were sometimes called the 'Ādhiriyya or 'excusers'.

A further theoretical point was made with regard to the common sins like theft and adultery. Thieves and adulterers need not be excluded from the community, because single acts did not relegate them to 'the people of Hell'. On the other hand, persistence in sin—even in lesser sins than theft and adultery—made a man a *mushrik* or 'idolater', and this excluded him from the community and implied that he would go to Hell. In contrast the occasional sinner who did not persist in sin might be punished by God in accordance with the extent of his sin; but the punishment would not be in Hell and would not be eternal, so that he would finally enter Paradise. This discussion of the status of sinners is linked with the conception of the community. Najda presumably accepted the principle ascribed to the Azraqites : 'we bear witness by God that of those professing Islam in the camp (*dār al-hijra*) all are approved by God'.[27] The last phrase might be held to apply to occasional sinners in so far as they were eventually to reach Paradise.

One or two other points are recorded of Najda. He rejected the view of Ibn-al-Azraq that 'those who sit still' are unbelievers, but regarded them as 'hypocrites' (*munāfiqūn*). He also appears to have allowed to his followers the practice of *taqiyya* or 'prudent fear', that is, the concealment of one's true beliefs when among enemies who might kill one if they knew;[28] this presumably refers to Khārijites who were living among non-Khārijite Muslims, or to Najda's followers living among Azraqites, or it may merely be a mark of opposition to Ibn-al Azraq.

In some respects Najda and his followers exhibit attitudes typical of the nomadic Arabs. On the question of appropriating captive women Najda himself is said to have made the decision; but his followers may have been unwilling to concede to him any special right in this matter, for we are told that the Najdites held that an imam was unnecessary—in practice they made frequent changes—and that all men had to do was to follow the Qur'ān.[29] This suggests the egalitarianism of the nomads, and the readiness of each man to put forward his views in the council of the clan or tribe In contrast to the Azraqites who thought the *ẓāhir* or 'obvious meaning' of the Qur'ān met all practical needs,[30] the Najdites were aware of the complexities of actual life and recognized the need for *ijtihād* or 'personal effort' in the application of Qur'ānic rules to particular situations. It is perhaps also worth considering whether the Najdite toleration of occasional theft, adultery and wine-drinking may in part spring from the toleration of these, at least in certain circumstances, by the pre-Islamic nomads, so that the Qur'ānic punishments were in some ways a novelty. The attitude of Najda to wine-drinking in practice is not clear; one report says he was criticized for not punishing it, but another seems to assert that he was strict.[31] If these points are sound, they would support the general contention that the early Khārijites were attempting to reconstitute on a religious basis the small closely-knit group familiar to them in the old desert life.

d) *Later risings against the Umayyads*

There were several later risings against the Umayyads which are reckoned as Khārijite.[32] The most important was that of Ṣāliḥ ibn-Muṣarriḥ; though he himself fell in battle in 695, he was long regarded as a hero; the rising was continued by Shabīb ibn-Yazīd ash-Shaybānī for a year or more until he was drowned. Though Ṣāliḥ is counted as belonging to the sect of Ṣufriyya, no significant doctrinal developments took place in connection with this or any other actual rising.

4

The theoretical or moderate development of Khārijite doctrine

a) *The sub-sects and men involved*

Before and during the rising of Ibn-al-Azraq many moderate Khārijites remained in Basra. These were religious-minded men, who wanted to see the Islamic state and community based on Qur'ānic principles, but who disapproved of the Azraqite practice of *isti'rāḍ* or the killing of Muslims who differed from them on points of doctrine or who refused to join them. The leader of those who thus 'sat still' (on the Azraqite view) was Abū-Bilāl Mirdās ibn-Udayya at-Tamīmī. Though in general he disapproved of insurrection, he was apparently provoked shortly after the death of Mu'āwiya in 680 to revolt with forty men against the governor of Basra, 'Ubayd-Allāh ibn-Ziyād; after a success in al-Ahwāz he was defeated and killed in 681.[33] There is a report that the alleged founders of the sects about to be mentioned were 'agreed on the view of Abū-Bilāl';[34] and from this report we may infer that the later developments were regarded as derived from the position of Abū-Bilāl.

Many items of information show that there was considerable theological discussion in Basra from about 680 onwards, and in this the Khārijites played a part. At this point, however, we come upon a phenomenon that is almost unique in Islamic heresiography, namely, that the existence of the sects is better attested than the existence of their founders. Out of the confusion at Basra there emerged three sects of moderate Khārijites, the Ibāḍites (Ibāḍiyya), the Ṣufrites (Ṣufriyya) and the Bayhasites (Bayhasiyya). The first two are known to have existed from numerous references in the historians; and indeed the Ibāḍites still exist and there is much material about them, including writings by Ibāḍite scholars. One important account of the founders of the three sects is that among those who helped Ibn-az-Zubayr at Mecca and then returned to Basra with Ibn-al-Azraq about 684 were 'Abd-Allāh ibn-Ibāḍ (of B. Ṣarīm, a subdivision of Tamīm), 'Abd-Allāh ibn-Ṣaffār as-Sa'dī (also of B. Ṣarīm) and Ḥanẓala ibn-Bayhas.[35] Ibāḍite material now gives something of a picture of Ibn-Ibāḍ, but even the names of the other two founders are disputed. The Bayhasiyya are usually said to derive their name from Abū-Bayhas al-Hayṣam ibn-Jābir, who is known to have been put to death by the caliph in 713.[36]

The Ṣufrites are also said to have been founded by Ziyād ibn-al-Aṣfar or 'Ubayda while some scholars held that the name did not come from a person at all.[37] The heresiographer al-Baghdādī, though he calls the Ṣufrites followers of Ziyād ibn-al-Aṣfar, treats Abū-Bilāl as their first imam. Since Abū-Bilāl is not mentioned by al-Ash'arī, al-Baghdādī must have had an independent source of information, and this seems to have been accurate in many points. The two persons named as founders of the Ṣufrites, however, are otherwise unknown, and their names would not normally produce the form *ṣufriyya*; they may therefore be eliminated. The probability is that the name was originally a discreditable nickname—perhaps even *ṣifriyya*, meaning 'empty (of religion)'—and that the suggested derivations are attempts to make it less objectionable. It is common to find several explanations of the early names of sects, and this is doubtless because those to whom a name was applied wanted to make it more honourable, while their opponents wanted to increase the discredit. It would appear, therefore, that the term 'Ṣufrite' was applied to early Khārijites who were neither Najdites nor Azraqites. If this were so, it would be natural to find that there was no very definite Ṣufrite doctrine ; and this is the case. It would also be natural to regard Abū-Bilāl as imam of the Ṣufrites.

Considerable importance is to be attached to the statement of al-Ash'arī (101.10) : 'the source of Khārijite doctrine is the doctrine of the Azraqites, the Ibāḍites, the Ṣufrites and the Najdites ; and all the subdivisions apart from the Azraqites, the Ibāḍites and the Najdites branch off from the Ṣufrites'. This is not altogether obvious, however, from his statements of detail. The largest number of sects is traced to the followers of Ibn-'Ajarrad, who was himself the follower of a successor of Najda. The place of Abū-Bayhas in this is obscure, but, since Ibn-'Ajarrad is said to have been a follower of his, [38] he was probably a follower who returned to Basra. Indeed most of the Khārijites in Basra after 684 were probably influenced by Najda. A statement that a letter from Najda to the people of Basra was read jointly by Ibn-Ibāḍ and 'Ubayda (head of the Ṣufriyya) seems to be a genuine piece of early information. This is evidence for the existence of the Ṣufrites before 692, the date of Najda's death. This is in keeping with reports that the insurgent Ṣāliḥ ibn-Musarriḥ (d. 695) was a Ṣufrite.

Besides this scanty and uncertain information about the origins and early stages of the subdivisions of the non-rebellious Khārijites, there is information about particular scholars who held Khārijite views. One early scholar was Jābir ibn-Zayd al-Azdī with the *kunya* Abū-sh-Sha'thā'. From Ibāḍite sources it is clear that he was regarded as the man who, following on Ibn-Ibāḍ, made the greatest contribution to the development of distinctive Ibāḍite doctrines. [39] On the other hand, he is regarded by Sunnites as an important Traditionist, [40] though it is sometimes added that he was claimed by the Ibāḍites as one of them, but denied this. [41] There are two explanations of this apparent contradiction. The first is that he may really have been an Ibāḍite (especially since he is said to have been exiled to Oman towards the end of his life—though there is also some dubiety about the date of his death), and the Sunnite biographers may have tried to conceal this fact because they made use of him as a Traditionist; on the whole this is perhaps the most likely. There is a second possibility, however, namely, that, though his views were close to those of the Ibāḍites, he did not fully accept them, but that they later claimed to be following him to give their doctrines greater 'respectability' in the eyes of the main body of Sunnites.

Another important scholar who held Khārijite views was ʿIkrima (d. c. 725), a pupil of Ibn-ʿAbbās and an authority on the Qur'ānic text.[42] His heretical views do not appear to be denied or concealed, but it is stated that Mālik ibn-Anas and Muslim did not accept Traditions from him.[43] Other scholars mentioned along with him by al-Ashʿarī (109) as holding Khārijite views are Mujāhid (d. 721) and ʿAmr ibn-Dīnār (d. 743), but this point seems to be passed over in silence by other writers, and the two scholars were in high repute. At a later date the great philologist Abū-ʿUbayda (d. 824) was a Khārijite, and in particular a Ṣufrite, but this was not held to detract from the value of his collection of material about pre-Islamic Arabia.[44] Other Khārijite scholars are also named who seem to have engaged in discussions with the Muʿtazilites in the later eighth and early ninth centuries.[45]

All these facts indicate that many of those holding Khārijite views in Basra after about 690 were members of the 'general religious movement' (to be described in chapter 3), who discussed with other scholars and were usually on good terms with the government. The reports of some of the disputes leading to the subdivisions, especially among the ʿAjārida, suggest the internal quarrels of a small coterie, but this may be a misleading impression, since there is little historical information about the men involved. The Khārijite theorists of Basra were certainly not rebels, but engaged in religious discussions in much the same way as other members of the general religious movement.

b) *General features of the doctrinal development*

The distinctive feature of the Khārijite theorists was that they were prepared to live under a ruler who did not share their principles in detail. They continued to maintain the ideal of a body politic administered according to the Qur'ān and consisting only of those who held the true beliefs (in their eyes), but there was no question of putting this into practice immediately by actual rebellion, though when the Umayyad government was obviously tottering, some of them were not averse to an attempt to replace it by Khārijite rule in at least a part of the caliphate. Apart from this period, however, they fully acquiesced in practice in the Islamic state, but were doubtless trying to make it more Islamic. They used a curious terminology to justify continuing to live under non-Khārijite rule. Some said their lives were being lived 'among the people of war', or that they were in 'the sphere of prudent fear' (*dār at-taqiyya*) or the like.[46] Their actual position was thus contrasted with 'the sphere of Islam' (*dār al-islām*) or 'the sphere of openness' (*ʿalāniya*), that is, a state where the true principles are observed by the sovereign; and there might be a difference between what was permissible in 'the sphere of prudent fear' and what was permissible in 'the sphere of openness' or 'the sphere of the Hijra'.[47] In the former there was, strictly speaking, no imam, that is, no political sovereign following Qur'ānic principles; but it was possible to appoint someone to administer the affairs of the true believers who would be an imam of sorts—the Ibāḍites spoke of him as *imām ad-difāʿ*, 'the imam for defence' in distinction to the true imam to whom allegiance was owed (*imām al-bayʿa*).[48]

The views of Ṣufrites, as noted above, are not clearly defined. In accordance with their acceptance of a non-Khārijite ruler, it is reported that they did not regard 'sitting still' as unbelief, and that they allowed 'Muslim' (that is, Ṣufrite) women to marry 'unbelievers' (that is, non-Ṣufrites) of their own tribe.[49] Apart from these points most of the reports of their views deal with the question of the grave sinner or criminal. Some of the Ṣufrites clung to the original Khārijite view that grave sin made a man an unbeliever or idolater (*kāfir*, *mushrik*). In the case of sins or crimes, like adultery and theft, for which a penalty was prescribed in the Qur'ān, some held that the sinner was not a *kāfir* until he had been punished by the governor. Others, again, tried to distinguish between such sins, and those with no fixed penalty, like omitting the prescribed worship (*ṣalāt*) or the fast of Ramaḍān, and maintained that the latter made a man a *kāfir*, whereas the former made him an adulterer or a thief but not a *kāfir*.[50] According to this last view the criminal had ceased to be a believer, but had not become an unbeliever; or, in other words, adultery and theft do not lead to a man's exclusion from the community.

Early Ibāḍite views, as described by the heresiographers, introduced a refinement into the discussion of whether the thief or adulterer was a *kāfir* and a *mushrik* by distinguishing between these terms and insisting that the latter ('idolater') could only be applied where there was ignorance or denial of God.[51] In accordance with this distinction they allowed that other Muslims were 'monotheists' though not 'believers' (*muwaḥḥidūn*, not *mu'minūn*), and that they were in 'the sphere of monotheism' (*dār at-tawḥīd*), not that of 'prudent fear'.[52]

This partial acceptance of Muslims of other sects led in time to further problems, such as whether it was lawful to sell 'believing' slave-girls to 'unbelievers' (other Muslims). There is a story about how a man called Ibrāhīm was kept waiting by a slave-girl, and swore he would sell her to the bedouin, and how a fellow-Ibāḍite called Maymūn challenged him on the legality of this.[53] It does not matter whether the story is true or not. It raises in concrete form the question of the application of a Qur'ānic rule to the sect-community. The Qur'ān forbids marriage between a Muslim man or woman and an idolater, but permits a Muslim man to marry a woman from 'the people of the Book'.[54] The stricter rule for women may correspond to some deep-rooted feeling about not allowing a woman to marry outside her tribe. Since a slave-girl sold to an 'unbeliever' would presumably have marital relations with him, to sell her was tantamount to permitting the marriage of a Muslim woman with an 'unbeliever', and so was contrary to the Qur'ān. The discussion of this case thus raises the issue of the relationship of the Ibāḍites to the rest of the community of Muslims. Were they to keep themselves entirely aloof and separate from their fellow-citizens, or were they to have certain forms of association with them? In places like Basra the majority seem to have followed Ibrāhīm and remained members of the wider community despite theological differences.

Besides those who opposed the sale of slave-girls to 'unbelievers', there was a party which suspended judgement (*waqafa*) on the question and on some similar questions, and which was called by some opponents 'the party suspending judgement', Wāqifa or Wāqifiyya.[55] From the little that is said by the heresiographers, it would seem that the main conception is that, in so far as men live in 'the sphere of mixing' (*dār al-khalṭ*),[56] everything cannot be precisely stated, and it is necessary to have a measure of compromise or perhaps rather of indefiniteness and imprecision.

Behind this conception of the Wāqifa lies the tendency of the early Muslims to think in communalistic, not individualistic terms; that is to say, salvation is thought of as being given not to individuals but to a group or community. The Qur'ān contains both communalistic and individualistic thinking about the Last Judgement. The Tradition discussed in the Introduction according to which Muḥammad's community will be divided into seventy-three sects, of which only one will be saved, links up with the idea that salvation is attained through membership of 'the saved sect' (*al-firqa an-nājiya*). In reports of Khārijite views the phrase is often used 'people of Paradise' (*ahl al-janna*), and this is a sharply defined group which is contrasted with another sharply defined group, 'the people of Hell' (*ahl an-nār*).[57] It was of supreme importance for a man to belong to 'the people of Paradise' and to have nothing to do with 'the people of Hell'; and so we find the Khārijites constantly deciding that they 'associate with' or 'dissociate from' (*tabarra'a, tawallā*) certain persons. If one 'associated with' the people of Hell and accepted them as members of one's group, one imperilled the whole group's chances of attaining Paradise. This thought was presumably present in the exclusion of grave sinners from the community.

The early Khārijite rebels were apparently prepared to live in a small band of the people of Heaven and to regard all other men, the people of Hell, as enemies or potential enemies. For peaceful Khārijites, however, who were prepared to live where most of their neighbours did not belong to the people of Paradise, great efforts were needed to bring theory and practice into line with one another. In deciding to live among non-Khārijite Muslims they had implicitly ceased to treat them as potential enemies; and in course of time they came to approve of intermarriage. The changes of practice led to a change in the description of the 'sphere' in which they were living. It ceased to be 'the sphere of war'. To call it 'the sphere of prudent fear' was also unsatisfactory in that it suggested that the neighbours were potential enemies. Other terms, therefore, came into use such as 'the sphere of unbelief' (as distinct from idolatry), 'the sphere of mixing' and even 'the sphere of monotheism'. Some men likewise distinguished 'dissociation' from 'hostility'.[58]

In essence, then, it would seem that the Wāqifa were insisting that it is undesirable, perhaps impossible, to draw a firm line of demarcation between 'the people of Paradise' and 'the people of Hell'. In practice most Khārijites had found that natural feelings and commonsense considerations prevented them from excluding wrongdoers from their community; but they had also found it difficult to regard wrongdoers as belonging to 'the people of Paradise', since the

Qur'ān taught that sinners were punished in Hell. This difficulty had been obviated by Najda by the assertion that God might pardon members of his sect who committed grave sins and that, if he punished them, this would not be in Hell and would be followed by admission to Paradise; in this way continued 'association with' sinners was justified, and 'dissociation' forbidden.[59] It could have been argued that an attitude like that of Najda encouraged men to belittle crime and other forms of antisocial conduct. The Wāqifa were apparently anxious that crime should be taken seriously, and they therefore maintained that wrongdoers should be punished but not excluded from the community. This non-exclusion they based on their suspension of judgement or refusal to pronounce on the ultimate fate of the wrongdoer.

In opposition to the Wāqifa were the followers of Abū-Bayhas, who continued in a doctrinaire adherence to the idea of a community based on the Qur'ān.[60] Abū-Bayhas is said to have been a follower of Abū-Fudayk, who led a section of the Najdites after Najda's death, and was killed in 693; and he himself was executed at Medina in 713. His distinctive position became manifest in the discussions about the sale of slave-girls. He thought Ibrāhīm right in considering it lawful, but wrong in not 'dissociating' himself from the Wāqifa who suspended judgement on the matter. He argued that 'there is no place for suspension of judgement in respect of bodies (*sc.* outward acts) but only in respect of the decision proper (*ḥukm*) so long as no Muslim has pronounced it; when once a Muslim has pronounced the decision, those who are present are bound to recognize (*sc.* and distinguish between) the man who has declared truth and acted on it and the man who has declared falsehood and acted on it'. Implicit in this argument is the idea that the community of Islam comprises only those who hold true beliefs and act on them, and also the egalitarian idea that almost any Muslim can give the solution of a problem on behalf of the whole body. A number of groups claimed to follow Abū-Bayhas, but they were less clearly defined than other subdivisions of the Khārijites, and seem gradually to have faded out.

It was probably during the lifetime of Abū-Bayhas that one of his followers Ibn-ʿAjarrad criticized him on certain points and evolved distinct views. Ibn-ʿAjarrad is reckoned the founder of the sect of ʿAjārida, to which the heresiographers attach some fifteen sub-sects.[61] Almost all that is known about him is that he was imprisoned by

Khālid ibn-ʿAbd-Allāh al-Qasrī, governor of Iraq from 724 to 738, and seems to have died in prison. The rupture with Abū-Bayhas was due to differences over the attitude towards opponents' children. Previously the Khārijites had usually assigned to children the same status as their parents. The children of unbelievers were also unbelievers from the cradle upwards, and could be treated as such. This was a communalistic way of thinking and Ibn-ʿAjarrad was protesting against it from an individualistic standpoint. The basic principle was that children were neither believers nor unbelievers until they had come of age, been summoned to embrace Islam, and then either accepted or rejected it for themselves. Within the ʿAjārida there were different views about the attitude to be adopted to children. Some men, for example, held that one ought to 'dissociate oneself' even from one's own children until they professed Islam for themselves, while others, though admitting that their children were not Muslims, felt that 'dissociation' was not appropriate, and suggested an attitude between 'association' and 'dissociation'.

Individualism also appears at one or two other points in the reports of Khārijite views. Thus it may be said to underlie the doctrine of some groups that they only 'associate' with 'those of the professors of Islam or people of the *qibla*' whom they know to be 'believers',[62] since the form of words implies 'those individuals', and it is known that some sects held that belief and unbelief were within the scope of man's free will. In general those groups which emphasized freedom of the will were also individualistic in outlook. Some Khārijites appear to have taken part in the earliest discussions of free will and kindred topics, but these matters will be reserved for chapter 4. The later Khārijite scholars who debated with the Muʿtazilites do not appear to have made any distinctive contributions to the main development of Islamic thought, and need not therefore be described in detail.

c) *The later history of the Khārijites*

The important creative period of Khārijite thought was during the intellectual ferment in and round the circle of al-Ḥasan al-Baṣrī. Khārijites subsequently played minor parts in political events, but without making any notable theological contributions.

Before the fall of the Umayyads, apart from risings in the north of Iraq, refugees from Basra had carried the Ibāḍite and Ṣufrite creeds to the Berbers of North Africa, and effectively propagated them.

There were Ibāḍites in Oman, the Yemen and other parts of Arabia. In the eastern half of the caliphate, apart from remnants of the Azraqites and Najdites who had retreated eastwards, there were pockets of moderate Khārijites established there at a later date.[63] Some groups seem to have accepted certain Persian ideas. Thus a man called Maymūn, a follower of Ibn-ʿAjarrad, permitted marriages with certain close relatives in accordance with Persian custom, though these were regarded as incestuous by the Arabs.[64] The same person, in a dispute about free will, emphasized the words 'we do not fix evil upon God' in a way that might link up with the Zoroastrian dualism of good and evil.[65] An Ibāḍite called Yazīd ibn-Unaysa held that there would be a Persian prophet (*rasūl min al-ʿajam*) with a revelation from God which would abrogate Muḥammad's.[66]

The readiness of Berbers and Persians to accept Khārijite doctrines may be due to the justification these gave for rebelling against the central government and also for considering oneself superior to other Muslims. Once Khārijite doctrine had been accepted, communities which wanted relative isolation from their neighbours, found that it gave them this. Where small states were established on Khārijite principles, these were in the moderate Ibāḍite and Ṣufrite forms.[67] Some doctrinal elaboration took place in these states in the course of centuries, but it has contributed nothing to the main stream of Islamic thought. The gradual disappearance of the Khārijite movement in the heartlands of the caliphate may be assigned to two causes. One is the acceptance by other schools of what is valid in the Khārijite standpoint; the insistence that the Islamic community should be based on revealed truth was continued by the general religious movement, and the concern for justice and the punishment of wrongdoing was taken up by the Muʿtazila, while the views of the Wāqifa are not far from those of the Murji'ites. The other reason was that in the ferment of the early ʿAbbāsid period new problems kept arising on which no light was shed from the distinctive Khārijite position, and those who clung to that position were left, as it were, in a backwater.

5

The significance of the Khārijite movement

After this study of some of the more important details of the Khārijite movement it is advantageous to stand back and look at the movement as a whole and its place in the development of Islamic thought.

The first point to notice is that an essential of the Khārijite position was the insistence that the Islamic community must be based on the Qur'ān. Presumably there were also other Muslims who believed this in some form, but they may not have formulated it explicitly even to themselves, and they were probably not prepared to make any stand when they saw the possibility of a Qur'ānic polity being whittled away by the actions of those in authority. If everyone had acquiesced in ʿUthmān's failure to inflict Qur'ānic penalties, and the apparent return to pre-Islamic principles in the dispute between ʿAlī and Muʿāwiya and the appointment of arbiters, there might never have been any genuinely Islamic empire. It is difficult to estimate the numerical strength and the influence of these presumed moderate religious-minded Muslims; but it seems likely that without the actions of the Khārijites they might well have allowed the caliphate to become a secular Arab state. The Khārijites, in their zeal for a community based on the Qur'ān, went too far in some directions, as when they asserted that the grave sinner was excluded from the community. Sects other than the Shīʿites, however, when they criticized the Khārijites, accepted the idea of a community based on Qur'ānic principles (even if expanded by Traditions), and aimed at correcting the excesses of the earlier Khārijites. While it was manifestly impossible to exclude men from the community for every grave sin, there was general agreement that membership of the Islamic community presupposed some minimum standard of belief and conduct.

Closely connected with this is a second point, namely, that the distinctive Khārijite views belong to a communalistic and not individualistic way of thinking. Although there was no word in normal use for 'group' or 'community', they discussed most matters in terms of groups or communities. They themselves were 'the believers' (*mu'minūn*) or 'the people of Paradise', while the other party was 'the unbelievers' (*kāfirūn*), 'the idolaters' (*mushrikūn*) or 'the people of Hell'. The reference to Paradise and Hell further shows that the Khārijites regarded ultimate salvation or damnation as linked with membership of the group. Because of this linking the Khārijites were much concerned about 'associating' only with 'the people of Paradise' and 'dissociating' from 'the people of Hell'. Some went further and held that not all grave sins would lead to an eternity in Hell.

Najda, for example, distinguished between what was fundamental in religion and what was not, and insisted that for sins in non-fundamentals God's punishment would not be in Hell and would not be eternal; that is, a man who committed a single act of theft or adultery would not thereby become one of 'the people of Hell'. In short, from this communalistic standpoint membership of the community leads to salvation provided a man does not hold views or perform acts which the other members regard as incompatible with membership.

The community as thus conceived may be called a 'charismatic community'. Its charisma is that it is capable of bestowing salvation on those who become members of it. It possesses this charisma because it has been divinely founded (through the revelation given by God to Muḥammad) and because it is based on and follows the divinely given rule of life or Sharīʿa (which has been developed from the Qur'ān and the example of Muḥammad). In other words, it is through belonging to the community that a man's life becomes meaningful. The community is the bearer of the values which constitute meaningfulness, and so transmits some of this meaningfulness to the members. While the Khārijites thought that this charisma was attached to their small sect-community, one result of their striving was that the Islamic community as a whole (or at least the Sunnite part of it) came to regard itself as a charismatic community. Much of the strength and solidarity of the Islamic community today comes from the belief of Sunnite Muslims in its charismatic character.[68]

This communalistic thinking about the Islamic community found among the Khārijites is closely paralleled by the thinking of the pre-Islamic Arabs about the tribe. For the nomads the tribe was the bearer of the values they recognized, summed up in the conception of *muruwwa* or 'manliness'; and it was the tribal stock which transmitted genetically the capacity for manliness. If an Arab performed a noble deed it was because he came of noble stock, that is, of a noble tribe, and his deed redounded to the glory and honour of the tribe. This parallelism of the communalistic thinking in Islam and that among the pre-Islamic Arabs further suggests (as noted above) that the early Khārijites may be regarded as attempting to reconstitute in new circumstances and on an Islamic basis the small groups they had been familiar with in the desert. If this is so, then through the Khārijite movement the feeling of the desert Arab for his tribe came to be experienced by Muslims towards the Islamic community as a whole. This feeling comprised a deep loyalty and devotion to the group which was the bearer of values, and also a sense of really belonging to it.

In so far as the Khārijites are considered to have emphasized the charismatic nature of the community, there is implicit a contrast with the Shīʿites who placed great emphasis on the charismatic character of the leader. It is true, of course, that in actual practice leaders were important in the various Khārijite revolts. Success followed strong leadership, and when the strong leader was killed the revolt often broke up. The Khārijites, however, differed from the Shīʿites in that they never assigned any special charisma to the leader. The leader might be indispensable in practice, but never was so in theory. On the contrary he was only *primus inter pares* like the Arab *sayyid*. With true nomadic egalitarianism the leader might be chosen from any tribe, or might even be a non-Arab. There was no special position for the family of Muḥammad or the house of Hāshim, or even for Quraysh as a whole.[69]

Finally there would seem to be a special connection between the Khārijite movement and certain northern Arab tribes, notably Tamīm, Ḥanīfa and Shaybān. This point can best be made, however, when the Shīʿite movement also has been studied, and will therefore be deferred to the next chapter.

2

Proto-Shī'ite Phenomena under the Umayyads

1
The nature of the problems

There is a special difficulty in respect of the use of the words *shī'a* and *tashayyu'* during the Umayyad period and indeed up to the last quarter of the ninth century. This is in addition to the usual difficulties which arise from the fact that different groups of people use words in different ways. The special difficulty consists in the fact that the Imāmite or Ithnā'asharite form of Shī'ism put out propaganda in which it insisted on a version of events during the first two Islamic centuries which supported its doctrinal position but was not necessarily in accordance with the facts. This version of events has been largely accepted by Sunnites, since it was directed not so much against them as against other forms of Shī'ism. The distorting influence of this propaganda on historical conceptions has gradually been made manifest by occidental scholars, and notably by Claude Cahen in a recent article;[1] and so in the present study it seems best to assume without argument the general soundness of this critique of the sources and to allow the later discussions to present the details which confirm it. It will be useful, however, to begin with a short statement of the chief points.

The first main point is that Shī'ism, as it is described by the heresiographers, did not exist before the last quarter of the ninth century. It is obvious that the Imāmite theory of twelve imams could not have been formulated before the death of the eleventh imam in January 874 and the disappearance of the twelfth imam about the same time. Other considerations show that the Imāmite imams from the fourth onwards did not during their lifetimes have the position which Imāmite theory postulates. To avoid confusion it has thus seemed best to avoid the term 'Shī'ite' as far as possible in the period before

874. As a substitute 'proto-Shīʿite' has been used with the intention that it should cover not only all the phenomena brought under the heading of Shīʿism by the heresiographers but also some milder forms of respect for 'the family'.

The second point is that, as Claude Cahen has maintained, certain other men than the Imāmite imams were in some sense recognized as heads of 'the family' at various times and at least by important sections of it. This means that 'the family' can be understood in narrower and wider senses. Thus it may mean the descendants of ʿAlī and Fāṭima only, or all the descendants of ʿAlī, or all the descendants of Hāshim (the clan of Hāshim). The Umayyads even seem to have tried to include themselves in 'the family' by holding that it consisted of all the descendants of ʿAbd-Manāf. In the Umayyad period those who were moved by reverence for 'the family' may not have distinguished these senses clearly. Here an attempt will be made to use the terms with precision. The descendants of ʿAlī will be called ʿAlids, those of al-Ḥasan Ḥasanids, those of al-Ḥusayn Ḥusaynids and those of al-ʿAbbās ʿAbbāsids. Those who follow and support them will be called ʿAlid supporters and so forth.

Since the clan of Hāshim is an adequate way of referring to the descendants of Hāshim, the term 'Hāshimite' will here be used for those who believed that special qualities of some sort were transmitted within the clan of Hāshim. For most of the Umayyad period this belief was held in a vague form; that is, it was not restricted to the descendants of ʿAlī, and the 'special qualities' were not necessarily thought of as the charisma later ascribed by Shīʿites to their imams. In ʿAbbāsid times Ḥāshimiyya could mean either the descendants of Hāshim (and in particular the ʿAbbāsids in so far as they held the caliphate as members of 'the family') or those who approved of ʿAbbāsid rule. Yet a third use is found, namely, for the sect which believed that the imam after Muḥammad ibn-al-Ḥanafiyya was his son Abū-Hāshim; but this is probably later Ḥusaynid or Imāmite propaganda to weaken the ʿAbbāsid claim to the caliphate by making it depend on the testament of Abū-Hāshim and not on membership of the clan of Hāshim. This third usage is found in the Imāmite writer an-Nawbakhtī (early tenth century); but the poet Kumayt (d. 743) applied the term *Hāshimiyyāt* to poems in praise of Muḥammad, ʿAlī and the ʿAlids, so that the third use cannot have been general in his time.[2]

2

The Arab share in proto-Shīʿism

Because of later events it is sometimes thought that Shīʿism is more a Persian than an Arab attitude; but careful examination of the early historical sources shows that many of the phenomena of proto-Shīʿism are first found among Arabs. In particular most leaders of revolts (other than Khārijite) during the Umayyad period made vengeance for 'the family' one point in their programme for action; and this is a typically Arab idea. With this was usually linked the further idea that 'the family' possessed special qualities—an idea in accordance with the common Arab belief that good and bad qualities like nobility and meanness were transmitted genetically through the family stock; from the exceptional gifts seen in Muḥammad, it might be inferred that there was something exceptional about the clan of Hāshim.

The idea most characteristic of later Shīʿism, however, was that of the imam or charismatic leader; and this implies that a series of men, each usually designated by his predecessor, had a special charisma over and above the general charisma of the clan of Hāshim, though doubtless connected with it. The first expression of this idea (if a historian's report may be accepted) occurred in 658 when some of ʿAlī's followers went to him and said that they would be 'friends of those whom he befriended and enemies of those to whom he was an enemy'.[3] This records a willingness to accept ʿAli's judgement in these matters and presumably also in others, and so implies, at least to a slight degree, the belief that ʿAlī was a charismatic leader. Such a belief cannot always be clearly distinguished from the belief that in a time of crisis a member of 'the family' is the wisest guide. As the phenomena of the Umayyad period are examined, however, it will be found that the idea of the charismatic leader becomes more prominent until it dominates the thinking of the supporters of 'the family'.

When ʿAlī was killed in January 661 by a Khārijite in revenge for his comrades slaughtered at an-Nahrawān, his son al-Ḥasan with Hāshimite support from Kufa made a half-hearted attempt to claim the caliphate. He was defeated by Muʿāwiya, but allowed to retire to a life of luxury in Medina. Ten years later in 671 there was an abortive revolt in Kufa led by Ḥujr ibn-ʿAdī al-Kindī. Next, after the death of Muʿāwiya and accession of Yazīd in 680, came the bid for the caliphate by al-Ḥusayn, the full brother of al-Ḥasan. Though he received only a fraction of the support he expected, he refused to give up, and his small band of about a hundred, mostly members of 'the family', was massacred at Kerbela, halfway between Kufa and the site of the later Baghdad. This martyrdom of 'the family' has dominated the imagination of Shīʿites in later times. During the four troubled years that followed Kerbela nothing is heard of the Hāshimites in Iraq, perhaps because anti-Umayyad feelings had found a focus in Ibn-az-Zubayr at Mecca, who was claiming the caliphate.

The death of Yazīd in 684 produced a new situation, for his son Muʿāwiya, though acclaimed as caliph in Damascus, was a minor, and in pre-Islamic Arab practice minors had never succeeded. Some of the older Hāshimites of Kufa therefore prepared for military action under the leadership of Sulaymān ibn-Ṣurad al-Khuzāʿī. The aims of this movement were twofold : the men involved wanted to show that they repented of their betrayal of al-Ḥusayn (and so they are known as the *tawwābūn* or Penitents) ; and they undertook to seek vengeance for his blood. Most of those responsible for the massacre at Kerbela were living in Kufa, but the governor who had despatched the army against al-Ḥusayn, ʿUbayd-Allāh ibn-Ziyād, had been forced to withdraw to the Syrian border. After some debate, the Penitents with their 4000 men decided to march against the ex-governor's army, but they were defeated and several of their leaders killed in January 685. Before the end of the year there was another rising in Kufa, but this belongs to the next section since it involves non-Arabs.

It is clear from the lists of participants in these risings that nearly all were former nomadic tribesmen. During his lifetime ʿAlī had indeed been supported by many of the Anṣār or Muslims of Medina.[4] They had a common interest with him in emphasizing the principle of *sābiqa* or 'priority' (*sc.* in acceptance of Islam and in service of the community). This principle had been made the basis of the grading in the *dīwān* or stipend-roll, and had placed ʿAlī and the Anṣār above the groups of Quraysh which were now aiming at supreme power, namely, the Umayyads and the party first of Ṭalḥa and az-Zubayr and then of Ibn-az-Zubayr. The Anṣār, however, are not found among the participants in the early ʿAlid or Hāshimite risings, presumably because as townsmen they had not experienced so great a change in their lives as the nomads, and did not feel the same tensions. Thus both the Khārijite and proto-Shī'ite movements came not from the Muslims of Mecca and Medina, but from former nomads.

Basically it would appear that proto-Shī'ite activities, like those of the Khārijites, were reactions to the abrupt change from nomadism to life as the superior military caste of a large empire. In this situation those who first began to treat 'Alī as a charismatic leader were looking for a man whom they could trust utterly to have the wisdom to guide them through their difficulties. In contrast to those who thus looked for an individual with charisma, the Khārijites considered that there was a charisma spread through the whole group of 'the people of Paradise'. At the same time they doubted whether any leader had such a charisma as was claimed and thought that a leader by himself might easily lead the community astray. Similarly those who looked to a leader denied the charisma shared in by ordinary members of the community, and insisted that decisions made by ordinary men, and not by a charismatic leader, would be sure to bring disaster. In this way proto-Shī'ites and Khārijites were diametrically opposed and each felt threatened by the other. Yet both groups were reacting to the same tensions, and it is tempting to look for further differences which might explain the contrast.

In the first place, then, there appear to be more proto-Shī'ites and fewer Khārijites from certain tribes, and fewer proto-Shī'ites and more Khārijites from certain other tribes. The first group of tribes are those called Yemenite, while the second may be called 'northern' but its precise identity will have to be considered further. The following are some statistics. In a list of twelve men who revolted with Ḥujr in 671, six were from Yemenite tribes : Bajīla (2), Ḥaḍramawt (1), Khath'am (1), Kinda (2) ; the rest were from 'Abs (1), 'Anaza (2), Shaybān (1), Tamīm (2).[5] Again among the Penitents and their associates in 684–85 the Yemenites account for nine out of sixteen : al-Ash'ar (1), Azd (1), Bajīla (3), and one each from Hamdān, Ḥimyar, Khuzā'a, Kinda ; the others were 'Abd-al-Qays (2), and one each from 'Abs, Asad, Bakr b. Wā'il, Fazāra, Muzayna.[6] There is a marked contrast to these proportions in the lists of Khārijites. In a list of Ḥarūriyya from Khārijite sources only seven men are clearly Yemenite (three from Azd, two from Khuzā'a, one from Ṭayyi', one Anṣārī) as against twenty definitely from other tribes.[7] Similarly, out of nineteen leaders of revolts against 'Alī and

Muʿāwiya whose tribe is known, only five are Yemenite (three from Ṭayyi', and one each from Bajīla and Azd); of the remainder six are from Tamīm, and there is one from each of eight other tribes.[8] It also appears to be the case that the chief leaders of later revolts and those who were important in the history of doctrine came mainly from the 'northern' tribes of Tamīm, Ḥanīfa and Shaybān.[9]

These data make it clear that a higher proportion of men from Yemenite tribes followed 'the family', while most of the leading Khārijites were from one or two 'northern' tribes. Does this help us to understand why some nomads adopted the proto-Shīʿite reaction to the contemporary situation, while others adopted the Khārijite? There do not appear to be any great economic differences between the two groups. On the whole the 'northern' tribes began raids on non-Arabs at an earlier date, but there was also a large force of the Yemenite Bajīla among the first raiders.[10] Again, though ʿAlī performed administrative functions in South Arabia about 631, there is no evidence of his gaining special affection.[11] Another possibility is that the two groups might somehow be linked with the contrast between Jewish and Christian influences or with that between Nestorians and Monophysites; and there is some similarity of ideas between Khārijites and Nestorians and between Shīʿites and Monophysites. Yet in the end a significant degree of linkage cannot be established. There may also be other factors which have contributed to the result, such as the chances which led some tribes to settle in Kufa and others in Basra, for Kufa was the main centre of proto-Shīʿism as Basra was of Khārijism.

In the absence of anything like a complete explanation of the two contrary reactions, it may be suggested as a hypothesis that an important factor in the final result was a difference in the traditional culture of the two groups. The Yemenites came from South Arabia, the land of an ancient civilization, where for a thousand years kings had succeeded one another according to a dynastic principle and had been regarded as having superhuman qualities.[12] Even if the seventh-century Arabs had no personal experience of kingship, the Yemenites came from a land where civilization had been based on charismatic leaders, and they must somehow have been influenced by the tradition. The 'northern' tribes, on the other hand, had come under no comparable influence. Though some had known the Lakhmid rulers of al-Ḥīra, the latter stood in the nomadic egalitarian tradition according to which all the adult males of a tribe were roughly equal and had a right to share in the business of the tribe. This nomadic tradition was dominant in the Arabian deserts at that time, and there are traces of 'democratic' communities in Iraq in the distant past.[13] The hypothesis here suggested, then, is not that there was any conscious attempt to re-create a former polity, but that in a time of stress and tension men's conduct was controlled by deep-seated urges, varying according to the tradition to which they mainly belonged. In some men the unconscious urge was to rely on the charismatic leader, and they eagerly searched for such a person and, when they thought they had found him, fervently acclaimed him without giving too much thought to evidence of his unsuitability. Others looked rather to the charismatic community, and again assumed too readily that they had found it and understood how it should be constituted.

3

Al-Mukhtār and the Mawālī

Until about 685 proto-Shī'ite phenomena had been entirely among Arabs, but with the revolt of al-Mukhtār non-Arabs became involved. Al-Mukhtār ibn-Abī-'Ubayd ath-Thaqafī was a man of 'Alid and Hāshimite sympathies who had not joined the Penitents in 684. For his part in a movement in favour of al-Ḥusayn he had had to go into exile shortly before the battle of Kerbela, but by 684 or 685 he was back in Kufa organizing like-minded persons. In a letter to the remnants of the Penitents he said he would base his policy on 'the Book of God, the Sunna of the Prophet, vengeance for "the family", defence of the weak, and the *jihād* against the evildoers'.[14] Thus al-Mukhtār claimed not merely to follow the Book and the Sunna, the central principles of any Islamic government, but also to pursue the aims of the Penitents; and when he got control of Kufa he actually executed those responsible for killing 'the family' at Kerbela. The phrase 'defence of the weak' referred especially to activity on behalf of the clients or *mawālī*. In addition—and this was a novel feature—al-Mukhtār claimed to act as the agent of a son of 'Alī, Muḥammad ibn-al-Ḥanafiyya ('the son of the woman of Banū Ḥanīfa', probably so known to distinguish him from another son of 'Alī also called Muḥammad and likewise from the sons of Fāṭima). Ibn-al-Ḥanafiyya probably had nothing to do with originating al-Mukhtār's movement; but, when he was imprisoned by Ibn-az-Zubayr after al-

Mukhtār had broken with the latter, he accepted help from his 'agent'. After the revolt had failed he continued to live peacefully in the Hejaz.

By some point in the year 685 al-Mukhtār had collected a sufficient army to make a successful attempt to gain control of Kufa. An Umayyad army from Syria defeated his forces in July 686, but in the following month a second army from Kufa defeated and killed the former Umayyad governor, 'Ubayd-Allāh ibn-Ziyād, at the battle of the Khāzir. Al-Mukhtār also refused to acknowledge Ibn-az-Zubayr as caliph, who was represented in Iraq by his brother Mus'ab, and the latter defeated and eventually killed al-Mukhtār, probably in the first half of 687. In view of his claim to be 'defending the weak', it seems likely that from the first al-Mukhtār had considerable support from *mawālī*, but the conflict of interest between Arabs and *mawālī* created difficulties for him. The *mawālī* accused him of favouring the Arabs, and the Arabs objected to the *mawālī* receiving any share at all of the spoil.[15] Some influential Arabs withdrew their support, and in the later stages of the revolt al-Mukhtār came to rely more on *mawālī*. It is noteworthy that his followers, though sometimes called Mukhtāriyya by the heresiographers, are more usually spoken of as Kaysāniyya. Various explanations are given of this name, as is the case with several of the older sect-names; but the Kaysān in question was almost certainly the man with the *kunya* Abū-'Amra, who was the most distinguished of the *mawālī* supporting al-Mukhtār and chief of his bodyguard.[16] The name was widely given to men of 'Alid sympathies during the latter part of the Umayyad caliphate, and was presumably a pejorative nickname first applied by opponents in order to discredit the group.[17]

It has been maintained by Julius Wellhausen and accepted by other scholars that an important result of the rising of al-Mukhtār was to bring the *mawālī* to fuller awareness of themselves as a political force.[18] Juridically there were three classes of *mawālī* : *mawlā raḥim*, *mawlā 'atāqa*, *mawlā l-'ahd*; that is, a man became a *mawlā* (sing. of *mawālī*) by kinship, by emancipation from slavery or by a covenant.[19] Of these the first is conceivably a way of incorporating matrilineally related persons into a patrilineal society; the second type is the freedman who would often be free born but enslaved through capture in war; while the third type is the man who by a compact or covenant voluntarily accepts the position of 'client' to a 'patron'.

The first type is hardly ever met with in the Umayyad period. In the biographical notices given by Ibn-Sa'd[20] of the numerous *mawālī* at Mecca, Medina, Kufa, Basra and elsewhere only a few are said to have had this status by emancipation; and the presumption is that most belong to the third type. It would appear that the caliphate was regarded as a federation of Arab tribes, so that before a non-Arab on professing Islam could be accepted as a citizen of the caliphate he had to become a client of an Arab tribe, and this could most simply be done by a covenant. There was nothing to prevent an Arab becoming a client of another Arab, and instances of this are found.[21]

The *mawālī*, then, whose discontent at their status was a factor in the downfall of the Umayyads were Muslims of non-Arab origin attached by covenant to Arab tribes. In a history of Islamic thought we are specially concerned with those from southern Iraq. Here at the Arab conquest the population had been predominantly Aramaean, but with an upper stratum of Persian landlords and officials. In several areas the peasants had helped the Muslims against the Persians.[22] Many of the *mawālī* here must have been of Aramaean (and also Christian) origin. The important scholars who were *mawālī* had doubtless had some connection with the Christian institutions of higher education in Iraq. Some proto-Shī'ite ideas are similar to pre-Christian ideas (like the death of Tammuz), and this suggests that many proto-Shī'ites were from the old stock of the land (and persons assimilated to it) rather than from more recent Persian immigrants. Aramaean-Christian influence is to be seen in the case of Abū-Manṣūr (head of the Manṣūriyya) who was an illiterate desert Arab, probably of the tribe of 'Abd-al-Qays, yet who heard God speaking to him in Syriac (*suryānī*), and who assigned a special place in his cosmology to 'Īsā and the *kalima* or 'Word of God'.[23]

Although it is thus plausible to think of the *mawālī* of southern Iraq as mainly of Aramaean and Christian origin, it must be noted that there was also a Persian element. One man is said to have allowed the Persian practice of marriage to daughters.[24] The father of another sectarian is said to have been a *zindīq*, which probably implies that he was a Persian or persianized Aramaean.[25] The persianizing tendency is also illustrated by the statement that part of the tribe of 'Ijl had 'completely passed into the Persian nationality'.[26] This becomes more significant when it is realized that towards the end of the Umayyad period several leaders of Hāshimite supporters were from ʿIjl. Al-Mughīra ibn-Saʿīd was of ʿIjl, though he had become a client of Khālid al-Qasrī (of Bajīla); Abū-Manṣūr is sometimes said to be of ʿIjl, sometimes of ʿAbd-al-Qays; and Abū-Muslim, the architect of the ʿAbbāsid victory, was a *mawlā* of ʿIjl and said to be of Persian stock. It must also be kept in mind that Persian influence had been spreading among the Arabs long before the Muslim conquest of Iraq. Evidence of this influence is to be seen in the Persian words which are found in the Qur'ān and in pre-Islamic poetry.[27] In the half-century before the break-up of the Persian empire there were pro-Persian groups in power in various little states in the Persian Gulf, while a Persian army occupied the Yemen; it is known that the latter became arabized, but some Persian influence must also have emanated from them.[28] Mecca had trade contacts with the Persian empire, and one Meccan pagan claimed to have a knowledge of Persian stories that was comparable to the Qur'ān.[29] Among the Muslims at Badr were two or three *mawālī* of Persian extraction.[30]

The discontent of the *mawālī*, however, even if raised to self-awareness by al-Mukhtār, did not become an effective political force until much later.

4

The period of quiescence

After the death of al-Mukhtār there is no record of any Hāshimite revolt until 737, but this half-century of quiescence is a period containing important proto-Shīʿite phenomena. The term 'Kaysānite' is common in early sources, and various sub-sects are listed by the heresiographers.[31] This would seem to show not merely a continuing belief in the imamate of Ibn-al-Ḥanafiyya but also some persistence of al-Mukhtār's movement.[32] The political aspects may be left aside for the moment while attention is drawn to the appearance of novel religious ideas about the charismatic leader.

It was presumably after the death of Ibn-al-Ḥanafiyya in 700 that messianic ideas about him began to spread. We know the name of at least one man involved in this messianism, the poet Kuthayyir; he is reported to have been present at the caliphal courts of ʿAbd-al-Malik (685–705) and his son Yazīd (720–24) in Damascus, though he mostly lived in Medina; the date of his death is given as 723.[33] He is sometimes said to have belonged to a sub-sect of the Kaysāniyya called the Karbiyya or Karibiyya about whose founder nothing seems to be known. The view propagated by Kuthayyir was that Muḥammad ibn-al-Ḥanafiyya had not died but was in concealment at mount Raḍwā, seven days' journey from Medina, nourished by springs of water and honey and protected by a lion and a leopard; he would return at the appropriate time and fill the earth with justice as it was now filled with wickedness. There were other versions according to which the place of concealment was unknown.

This appears to be the first occurrence among Muslims of ideas of this kind, though they afterwards came to be held by Shīʿite groups in many forms. For the present, it was held, the imam or charismatic leader was in concealment (*ghayba*), but his return (*rajʿa*) was confidently expected; and when he returned he would be the Mahdī, 'the guided one' (a kind of Messiah), who would right all wrongs and establish justice on the earth. The similarity of these ideas to Judaeo-Christian messianic ideas has often been noted; but this is no mere imitation. Such ideas gave a measure of hope to men in an almost impossible situation, and yet helped them to accept the situation in so far as it was inevitable. Believers in a 'hidden imam' are not required to do anything in the present, not even to work for the reform of any particular abuse. There has always been among Muslim scholars a strain of quietism, manifesting itself in a tendency to accept any actual or *de facto* authority, without asking about its legitimacy. This is well illustrated by Ibn-Ḥazm's account of the obligation of 'commanding the right and prohibiting the wrong' (*al-amr bi-l-maʿrūf wa-n-nahy ʿan al-munkar*). According to many scholars this obligation was to be fulfilled in a man's heart only in the first place, though there were no exceptions to this; if there was an opportunity, he was to fulfil the obligation by his tongue; but he was never to do it by his hand and by drawing swords. Ibn-Ḥazm then adds that all the 'Rāfiḍites' held this to be so, even if all were to be killed, but they restricted it to the time before 'the speaking (*nāṭiq*) imam' had raised his standard; when he did so, he must be supported by the sword.[34] There are curious reports about how some of the Kaysāniyya who wanted to be active before the appearance of the imam armed themselves with wooden clubs instead of swords.[35]

Not many names are known of actual persons who held messianic ideas. One such was Ḥamza ibn-ʿUmāra (or 'Ammāra) of Medina, who had followers in both Medina and Kufa. In general his views were those of the Kaysāniyya and Karbiyya, but he is also alleged to have held that Muḥammad ibn-al-Ḥanafiyya was God and he himself his prophet.[36] This last is probably a hostile exaggeration of some statement of his about his relation to Muḥammad ibn-al-Ḥanafiyya. Similar to the views of Kuthayyir were those of another later poet, as-Sayyid al-Ḥimyarī (723–89).[37] While the two poets held that their imam was concealed at Raḍwā, Ḥamza maintained that his place of concealment was not known.

It would further appear that, if the Saba'iyya are really connected with ʿAbd-Allāh ibn-Saba', he should be placed in the half-century of quiescence. Ibrāhīm an-Nakhaʿī (to be discussed presently) is reported to have denied being a Saba'ite;[38] and the insurgent al-Mughīra, who was executed in 737, is said to have been one originally.[39] This shows that the name was in use before that time. The report in al-Ashʿarī about the Saba'iyya only states that they believe that ʿAlī is not dead but will return before the day of resurrection to institute a reign of justice; and from the mention of the belief of the Saba'iyya in the 'return' from the dead he passes to a mention of as-Sayyid al-Ḥimyarī holding this belief.[40] The conjunction of the reports and the similarity of view suggest that the Saba'iyya are not too distant in time from as-Sayyid al-Ḥimyarī.

Those persons just mentioned with messianic views are in a sense precursors of later Shīʿism. Proto-Shīʿite phenomena, however, also comprise the 'activists' to be considered in the next section, and certain 'quietists' who are not Shīʿite in the later sense, but who are included by Ibn-Qutayba in his list of 'Shīʿa'. The significance of the list as a whole will be discussed later (pp. 58, 61). For the moment it will be sufficient to look at those men on the list who lived during the Umayyad period. Like the later men also they are all respected Traditionists or, as we shall say, members of the general religious movement. One is described by Ibn-Saʿd as a *shīʿī*, but this is probably only in respect of his close association with ʿAlī in the administration of the caliphate.[41] Another joined the rising of Ibn-al-Ashʿath against al-Ḥajjāj in 701, fled to Khurasan and was captured; on being asked to curse ʿAlī he refused and was punished.[42] Another was critical of al-Ḥajjāj but remained on good terms with the régime, so that the caliph Hishām gave the funeral address for him in 724.[43] Apart from these rather slight points we are told nothing about the political views of the men in question with one exception.

The exception is Ibrāhīm an-Nakhaʿī (d. c. 714), who is the first important figure among the scholars of Kufa. If we may accept as authentic one or two sayings attributed to him, they give an idea of the content of the Shīʿism attributed to him. In general he is known to have been bitterly opposed to the Murji'ites, and to have disliked al-Ḥajjāj. On one occasion a pupil was perplexed by the discussions about ʿAlī and ʿUthmān, and asked his view; he replied that he was neither a Saba'ite nor a Murji'ite. This probably means, on the one hand, that he did not regard ʿAlī as being a messianic figure or in some way charismatic, and, on the other hand, that he did not attribute any special merit to ʿUthmān. This interpretation is in line with two further sayings. He reproached a man who said that ʿAlī was dearer to him than Abū-Bakr and ʿUmar, and asserted that this view would have been objectionable to ʿAlī himself. He also said that for his own part ʿAli was dearer to him than ʿUthmān, but that he would rather forfeit Heaven than speak ill of ʿUthmān.[44] This seems to indicate that he accepted the first four caliphs, but considered the merits of ʿAlī greater than those of ʿUthmān. The significance of these views can only be discovered when the phenomena of the ʿAbbāsid period are examined. For the moment Ibrāhīm's views illustrate the complexity of the attitudes towards ʿAlī.

5

The Hāshimite revolts during the Umayyad decline

A series of revolts from about 737 onwards may be regarded as the 'activist' aspect of proto-Shīʿite phenomena. The growing weakness of the dynasty was doubtless becoming obvious to the more perceptive. Some men hoped to turn this situation to their personal advantage; others seem without actually plotting to have given sufficient expression to their discontent to rouse the suspicions of the authorities in their anxious state. More than previously the ordinary man in this crisis was looking for some member of 'the family' to give him a lead. Several men of the clan of Hāshim are named as actual or nominal leaders of revolts, but there are inconsistencies in the accounts. The material will be presented briefly in this section, and the credibility of the Imāmite version will be discussed in the next section.

One of the first to suffer, though his activity did not lead to an actual revolt, was Bayān ibn-Simʿān, a straw-dealer of Kufa belonging to the Yemenite tribe of Nahd (or to Tamīm). He was a follower of the quietist Ḥamza ibn-'Umāra, and at first claimed to be an emissary of Abū-Hāshim, whom some held to have succeeded his father Muḥammad ibn-al-Ḥanafiyya as imam.[45] It was perhaps later that, according to a report, he wrote to the Ḥusaynid Muḥammad al-Bāqir (d. 731–37) and called on him to accept himself (Bayān) as a prophet. At another point—conceivably after the death of al-Bāqir if that was before Bayān's—he claimed that al-Bāqir had appointed him as his emissary. It is also reported, however, that he was hostile to al-Bāqir. Other versions are that he was planning a revolt, perhaps in conjunction with al-Mughīra (who is about to be mentioned) and that this was in the name either of al-Bāqir's son Ja'far aṣ-Ṣādiq or of an-Nafs az-Zakiyya, a Ḥasanid who actually revolted in 762.[46] Some of this activity came to the ears of the governor of Kufa, who decided that it was sufficiently serious to have Bayān and al-Mughīra arrested and then executed by burning in 737.

The full name of this apparent associate of Bayān was al-Mughīra ibn-Sa'īd al-'Ijlī.[47] An anthropomorphic account of the creation is ascribed to him, and he also claimed to know the greatest name of God and to gain various powers from this knowledge. He is said to have for a time looked to Muḥammad al-Bāqir as his imam, then on his death to have turned to an-Nafs az-Zakiyya; but the latter, since he was only 19 in 737, may not have acknowledged al-Mughīra as his agent in any way. Jābir ibn Yazīd al-Ju'fī (d. c. 745) is said to have been a follower of al-Mughīra; he was highly thought of as a Traditionist by some, but severely criticized by others.[48]

Yet a third man is said to have professed himself a follower of Muḥammad al-Bāqir and to have claimed to be his legatee. This was Abū-Manṣūr of the tribe of 'Ijl or 'Abd-al-Qays, who lived in Kufa.[49] For a year or two before his execution by the governor of Iraq in 742 he seems to have been active in propagating his teaching. Of the followers he gained some practised strangulation. There was a revival of his teaching about 780. Like the two previous leaders, he showed special interest in the descendants of al-Ḥusayn. He was not content to be merely an agent, however, but asserted that he was the *waṣī* or 'legatee' of Muḥammad al-Bāqir, and so his successor. He gave further support to this claim by maintaining that he had experienced an ascension to heaven, in the course of which he had been commissioned by God as a prophet and messenger. He seems to have been the first to attach cosmic importance to 'the family of Muḥammad', for in some strange way he identified 'the family of Muḥammad' with heaven and 'the party' (*shīʿa*—presumably his own following) with earth. He was probably only a client of the Arab tribe, for (as noted above) during the ascension God is said to have addressed him in Syriac, while the last points of teaching are reminiscent of ancient Mesopotamian mythology.

If the reports of Bayān, al-Mughīra and Abū-Manṣūr are authentic, they show that by 737 there was a growing interest in the family of al-Ḥusayn, at least among some of the groups of proto-Shīʿites. The possibility must be kept in mind, however, that these reports are later Imāmite inventions to support the contention that Muḥammad al-Bāqir was recognized as imam during his lifetime. It is difficult to determine whether towards the end of his life Muḥammad al-Bāqir was personally giving some attention to politics. Propaganda for the ʿAbbāsids had probably begun by that time; and his son Jaʿfar aṣ-Ṣādiq may also have been putting forward claims on his own behalf. In the latter case Bayān and the other two may have been trying to counter the claims of Jaʿfar and the ʿAbbāsids; and the story that Bayān called on Muḥammad al-Bāqir to follow him and was roughly rejected may be an invention (perhaps by an associate of Jaʿfar) to parry Bayān's claim.

The first descendant of the Prophet to lead a revolt personally was Muḥammad al-Bāqir's brother Zayd ibn-ʿAlī, who rose against the Umayyads in 740, but was killed almost at once. The sect of Zaydites, called after this Zayd, is still in existence, but its real rise to importance and its attainment of a distinctive body of doctrine belong to the early ʿAbbāsid period (cf. chapter 6), and it is not clear how far these later doctrines coincide with the views of Zayd himself. It seems certain that he and his followers rejected any idea of a quiescent or hidden imam, and insisted that the imam is not entitled to claim allegiance until he has publicly asserted his imamate. He is said to have held that the imam must be a descendant of ʿAlī and Fāṭima, though this may rather be the teaching of later Zaydites. In general Zayd was trying to mobilize a wide band of proto-Shīʿite feeling behind his attempt to gain control of the caliphate, as it slipped from the hands of the Umayyads. The messianic movements just considered had been irrational, giving vent to material grievances and spiritual yearnings but having no considered plan for taking over the administration of the caliphate. Zayd, on the contrary, was over-rational. He saw that, in order to rule the caliphate effectively, he must have the main body of Muslim opinion behind him, and must therefore accept the views of this body. In particular he took the view that Abū-Bakr and 'Umar had been rightful caliphs and imams, but qualified this—to placate the upholders of 'Alī's rights—by adding that, though 'Alī was superior, this was an instance where 'the imamate of the inferior' (*mafḍūl*) was permissible to secure certain immediate advantages. Even this modified acceptance of Abū-Bakr and 'Umar, however, seemed to some to involve a partial denial of the charismata of 'Alī and the clan of Hāshim, and probably lost Zayd the support of many who believed in these charismata.

The last Hāshimite to lead an unsuccessful revolt against the Umayyads was 'Abd-Allāh ibn-Mu'āwiya, great-grandson of 'Alī's brother Ja'far. The revolt began in Kufa in 744, and continued until the assassination of 'Abd-Allāh by Abū-Muslim, probably in 747. There is much confusion about the theological doctrines connected with this man. Apparently a certain follower of Bayān, connected with the quietest section of the Kaysāniyya, by name 'Abd-Allāh ibn-'Amr ibn-Ḥarb al-Kindī, had propagated in Kufa ideas about the hidden imam and the transmigration of souls. Some of those who accepted these ideas then became followers of 'Abd-Allāh ibn-Mu'āwiya, and applied them to him, especially after his death.[50] The connection with the Kaysāniyya is further supported by the claim that 'Abd-Allāh ibn-Mu'āwiya was the legatee of Abū-Hāshim, the son of Muḥammad ibn-al-Ḥanafiyya. It is not clear how far 'Abd-Allāh ibn-Mu'āwiya approved even of the claims made for him during his life. He does not appear to have had a clear and definite set of ideas as a basis for his movement, and this doubtless contributed to his failure. At first the remnants of Zayd's forces are said to have been a more important part of his army than those who held messianic ideas derived from the Kaysāniyya; and later, when he had to move from Kufa into Persia and controlled a large area there, his supporters included almost every shade of Muslim religious and political opinion.

Finally there was a revolt which destroyed the Umayyads and brought the 'Abbāsid dynasty to the caliphal throne, but this will more appropriately be discussed in chapter 6.

6

The significance of proto-Shī'ite phenomena

a) *The various aspects of the phenomena*

Under the term 'proto-Shī'ite' here there have been brought together a number of phenomena which hitherto have been described as the beginnings of the Shī'ite movement. Such a description, however, would read into the phenomena a greater unity than one is justified in assuming that they possess during the Umayyad period. We have in fact several groups of disparate phenomena. It may well be that they arise from common factors, and that most of them contribute to the Shī'ism of the tenth (fourth Islamic) century as that is conceived by the heresiographers. Until after the year 750, however, and indeed until after 874, one should avoid assuming the existence of connections unless there is good evidence for them.

The minimal form of belief which may be called proto-Shī'ite is a belief in the personal worthiness of 'Alī. Such a belief, as has been seen, may be ascribed to Ibrāhīm an-Nakha'ī. One would also seem to be justified in supposing that such a belief was held by many of those who supported 'Alī during his lifetime. From such a belief the element of special charisma is presumably absent.

From this minimal belief there is to be distinguished any form of belief in which charismatic qualities are held to be present in the clan of Hāshim or in some members of it. These charismatic qualities might be conceived in different ways, varying from a supremely high degree of human excellence, including gifts of leadership, to a supernatural or divinely given endowment. Belief in an inheriting of special human excellence through the clan stock would be in accordance with the ideas of the pre-Islamic Arabs, whereas the idea of the manifestation in men of superhuman qualities may rather have come from Aramaean and Persian elements among the Muslims. In some form or other, however, the charismatic leader of the house of Hāshim had an appeal for masses of Muslims during the period from 700 to 850 and later. It was only gradually that belief in charismata restricted to the descendants of al-Ḥusayn became predominant. For several decades Muḥammad ibn-al-Ḥanafiyya and his son Abū-Hāshim attracted more attention. The poet Kuthayyir speaks of 'Alī and his three sons, who are of course al-Ḥasan, al-Ḥusayn and Muḥammad ibn-al-Ḥanafiyya, and the impression is given that the three are roughly equal. Indeed it is the third who is said not to have died but to be in concealment; and from this it may be inferred that the poet and doubtless other men were not interested in the descendants of al-Ḥusayn. Moreover even in the years round 750 it was still possible to claim charismata for other members of the clan of Hāshim, notably ʿAlī's brother Jaʿfar and Muḥammad's uncle al-ʿAbbās. This wide extension of the charismata is a distinctive feature of proto-Shīʿism.

General considerations of this kind throw doubt on the Imāmite version of events during the Umayyad period. According to this version one of the descendants of al-Ḥusayn was always from the time of Kerbela recognized as 'imam'; and it is indicated or implied that by the use of this term it is meant that he was head of 'the family' and in some sense leader of a movement. Many accepted facts, however, contradict this conception. Even in the Imāmite accounts it is clear that the imams were not seriously engaged in politics, at least until near the end of the Umayyad rule.[51] The first reliable account of political activity by a Ḥusaynid is that of the revolt of Zayd ibn-ʿAlī in 740. Before that date, however, the later Imāmites and Ismāʿīlites held that three men had been 'recognized as imams': (1) ʿAlī known as Zayn-al-ʿĀbidīn ('ornament of the worshippers'), the elder surviving son of al-Ḥusayn, who died in 712; (2) his eldest son Muḥammad, known as al-Bāqir ('the ample', *sc.* in knowledge), who died between 731 and 737; (3) the latter's son Jaʿfar, known as aṣ-Ṣādiq ('the truthful'), who lived into the ʿAbbāsid period and died in 765.

The first of these men, ʿAlī Zayn-al-ʿĀbidīn, had a reputation for piety and uprightness of life, but even in the later literature is seldom mentioned in a way that implies leadership of any kind. One of the rare notices about him, however, occurs in al-Ashʿarī, and directly contradicts the Imāmite version, for it speaks of a sect which recognized as imams first Muḥammad ibn-al-Ḥanafiyya, then his son Abū-Hāshim, and only then Zayn-al-ʿĀbidīn.[52] This is all the more remarkable, since it implies that Ḥusaynid supporters recognized two non-Ḥusaynid imams. This clinches the other arguments for Claude Cahen's view that after the death of al-Ḥusayn the man widely recognized as imam or head by 'the family' and their supporters was Muḥammad ibn-al-Ḥanafiyya.[53] This view makes sense of a great many details: he was the most capable of the surviving sons of ʿAlī; numerous sects are associated with his imamate, namely, the sub-sects of the Kaysāniyya, and the Kaysāniyya was for long the most important proto-Shīʿite group; messianic ideas were apparently first attached to his name.

On the assumption that this view is correct it is further probable that on Ibn-al-Ḥanafiyya's death many who had accepted him as imam accorded a similar recognition to his son Abū-Hāshim. This recognition, however, could hardly have been more than recognition of him as official representative and spokesman of 'the family' (here presumably the descendants of ʿAlī) in specifically family matters. It cannot have included any political role, since neither father nor son was molested by the Umayyads. The fact that in 750 the ʿAbbāsids claimed that the headship of the family had passed from Abū-Hāshim to one of them shows that Abū-Hāshim must at one time have been widely recognized (even if only in a non-political role), and that this former recognition still had some residual importance.

Towards the end of the Umayyad period changes were taking place in the form of political expression given to Hāshimite sympathies. There was no general recognition of any one man as imam in a political sense, but many seekers for power tried to use Hāshimite sympathies for their own ends and to gain support for some political programme by appealing to these sympathies as well as to the dissatisfaction with Umayyad rule. The most serious problem was perhaps to prevent the dissipation of a potentially significant political force into many small insurrectionary movements headed by almost any member of the clan of Hāshim or indeed by anyone claiming to be the agent of a member. One of the methods adopted to counter this loss of effectiveness was to propound the idea that there was only one possessor of Hāshimite charismata in the full sense at any one time, and that this person appointed or designated (*naṣṣa*) a successor; the word *awṣā*, 'appoint as legatee' (*waṣī*), was also used. The person so appointed was of course the *imām* or leader.

It is difficult to know how prevalent in the earlier Umayyad period was this practice of designating a successor. Both the contemporaries of the Umayyads and also later Shīʿites claimed in numerous cases that so-and-so had made so-and-so his legatee; and such claims might be made long after the events. We have thus to distinguish: (a) the claim that a particular appointment was made; (b) the date at which the claim was made public; (c) the factual question whether there was such as appointment. In one important case, the alleged appointment of an ʿAbbāsid as heir by Abū-Hāshim about 716, it is clear that the claim or allegation had been made public by about 750. By this time, then, the idea that the imam designated his successor must have been widely accepted. The success of the ʿAbbāsids in gaining supreme power suggests that they may have been either the inventors or the first outstanding exponents of this idea.

Another aspect of proto-Shīʿite phenomena, the messianic ideas, had been present in Iraq and neighbouring lands for centuries. As held by Muslims these ideas had a distinctive Islamic colouring and are a new phenomenon; but they may also be regarded as an adaptation of older ideas. For the student of Islamic thought, however, the focus of interest is rather the function of these ideas within Islamic society and their contribution to the later forms of Shīʿism. In the Umayyad period the idea of the Mahdī was often associated with political quietism and the acceptance of existing circumstances despite various drawbacks. Yet it was always possible, at least in theory, that the Mahdī or his agent might appear and summon men to arms, so that they would pass from quietism to active insurrection. Whether in any given case this possibility was realized depended on the temperament of the believers in the Mahdī. It may also be noted that along with the idea of the Mahdī there entered Islam other old ideas of the Middle East and India, such as that of the transmigration of souls (*tanāsukh*).

b) *The use of names*

The later and now normal usage of Shīʿa is well defined by ash-Shahrastānī : 'the Shīʿa are those who "follow" (*shāyaʿu*) ʿAlī—peace be on him—in particular, and assert his imamate and caliphate by appointment and delegation (*naṣṣ, waṣiyya*) made either openly or secretly, and who believe that the imamate does not depart from his descendants'.[54] This is a more careful and comprehensive definition than that of al-Ashʿarī, who merely says that 'they are called the Shīʿa because they "follow" (*shāyaʿu*) ʿAlī—may God approve of him—and place him before the other Companions of the Messenger of God'. Al-Ashʿarī rarely used this term, however, and for his heading has the plural *shiyaʿ*, 'parties', though he is also familiar with the abstract noun *tashayyuʿ*, which might be rendered 'Shīʿism'.[55] The later Ashʿarite al-Baghdādī in *Al-farq bayn al-firaq* almost completely avoids Shīʿa except in virtual quotations, and uses Rāfiḍa or Rawāfiḍ instead.[56] Similarly the ninth-century Muʿtazilite al-Khayyāṭ only has Shīʿa where he is quoting from Ibn-ar-Rāwandī.[57] About the same time Ibn-Qutayba, as noted above, only uses Shīʿa in a specially mild sense. Both these authors normally speak of the Rāfiḍa. Perhaps this reluctance to speak of heretics as the Shīʿa is due to the fact that it is a 'good' word; Aḥmad ibn-Ḥanbal, for example, wanted to claim that the Ahl as-Sunna wa-l-Ḥadīth were the true *shīʿa* of ʿAlī since they had due affection for the family of Muḥammad and recognized the rights of ʿAlī.[58] The Ḥanbalite al-Barbahārī (d. 940) distinguished between *shīʿī*, as the man who acknowledges Abū-Bakr and ʿAlī and does not decide between ʿAlī and ʿUthmān, from the *rāfiḍī* who puts ʿAlī above ʿUthmān;[59] this is in line with Ibn-Ḥanbal's remark. About the same period the 'normal' sense of Shīʿa is found in Ibn-an-Nadīm and at least occasionally in al-Masʿūdī.[60]

These references show that *shīʿa* was originally a term in use mainly among some proto-Shīʿite groups, though certain Traditionists wanted to lay claim to it. It seems likely that ʿAlī had the habit of calling certain close associates—or perhaps all who followed him against Ṭalḥa and az-Zubayr—*shīʿatī*, 'my party'.[61] A non-technical use—that is, *shīʿat N* in the sense of 'the party of N'—seems to have been common among proto-Shīʿites. An-Nawbakhtī in *Firaq ash-shīʿa*, though he adopts the later general sense, sometimes also uses the word in a non-technical way.[62] Although an-Nawbakhtī and other heresiographers define the Shīʿa as the followers of ʿAlī, they include among the Shīʿa the sects connected with the descendants of Jaʿfar ibn-Abī-Ṭālib and of al-ʿAbbās. An early example of the general use of the term is found in a quotation from the Shīʿite Ibn-ar-Rāwandī where he states that the *umma* or Islamic community consists of five sects: Shīʿa, Khawārij, Murji'a, Muʿtazila and Aṣ'ḥāb al-Ḥadīth.[63] With this may be compared a statement ascribed to Ibn-al-Mubārak (d. 797) that the four fundamental sects are Qadariyya, Murji'a, Shīʿa and Khawārij.[64] Ibn-al-Mubārak cannot have regarded himself as belonging to the Shīʿa, though he is linked with men in Ibn-Qutayba's list of Shīʿa, for he is reported as praising the piety of Muʿāwiya;[65] so he presumably considered all four sects heretical.

From this material it is apparent that Shīʿa, unlike most early names of sects, did not originate as a nickname given by opponents, but was normally used by men of themselves. It was frequently used non-technically. Moreover it was not objectionable to the main body of the Traditionists, as is shown by Ibn-Qutayba's list, and by the fact that all the men on the list are given biographies by Ibn-Saʿd in his *Ṭabaqāt*. Ignaz Goldziher pointed out that *tashayyuʿ* or affection and admiration for the house of ʿAlī might be either good or bad (*tashayyuʿ ḥasan, qabīḥ*), and only became heretical when it went to excess.[66] The term Shīʿa was gradually restricted to the followers of ʿAlī and the ʿAlids, and by the later ninth century Ibn-ar-Rāwandī was prepared to accept it as a fundamental division of the Islamic community; and this implied that he was prepared to regard all or most of the strange proto-Shīʿite groups as in some sense forerunners of himself and his associates.

During the Umayyad period, then, the term 'the Shīʿa' was not used in the comprehensive sense later given to it. The nearest term to this was probably Kaysāniyya, which, though by most heresiographers restricted to followers of Muḥammad ibn-al-Ḥanafiyya, is used by an-Nawbakhtī at least once without any reference to him.[67] It is also possible that Sabaʾiyya was another early general term in view of its use by Ibrāhīm an-Nakhaʿī (as noted above). The term Rāfiḍa, on the other hand, probably did not come into use until after 750, and will be dealt with later.

ANNEX A. *ʿAbd-Allāh ibn-Sabaʾ and the Sabaʾiyya*

The evidence available at the beginning of the century concerning ʿAbd-Allāh ibn-Sabaʾ was carefully examined by Israel Friedlaender in a long article entitled "Abdallāh b. Sabā, der Begründer der Sīʿa, und sein jüdischer Ursprung'.[68] He rightly considered that the fundamental parts of this evidence were extracts from aṭ-Ṭabarī (i. 2858f., 2922, 2942, 2944, 2954, 3163ff.), the notice of ash-Shahrastānī (132, or i.289–91), and that in the *Farq* of al-Baghdādī (223–6). He pointed out the inconsistencies and contradictions of this material, and also argued that the particular form of messianic ideas involved was similar to that of Jews in the Yemen and the Falashas of Abyssinia. Other European views are briefly mentioned in the article by Marshall Hodgson in *EI*[2] ('Abd Allāh b. Sabaʾ). Since the time Friedlaender wrote further material has become available, notably the accounts by al-Ashʿarī,[69] an-Nawbakhtī,[70] al-Malaṭī (quoting Khushaysh)[71] and an-Nāshiʾ;[72] in addition the *Ṭabaqāt* of Ibn-Saʿd have been completed and the valuable index added. The purpose of this Annex is to justify the neglect of the Saba'iyya in the main account of proto-Shī'ite phenomena, and it will be sufficient, without going over again the ground covered by other writers, to underline some of the conclusions.

1) It is suspicious that no one is named as belonging to the sect except 'Abd-Allāh ibn-Saba', an Ibn-Sawdā' (who may be the same) and an obscure Companion, Rushayd al-Hajarī. Because of this, too, no continuity can be shown between the Saba'iyya and other proto-Shī'ite and later Shī'ite phenomena. It follows that the Saba'iyya cannot be considered the beginning of Shī'ism. They have therefore been neglected in the preceding chapter.

2) Al-Ash'arī knows nothing of an early date. He mentions (i.15) the Sabā'iyya, the followers of 'Abd-Allāh ibn-Sabā', as the fourteenth sect of the Ghāliya or extreme Shī'a. He also mentions, as holding some of the same views (but not necessarily as a member of the sect), as-Sayyid al-Ḥimyarī, who lived from 723 to 789. On general grounds the views ascribed to the Saba'iyya might be dated as having been first propounded about 700. The report in Ibn-Sa'd (vi.192) that Ibrāhīm an-Nakha'ī (d. c. 714) said he was neither a Sabā'ī nor a Murji'ī shows the name must have been in use by about 710. Another point linking the name with the early eighth century is that az-Zuhrī (d. 742) said that Abū-Hāshim (d. 716), son of Ibn-al-Ḥanafiyya, made a collection of *aḥādīth as-sabā'iyya.*[73]

3) It is not necessary that the name should be derived from a real individual of any importance. There is a similar obscurity about the origin of the name Kaysāniyya. Friedlaender notes that Saba' is unusual as a name. Saba'ī could be the adjective from the tribe of Saba'. Yāqūt (*Buld.*, iii.27) says the tribe had become proverbial for going in different ways.

4) An-Nāshi' (1/§33), probably using material from the early ninth century, describes the Saba'iyya as those who denied 'Alī's death and regarded him as a messianic figure.

5) In the light of these points the following hypotheses may be put forward. (a) The name is a nickname and may well overlap other names. It could be derived from the tribe, perhaps with reference to the proverb, or to indicate someone with extreme views. In this case the individual could have been invented to make the name less unpleasant. It is also possible that some element of truth underlies the names of the sect and the individual. (b) The story of the punish-

ment of Ibn-Saba' by ʿAlī was probably invented later by followers of ʿAlī who wanted to discredit extreme Shīʿite ideas. The Shīʿites constantly project later claims back into the past; e.g. an-Nawbakhtī (p. 2) speaks of ʿAlī as having been put forward as a claimant for the caliphate on the day Muḥammad died, though there is no mention of this in the usual historical sources. (c) This view gains some support from the fact that Abū-l-ʿAbbās, in the first Friday address after his proclamation as caliph, is reported to have violently attacked the followers of Ibn-Saba'.[74]

ANNEX B. *Ibn-Qutayba's list of the Shīʿa—earlier members*

The following are the men included in Ibn-Qutayba's list of the Shīʿa (*Maʿārif*, 301) who died during the Umayyad period. All have notices in Ibn-Saʿd (IS), and some at an earlier point in *Maʿārif* (*M*). All are from Kufa except no. 7.

1) Ṣaʿṣaʿa b. Ṣuḥan : with ʿAlī at battle of the Camel; d. in reign of Muʿāwiya (IS, vi. 154)

2) al-Aṣbagh b. Nubāta : associate of ʿAlī, but held to be weak in Traditions related from ʿAlī and others; called *shīʿī* by Fiṭr b. Khalīfa (d. 155) (IS, vi. 157)

3) Ḥabba b. Juwayn : related Traditions from ʿAlī and (?) Ibn-ʿAbbās, but held weak; d. 76 (IS, vi. 123)

4) al-Ḥārith al-Aʿwar : related from ʿAlī and Ibn-Masʿūd; weak as Traditionist, but approved by no. 13; d. at Kufa under Ibn-az-Zubayr (IS, vi. 116f.)

5) Ibr. an-Nakhaʿī : important jurist of Kufa (see above); d. 95/6 (IS, vi. 188–99; *M*, 235)

6) Sālim b. Abī-Jaʿd : d. 100/1 or earlier (IS, vi. 203) *M*, 230)

7) Ṭā'ūs : critical of al-Ḥajjāj; caliph Hishām gave funeral address; d. 106 (IS, v. 391–5; *M*, 231)

8) ʿAṭiyya b. Saʿd al-ʿAwfī : joined Ibn-al-Ashʿath against al-Ḥajjāj; fled; later returned to Kufa; d. 111 (IS, vi. 212f.)

9) al-Ḥakam b. ʿUtayba : sound Traditionist; d. 115 (IS, vi. 231; *M*, 235)

10) Ḥabīb b. AThābit : a leading scholar; d. 119 (IS, vi. 223)

11) Salma b. Kuhayl : d. 122, when Zayd b. ʿAlī killed in Kufa (IS, vi. 221)

12) AṢādiq al-Azdī : ascetic (IS, vi. 206f.)

13) AIs'ḥāq as-Sabīʿī : Traditionist; d. 128/9 aged over 98 (IS, vi. 219f.; *M*, 230)
14) Manṣūr b. al-Muʿtamir : d. 132 (IS, vi. 235)
Ibn-Qutayba also lists (p. 300) the following sects of the Rāfiḍa : Khashabiyya, Kaysāniyya, Sabā'iyya, Mughīriyya, Manṣūriyya, Khaṭṭābiyya, Ghurābiyya, Zaydiyya, Ghāliya.

He gives (p. 301) as the names of the Ghāliya : Abū-ṭ-Ṭufayl (with al-Mukhtār), al-Mukhtār, Abū-ʿAbd-Allāh al-Jadalī, Zurāra b. Aʿyan, Jābir al-Juʿfī.

3

The General Religious Movement

1

Intellectual aspects of the movement

a) *The standard Muslim view and occidental criticism*

The standard Muslim view of the early period of Islamic thought is dominated by the conception of the unchangeability of true religion and the special Arab and Islamic conception of the nature of knowledge. According to the latter the knowledge which is important for the conduct of life—and this is knowledge in the fullest sense—is contained in the revealed words of God and in the sayings of prophets and other specially gifted men. From this conception of knowledge it follows that the work of the scholar is to transmit accurately the revealed text and the other wise sayings. It is therefore assumed that during the Umayyad period there was a body of devout and learned men who spent much time in mosques and other places of assembly handing on anecdotes about Muḥammad and authoritative interpretations of the Qur'ān from persons like Ibn-ʿAbbās. They also considered the relevance to contemporary legal problems of the Qur'ānic rules and the practice of Muḥammad as reflected in the anecdotes (technically known as *ḥadīth* or Traditions). The standard Muslim view also assumed that these devout men remembered from whom they had heard each anecdote or interpretation and mentioned the name when they retold it to others. In this way each item of knowledge came to be supported by a chain of authorities or *isnād*. In the course of time it was recognized by Muslim scholars that Traditions about Muḥammad could easily be distorted or even fabricated out of nothing; but it was held that, if there was an unbroken *isnād* back to Muḥammad himself, containing only the names of reputable men, the Tradition was trustworthy. When the 'sound' Traditions were written down in the later ninth century each was provided with such an *isnād*. This implied that scholarly activity in the later seventh century was similar to that in the ninth century except that the scholars were fewer and less spread out geographically.

Occidental scholars have made devastating criticisms of this standard Muslim view, notably Ignaz Goldziher in the second volume of his *Muḥammedanische Studien* (1890) and Joseph Schacht in his *Origins of Muhammadan Jurisprudence* (1950). The latter in particular showed that up to the time of ash-Shāfiʿī (d. 820) a complete *isnād* was in no way regarded as essential, and that earlier writers gave anecdotes about Muḥammad with a partial *isnād* (e.g. only their immediate source) or none at all. Schacht also claimed to be able to show that in some cases an *isnād* had been 'produced backwards', that is, the earlier names in the chain had been added conjecturally. Goldziher showed how Traditions had been affected by political and other sectional interests, and were far from being objective accounts of sayings and actions. The arguments of these occidental critics may be considered weak on some particular points, but one is bound to accept the general conclusion that there was no systematic transmission of Traditions in the seventh century.

The occidental scholar's picture of the Umayyad period thus comes to be somewhat as follows. Although there was no such systematization and specialization as the standard Muslim view assumes, all the leading men in the Islamic community were religiously oriented. Inevitably the conceptions of Islam and of the Qur'ān dominated all the thinking of the Muslims. Most of those deeply involved in political and administrative matters were not specially concerned with religious learning, but the Islamic intellectual outlook was the background of all their practical thinking. Some of this stratum, however, and many men in lesser positions of power or wealth devoted much time and energy to the pursuit of religious learning. The outstanding representative of the earlier religious scholars is al-Ḥasan al-Baṣrī (d. 728) who participated in most aspects of the intellectual activity of his time (as will be seen from the account of him in the third section of this chapter). Meanwhile, in presenting a general account of religious learning under the Umayyads, it is convenient to distinguish three aspects, law, the Qur'ān and the Traditions, even though there was no high degree of specialization.

b) *Early legal thought*

In later centuries jurisprudence or *fiqh* was the central discipline of

Islamic higher learning, and it seems to have been prominent from the beginning. On Muḥammad's death in 632 the Muslims took over a legal system that was already functioning. The rapid expansion of the following century placed a great strain on the administration of justice, but the caliphs and their subordinates managed to adapt the relatively simple structure of laws and courts to the complex needs of a large empire. The caliphs had inherited a system based partly on specific rules from the Qur'ān and partly on traditional Arabian practices, and they were aware of the spirit in which Muḥammad in his decisions had tried to fuse together Arab custom and Qur'ānic principle. Their primary concern, of course, was with efficient government, and judicial decisions were seen as a part of government both at the capital (Medina or Damascus) and in the provinces. Men were appointed both centrally and provincially, with the title of *qāḍī* or 'judge', but these were not specialists in jurisprudence and could be transferred from and to non-judicial administrative appointments. Where a case came up not fully covered by the accepted rules, the judge had to give a decision according to what he thought best.

Both under the first four caliphs, the Rāshidūn or 'rightly-guided', and under the Umayyads there was a serious attempt to continue the judicial practice of the Islamic state as it had been during Muḥammad's lifetime. It was inevitable, however, that as time went on administrative convenience should sometimes come before strict Islamic principle, or at least should appear to have done so to those who were adversely affected. In the chief cities of the empire groups of men with a religious concern seem to have met together to discuss the application of Islamic principles to the fresh problems that were arising. In course of time these groups acquired a certain stability in doctrine and in membership, sufficient to justify the name of 'ancient schools of law'. This was the beginning of jurisprudence, though it was far from being a systematic discipline. A measure of agreement was reached in each group and referred to as 'the doctrine' of the school. Detailed knowledge of the early stages of this process is necessarily conjectural, since there is little reliable information about the views of individual scholars.

Even where the sources ascribe doctrines to early jurists, the ascription is not necessarily correct. Joseph Schacht, who made the fullest study of this subject, maintained that there was a tendency for a school to ascribe its current doctrines to the leader of the school in the previous generation. Thus the leading scholar at Kufa for a time was Ibrāhīm an-Nakhaʿī (d. c. 714). Schacht considers that he 'did no more than give opinions on questions of ritual, and perhaps on kindred problems of directly religious importance, cases of conscience concerning alms tax, marriage, divorce and the like, but not on technical points of law'; and that anything else ascribed to him is rather the teaching of the school of Kufa in the time of Ḥammād ibn-Abī-Sulaymān (d. 738).[1] Similarly the teaching of the school of Medina about the end of the Umayyad period was projected back to the 'seven lawyers of Medina': Saʿīd ibn-al-Musayyab, ʿUrwa ibn-az-Zubayr, Abū-Bakr ibn-ʿAbd-ar-Raḥmān, ʿUbayd-Allāh ibn-ʿAbd-Allāh ibn-ʿUtba, Khārija ibn-Zayd ibn-Thābit, Sulaymān ibn-Yasār and Qāsim ibn-Muḥammad ibn-Abī-Bakr. Schacht also holds that there was a minority group in each centre which justified its views by Traditions (sayings or decisions of Muḥammad himself).

In its broad outlines the theory of Schacht appears to be justified, though in places he may have worked it out too radically. It may well be, for example, that in the time of Ibrāhīm an-Nakhaʿī at Kufa some technical legal points were discussed and the later solutions at least adumbrated. It is probable, too, as Schacht suggests, that the circulation of Traditions began among the opponents of the dominant party in each 'ancient school', and that the Ahl al-Ḥadīth 'were distinguished from the lawyers and muftis' and other groups.[2] In so far as the achievement of ash-Shāfiʿī was to make 'the essential thesis of the traditionists prevail in legal theory' the distinction between 'traditionists' and lawyers tended to disappear, since most scholars studied both Traditions and law. Indeed, ash-Shāfiʿī himself blurred the distinction by claiming that many earlier Medinan and other lawyers had accepted his view of the importance of Traditions.

The chief observation to be made here is that it seems unfortunate that Schacht should have rendered the Ahl al-Ḥadīth (or Aṣ'ḥāb al-Ḥadīth) as 'traditionists' since this word is better reserved for *muḥaddithūn*. The latter is a neutral term applicable to all scholars participating in the transmission of Traditions; and according to later Muslim writers this included lawyers like Abū-Ḥanīfa, and even the Muʿtazilite theologian an-Naẓẓām. The Ahl al-Ḥadīth, on the other hand, are those who not merely transmit Traditions but who also believe in the great importance of Traditions in legal matters. The term could be rendered 'the party of Tradition', but it has seemed preferable in this study simply to retain it. It should be noted, however, that, like certain names of sects, it varies somewhat in meaning from writer to writer. This is one of the reasons for adopting here the term 'general religious movement' to cover all the religious-minded men of the Umayyad period. This retains the monolithic façade presented by Islamic scholarship, while leaving us free to discover what we can about internal divisions.

From the first a majority in the ancient schools of law was critical of Umayyad practice, even if the Umayyads had their legal supporters. As time went on, disapproval moved into hostility, and by 750 most of 'the general religious movement' were disaffected towards the Umayyads and sympathetic towards the 'Abbāsids.

c) *Qur'ānic studies*

From Muḥammad's lifetime onwards many Muslims knew by heart the whole Qur'ān or large parts of it. When political, social, judicial or other problems were discussed, it would be natural for a man to find a Qur'ānic verse to support his view. Thus reports of some of the early arguments about free will and predestination (to be given in the next chapter) show that Qur'ānic verses have an important role. These arguments mostly turned on the interpretation of the text officially fixed under the caliph 'Uthmān about 650, but sometimes there would be variant texts. Variant readings were sometimes used to avoid difficulties of interpretation, as can be seen from examples given by Ignaz Goldziher in the first chapter of *Die Richtungen der islamischen Koranauslegung* (Leiden, 1920). In so far as the variants were due to the defective writing originally employed they were gradually obviated by improvements such as dots, vowelsigns and other diacritical marks. Even when there was agreement about the text Arabic lends itself to alternative interpretations. Attention was doubtless first drawn to these when rival interpretations had different practical consequences. At a relatively early period, however, it was realized that the proper understanding of the Qur'ān was of the highest importance and worthy of study for its own sake.

The outstanding authority on Qur'ānic exegesis in the generation after Muḥammad was his cousin 'Abd-Allāh ibn-al-'Abbās, often known as Ibn-'Abbās (d. 687). The great commentary on the Qur'ān by aṭ-Ṭabarī (d. 923) contains interpretations of most passages of the Qur'ān ascribed to Ibn-ʿAbbās through his various pupils such as Saʿīd ibn-Jubayr (d. 713), Mujāhid (d. 721) and ʿIkrima (d. 724). Since in some cases contradictory interpretations are ascribed to Ibn-ʿAbbās, it would seem that these interpretations are actually those of later scholars projected back in a similar way to legal doctrines. There are also careful lists of those who were authorities on the text of the Qur'ān in their time; and it is interesting to find in these lists some of the jurists already mentioned like Ibrāhīm an-Nakhaʿī and three of the lawyers of Medina. [3]

d) *The study of Tradition*

The word 'Tradition' (spelt with a capital) is here restricted to anecdotes about Muḥammad himself, which are called *ḥadīth* or *akhbār* in Arabic. Similar anecdotes about political or religious leaders were also transmitted with an *isnād*, but these are distinguished by Muslim scholars from the Traditions proper, being often called *āthār*. [3a] It has been asserted above that during the earlier Umayyad period there was no systematic transmission of Traditions such as occurred later. This does not mean that there was absolutely no recounting of anecdotes about Muḥammad. Anecdotes were certainly passed on. In particular the stories connected with Muḥammad's campaigns or *maghāzī* were collected and written down by scholars such as ash-Shaʿbī (d. 721), ʿUrwa ibn-az-Zubayr (d. c. 712), ʿĀṣim ibn-ʿUmar ibn-Qatāda (d. 737) and az-Zuhrī (d. 742). Other materials about the *sīra* or life of Muḥammad were also collected. Most of the Traditions, however, which appear in the standard 'canonical' collections of the later ninth century added little to the biography of Muḥammad but were very important for their bearing on legal or theological questions.

In the field of the latter type of Tradition, there must have been some activity, but it was informal in character. It was not usual to support a Tradition with an *isnād* until about the time of az-Zuhrī, for the latter is said to have been the first to give an *isnād*. [4] There is inevitably some vagueness about the matter. It may be concluded, however, that until near the end of the Umayyad period whatever study of Tradition there was remained informal and was pursued by scholars who had also juristic and exegetical interests. That is to say, it is impossible to make a clear distinction between Traditionists and other members of the general religious movement.

2

Political attitudes in the movement

While the Muslim sources tend to give the impression of a vast monolithic body of scholarship during this early period, attentive study of the sources shows that there were many different groups or parties. Some of these can be clearly marked off, such as the supporters of Ibn-az-Zubayr, and these will be dealt with first. The question will remain, however, whether there is justification for speaking of a moderate or central party.

a) *The Zubayrid party*

The civil war or *fitna* of Ibn-az-Zubayr may be said to have begun on the death of the first Umayyad caliph Muʿāwiya in 680, when (ʿAbd-Allāh) Ibn-az-Zubayr went to Mecca and refused the oath of allegiance to the new caliph, Yazīd I. The war continued until 692 when the Umayyads regained Mecca. From about 684 until 691 Ibn-az-Zubayr also ruled much of Iraq. There was thus an extensive, if short-lived, Zubayrid state, within which were numerous members of the general religious movement, some of whom at least supported Ibn-az-Zubayr. Moreover this *fitna* was not an isolated event. In a sense it continued the same group's attempt to wrest power from ʿAlī in 656, when the father, az-Zubayr, in association with Ṭalḥa and ʿĀ'isha, was defeated at the battle of the Camel. The group seems to have come mainly from one or two minor clans of the tribe of Quraysh, notably Taym and Asad.[5]

An interesting example of a scholar who supported Ibn-az-Zubayr is Ibn-Abī-Mulayka (d. 735) of the clan of Taym, who was *qāḍī* of Mecca under the anti-caliph. Among material which he transmitted is the story that, when Abū-Bakr was addressed as *khalīfa* of God, he objected and insisted that he was only *khalīfa* (presumably here 'successor') of the Messenger of God.[6] The story was doubtless first circulated to counter Umayyad claims to have divine sanction for their rule and to indicate this by the title 'caliph of God'.

Other scholars belonging to this group are ʿUrwa ibn-az-Zubayr (d. c. 712), his son Hishām ibn-ʿUrwa (d. c. 763) and az-Zuhrī. ʿUrwa was a brother of the anti-caliph ʿAbd-Allāh, and on the latter's death is said to have hastened to the Umayyad caliph ʿAbd-al-Malik and on behalf of their mother to have begged to be given the body for burial. With other Zubayrid supporters he was reconciled to the Umayyads and lived quietly in Medina. Among other occupations he collected materials for the biography of Muḥammad. Parts of a letter of his to ʿAbd-al-Malik on this subject are preserved in aṭ-Ṭabarī's history, and are a precious early source. Other materials transmitted by him include anecdotes about his own family (e.g. Abū-Bakr his maternal grandfather) and persons associated with it. There were also stories tending to discredit members of clans hostile to Taym and Zuhra, and these included members of Umayya. Even the letter to ʿAbd-al-Malik may exaggerate the extent of the persecution of Muslims before the migration to Abyssinia, since the persecution was largely the work of these hostile clans.[7] His son Hishām transmitted material from his father, but otherwise seems to have been a sound middle-of-the-road scholar.[8]

Az-Zuhrī (Muḥammad ibn-Muslim . . . ibn-Shihāb) was the son of a man who had supported the anti-caliph's brother and lieutenant Muṣʿab ibn-az-Zubayr.[9] He became the greatest scholar of Medina in his day in various studies. Since he was born in 670 or 671, his formative years must have been spent in Medina under Zubayrid rule. Although he later gave allegiance to the Umayyads, he transmitted some materials which were not very favourable to them, including some of those from ʿUrwa.[10] On the other hand, so far as the struggle between ʿAlī and Muʿāwiya is concerned, his version is broadly pro-Umayyad.[11] He is reported to have said that of the scholars of the previous generation he admired Saʿīd ibn-al-Musayyab (Medina, d. 709 or later), ash-Shaʿbī (Kufa), al-Ḥasan (Basra) and Mak'ḥūl (Syria).[12] Of these the last three at least were somewhat critical of the Umayyads, so that, even if the report is a later invention, it shows that men thought of him as one of those who disapproved of the Umayyads. In ʿAbbāsid times, of course, this was a point of commendation. Long before az-Zuhrī's death in 742, however, the distinctive Zubayrid element had disappeared.

b) *Wholehearted supporters of the Umayyads*

As the eighth century proceeded those linked with the former Zubayrid party became supporters of the Umayyads, though perhaps lukewarm supporters. There were other scholars and literary men, however, who helped to work out and present to the public the Umayyad justification and defence of their rule. These may be called the wholehearted supporters of the Umayyads. A full account of the Umayyad case will be reserved to the next chapter, but some typical figures among the scholars involved may be mentioned here. Since in its beginnings the Qadarite heresy was a political movement against the Umayyads with a tendency to engage in active revolt, the pro-Umayyad scholars are found arguing against Qadarite doctrine.

The caliph ʿUmar II ibn-ʿAbd-al-ʿAzīz (717–20) was himself something of a scholar, and argued against the Qadarites. A little later, in the caliphate of Hishām (724–43), arguments for the official point of view against a Qadarite leader Ghaylān were conducted by Maymūn ibn-Mihrān (d. 735) and al-Awazāʿī (d. 773). This Maymūn was in charge of justice and the tribute in the Jazīra under ʿUmar II, and is said to have been reproved by Ghaylān for taking such offices under the Umayyads. Nevertheless he was well thought of by later scholars, and a Ḥanbalite writer has a quotation from him which suggests that Maymūn accepted the principle of recourse to the Book and Sunna in cases of difficulty.[13] Al-Awzāʿī was the most prominent jurist of Damascus during the later Umayyad period, and his views seem to have been more or less officially accepted. They continued to be influential under the Umayyads of Spain until about the end of the eighth century. He had studied under Maymūn among others. After the fall of the Umayyads in 750 he became reconciled outwardly with the ʿAbbāsids and retired to Beirut where he seems to have lived quietly without much influence.[14] He is precisely the kind of scholar whom one would expect to support the Umayyads by his scholarship.

c) *Active opponents of the Umayyads*

Many of the revolts against the Umayyads were allegedly based on Khārijite doctrine. Some of the proto-Shīʿites were potential revolutionaries, but remained passive until after 740. There were some other revolts, however, which lacked a clear doctrinal basis and yet were important in the development of doctrine.

Outstanding among these was the rising of Ibn-al-Ashʿath, which lasted from about 701 to 704 (81 to 84/5 A.H.).[15] The chief reason for the revolt, according to Wellhausen, was that the Iraqi armies disliked the Syrian troops and thought that the latter were being favoured at their expense. Apart from this the strict rule of al-Ḥajjāj was generally hated and he himself, as belonging to the tribe of Thaqīf, was looked down on by Quraysh and others who prided themselves on their descent. Other material and social factors may have been present. Although Ibn-al-Ashʿath did not put out any clear statement of religious principle, the soldiery commonly referred to al-Ḥajjāj as 'the enemy of God', while he in turn after his victory only pardoned those prisoners who confessed that they had been 'unbelievers'. This was justified in that Ibn-al-Ash'ath had the support of men who had been prominent in theological and other religious discussions; but the matter is complicated by the fact that these scholars differed among themselves. One was Ma'bad al-Juhanī, the reputed founder of the Qadarite sect, and his presence is understandable. At least three others, however, are reckoned as Murji'ites, while one was the prominent scholar ash-Sha'bī, who is not accused of any heresy.

Somewhat similar was the short-lived rising of Yazīd ibn-al-Muhallab in 720.[16] Personal factors were involved, but Yazīd summoned the religious men of Basra to the holy war against the Syrians in the name of the Book of God and the Sunna of the Prophet. Many responded to the summons, but al-Ḥasan al-Baṣrī publicly opposed it. Among those who took part in it a Khārijite and a Murji'ite are mentioned, but no scholar of importance is named. Yazīd was killed in August 720, but other members of the family continued the revolt for a time. This rising, like that of Ibn-al-Ash'ath though to a lesser extent, was important in that it forced religious-minded men who were critical of the Umayyads to decide whether to join the rising or to continue to support the government.

d) *The question of a moderate or central party*

The idea that during the Umayyad period there was a moderate or central party, to which most members of the general religious movement belonged, is one that at once commends itself when it is suggested, but which it is difficult to work out in detail. We can perhaps say that this party included men who were neither Khārijites nor extreme Shī'ites, neither out-and-out supporters nor out-and-out opponents of the Umayyads; but can we give any positive description of them? What did they believe? Did they hold the basic Sunnite doctrine? But, if so, how was it formulated at this time? If we say that the state was to be administered 'according to the Book of God and the Sunna of the Prophet', was there a clear interpretation of what this meant in practice? Before trying to answer these questions it will be useful to look at one or two particular men.

One who is frequently named as a representative of a neutralist position is 'Abd-Allāh ibn-'Umar (d. 693), the son of the second caliph.[17] He remained neutral in the struggle between 'Alī and

Muʿāwiya after the death of ʿUthmān. Later he refused Muʿāwiya's demand to take an oath of allegiance to his son Yazīd as heir apparent, because he held this to be an innovation, but after Muʿāwiya's death he did take the oath unlike Ḥusayn and Ibn-az-Zubayr. On the whole he lived quietly in Medina, and his neutrality seems to have consisted chiefly in avoiding involvement in politics. This is indeed an attitude found right through Islamic history. The genuine scholar must avoid 'soiling his hands' in politics; he must even refuse judicial appointments and gifts from dubious rulers. There were always, of course, others who saw the need of political involvement; in their own terms they recognized the obligation of 'doing what is approved and forbidding what is disapproved'.

Next may be considered two scholars of Kufa. One, Ibrāhīm an-Nakhaʿī (d. c. 714), appears in Ibn-Qutayba's list of Shīʿa, and his views have been described above (50f.). The other, ash-Shaʿbī (d. c. 722), though his views are somewhat similar, does not appear in Ibn-Qutayba's list, and is said to have ceased to be a Shīʿite.[18] His views are indicated in a saying reported of him by Ibn-Saʿd: 'love the upright one of the believers and the upright one of Banū-Hāshim, and do not be a Shīʿite; "postpone" what you do not know and do not be a Murji'ite; know that the good is from God and the evil from yourself and do not be a Qadarite; and love him whom you see acting uprightly, even if he is a Sindī'. The first point is presumably intended to be a denial of any special charisma in the clan of Hāshim, and is comparable to Ibrāhīm's denial that he was a Saba'ite. The Qadarites and Murji'ites will be discussed in the next two chapters, and the conclusions have to be assumed here. By not being a Murji'ite Ibrāhīm probably meant not making ʿAlī inferior to ʿUthmān; and ash-Shaʿbī doubtless meant something similar, perhaps with the further implication that in politics some moral judgements were possible. By not being a Qadarite ash-Shaʿbī presumably meant not revolting against the Umayyads.

One or two further facts are known about ash-Shaʿbī which fill in this picture. For a time he seems to have been on good terms with the caliph ʿAbd-al-Malik and the governor al-Ḥajjāj,[19] but his attitude must have changed for he took an active part in the rising of Ibn-al-Ashʿath and also refused the office of *qāḍī*.[20] In 721, near the end of his life, when a new governor Ibn-Hubayra made a strong statement of the Umayyad claim to be divinely appointed, he did not criticize but expressed approval and was given a reward.[21] In view of this approval it is noteworthy that he is reported to have said : 'when men obey their authority (*sulṭān*) in an innovation he imposes, God drives faith from their hearts and sets there fear'.[22] If this is genuine, and if ash-Sha'bī felt justified in acquiescing with Ibn-Hubayra, then he cannot have regarded as an 'innovation' (or 'heresy') the assertion that the Umayyads were divinely appointed; to lose faith (*īmān*) implied ceasing to be a believer (*mu'min*). These glimpses of his story, however, show the trials and difficulties a scholar had to meet in the early eighth century.

Another source of information about ash-Sha'bī's political attitudes is the material from him included in the works of later historians, especially aṭ-Ṭabarī. Ash-Sha'bī is the earliest representative of the historical tradition of Kufa. His account of the struggle between 'Alī and Mu'āwiya[23] has distinctive features which are in keeping with his attitudes as already described. He insists that 'Alī was validly elected caliph by the Emigrants and Anṣār in Medina, that his alleged complicity in the murder of 'Uthmān was false, and that Mu'āwiya's claim as effective next-of-kin to 'Uthmān to have a right to oppose 'Alī as partly responsible for the murder was unfounded. It followed that Mu'āwiya had resisted by arms the head of the Islamic community. This placed the Umayyad dynasty in a bad light, and gave some justification for revolting against them. Ash-Sha'bī's version of the events is in contrast at certain points with that current in Syria and Medina, represented by az-Zuhrī (d. 742) and Ṣāliḥ ibn-Kaysān (d. 758). In this version 'Alī's complicity in the murder was admitted, so that Mu'āwiya was justified in seeking vengeance for 'Uthmān; and moreover Mu'āwiya claimed homage only as governor (*amīr*) not as caliph.[24] In this historical material, then, ash-Sha'bī is shown as accepting the caliphate of 'Alī, though without attributing any special gifts to 'Alī or the clan of Hāshim, and as being critical of the Umayyad dynasty.

Finally we may look briefly at al-Ḥasan al-Baṣrī's political attitudes, although he is to be discussed more fully in the next section. The two chief points to notice are that, firstly, he was on friendly terms with several scholars who were critical of the Umayyads and even actively opposed them, but that, secondly, he strongly disapproved of the armed risings of Ibn-al-Ash'ath and Yazīd ibn-al-Muhallab, and urged men not to participate in them. On the other hand, if we may trust a report, he did not advocate obedience to authority in absolutely all circumstances, for he said, 'there is no obedience (owing) to a creature in respect of a sin against the Creator';[25] that is, there is no obligation to obey a ruler who commands something sinful. Presumably, however, his criticisms of the Umayyads were in respect of less serious matters, and he regarded them as having seldom or never issued wrongful commands.

In the light of what has been said about the various scholars mentioned it is possible to give a more positive account of the central or moderate party. There was, of course, no organized party; but various facts (such as Yazīd ibn-al-Muhallab's summons to fight) show that there was a large body of opinion which thought that the Islamic state should be based on 'the Book of God and the Sunna (standard practice) of the Prophet'. For most of the Umayyad period the latter phrase was probably loosely interpreted and only meant the practice approved by the scholars of the town in question. In this respect the Khārijites differed, since they attempted to base the conduct of affairs on the Book of God alone. A few extremists among the proto-Shī'ites tended to neglect the Book of God and to make the charismatic imam the fount of all practice, at least in theory. In this central body of opinion, then, there was special concern to maintain the Islamic character of the caliphate and empire. This was to be based on the principles of uprightness and fairplay in accordance with the Qur'ān and with previous practice, but there was to be no perfectionism. Beyond these points of agreement there were many differences within the membership of the 'moderate party'. One had to decide how far one was prepared to promote this conception of the state actively. Some preferred to keep entirely clear of politics, and to witness to Islamic ideals by frugal and blameless lives. Some were prepared to work for the state provided there was no glaring wickedness.

The basic positive feature of the 'central party' may be said to have been the attitude to community and state. Their common attitude was one of attachment to the state and to the underlying Islamic principles; and this attachment usually led to devout loyalty or even to a practical zeal for the maintenance and advancement of the community.

e) *The 'Uthmāniyya*

The 'Uthmāniyya might well have been included among the supporters of the Umayyads, but since they raise special problems, it is convenient to deal with them separately. They are hardly a sect, and, though it is clear that the adjective *'Uthmānī* was applied differently at different periods, precise information is scanty.

Immediately after the murder of the caliph in 656 a group of his supporters were active in Egypt, and were known as 'the party of 'Uthmān' (*shī'at 'Uthmān*).[26] Individuals in this group are spoken of as 'Uthmānī.[27] The same term is applied to the poet Ḥassān ibn-Thābit, who wrote an elegy for 'Uthmān containing the following lines:

> They murdered the old man on whose forehead shone piety,
> who spent the night in prayers and litanies.
> Soon in their own land will be heard the cry,
> 'God is great! up to avenge 'Uthmān!'[28]

In these cases the term 'Uthmānī appears to mean one who thought that 'Uthmān was legitimate caliph and that his murder was to be condemned, and who did not support 'Alī. It is to be noted, however, that they were not necessarily supporters of Mu'āwiya.

A somewhat similar position was probably held by two other men a little later. Ṣuḥār al-'Abdī, known as a writer and orator in the time of Mu'āwiya, is described as both Khārijī and 'Uthmānī.[29] This is puzzling, since most Khārijites regarded the murderers of 'Uthmān as their spiritual ancestors; but it is conceivable that he took part in one of the 'Khārijite' risings against 'Alī, and that his anti-'Alid views, perhaps later, made him speak good of 'Uthmān. Also described as an 'Uthmānī about the same time was Kathīr ibn-Shihāb al Ḥārithī, who held appointments under Mu'āwiya. He spoke of 'Alī in abusive terms and kept men away from al-Ḥusayn; and he in turn was satirized in verse by al-Mukhtār.[30] Though Kathīr was a supporter of the Umayyads, the designation 'Uthmānī seems rather to indicate that he contrasted 'Uthmān and 'Alī to 'Alī's disadvantage.

From this time onwards 'the affair of 'Alī and 'Uthmān' was a common subject of discussion,[31] and the 'Uthmānī was regularly contrasted with the 'Alawī or supporter of 'Alī.[32] Once Mu'āwiya was securely established as caliph, it is unlikely that any 'Uthmānī did not give him full support. The name 'Uthmānī, however, was presumably not given to all supporters of the Umayyads but only to those who spoke much of the merits of 'Uthmān and the demerits of 'Alī. Among the few persons described as 'Uthmānī in the sources are a scholar in Egypt who collected the information about the *shīʿa* of ʿUthmān,[33] and a follower of Ibrāhīm an-Nakhaʿī in Kufa who attacked ʿAlī though Ibrāhīm had considered him superior to ʿUthmān.[34] Support of the Umayyads seems to be indicated by the report that a certain ʿUthmānī did not greet a Qadarite, for Qadarite views (as will be seen in the next chapter) were linked with hostility to the Umayyads.[35]

The last point may refer to the early ʿAbbāsid period, since the man lived on until then. Certainly the change to the ʿAbbāsid dynasty must have altered the significance of being an ʿUthmānī. As there was no possibility of an Umayyad restoration, it probably indicated a critical attitude towards the dynasty in power. The reappearance of the term in connection with al-Jāḥiẓ will be considered later. Here it may simply be noted that in the first half-century of ʿAbbāsid rule there were a number of ʿUthmānī scholars in Basra.[36]

This study of a little-used term thus gives further insight into the complex character of the general religious movement and the variety of political attitude to be found in it, even among men who were otherwise associated with one another.

3
Al-Ḥasan al-Baṣrī

In his lifetime al-Ḥasan al-Baṣrī was only one of several distinguished scholars, but many men in later generations came to feel that he stood head and shoulders above all his contemporaries. This has meant that source-material is plentiful and that there have been a number of modern studies.[37] Without necessarily subscribing to the most laudatory views, it is convenient here to select him for special study.

a) *His life and political attitudes*

Al-Ḥasan—more fully Abū-s-Saʿīd al-Ḥasan, son of Abū-l-Ḥāsan Yasār—was born in Medina in 642 (21 A.H.) and died in Basra in October 728. His father was a Persian or a persianized inhabitant of Iraq, who was taken prisoner by the Muslims in 635 and brought to Medina, where he eventually gained his freedom and married. Al-Ḥasan was most probably brought up in Wādī l-Qurā near Medina. He is said to have gone to Basra about 657 during the first civil war, and most of the rest of his life was spent there. He was too young to have a distinctive personal view about the rights and wrongs of ʿAlī's position, but like many others in Basra he adopted a course of neutrality in the rising of Ṭalḥa and az-Zubayr. Among those with whom he came in contact and who influenced him was the *qāḍī* ʿImrān ibn-Ḥuṣayn al-Khuzāʿī (d. 672), who was noted for his patient endurance of suffering and his serenity of spirit.[38] For about three years from 663 to 665 al-Ḥasan was engaged in a campaign in the region round Afghanistan. He also acted as secretary to a governor of Khurasan shortly after this, from which it may be deduced that he was familiar with the Persian script.

It is not known when he returned to Basra. It may have been shortly before the death of Muʿāwiya in 680, since he is said to have protested against the oath of allegiance to Yazīd as heir apparent.[39] He does not appear to have played any part in the fighting or in the political debates which followed on the death of Yazīd in 684. Al-Ḥajjāj became governor of Iraq in 694, and for a time al-Ḥasan seems to have served him loyally and to have been on good terms with him. In particular he helped with the improvement of the pointing of the Qur'ānic text which was initiated by al-Ḥajjāj. It was at this period that the rising of Ibn-al-Ashʿath took place (701–4); and al-Ḥasan not merely himself remained loyal, but urged his friends not to join the rising. In 705, however, something occurred which ended the good relationship between the governor and the scholar, and al-Ḥasan went into hiding until the death of al-Ḥajjāj in June 714. The cause of the rupture was probably al-Ḥasan's criticisms of the arrangements made for the founding of the new city of Wasit;[40] but this may have been an irritating instance of his fulfilment of the duty of criticizing those in authority.

The years from about 684 until 705 were doubtless, as Massignon asserts, the most important years in his career. His discussion-circle was frequented by the chief members of the general religious movement in Basra such as Muṭarrif.[41] It was presumably at this time that his thought became fully worked out. The years from 705 to 714, however, may also have led to a deepening. After 714 he was something of an elder statesman, and became *qāḍī* of Basra for a short time in 717 on the assumption of the caliphate by ʿUmar (II) ibn-ʿAbd-al-ʿAzīz. When ʿUmar died early in 720 and was succeeded by Yazīd II, al-Ḥasan supported the governor in his dealing with the Muhallabids. He publicly criticized Yazīd ibn-al-Muhallab after he had gained control of Basra and was calling men to fight against the Umayyads, and he urged his fellow-citizens not to respond to this appeal. Despite this show of hostility the Muhallabids took no repressive measures against him, presumably because he was so widely respected in Basra. Al-Ḥasan was publicly honoured after the quelling of the Muhallabid rising later in 720. Yet there is a story of him giving a bold answer to the new governor Ibn-Hubayra, and bidding him fear God more than the caliph, since God could protect him against the caliph, but the caliph could not protect him against God.[42] Nothing more is recorded of al-Ḥasan until his death on 10 October 728 at the age of 86 (solar) years.

b) *His general doctrinal position*

While al-Ḥasan was one of the best all-round scholars or intellectuals of his time, cultivating all the embryonic disciplines of the new thought-world of Islam, it is his ascetic and mystical sayings which have been best preserved. The fullest collection of them is that contained in the article of Hellmut Ritter. Although the sayings are not primarily concerned with his doctrinal position, they throw some light on it.

The eschatological or other-worldly interest is dominant in al-Ḥasan. This does not imply a sheer rejection of worldly and material things, though he advocates using such things sparingly and, for example, criticizes a man who eats until he desires nothing more. It would be more exact to say that he is constantly aware of the eschatological relevance of this-worldly acts, that is, the possibility of employing them in fulfilling God's commands. Thus al-Ḥasan constantly insists on upright conduct both in himself and in other people. At the same time he is sufficiently realistic to know that human acts will often fall short of God's standards, and warns a man not to allow his fulfilment of God's command to wait on the perfect fulfilment of his duties by someone else. When men were guilty of definite 'innovation' or heresy, however, he refused to perform various liturgical acts along with them. In this respect and in others he may be said to be fully aware of the brotherhood of all Muslims, and he was always generous in giving material help to others. He also regarded it as a duty of the Muslim scholar to warn his fellow-Muslims, even those in positions of authority, about the danger of being committed to the fire of Hell.

His attitude to caliphs and governors is in accordance with this general position. Even when they are bad they are to be obeyed. Some men spoke to him about various misdeeds of al-Ḥajjāj at the time of Ibn-al-Ashʿath's rising and asked for his view on taking up arms against the governor. His reply was that, if the matters named were a punishment from God, they could not with their swords deflect God's punishment, and that, if they were a trial, they should patiently await God's judgement; thus in neither case should they fight.[43] The one concession he made was that (as noted above), if those in authority commanded men to do something contrary to God's command, there was no obligation to obey them.[44] He seems to have taken seriously the scholar's duty of warning those in power, and on several occasions preached to al-Ḥajjāj and his successors. It has been suggested that it may have been regarded as good form by Muslim rulers to allow vigorous and penetrating sermons to be addressed to them on specified occasions.[45] All this is linked up with al-Ḥasan's deep sense of the unity and brotherhood of all Muslims. His remark that a Khārijite who tries to right a wrong (*munkar*) commits a greater wrong[46] should probably be taken to mean that this last is the rupture of the community.

Although al-Ḥasan is apolitical in the sense of avoiding active participation in the politics of the time, yet as things were in the Umayyad period his religious teaching necessarily had political implications. One criticism of the Khārijites has just been mentioned. Another is present in his doctrine that the grave sinner (*ṣāḥib kabīra*) is a 'hypocrite' (*munāfiq*).[47] This doctrine is contrary both to that of the Khārijites that the grave sinner is an unbeliever and excluded from the community and to that of the Murji'ites (see chapter 5) that he is a believer or to be treated as such. The original 'hypocrites' were those persons in Medina during Muḥammad's lifetime who had professed Islam but were politically opposed to Muḥammad and wanted to drive him out of the town. In one passage (quoted by Ritter) al-Ḥasan describes the hypocrite as the man who says, 'the people as a whole are numerous, so I will be pardoned and nothing will happen to me', and who then does evil deeds and hopes that God will give him what he desires. Al-Ḥasan thus regards the hypocrite as one who through lack of concern for uprightness of life (and failure to repent) is in danger of hell-fire; but at the same time the hypocrite is a man who is accepted as a member of the community in externals.

While al-Ḥasan thus criticizes the moral laxity shown by some Murji'ites, at other points he comes near to Murji'ite teaching. He held that it was important that a dying man should repeat the first part of the Shahāda, that 'there is no god but God'; and he himself is said to have dictated this as his last testament.[48] This is reminiscent of the view of some Murji'ites that the man who retained his belief in God free from any trace of *shirk* or polytheism was assured of paradise. Any such thought is far from al-Ḥasan, who always insisted that inner attitudes were more important than mere externals. For him the purpose of this last repetition of the Shahāda is presumably to strengthen and renew the inner faith; he certainly could not have thought that it wiped out unrepented sin.

Al-Ḥasan cannot be said to adopt any attitude over against political Shīʿism, since (as the previous chapter has shown) it was not a live issue during the period of his mature activity. He could not, however, avoid having views on the question of ʿAlī and ʿUthmān. According to Massignon,[49] he held that ʿUthmān had been unjustly killed; and further that ʿAlī, though validly elected, shared with Ṭalḥa and az-Zubayr the guilt of introducing fratricidal conflict into the community, and that, because he was validly elected, he was wrong in accepting the arbitration, though justified in killing the rebels at Nukhayla.

The problem of al-Ḥasan's relation to the Qadarite heresy is a difficult one and is best left to the next chapter. A word may be said here, however, about Massignon's claim that he 'was the first to formulate the "Sunnite" solution of the crisis of the years 656–661'.[50] This claim is exaggerated, since Sunnism did not come to full self-awareness until at least a century after al-Ḥasan's death (cf. chapter 9); but there is justification for the lesser claim that it was 'a manifestation of Sunnism'. The moderate or central party in the general religious movement was the precursor of the later explicit Sunnism; and al-Ḥasan is both a typical example of that movement and also a formative influence in it as it developed, especially by his insistence on the duty of not rupturing the community and by his acceptance as legitimate rulers of both the four rightly-guided caliphs and the Umayyads.

4

God's Determination of Events

During the Umayyad period there was much discussion among Muslims of what the modern West calls the question of free will and predestination. The terms in which the discussion took place were rather different, however. The central conception was that of God's Qadar or power to determine events, including human acts. The standard Sunnite doctrine eventually came to be that God by his Qadar determined all happenings and acts. Somewhat illogically, however, the name 'Qadarite' in standard usage was applied, not to those who held that doctrine, but to those who denied it. Thus a Qadarite is, roughly speaking, a believer in human free will. Like all the early Islamic theological discussions, however, this was not purely academic, but was linked with political concerns, namely the Umayyad justification of their rule and the contrary arguments of their opponents. In so far as Qadarism meant opposition to Umayyad rule, its character was bound to change with the advent of the ʿAbbāsid dynasty in 750. The present chapter will be restricted to the Qadarites of the Umayyad period and the first half-century of the ʿAbbāsid. The name Qadarite continued to be used by some writers, such as the heresiographer al-Baghdādī, but is then virtually synonymous with Muʿtazilite and does not require separate consideration.

1
The political background

a) *The Umayyad claim to divine authority*

Occidental scholars have shown remarkably little interest in the ways in which the Umayyads defended and justified their rule, although there is adequate material, notably in the *Dīwāns* of Jarīr and al-Farazdaq.[1] The main argument was that the Umayyad family, and in particular the Marwānid branch which ruled from 684 to

750, had inherited the caliphate from their kinsman 'Uthmān. This partly countered the charge that they had gained the caliphate by force; and they further emphasized that 'Uthmān had become caliph as the result of the decision of a council (*shūrā*). The succession of Mu'āwiya was justified by his readiness to accept the responsibilities of avenger of blood when 'Alī refused to punish 'Uthmān's murderers, for according to old Arab ideas the heir was ideally the avenger of blood. It was also asserted that the Umayyad family was worthy of the caliphate because of their many noble deeds.[2] An attempt was even made to counter the propaganda about the special charisma of the Prophet's clan (usually taken to be Hāshim) by speaking of the larger clan of 'Abd-Manāf, which contained both Umayya and Hāshim.

> 'You (pl.) have inherited the staff of *mulk*, not as distant relatives, from the two sons of ('Abd-)Manāf, 'Abd-Shams and Hāshim.'[3]

A second line of argument is of greater theological importance, namely, that the caliphate has been bestowed on the Umayyad family by God:

> 'The earth is God's; he has entrusted it to his *khalīfa*;
> he who is head in it will not be overcome.'[4]
> 'God has garlanded you with the *khilāfa* and guidance;
> for what God decrees (*qaḍā*) there is no change.'[5]

Other verses show that these are not mere verbal compliments, for important religious functions are ascribed to the caliphs:

> 'We have found the sons of Marwān pillars of our religion,
> as the earth has mountains for its pillars.'[6]
> 'Were it not for the caliph and the Qur'ān he recites,
> the people had no judgements established for them and
> no communal worship.'[7]

The corollary of such statements is that to disobey the caliph or his agents is a refusal to acknowledge God and so is tantamount to unbelief. In addressing al-Ḥajjāj the poet says:

> 'You regard support of the Imam as a duty laid upon you . . .'[8]

It has been seen, too, that, when al-Ḥajjāj was dealing with the men taken prisoner in the rising of Ibn-al-Ash'ath he refused to free them until they confessed that they were unbelievers, and that he executed those who did not confess.[9] His enemies are referred to in a poem as 'opposing the religion of the Muslims',[10] while various words implying unbelief — *mulḥidūn, munāfiqūn, mushrikūn, kuffār* — are applied to opponents of the régime.[11]

In this general climate of thought it is not surprising that Jarīr and a number of other persons are found using the phrase 'God's caliph' (*khalīfat Allāh*). In accordance with the assertion just quoted that God entrusted (*wallā*) the earth to his *khalīfa*, the phrase was presumably interpreted to mean 'God's deputy'. This interpretation is confirmed by the report that al-Ḥajjāj maintained that the caliph was superior to angels and prophets; in proof of this he quoted the passage in the Qur'ān (2.30/28) in which God makes Adam a *khalīfa* in the earth and gives him the ability to instruct the angels about the names of things.[12] This report implies that by the time of al-Ḥajjāj *khalīfa* was being taken to mean 'deputy', at least by friends of the Umayyads. Other commentators on the Qur'ān, however, exercised great ingenuity to avoid this interpretation; thus al-Ḥasan al-Baṣrī held that in 2.30/28 *khalīfa* meant 'a posterity who will succeed one another' while others suggested 'successor'.[13]

Later scholars discussed the propriety of the title 'God's caliph' and mostly held that it should not be used. There are fewer instances of its use under the ʿAbbāsids than under the Umayyads, but it does occur, and other titles with a reference to God, such as 'the shadow of God on earth', are common.[14] As noted on p. 69 a story was circulated about Abū-Bakr according to which, when he was addressed as *khalīfat Allāh*, he objected and insisted that he was only *khalīfa* of the Messenger of God. This story was almost certainly invented to support the interpretation of *khalīfa* as 'successor' and not 'deputy'. The earliest version of it appears to be that in the *Musnad* of Aḥmad ibn-Ḥanbal; and it is significant that the first name in the *isnād* of the report is that of Ibn-Abī-Mulayka, a Zubayrid supporter who must have been an opponent of the Umayyads.[15]

Apart from the material in the poets, there are some other indications of a similar kind. The caliph ʿAbd-al-Malik, after talking to some Khārijite prisoners, is reported to have said that they had almost convinced him that they were the 'people of Paradise' and that he was destined for Hell, until he remembered that God controlled both this world and the next, and had made him ruler on earth; and so it has been suggested that ʿAbd-al-Malik, because he was not strictly an heir of Muʿāwiya, tended to regard the divine decision as the legitimation of his rule.[16]

We also possess the text of a letter (*kitāb*) written by the caliph 'Umar (II) ibn-'Abd-al-'Azīz to a group of people of Qadarite views (though the actual term is not used). The arguments used, like those of al-Ḥasan, are based on verses of the Qur'ān.[17]

The importance of the material mentioned here is that it shows that the Umayyads made use of theological arguments to justify their rule. The idea that the Umayyads were bad Muslims who did not care at all about theology or the religious point of view is chiefly an exaggeration of 'Abbāsid propaganda and should be discounted. In particular it was the theological standpoint of the Umayyads which forced their opponents also to adopt various theological positions.

b) *The first Qadarite opposition*

The name of the founder of the Qadarite heresy is regularly given as Ma'bad al-Juhanī, that is, of the tribe of Juhayna. Little is known about him, and there are several variants of his father's name.[18] He is said to have derived his views from an Iraqi Christian called Sūsan who became a Muslim and then reverted to Christianity; there may be truth in this, or it may be an invention to discredit the Qadarites. It is not known exactly how Ma'bad formulated Qadarite doctrine. Presumably he held that at least some human acts were free, especially those that were wrong or dubious, because he denied that the wrong acts of the Umayyads were determined by God. A significant point is that he joined the rising of Ibn-al-Ash'ath in 701 along with some men of similar views from the general religious movement.[19] Most of these men had been in contact with al-Ḥasan al-Baṣrī, though the latter had refused to join. Because of his participation in the rising Ma'bad was executed, probably in 704 when it was more or less quelled. Perhaps the most interesting thing about Ma'bad is that he gained the reputation of being the first to discuss the question of God's Qadar despite the fact that little was known about him. This singling out of Ma'bad could be part of an attempt by later Sunnite writers to conceal the fact that the Qadarite heresy began among devout Traditionists. The other Qadarite participants in the rising will be mentioned later; the leader and many of his supporters were not Qadarites.

c) *Ghaylān ad-Dimashqī*

The second important name among the Qadariyya is that of Ghaylān, more fully Abū-Marwān Ghaylān ibn-Muslim (or ibn-Marwān) al-Qibṭī ad-Dimashqī. Qibṭī may mean either 'Copt' or member of Qibṭ, a subdivision of Ḥimyar.[20] His father was a freedman of the caliph ʿUthmān, and he himself had a position as secretary in the Umayyad administration at Damascus.[21] He left a collection of letters or epistles (*rasāʾil*), which came to be well known and consisted of over 2000 leaves, and which Massignon thinks have been 'amalgamated' with *rasāʾil* attributed to al-Ḥasan al-Baṣrī[22] The heresiographers have some difficulty in classifying Ghaylān, and assign him to both the Qadariyya and the Murji'a, while al-Khayyāṭ claims him for the Muʿtazila. The significance of these points will be considered later.

Ghaylān's opposition to the Umayyad government appears to have been manifest as early as the reign of ʿUmar (II) ibn-ʿAbd-al-ʿAzīz (717–20). He is said to have written to the caliph in a critical vein, presumably urging him to bring about certain reforms.[23] ʿUmar, who is known as a bitter opponent of the Qadarite doctrine,[24] is said to have questioned Ghaylān about his view and to have warned him of its danger, and also to have warned others not to hold Ghaylān's doctrine of Qadar.[25] His views again brought him into trouble in the caliphate of Hishām (724–43), and he is said to have fled to Armenia with a companion.[26] Eventually he was captured and executed, probably towards the end of the reign of Hishām.[27]

Brief accounts are preserved of the arguments used against him. The caliph ʿUmar II made him recite the first nine verses of Sūrat Yā-Sīn (36), which end with the words : 'We have set before them a wall, and likewise behind them, and (thus) covered them so that they do not see.' This, most improbably, is said to have convinced Ghaylān of his error.[28] Arguments before Hishām are said to have been conducted by Maymūn ibn-Mihrān (d. 735) and al-Awzāʿī (d. 773). That with Maymūn is said to have begun with a question from Ghaylān, 'Does God will that sins should be committed ?'; and to this Maymūn retorted, 'Are they committed against his will ?' The account concludes by saying that Ghaylān was silenced at this but that again seems improbable. The general tenor of the report, however, is confirmed by al-Ashʿarī's account of the view of al-Faḍl ar-Raqāshī on this question, to which Ghaylān's view, he says, was similar.[29] Al-Faḍl seems to answer Maymūn's question by distinguishing between a previous willing of human acts (which he denies) and a contemporaneous willing; and also by allowing that God may bring about (*yafʿal*) things even when he did not will them.

The Muʿtazilite claim that the caliph Yazīd III an-Nāqiṣ, who reigned for some months in 744, was a follower of Ghaylān appears to be true. Ghaylān is reported to have said that 'the common people of Syria think that evildoing is by God's determination (*qaḍā' wa-qadar*)', and Yazīd agreed that the acts of the Umayyads were wrong acts (*maẓālim*) and tried to put them right.[30] The group of Qadarites of Damascus, followers of Mak'ḥūl, who supported Yazīd in the insurrection which brought him to the throne, are sometimes called Ghaylāniyya; and Yazīd seems to have intended to follow a policy similar to that previously advocated by Ghaylān.[31] In giving a letter of safe-conduct to al-Ḥārith ibn-Surayj he promised to act according to the Book and the Sunna, and in particular to return the confiscated property of al-Ḥārith's followers.[32]

Certain other views ascribed to Ghaylān may be mentioned briefly. In line with his political opposition to the Umayyads is the doctrine that the imamate (the position of head of the community of Muslims) may be conferred on a man who does not belong to the tribe of Quraysh provided he knows the Book and the Sunna and provided it is conferred by consensus (*ijmāʿ*).[33] Thus he is concerned with religious and not genealogical qualifications. His views on faith (*īmān*) are similar to those of the Murji'a, and will be more fully discussed in connection with the latter. Ghaylān held that faith is indivisible and cannot increase or decrease.[34] He also made a distinction between primary knowledge which a man had of necessity (*iḍṭirār*) and secondary knowledge which was something acquired (*iktisāb*); but this distinction did not find general acceptance.[35]

Finally, it may be noticed that al-Awzāʿī is reported to have said that 'the first to speak about the Qadar was Maʿbad al-Juhanī, and then Ghaylān after him'.[36] If al-Awzāʿī is one of the early sources of this common belief, it may serve to explain why these two men are singled out to be branded as Qadarites when many others held not dissimilar views. These two were rebels or supposed rebels against the Umayyads, and it was therefore natural for a supporter of the Umayyads to try to connect the Qadarite doctrine with rebellion so as to place it in a bad light. The chief discussions about Qadar seem to have been within the general religious movement, since the discussions among the Khārijites (to be described below) were probably apart from the main stream. When later generations wanted to foster and commend the image of the unity of the general religious movement, they minimized the Qadarite sympathies of other members of the general religious movement, and allowed the odium to fall chiefly on these two;[37] and they further encouraged the belief that their heresy was due to Christian influences rather than to politico-religious differences within the movement.

d) *Qadarism among the Khārijites of Basra*

Certain subdivisions of the Khārijites of Basra are reported to have held Qadarite views. This has no political significance, however, for the earliest group involved is from about the beginning of the eighth century,[38] and by this time the Khārijites of Basra had ceased to be revolutionaries. The scholars considered to have Khārijite sympathies were often respected members of the general religious movement, who participated in the many discussions which took place in Basra.[39] Khārijites with their moral earnestness and their emphasis on God as righteous judge might have been expected to find some forms of Qadarism attractive; yet among the Khārijites those who opposed it were as numerous as those who accepted it.[40] Though there are some reports about the arguments of these Qadarite Khārijites,[41] they were mostly obscure persons and not all of them lived in Basra.

2
The background of the discussions

a) *The pre-Islamic background*

The discussions about Qadarite views in Islam took place in an environment in which there had previously been a large element of fatalism or belief in predestination. This matter has been studied by many scholars, notably in recent times by Helmer Ringgren in *Studies in Arabian Fatalism*.[42] The chief points may therefore be made here very briefly.

Pre-Islamic poetry is full of references to the determination or control of human life by 'time' (*dahr*, *zamān*). All that happens to a man is brought about by Time. From Time come his successes and still more his misfortunes. Time shoots arrows which never miss the mark. Although in such a phrase as the last there is personification, this is only poetic form. Time was regarded as essentially an abstract, impersonal force. The Arabic words might be rendered by 'fate' or 'destiny', except that one finds as variants 'the days' and even 'the nights'. Moreover this impersonal force was simply a fact of nature, like gravitation, of which account must be taken; it was not something to be worshipped. Though the name of the goddess Manāt is connected with a word meaning 'fate', in the actual worship it is probable that the thought of the providing mother is uppermost.[43]

This conception of Time had parallels in the Iranian conception of Zurvan and may owe something to that, though there are also specifically Arabian elements. The conception, too, is appropriate to the life of nomads in the desert; when a man knows that everything is predetermined and the final outcome will not be affected by his activity, he is released from undue anxiety which is a factor leading to disaster in desert conditions. Experience of life in the Arabian desert also suggests the uselessness of guarding against future contingencies. In other parts of the world men come to rely on the regularities of nature; but in Arabia even natural phenomena like rainfall are highly irregular. If one tried to guard against every chance of misfortune one would become a nervous wreck; but if one cultivates the attitude of accepting what 'the days' bring, one has some hope of success. Thus fatalism helps the nomad to succeed in his attempt to live in the desert.

The fatalism of the Arabian nomad was limited in the sense that it was primarily the outcome of man's acts that was fixed, not the particular acts themselves. He might decide to take part in some fighting or to keep aloof from it, but, whatever he decided, he would die if it was the predetermined day of his death. Above all, then, what was predetermined was a man's good fortune or evil fortune, and also his 'term' (*ajal*), that is, the date of his death. In a land where men often went hungry it would also seem that a man's *rizq* or 'sustenance' was beyond his control and predetermined by Time.

This fatalism, of course, was not the whole of the outlook of the pre-Islamic Arabs, though it is the most important aspect in a consideration of Qadarism. There was some vestigial paganism, but it probably had little influence on men's lives, though Muḥammad's opponents tried to appeal to it in their efforts to rouse the Meccans against him. Some of the more thoughtful men in Mecca were moving towards a kind of monotheism. For the bulk of the nomads, however, the chief religious factor was what I have called 'tribal humanism', that is, a belief in the ultimate value of human excellence but one in which this excellence was regarded as the possession not of the individual but rather of the tribal stock. In other words, a man can only do a noble deed when he comes of noble stock. The focus of this quasi-religion of tribal humanism was the conception of the honour of the tribe.

b) *The Qur'ān*

The kerygma or essential message of the Qur'ān presupposed the thought-world of the pre-Islamic Arabs even when it tried to modify their ideas. The kerygma itself has been often described, and may be briefly summarized here. In its earliest form it consists mainly of the following five points:[44] (1) God is good and all-powerful; (2) man returns to God for judgement on the Last Day; (3) man's attitude to God should be one of gratitude and worship; (4) this should further lead man to be generous with his wealth; (5) Muḥammad has been commissioned by God to convey this message to his fellows. The most important point added in later passages was the one which came to occupy the centre of Islamic religious thought, namely, that 'there is no deity but God'.

The first comment to be made here is that the Qur'ānic conception of God may be said to include the pre-Islamic belief that a man's life is controlled by a power beyond himself. Just as Time was the source of man's fortune or misfortune, and brought about his death on the appointed date, so activities which are in effect the same are ascribed to God. One passage describes the pagan view of death as caused by Time, and then goes on to assert that death is from God:

> (The idolaters) say, There is only our present life; we die and we live, and Time (*dahr*) alone destroys us. (The idolaters) have no knowledge of that; they have only (baseless) opinions . . .
>
> Say (to them, Muḥammad), It is God who makes you live, then makes you die, then gathers you for the day of resurrection, about which is no doubt; but most of the people do not know. (45.24/23, 26/25)

Similarly misfortune is from God:

> No misfortune has happened in respect either of the land or of yourselves but it was in a book before we (God) brought it about. (57.22)

In the Qur'ānic perspective the greatest fortune and misfortune are for men to be assigned to heaven and hell respectively, and the decision follows on what a man deserves, and this in turn depends on whether God guides him or leads him astray; and God 'leads astray whom he wills, and guides whom he wills' (16.93/95).

The similarity of function between Time, as conceived by the pre-Islamic Arabs, and the Qur'ānic God was expressed in a Tradition which occurs in slightly different forms. The simplest is : The Messenger of God said, God said, The sons of Adam insult *dahr*; but I am *dahr*; in my hand are night and day.[45] Though this is a *ḥadīth qudsī* and so of doubtful authenticity, it would seem to have been in circulation by the time of az-Zuhrī (d. 742), whose name appears in more than one *isnād*. Later scholars were perplexed by this identification of God with Time, and used various devices to avoid it. One was to read *anā d-dahra* instead of *anā d-dahru*, and to render this variant reading 'I am eternal'.[46] Ibn-Qutayba preferred to imagine an incident in which the phrase 'Zayd is Fat'ḥ' meant that Zayd was responsible for a murder since he had commanded his slave Fat'ḥ to do it; in this way Time becomes, as it were, an agent of God.[47]

The Qur'ānic idea of God, of course, contains besides the aspect of supreme control of events, that of the goodness or benevolence towards mankind of this supreme power, and that of this supreme being's concern with uprightness of conduct (through issuing commands and sitting in judgement on the Last Day). This belief gives a completely different complexion to the whole of human life, and becomes one of the distinctive notes of Islam.

Despite this new emphasis many old ideas persist in the Qur'ān, both those found in pre-Islamic poetry and others which seldom or never appear there. Since the latter are presupposed by the Qur'ān and not part of its kerygma, it would seem that they must have been current in the 'oral culture' of Mecca or at least have been familiar to some people there. An example of this last group is the idea that what has been predestined for a man has been written down somewhere—'in a book' in the verse quoted above (57.22). Similarly Muḥammad is instructed to say, 'Nothing will befall us except what God has written for us' (9.51). The idea of such a book is specially connected with the end of life : 'no man becomes long-lived nor has any of his life cut short but it is in a book' (35.11/12); 'it is not for any person to die but by God's permission according to a fixed writing' (3.145/139, *kitāb mu'ajjal*). In one verse the idea of a written term-of-life is combined with the pre-Islamic belief that a man cannot escape his term by any 'avoiding action'; Muḥammad is told to say to those who criticized the decision to fight at Uḥud, 'If you had been in your houses, those for whom killing was written down would have sallied out to the places of their falling' (3.154/148).[48]

Another common idea in the Qur'ān is that of the fixed term-of-life or date of death, *ajal*. In general social contexts *ajal* can mean any prescribed term; for example, that for the repayment of a debt (2.282). Mostly, however, the *ajal* is the end of something, though the aspect emphasized is sometimes death, sometimes earthly punishment (as in the case of disobedient peoples), and sometimes the Last Judgement.[49] What is relevant here is the *ajal* as the fixed term-of-life for the individual. An example is 63.11: 'God will not defer (the death of) any person when his term comes.' It is to be noted, however, that in the Qur'ān God is not merely the one who brings about the man's death but also the one who fixes the date beforehand: 'He is the one who created you from clay then fixed a term; and a stated term is in his keeping' (6.2).

Another idea whose predestinarian relevance is not so obvious but which was mentioned with *ajal* in later discussions is that of *rizq*, 'provision', 'sustenance' or roughly 'food'. 'God is the one who created you, then made provision (*razaqa*) for you, then causes to die, then brings you to life' (30.40/39). 'God lavishes provision (*rizq*) on whom he wills and stints it' (30.37/36; and other eight verses). The idea that provision may thus be plentiful or scarce is frequent in the Qur'ān and is presumably linked with experience of the erratic character of life in the Arabian desert. Though the conception is implied rather than explicitly mentioned in pre-Islamic poetry, its frequency in the Qur'ān and in later discussions shows that it had a prominent place in the Arab's thoughts.[50]

In these ways, then, and perhaps in others the Qur'ān preserves some of the predestinarian conceptions of the pre-Islamic Arab, though it modifies them in that the ultimate control rests not with impersonal and 'unfeeling' Time but with God who is above all merciful. These conceptions are still more decisively modified by another note of the Qur'ānic kerygma, namely, that God will judge men on the Last Day and that this judgement will be based on the moral quality of their conduct. This matter is too well known to require illustration.[51] Some of the earliest passages speak of a balance to weigh a man's good and bad deeds, and it is implied that the decision about his case depends solely on the balance. Later, however, it comes to be allowed that God of his own accord may forgive a man, or may do so in response to the intercession of some privileged person. In a discussion of Qadarism the most important point in this whole body of ideas connected with the Last Judgement is that human responsibility is implied. A man is punished or rewarded for his acts because they are *his* acts. Responsibility or accountability in some sense is implicit in the ideas of punishment and reward. This point was insisted on by the Qadarites, but their opponents had to allow some weight to it and were not prepared to deny it outright.

More and more in the later discussions the main point of conduct came to be whether a man believed in God or had fallen into idolatry or polytheism (*shirk*) and had 'associated' other beings with God. Yet there are verses in the Qur'ān which suggest that man's faith or unbelief is determined by God in that he may either 'guide' him or 'lead him astray'.

> If God wills to guide anyone, he enlarges his breast for Islam, but if he wills to lead him astray he makes his breast narrow and contracted as if he were climbing up into the sky. (6.125)
>
> If God had so willed, he would have made you one community; but he leads astray whom he wills and guides whom he wills; assuredly you will be asked about (held responsible for) what you have been doing. (16.93/95)

On the other hand there are verses in which God's guiding or leading astray is not the mere fiat of his will but is grounded in a man's previous good or bad acts:

> Those who do not believe in God's signs, God does not guide. (16.104/106)
>
> By it (the use of similes) he leads astray many and guides many; he leads astray none but the wrongdoers. (2.26/24)
>
> How will God guide a people who have disbelieved after believing, and (after) they testified that the Messenger is true and that the Evidences have come to them? God does not guide the wicked people. (3.86/80)

Another pair of concepts applicable in practical affairs are helping and abandoning (*naṣara, khadhala*):

> If God helps you there is none to overcome you, but if he abandons you who will help you after him?

There are other similar conceptions in the Qur'ān, but those mentioned, especially guidance and leading astray (*hudā, iḍlāl*), raise the important theological issues in the area.

3
The arguments of the Qadarites and their opponents
a) *Records of early discussions*

It is difficult to be certain about the earliest forms of the discussion of the Qadarite question. The main Qadarite doctrines were taken over and elaborated by the important sect and theological school of the Muʿtazilites, and heresiographers tended to describe the views of early scholars in terms which came into use only at a later period. There appears to be some pre-Muʿtazilite material about the Qadarites in the writings of al-Ashʿarī and of a slightly older scholar Khushaysh (d. 867), and it is convenient to begin with this.

Khushaysh has a long section on the Qadariyya, but it is nearly all a refutation of them. The main descriptive points are:[52]

1) One group (of the Qadariyya) holds that noble actions (*ḥasanāt*) and goodness (*khayr*) are from God, but wickedness and base actions from themselves, so that they may not attribute any base action or sin to God.

2) A section of the Qadariyya is called the Mufawwiḍa. They hold that they are entrusted (*muwakkal*) to themselves in such a way that they are able (*yaqdirūna*) (to do) everything good through this delegation (of power—*tafwīḍ*) they speak about, without God's help and guidance.

3) A section of them consider that God has made (*jaʿala*) the power-to-act (*istiṭāʿa*) in them perfect and complete, so that they do not require any increase in it but are able to believe and disbelieve, to eat and drink, to stand and sit, to sleep and wake, indeed to do what they will. They hold that men are (of themselves) able to believe. If this were not so, they would (when punished for disbelief, etc.) be punished for what they are not capable of.

4) A group of them, the Shabībiyya, also deny that the (God's) knowledge exists antecedently to what men do and what they become.

5) A group of them deny that God creates the child of adultery or determines (*qaddara*) him or wills him or knows him (? antecedently). They deny that the man who steals throughout his whole life or eats what is forbidden receives the sustenance of God; they assert that God does not provide any sustenance except what is lawful.

6) A group of them holds that God has appointed men their sustenance and their terms for a fixed time (*waqqata . . . li-waqt maʿlūm*), so that whoever murders a man precludes him from his term and his

sustenance to die at what is not his term, while of his sustenance there remains what he has not already received and fully obtained.

The first of these points seems to be basically the denial of an Umayyad argument. The Umayyads presumably argued that since they were caliphs or deputies of God, whatever they did was in effect decreed by God. Their opponents held that some of their acts were in fact bad acts, and from that it would follow on the Umayyad view that these bad acts were decreed by God. Thus to assert the general principle that good acts were from God and bad acts from men was to contradict an important part of the Umayyad apologia for their rule. The argument was doubtless felt to be the stronger since the general principle was widely held by Christians,[53] and those who advanced it against the Umayyads may well have been converts from Christianity.

The Umayyads possibly took advantage of an ambiguity in the meaning of 'decreed' or 'willed'. In one sense everything that happens is willed or decreed by God. In another sense only good human acts are willed or decreed by God; this sense can be made more explicit by saying that these good acts are what God has 'commanded' men to do. It will be seen in the next section that al-Ḥasan al-Baṣrī makes the assertion that God's *qadar* is his 'command'. Something similar is found in an early story about some Khārijites of Basra, which has been preserved by al-Ash'arī:[54]

> . . . the Shu'aybiyya, the disciples of Shu'ayb. He was a man who dissociated himself from Maymūn and his doctrine. He held that no one is capable of doing anything except what God wills, and that the acts of men are created by God.
>
> The cause of the cleavage between the Shu'aybiyya and the Maymūniyya was that Maymūn had some money owed to him by Shu'ayb and demanded its repayment. Shu'ayb said to him, I shall give it to you if God will. Maymūn said, God *has* willed that you should give it to me now. Shu'ayb said, If God had willed it, I could not have done otherwise than give it to you. Maymūn said, God *has* willed what he commanded; what he did not command he did not will, and what he did not will he did not command. Then some followed Maymūn and others Shu'ayb; and they wrote to 'Abd-al-Karīm ibn-'Ajarrad, who was held in prison . . ., to inform him of the views of Maymūn and Shu'ayb.

> ʿAbd-al-Karīm wrote : Our doctrine is that what God willed came about, and what he did not will did not come about; and we do not fix evil upon God. This letter reached them about the time of the death of ʿAbd-al-Karīm. Maymūn claimed that Ibn-ʿAjarrad had adopted his view when he said, 'we do not fix evil upon God', while Shuʿayb said that he had rather adopted his view in that he had said, 'what God willed came about and what he did not will did not come about'. Thus both associated themselves with ʿAbd-al-Karīm but dissociated themselves from one another.

The two disputants mentioned here were members of the ʿAjārida or disciples of Ibn-ʿAjarrad, who was imprisoned by Khālid al-Qasrī, governor of Iraq from 723 to 738. Even if the story has been touched up, the letter may well be authentic, and thus give relatively early information. Since all three men were Khārijites, the assertion of divine omnipotence (though not necessarily *pre*destination) cannot have been made out of love for the Umayyads, but rather suggests a reversion to pre-Islamic modes of thinking. The phrase about not fixing evil upon God, however, may be primarily anti-Umayyad.

The Mufawwiḍa mentioned in the second point are obscure. They are certainly distinct from the Shīʿite Mufawwiḍa, who were primarily political.[55] The use of the word is also to be distinguished from that found among the Ḥanbalites in respect of leaving to God alone the full understanding of certain mysteries.[56] Here the word must mean those who assert that God has delegated to men power and authority to act independently of himself. If this is applied to Umayyad politics, it might be the view adopted by persons who were critical of the Umayyads and denied their claim that their acts were decreed by God; it would imply that their rule was legitimate in that power was delegated to them by God but would not imply that they were beyond criticism. This doctrine of 'delegation' or *tafwīḍ* is ascribed by Massignon to al-Ḥasan al-Baṣrī, and this would fit in with what we know of his attitudes; but the evidence is late.[57] An isolated reference in Ibn-Qutayba[58] might conceivably refer to the same group, though he seems to contrast the *mufawwiḍ* with the Qadarī; this man's view is expressed by the Tradition, 'Act, for everyone easily achieves that for which he was created.' On the whole this *mufawwiḍ* seems to be different from those mentioned by Khushaysh.

The third point, namely that man has the power or ability to do an act or its opposite, may be a 'spelling out' of the concept of delegation; but the last sentence rather suggests that it is connected with the question of punishment, especially God's punishment in the life to come. A man cannot justly be punished unless the act for which he is punished is his own act. This might be described as one form of 'not fixing evil upon God', but it is not directly expressive of anti-Umayyad attitudes. The thought of God as the just judge is most appropriately linked with certain sub-sects of the Khārijites who adopted a Qadarite view, for the Khārijites in general were much concerned with the distinction between the people of heaven and the people of hell. The sub-sects in question are: the Maymūniyya (followers of the Maymūn just mentioned), the Ḥamziyya, the Ma'lūmiyya, the followers of Ḥārith al-Ibāḍī and the Aṣ'ḥāb as-Su'āl.[59] The last are the earliest for they are followers of Shabīb an-Najrānī, who is to be identified with Shabīb ibn-Yazīd ash-Shaybānī, who was drowned in 697.[60] As noted above, Maymūn's dispute with Shu'ayb probably took place between 723 and 738; and there is nothing to suggest that any of the others are earlier. All these Khārijites were anti-Umayyad, but the basic Khārijite objection to the Umayyads went back beyond the Umayyad claim to divine authority; and the Khārijite sub-sects which opposed Qadarite views were just as numerous as those which adopted them.[61]

The fourth point is a sort of inference from man's freedom. If a man is truly free in his actions, then God cannot know beforehand what he will do. In one of the few passages where al-Ash'arī uses the term Qadariyya he speaks of them holding the view that God cannot know a thing until it exists;[62] and it was held at a later period by most of the Rāfiḍites.[63] The Shabībiyya are presumably the followers of the well-known Shabīb who has just been mentioned.

The fifth and sixth points are somewhat illogical elaborations of the idea of not fixing evil upon God. The chief comment to be made is that John of Damascus describes his 'Saracen' as using this argument against a Christian (who is in a sense a Qadarite).[64]

These six points mentioned by Khushaysh, whether they were held by different people or not, appear to represent an early stage in the development of Qadarite doctrine before it had been amplified and made more subtle by the great Mu'tazilites like Abū-l-Hudhayl. That is to say, they belong to a time when the Qadariyya were one or more groups with distinctive views and not a heterogeneous mass of people who believed in free will.

Much the same seems to be true of the term Qadariyya as used by al-Ashʿarī. In the *Maqālāt* only three instances of this word have been noticed. In discussing the views of the Khārijites about the children of believers and unbelievers he gives the views of two groups without naming them, and then says that 'the third group of them, the Qadariyya' hold that both are in Paradise.[65] A second passage deals with the application of the name and will be mentioned later. The third states that 'along with the Muʿtazila except ash-Shaḥḥām the Qadariyya held that God has no power over a thing over which he has given power to men'.[66] The Qadariyya here, whether Khārijites or not, are regarded as distinct from the Muʿtazila, though that is not so clear of the Ahl al-Qadar three lines above. In both the *Ibāna* and the *Lumaʿ* the Qadariyya are mentioned less frequently than the Muʿtazila, and the impression is given that they are altogether distinct from them.[67] It also seems to be the case, however, that the views described in these last two books are less primitive than those described by Khushaysh.

The material preserved by Khushaysh and al-Ashʿarī thus gives the picture of a number of groups holding relatively simple views which, though differing from one another, may all be described as Qadarite. Two motives are to be discerned for the adoption of Qadarite views, and these motives were at first operative in separate groups. Some were opposed to the Umayyad claim to rule by divine appointment; others were concerned to have justice in the community and in what was asserted of God. The Qadarite opposition to the Umayyads was of historical importance for a time, but ceased to have this importance when the ʿAbbāsids came to power. The second motive retained and increased its importance as time went on. When the Muʿtazilites became the chief exponents of the doctrine of free will, the idea of God's justice was prominent in their thinking.

A word may be added about Christian influence in the development of Islamic dogma. Carl Heinrich Becker (1876–1933) in an article published in 1911 collected a number of points which showed, he argued, that Christian influences had played an important role in the formative period of Islamic theology; more recently a similar thesis has been argued by Morris Seale.[68] The parallels to which attention has been called certainly exist. It should be clear, however, from what has already been said here about the relation of theology and politics, and from what will be said in the rest of the book, that the elaboration of dogma in Islam was mainly due to internal political pressures. In other words Muslims did not take over the doctrine of free will because they heard Christians express it and thought it intellectually sound; on the contrary, in their struggle with the Umayyads or with fellow-Khārijites when they found that some Christian idea or principle was an effective stick with which to beat these opponents, they did not hesitate to use it. Some of those who first did so, though now Muslims, may well have been brought up as Christians or in a Christian environment. The Christian ideas which thus affected the course of development of Islamic thought were those which were in a sense already present in the Islamic community (in the thinking of its members), and which were also relevant to the community's main tensions. When they were incorporated into the Islamic world of discourse, they naturally took an Islamic form; and those which could not be linked with Qur'ānic concepts seldom found a permanent home there. At first sight the word *fawwaḍa* (Mufawwiḍa, *tafwīḍ*) is a promising way of expressing the doctrine of free will; but unfortunately the solitary instance in the Qur'ān is not concerned with God delegating power to men, but with man committing his affair to God; and this doubtless contributed to the ultimate rejection of the concept.

b) *Al-Ḥasan al-Baṣrī's treatment of the subject*

That al-Ḥasan was a Qadarite or nearly a Qadarite has been both firmly asserted and vehemently denied; and the debate began in his lifetime or shortly afterwards. In section 7 of his article on al-Ḥasan Hellmut Ritter claims that he was almost certainly a Qadarite. Writing a little earlier Louis Massignon said, 'je pense qu'on peut aller plus loin, et affirmer que le "qadarisme" prétendu de Ḥasan est une légende'.[69] The decision on this point would seem to depend on precisely what is meant by Qadarism. Before looking at the epistle on the subject ascribed to al-Ḥasan, which is almost certainly genuine,[70] it will be convenient to consider some statements by near-contemporaries.

Pride of place may be given to the important statement by Ibn-Qutayba:[71]

> He professed the doctrine of Qadar in some respects (*takallama fī shay' min al-qadar*), but later recanted of it. 'Aṭā'

> ibn-Yasār, a story-teller, who held the doctrine of Qadar and made mistakes in speech, used to frequent al-Ḥasan along with Maʿbad al-Juhanī; they would ask, 'O Abū-Saʿīd (*sc.* al-Ḥasan), these princes shed the blood of Muslims and seize their goods; they do (various things) and say, "Our acts occur only according to God's determination (*qadar*)." ' Al-Ḥasan replied, 'The enemies of God lie.'

This is one of several pieces of evidence of the contact between al-Ḥasan and Maʿbad al-Juhanī. ʿAṭā' also appears in Ibn-Qutayba's list of Qadariyya, but is regarded as a very sound Traditionist. Since Maʿbad died at latest in 704, it would seem that al-Ḥasan must have been criticizing the 'princes' before his break with al-Ḥajjāj in 705. It should be noted that, in the light of al-Ḥasan's identification of God's *qadar* and his *amr* or command, his remark at the end of the conversation means that the acts of the Umayyads are not in accordance with God's command.

The assertion that al-Ḥasan had once been inclined towards a Qadarite view and had then turned away from it is paralleled in another early report. Ayyūb as-Sikhtiyānī (d. 748) said, 'I took al-Ḥasan up time after time on the question of the Qadar so that I made him afraid of the authorities and he said, "From now on I shall keep away from this" '; Ayyūb also remarked that this was the only thing with which al-Ḥasan could be reproached, while a younger friend of his, Ḥumayd aṭ-Ṭawīl (d. 759), was greatly distressed because al-Ḥasan had held such a doctrine.[72] Another man of the same group, Yūnus ibn-ʿUbayd (d. 756), is reported to have said that at first al-Ḥasan denounced Maʿbad but that later Maʿbad won him over by subtlety.[73] All these reports are slightly suspect, but they nevertheless imply that al-Ḥasan was widely thought to have favoured Qadarite views. The last report is improbable, since al-Ḥasan was always sympathetic to some form of belief in human responsibility, but was never won over to Maʿbad's belief in insurrection; it seems to be suggesting that his Qadarism was due to somewhat underhand methods.

Another reported denial of al-Ḥasan's Qadarism is worth quoting. The transmitters are obscure persons, but for that reason they are more likely to reproduce al-Ḥasan's teaching as it was understood by his contemporaries.[74] A *mawlā* called ʿUmar said:

> The Ahl al-Qadar claimed that al-Ḥasan ibn-Abī-l-Ḥasan

> was one of their party, but his views differed from theirs. He used to say, 'O son of Adam, do not approve of anyone at (the price of incurring) God's displeasure; never obey anyone in disobeying God; never praise anyone for (something due to) God's grace; never blame anyone for some (fault) which God kept from you. God created creation and the creatures, and they proceeded according as he created them; if a man supposes that by taking thought (*bi-ḥirṣi-hi*) he can increase his sustenance, let him by taking thought increase his (span of) life or let him alter his colouring or add to his limbs or his fingers.'

Most of this is what might be expected from our knowledge of al-Ḥasan's general outlook. The various items are matters of individual piety, and yet the first two injunctions at least have also political applications. From statements elsewhere it appears that al-Ḥasan believed that a man's sustenance was predetermined,[75] but, while this sets limits to man's activity, it does not imply a complete denial of his essential freedom.

These statements by near-contemporaries of al-Ḥasan are a fitting background for a consideration of the *Risāla* ascribed to him of which the text was published by Hellmut Ritter in his article on al-Ḥasan. The ascription of the *Risāla* to al-Ḥasan was denied by ash-Shahrastānī;[76] but this was an inference from his belief that al-Ḥasan was not a Qadarite whereas the views of the *Risāla* were essentially Qadarite. Modern scholarship sees no good grounds for denying al-Ḥasan's authorship. Even if it were not his, however, it would still be an important early document of the Qadarite controversy.

The first point to notice about the *Risāla* is that practically all the argumentation is based on the Qur'ān. Ash-Shahrastānī indeed speaks of arguing from 'verses of the Qur'ān and proofs of reason'; but there appears to be only one passage[77] with purely rational arguments, namely, where it is said that the belief that their sustenance is predetermined does not stop those who so believe from irrigating their fields; and similarly they protect their cattle from wild beasts, they shackle their horses to prevent them straying, and they lock their houses and shops; thus it is illogical for these people to blame predestination for their not believing in God. Al-Ḥasan goes so far as to assert (68.13) that 'every view for which there is no proof (*burhān*) from the Book of God is erroneous', and quotes two verses in support. This almost exclusive reliance on the Qur'ān is probably due to the fact that the Traditions were not yet established. The Traditions are, of course, nearly all anti-Qadarite; [78] but it is most likely that they were propagated shortly after this period as a reply to arguments such as those of the *Risāla*.

The predestinarian party also argued from the Qur'ān, and al-Ḥasan replied to their arguments of this type. Thus they quoted part of 13.27, 'God sends astray whom he will', and al-Ḥasan countered by insisting that this must be interpreted in accordance with other verses such as 14.27/32, 'God sends astray the evildoers'. [79] In other words all such verses are to be interpreted on the principle that God's action always follows man's free choice of good or evil, and does not predetermine man to a good or evil course of action. In respect of 6.35 ('had God so willed he would have gathered them to the guidance') al-Ḥasan admits that God has power to compel men to believe but holds that he does not do so. [80] Similarly he holds to be mistaken the contention of the opponents that God's knowledge that a group will disbelieve prevents them from believing; what God knows is that they will be unbelievers by their free choice (*ikhtiyār*). [81] Most interesting is al-Ḥasan's treatment of 57.22, 'no mishap has happened to the land or to yourselves but it was in a book before we brought it to be'; he argues that this does not apply to belief, unbelief, obedience and disobedience as the opponents claim, but only to men's wealth, their bodies and their fruits. [82] In these material respects he accepts a predestinarian view.

Much of the *Risāla*, however, is taken up with the positive presentation of al-Ḥasan's own views. Thus from 51.56 ('I created jinn and men only that they might worship me') he argues that men must be able to worship God, since God does not wrong men and would not command them to do something and then prevent them from doing it. [83] This might be described as a denial of inconsistency in God, and it occurs in various forms, such as 'not approving what he has forbidden'. [84] On the basis of 33.38 (*wa-kāna amru llāhi qadaran maqdūran*) he claims that God's command is his determination or *qadar* and *vice versa*, and thus implies that God does not determine human acts except by commanding and forbidding. [85] He also quotes a number of verses which speak of man acting or willing, [86] and insists that man really does so and is not simply predetermined. He holds that guidance is from God (quoting 92.12) but that the contrary, 'error' (*ḍalāl*) or blindness, is from men :[87] by 'guidance' he probably means God's commands or more generally his revelation.

From these brief indications it may be seen, as a recent writer has put it, that the *Risāla* is 'an expression of a sincere, genuinely religious protest against the belief in divine predetermination of human actions, because it contradicts divine justice and has an adverse effect on human morals'.[88] In short many of the views expressed in it are in some sense Qadarite. The important question thus becomes : in what sense are these views Qadarite ?

It is instructive to compare the *Risāla* with the six Qadarite views listed by Khushaysh. The first view, that goodness is from God and wickedness from men, is not unlike the assertion that 'error' is from men ; but al-Ḥasan considered that men were able of themselves to do good actions, while God allowed misfortunes to happen to men in order to test them. With regard to the second point, the delegation of acts to men, the word *tafwīḍ* is not used in the *Risāla*, and one would hardly expect al-Ḥasan to give a central place to a non-Qur'ānic term, though he expresses something akin to a doctrine of delegation. The doctrine of the third section is close to al-Ḥasan's, and we find him speaking of man having 'power' to act (*qudra*).[89] The fourth point is about God's knowledge, and al-Ḥasan differs from this, for he allows that God has knowledge but holds it to be descriptive and not determinative. He is far from the fifth and sixth points ; though he speaks about the child of adultery, he takes a completely different view, and states that the man is punished for the act of disobedience in committing adultery and not for the child, which has grown by natural processes.[90]

If we look merely at descriptions of the Qadarites such as this of Khushaysh, it is clear that al-Ḥasan stands close to them. He is very near to the third section and not far from one or two others. We also know that he was critical of the Umayyads, though not ready to join in insurrection against them like Ma'bad and Ghaylān. On the other hand, his moral fervour leads him to adopt positions not usually associated with the Qadariyya. This duality in al-Ḥasan means that he can justifiably be regarded as a forerunner of two opposed groups of later scholars. The first of these groups is that associated with 'Amr ibn-'Ubayd, whose teachings were subsequently incorporated in those of the Mu'tazila. Opposed to him among the Ahl al-Ḥadīth in

Basra was a group of scholars who may perhaps be regarded as forerunners of the later Ahl as-Sunna. From what has been said above about the *Risāla* it is easy to see how al-Ḥasan's insistence on God's justice and man's responsibility could be developed into the later Muʿtazilite doctrines, and how they could claim to follow him.[91] Yet the other side of his teaching must not be neglected. He emphasized the importance of the Last Judgement and of the acts of obedience or disobedience taken into account at it; and he assigned a central place to the Qur'ān in fixing the norms of conduct, both private and public. Beyond this he urged his fellow-Muslims to accept misfortunes as a trial or test given to them by God. This last point was the one which was developed after al-Ḥasan's death among the Ahl al-Ḥadīth.

During al-Ḥasan's lifetime the two opposing lines in his teaching did not become distinct from one another. This was largely due (as will be argued presently) to the fact that any strong assertion of God's control of events would have been felt by many as expressing approval of all Umayyad policies. Yet readiness to accept without complaint all circumstances, favourable or unfavourable, was one of the strong features of the Arab outlook as that had developed in the desert, for it enabled men to face the difficulties of life without anxiety. After the coming to power of the ʿAbbāsids in 750 some of the Ahl al-Ḥadīth were gradually able to restore or recover this religious value, which has remained characteristic of Islam.[92]

c) *The support in Tradition for predestinarian views*

Strong arguments against the Qadarite position are to be found in the collections of Traditions about Muḥammad. Since al-Ḥasan does not attempt to refute them in the *Risāla*, it may be inferred that the Traditions were not widely circulated at this time, and also that the general religious movement did not regard such Traditions as existed as having any special validity. They had certainly not become one of 'the roots of law' (*uṣūl al-fiqh*). In the following section an attempt will be made by scrutinizing the *isnād* to determine the scholar chiefly responsible for putting a Tradition into circulation. Before doing so, however, it is convenient to present a selection from the predestinarian Traditions.

A conception found in several forms is that man's fate, or certain aspects of it, is predetermined by being written down at some previous time:

> Al-Walīd, the son of 'Ubāda ibn-aṣ-Ṣāmit, said, My father enjoined me saying, My son, I enjoin you to believe in (God's) determination of both good and bad, for if you do not believe God will put you into the Fire. He continued, I heard the Prophet saying, The first thing God created was the Pen; then he said to it, Write; it said, What shall I write; he said, Write what will be and what is in being until the coming of the Hour.[93]

Another group of Traditions speaks of certain matters being written while the child is in the womb:

> The Prophet said, God has entrusted an angel with the womb; and he says, Lo, my lord, a drop. . . . Lo, my lord, a blood-clot. . . . Lo, my lord, a tissue; and when God wills to determine its nature (or mode of existence) he says, Lo, my lord, is it male or female? is it unfortunate or fortunate? what is the provision (*rizq*)? what is the term-of-life? and (the child) is written down thus in the womb of its mother.[94]

The idea of a man being overtaken by his book or destiny is sometimes expressed independently, sometimes added to the Tradition just quoted:

> (The Prophet said:) . . . By God, one of you will work the work of the people of the Fire until there is between him and it less than an arm's length, and the book will overtake him and he will work the work of the people of the Garden and enter it; and another man will work the work of the people of the Garden until between him and it there is less than an arm's length, and then the book will overtake him and he will work the work of the people of the Fire and enter it.[95]

Some rather different points occur in the following anecdote ascribed to the Companion Ubayy ibn-Ka'b; when questioned about predestination, he said:

> If God should punish the inhabitants of his heavens and his earth, he would not thereby do injustice. And if you should spend in the path of God an amount larger than mount Uḥud, he would not accept it from you unless you believe in the decree and acknowledge that what reaches you could not possibly have missed you and what misses you could not possibly have reached you. And if you should die in a different conviction, you would go to Hell.[96]

The formula at the end of this anecdote is one which is found in certain later creeds, such as *Al-fiqh al-akbar I* and the creed of aṭ-Ṭaḥāwī. The first sentence of the quotation can be interpreted in various ways. It could conceivably mean that, if God punishes a man whose acts are mainly good, he is not unjust, since he is not obliged to reward good acts; and this would be a denial of the view that punishment implies predominantly bad deeds for which a man is responsible. On the other hand the sentence could mean that men are justly punished since they are responsible for their bad deeds. The former of these interpretations is perhaps the more likely, since the Traditions in general tend to deny that a man is responsible for actions which have been predetermined for him. Another example is a story Muḥammad is reported to have told about a meeting between Adam and Moses. Moses accused Adam of being the cause of mankind's expulsion from Paradise, but Adam replied that he had not received from God such favours as Moses had received and that he could not be blamed for what had been predetermined for him forty years before he was born; in this way Adam had the better of the argument.[97]

It is clear that the dominant trend among the Traditionists from about the year 700 was to insist that a man does not have full control of his destiny and that there can be no infringement of God's omnipotence. Apart from this, however, there are many divergences of detail. One or two Traditions have even crept in which oppose predestinarianism on certain points. Thus there is a saying of the Prophet's to the effect that everyone placed in a position of trust (or made caliph) has two intimate friends, one ordering and inciting him to good and one to bad; the concluding phrase, 'the protected is he whom God protects', does not cancel the necessity for choice.[98] There are also Traditions which condemn fatalistic inactivity.

> The Prophet said, There is no one whose seat in Paradise or Hell is not written. Someone said, Shall we not then resign ourselves (*sc.* and do nothing)? He said, No, perform acts; for everyone has it made easy for him. Then he recited, As for him who gives and is pious, and counts true the best (reward), we shall make it easy for him to the ease (or Paradise) . . .[99]

Another very interesting Tradition is the following:

> 'Ā'isha asked the Messenger of God about the plague. He

> said, It was a punishment God sends on whom he will; and he made it a mercy to the believers; if a man in a town where the plague is for a period remains there and does not leave the town, but is patient and reckons (on a divine reward) in the knowledge that nothing will befall him except what God has written for him, he will receive the like reward as for martyrdom.[100]

This saying suggests that whether something is a misfortune for a man or a blessing depends less on its intrinsic nature than on the man's attitude to God. If he has disobeyed God, the thing is a punishment; but if he trusts God, it becomes a blessing for him. Such an idea is perhaps implicit in much later Islamic thought, but it is not often made explicit. It is comparable to the Christian belief that 'all things work together for good to those who love God'.[101]

4
The transformation of Qadarism

In the seventh century and the first quarter or third of the eighth century, while some Qadarites were inclined to insurrection against the Umayyads, most Qadarites were respected members of the general religious movement. By about the middle of the ninth century, however, or perhaps earlier, Qadarism had become something reprehensible in the eyes of most religious scholars. Some light, it is hoped, will be thrown on this transformation by an examination of Ibn-Qutayba's list of Qadarites and some other pieces of relatively early evidence. A point to be kept in mind is that the replacement of the Umayyads by the ʿAbbāsids must have altered the relevance of the doctrine to current politics. It was no longer a sign of opposition to the government, but rather of support for it, especially during the period when al-Ma'mūn and his successors were giving official backing to certain Muʿtazilite doctrines. From about 800 onwards most persons who favoured the central Qadarite position presumably became Muʿtazilites. Later writers like al-Baghdādī the heresiographer make Qadarite and Muʿtazilite almost synonymous, but in the eighth century there were certainly Qadarites who were not Muʿtazilites. These are the people now to be examined. Among them will be included ʿAmr ibn-ʿUbayd; though later claimed by the Muʿtazilites as a founder (a point to be discussed below), in his lifetime he normally associated with members of the general religious movement, and for a time he was accepted as a transmitter of Traditions.[102]

a) *'Amr ibn-'Ubayd and the scholars of Basra*

'Amr ibn-'Ubayd was born about 699 and became a member of the circle of al-Ḥasan al-Baṣrī, though presumably not until after 713 when al-Ḥasan was 70. He doubtless also listened to other eminent scholars. Later he was friendly with al-Manṣūr before he became caliph. He refused to accept gifts from the caliph, but the latter continued to respect him and wrote an elegy after his death which took place about 761. Like many scholars of the period he devoted much time to Qur'ānic studies, and is known as the transmitter of the *tafsīr* or 'commentary' on the Qur'ān of al-Ḥasan.[103]

Interesting light has been thrown on 'Amr's position within the followers of al-Ḥasan by a text of ad-Dāraquṭnī (d. 995) recently published by Josef van Ess with accompanying studies.[104] The text consists of nineteen anecdotes about 'Amr and two about Ghaylān, all presenting criticisms of these two men and their views. Of the anecdotes about 'Amr numbers 3, 7, 11 and 16 may be described briefly. (3) In conversation 'Amr is alleged to have said that, if two verses of the Qur'ān (111.1; 74.11) implying the sin of Abū-Lahab and another man are in *al-lawḥ al-maḥfūẓ* (the eternal original of the Qur'ān), then the men cannot be blamed for their sins. (7) 'Amr denied the authenticity of an alleged Tradition; in this a man (who had lived a bad life) ordered his friends to burn his body when he died and to scatter the ashes, so that God could not punish him; but God collected the ashes and then pardoned the man. (16) Somewhat similar is the point of an argument between 'Amr and the philologist Abū-'Amr ibn-al-A'lā (d. c. 770). 'Amr held that, if God failed to punish a man who had done something he had said he would punish, then he had 'broken his word'; the philologist pointed out that the Arabs only spoke of 'breaking one's word' when one had promised to do something good. (11) Another story was of a dream in which a man had seen 'Amr turned into an ape with a chain round his neck and, on asking him what was the cause of this, had received the reply, 'My belief in Qadarism.'

These arguments are not on a high level. The last (11) is only the expression of a dislike for Qadarism. The second and third are not against Qadarism but against the associated belief that sins will certainly be punished in the world to come—a belief which is implicit in the thought of al-Ḥasan. More important than the arguments as arguments is the identity of the persons primarily responsible for the criticisms of ʿAmr. Van Ess noted that of the thirteen persons named in the stories six out of the eight older ones were disciples of al-Ḥasan, namely, Qatāda (d. 735), Ayyūb as-Sikhtiyānī (d. 748), Yūnus ibn-ʿUbayd (d. 756), Sulaymān at-Taymī (d. 760), Hishām ibn-al-Ḥassān al-Qardūsī (d. 763) and Ibn-ʿAwn (d. 768); the seventh was the philologist just mentioned, while the eighth was virtually unknown; the five younger men were all pupils of the above. From this, and from various other pieces of information about these persons and others, van Ess concluded that a cleavage had occurred within the school of al-Ḥasan, but that it had not been at all complete for at least a generation. For a time a number of men continued to accept ʿAmr as a reliable transmitter of Traditions. Even among his critics there were some like Qatāda and the younger Nūḥ ibn-Qays who could be described as Qadarites in some sense. This makes the bitterness of the attack on ʿAmr all the more remarkable. Van Ess, doubtless correctly, sees it as due to two facts: the greater zeal and vigour of ʿAmr as a propagandist for his ideas, and his elevation by the Muʿtazila to the position of one of their founders.[105]

These conclusions are based on the assumption that the material in ad-Dāraquṭnī is authentic; but there appear to be no reasons for questioning its authenticity. The picture derived from it by van Ess of discussions on Qadarism and other matters within the general religious movement is confirmed by the earlier material now to be examined.

b) *Ibn-Qutayba's list of Qadariyya*

Ibn-Qutayba (d. 889) knew something about the Muʿtazila, but to judge from the paucity of his references he must have regarded them as of minor importance.[106] He mentions Abū-l-Hudhayl, an-Naẓẓām and Thumāma, but does not speak of them as Muʿtazilites, though neither does he call them Qadarites.[107] He knows the story of ʿAmr ibn-ʿUbayd founding the Muʿtazila by going apart (*iʿtazala*) from al-Ḥasan, but apparently does not know Wāṣil ibn-ʿAṭāʾ. Thus the list to be considered contains only Qadarites who were *not* Muʿtazilites. ʿAmr ibn-ʿUbayd is an exception, but only in appearance, for it will be argued in dealing with the Muʿtazila, that the story of the withdrawal and the claim that he was their founder are later inventions. Ibn-Qutayba's list, arranged approximately in order of death-date, will be given in the notes, and here the relevant information available will be mentioned briefly.[108]

Sufficient has already been said about Maʿbad al-Juhanī (1) and Ghaylān (8). After Maʿbad the oldest person on the list is Naṣr ibn-ʿĀṣim (2) who died in 708. He was a philologist and student of the Qur'ān who is credited with having devised, at the instance of al-Ḥajjāj, the system of single and double points for distinguishing letters of a similar shape. ʿAṭā' ibn-Yasār (3; d. 721 or earlier), who lived mainly in Medina, also studied the Qur'ān, and among other things counted the verses, words and letters. He is said to have taken part in the rising of Ibn-al-Ashʿath, but lived for some time afterwards. Another student of the division of the Qur'ān into verses was Khālid ibn-Miʿdān (4) of Homs (d. 721), whose many prostrations in prayer were said to have left a mark on his forehead. Rather different was the distinguished writer on historical and other subjects, Wahb ibn-Munabbih (5), who was born at Sanʿa as the son of a member of the Persian occupying force in the Yemen, and who died as judge there in 728. He is said to have written a *Kitāb al-Qadar*, but then to have recanted of his Qadarite views. His Qadarism may be connected with his knowledge of the scriptures of other religions, especially the Jewish, despite a report to the opposite effect. In abandoning it he must also have abandoned any hostility he felt towards the Umayyads.

Next come two men who were clearly important scholars. Mak'ḥūl (6) was of eastern origin, probably Sindi, and could not pronounce Arabic properly. Yet az-Zuhrī, according to one report, considered him the greatest scholar of his time in Damascus, comparable to al-Ḥasan in Basra, Saʿīd ibn-al-Musayyab in Medina and ash-Shaʿbī in Kufa. He was primarily a jurist. Like Wahb he was stated, though not so definitely, to have abandoned his Qadarism, and he cannot have been openly hostile to the régime or even very critical. Qatāda (7), a man of pure Arab descent, was in some ways the chief disciple of al-Ḥasan al-Baṣrī, perhaps head of the main body of his disciples until his own death in 735. With ʿAmr ibn-ʿUbayd he was the chief transmitter of the master's Qur'ānic interpretations; but he was also learned in history, genealogy and poetry. A lesser scholar was Ibn-Abī-Najīḥ (10), a client who lived in Mecca (d. 749), and is known as transmitter of the Qur'ān-commentary of Mujāhid (d. 722).

No death-dates are given for ʿAmr ibn-Fā'id (12) and al-Faḍl ar-

Raqāshī (13), but they probably come about this point, though the latter may be roughly a contemporary of al-Ḥasan. They differ from the men just mentioned in that they were primarily preachers. ʿAmr ibn-Fā'id was widely rejected as a transmitter of Traditions because of his Qadarite views. Al-Faḍl came of a Persian family noted for its eloquence in Arabic. His views were similar to those of Ghaylān on various points; but it is perhaps significant that Sulaymān at-Taymī (d. 760), one of the pillars of the central party in Basra, became his son-in-law. Rather different again is ʿAbbād ibn-Manṣūr (15) in that he was judge in Basra for periods both before and after the change of dynasty in 750; but he is also said to have handed on al-Ḥasan's Qur'ān-exegesis. Ibn-Is'ḥāq (17) is the great historian of the career of the Prophet, who lived first in Medina and then in Baghdad, but who also travelled in search of information (d. 767). He was accused of being both a Shīʿite and a Qadarite, and was much criticized, especially in matters other than history.

The remaining men on the list are of less importance, and some are relatively obscure. Kahmas (16) and Hishām ad-Dastuwā'ī (18) were Traditionists in Basra; the former held views inclining to anthropomorphism. Thawr ibn-Yazīd (18a) of Homs was well versed in Qur'ānic and legal studies, and disliked ʿAlī. Saʿīd ibn-Abī-Arūba (19) was in some ways the successor of Qatāda in Basra especially in Qur'ānic studies, and was also said to have been the first to arrange Traditions in chapters. Next come four minor figures from Basra: Ismāʿīl ibn-Muslim al-Makkī (20), ʿUthmān ibn-Miqsam (21), Ṣāliḥ al-Murrī (22), who was also a preacher, and Humām (or Hammām) ibn-Yaḥyā (23). The first was called 'the Meccan' because he had spent some years there; he was closely associated with Yūnus ibn-ʿUbayd, another pillar of the centre, and was noted for his decisions on juristic questions. The shadowy ʿUthmān aṭ-Ṭawīl (24) is chiefly known from Muʿtazilite sources as a link between Wāṣil and Abū-l-Hudhayl. ʿAbd-al-Wārith at-Tannūrī (25) of Basra (d. 796) was widely regarded as a reliable transmitter despite his known association with ʿAmr ibn-ʿUbayd. Ghundar, Nūḥ ibn-Qays and ʿAbbād ibn-Ṣuhayb (26–8) were minor scholars in Basra; Ibn-Saʿd seems to feel he has to explain how the last (d. 827) was Qadarite at such a late date.

The results provided by this survey are perhaps not exciting, but they have a certain importance. All the men named may be regarded as members of the general religious movement, either as scholars in some field or as preachers. The point has not been noted specially, but a great many of them were also ascetics. We also have some impression of the variety of interest within the movement and the absence of extreme specialization. The central place of the study of the Qur'ān, which was a feature of the *Risāla* of al-Ḥasan, is seen to be a general characteristic from the frequent references to some aspect of it. The list also confirms Josef van Ess's conclusion that for a generation after the death of al-Ḥasan there was no sharp cleavage among his followers in Basra, and most of the alleged Qadarites mix happily with the others. The most significant result of the examination, however, is to make it clear that Qadarism was largely a phenomenon restricted to Basra, at least after 750. To begin with it had some exponents in Syria : Khālid ibn-Mi'dān, Mak'ḥūl and Ghaylān, with Thawr ibn-Yazīd a little later. Wahb was in the Yemen, 'Aṭā' ibn-Yasār in Medina, Ibn-Abī-Najīḥ in Mecca, and Ibn-Is'ḥāq partly in Medina and partly in Baghdad; but all the rest were essentially Basrans. This strange fact deserves further consideration, but that may be postponed until some further material has been examined.

c) *Some predestinarian Traditionists*

Examples have been given above (pp. 104–7) of predestinarian Traditions. It is theoretically possible to examine all the names in all the *isnāds* of the very numerous versions of these Traditions; but in the present state of the study of the *isnād* a small sample will probably give all the information that can be assimilated at the moment.

From the fact that al-Ḥasan's *Risāla* does not speak of Traditions it would seem to be justifiable to infer that at this period they were not being greatly used as a defence of the predestinarian position. From this it follows that they only began to be widely circulated during and after the first quarter of the eighth century. It should therefore be instructive to look at those persons named in the *isnāds* who died between 725 and 775. This procedure does not assume that any *isnād* has been 'produced backwards',[109] but simply that the scholars of this period were those by whose efforts the Traditions became more widely circulated, and who must therefore be supposed to have approved of the Traditions. The modern scholar, however, will at least in some cases find it difficult to resist the conclusion that the *isnād* has in fact been produced backwards.

A point of interest comes to light with the second Tradition quoted above, that about the four things written down by the angel while the child is in the womb. In the first form of this given by al-Bukhārī the transmitter who died in the period selected is al-Aʿmash (d. 765). The same scholar is also named in the *Ibāna* of al-Ashʿarī; and in Muslim's collection no less than six (or with variants ten) different *isnāds* are given for the transmission of this Tradition to Muslim from al-Aʿmash. In every case, however, the Tradition is said to have come to al-Aʿmash from one Zayd ibn-Wahb who had it from (ʿAbd-Allāh) Ibn-Masʿūd. Al-Aʿmash is a well-known scholar of Kufa, but Zayd ibn-Wahb, also of Kufa, is a very minor figure. Moreover he is said to have died in 703 when al-Aʿmash was about thirteen; and, though a boy of twelve might have remembered stories he heard then, one wonders whether al-Aʿmash really remembered something which cannot have been of great moment at the time he heard it.[110]

Other scholars whose names occur as transmitters of predestinarian Traditions may be mentioned briefly.[111] Manṣūr ibn-Muʿtamir (1) of Kufa was slightly earlier than al-Aʿmash for he died in 749. Basra was not unrepresented. Apart from Shuʿba (2), who handed on Traditions from al-Aʿmash and died in 776, there was Dāwūd ibn-Abī-Hind (3), who died in 757, and the important historian Maʿmar ibn-Rāshid (4). The latter was chiefly known as the man who handed on the historical material collected by az-Zuhrī (5); and this included some predestinarian Traditions. He had also connections with Sanʿa, and received some Traditions from Hammām (6), the brother of Wahb ibn-Munabbih. Az-Zuhrī (d. 742), who was mentioned in the previous chapter, lived mostly at Medina, and on the question of Qadarism presumably supported the Umayyads. Some of his predestinarian Traditions were also transmitted by Yūnus ibn-Yazīd al-Aylī (7), who died in 769. Another scholar of Medina was al-Aʿraj (8), who later went to Alexandria and died there in 735, while some of his material was handed on by Abū-z-Zinād (9), known chiefly as a jurist in Medina (d. 748). Yet another Medinan scholar was Abū-Ḥāzim (10), who had been on good terms with the caliph Hishām and lived until 757. Finally we may name as a scholar from Mecca Abū-z-Zubayr al-Makkī (11), who died in 745 and whose material was further transmitted in both Basra and Kufa.

This list is sufficient to show that by the early eighth century predestinarian Traditions were circulating in all the intellectual centres of the Islamic world. The rivalry of Kufa and Basra might make one suppose that Kufa led the way in the anti-Qadarite movement; but this is far from being demonstrated. The Traditions, of course, differ from one another in the degree of predestinarian feeling. Some, such as the last two quoted above, are opposed to passivity and drift, and insist that a man must 'work'. In part at least these might have been approved by al-Ḥasan. Thus the contrast between the Qadarites and the predestinarians must not be exaggerated.

d) *Conclusion*

In order to understand the change of attitudes which took place among Muslims in the course of the eighth century it is necessary to review the various stages represented by the pre-Islamic Arabs, the Qur'ān, the Umayyad régime and al-Ḥasan al-Baṣrī. Among the pre-Islamic Arabs, then, there was a belief in the inevitability of what might be called the framework of human life—such matters as the amount of food available and the date of death. In so far as it was genuinely accepted this belief had the positive value of removing anxiety, since one could not alter predetermined matters by 'being anxious' about them. This belief, of course, could easily be abused, especially when it was held not by nomads but by urban dwellers, for it could become an excuse for the inactivity that was further encouraged by the climate. The Qur'ān accepted the pre-Islamic belief in the inevitable framework of human life, but it saw this as ultimately the work of God who was merciful and compassionate. At the same time by its doctrine of the Last Judgement it regarded the eternal destiny of the individual man as depending on the moral quality of his actions.

The Umayyad claims that they were caliphs of God and their rule divinely predetermined are to some extent an abuse of predestinarian views; yet because this was mostly in line with the old Arab conception it preserved some of the positive value of that and doubtless helped to reduce anxiety in a time of rapid social change. The critics of the Umayyads were on the theoretical side concerned about their abuse of predestinarian ideas. Al-Ḥasan joined in this criticism when, in respect of the Umayyad assertion that their acts were by God's determination, he said, 'The enemies of God lie.' He was more concerned, however, with the ordinary man's tendency to use predestination as an excuse for inactivity and drift. Hence he emphasized individual responsibility, especially in the moral sphere, and held—or at least implied—that man was in general capable of fulfilling God's commands. This last was the central thesis of the Qadarites, and to this extent al-Ḥasan was a Qadarite. He balanced it, however, by his insistence on God's mercy and on his ultimate control of what happens to a man. To this extent, then, he was not a Qadarite. There was a danger, however, in al-Ḥasan's teaching, whether it was present in his own sermons or only in those of his followers. This danger was that ordinary men would place too much emphasis on the attainment of a satisfactory eternal destiny *by their own efforts*. Overinsistence on the moral quality of a man's acts leads in course of time to what may be called 'moral anxiety'; and this brings about a swing of the pendulum in the other direction.

The use of predestinarian ideas to justify Umayyad rule certainly ceased to be a relevant factor after the change of dynasty in 750; but even before that date these ideas may have been declining in importance. It is perhaps worth remembering that the poets Jarīr and al-Farazdaq died about the same time as al-Ḥasan. This new situation would remove some of the objections to the circulation of predestinarian Traditions. It may also be noted that it is more difficult to argue for Umayyad rule from the Traditions than it is from isolated verses of the Qur'ān. In this way the general trend towards supplementing the Qur'ān by Traditions would make it easier to oppose Qadarism without being pro-Umayyad. Indeed in the early ninth century some of the Muʿtazilites, who held a more sophisticated form of Qadarism along with other doctrines, stood close to the ʿAbbāsid government and influenced its policies.

It may be useful at this point to distinguish two 'degrees' of predestinarian doctrine. The first 'degree' would be the view that what happens to a man is determined by God, but that the man's reaction to circumstances is not necessarily determined. An expression of this is the assertion that 'what reaches you could not possibly have missed you, and what misses you could not possibly have reached you'.[112] In contrast to this the second 'degree' is the belief that a man's reaction to circumstances is also predetermined. This is expressed by saying that his place in heaven or hell is predetermined and known. It occurs also in the Tradition about a man doing good deeds for most of his life and then being 'overtaken by his book' and doing evil deeds in his closing years or months and so earning a place in hell. The first of these 'degrees' is not far from the position of al-Ḥasan; the second and more extreme 'degree' may be regarded as an attempt to counter moral anxiety.

It remains to try to explain why certain members of the general religious movement were given the name of 'Qadarites' by Ibn-Saʿd and Ibn-Qutayba. These two writers lived in the ninth century when most members of the general religious movement had accepted the first 'degree' of predestinarian doctrine and probably also the second, and also made some slight acknowledgement of man's responsibility for his actions. When a man was labelled a Qadarite, then, it must have been largely a matter of emphasis. The Qadarites, we may suppose, were those who in speaking of human responsibility emphasized the dependence of a man's destiny on his own efforts, and at the same time had little to say about the first form of predestinarian doctrine and nothing at all about the second. If this is the basis of the name, there is some justification for saying that al-Ḥasan was not a Qadarite. The disappearance of true Qadarism in the ninth century is doubtless due to the fact that men either accepted the predestinarian Traditions or else turned to Muʿtazilism.

The disappearance of Qadarism did not mean an end of discussion of the problems in this field. With the Muʿtazilites and the Ashʿarites there was a more elaborate analysis of human action. Moral anxiety was dealt with by the elaboration of the doctrine of Muḥammad's intercession for Muslims on the Last Day and by some aspects of Murji'ite doctrine, though it came to be generally accepted that it was wrong to assert that the moral quality of acts had no ultimate importance. In various ways later thinkers were trying to maintain a balance between the trustworthiness of God and the need for moral effort.

5

The use of the name 'Qadariyya' and its opposites

In a short article Carlo Nallino discussed how it came to be that the word 'Qadarī', which one would expect to refer to an upholder of God's *qadar*, in fact meant the opposite. His suggestion was that the term was applied to men who spent much time debating about the Qadar and so made it an important question, irrespective of the precise view they held.[113] The suggestion may be sound up to a point; but it is more important to notice that 'Qadarite' quickly became an abusive nickname which each side tried to fasten on the other. Thus 'Amr ibn-'Ubayd, though widely attacked for his Qadarite views, is found writing a 'Refutation of the Qadariyya', while al-Jāḥiẓ, who was Mu'tazilite, spoke of the caliph 'Umar ibn-'Abd-al-'Azīz writing books on the Qadar in the fashion of the Jahmiyya.[114] The correct use of the name is discussed by al-Ash'arī thus:

> The Qadarites consider that *we* deserve the name of Qadar, because we say that God has determined (*qaddara*) evil and unbelief, and whoever affirms (*yuthbit*) the Qadar is a Qadarite, not those who do not affirm it. The reply to them is: The Qadarite is he who affirms that the Qadar is his own and not his Lord's, and that he himself determines his acts and not his Creator. This is the proper use of language . . .[115]

An examination of the ways in which al-Ash'arī uses the word *qadar* shows that he gives it the meaning of 'determination' (in an active sense) or 'power of determining'; he sometimes has *taqdīr* as an alternative, as in the phrase *man athbata t-taqdīr li-llāh*, 'he who affirmed the determination as God's'.[116] Belief in free will is also called 'the doctrine of the Qadar according to the view of the Mu'tazilites'.[117] The opposing view is expressed by *athbata*, as in the phrase just quoted, or by the verbal noun *ithbāt*, 'affirmation', in such phrases as: *qālū fi-l-qadar bi-l-ithbāt* or *bi-thbāt al-qadar*, 'they held the affirmation of Qadar (*sc.* as belonging to God)'.[118] When al-Ash'arī uses the phrase 'the doctrine of the Qadar' to mean the doctrine of free will, he always adds a qualification; and the same is probably true of later Ash'arites like ash-Shahrastānī.[119] The latter has sometimes an expanded form of the phrase which leaves no dubiety: *ithbāt al-qadar khayri-hi wa-sharri-hi min al-'abd*, 'affirmation of the Qadar, both good and bad, as being from men'; *aḍāfū l-qadar khayra-hu wa-sharra-hu ilā llāh*, 'attributed the Qadar, both good and bad, to God'.[120]

On the other hand, al-Ash'arī uses *ithbāt* only of those who affirm that the Qadar is God's, whereas ash-Shahrastānī (as in one of the examples given) can use it of those who affirm that the Qadar is man's. Al-Ash'arī also has the name Ahl al-Ithbāt in an absolute sense for the believers in God's Qadar, as in the following passage:

> The Qadariyya revile those who oppose them in respect of the Qadar; the Ahl al-Ḥaqq ('the people of truth' or those whom he himself approved) call them Qadariyya, and the

> latter call them (the Ahl al-Ḥaqq) Mujbira, although they themselves are more appropriately called Qadariyya than the Ahl al-Ithbāt.[121]

Ibn-Qutayba speaks both of *ithbāt* and Ahl al-Ithbāt in this sense.[122] The only members of the Ahl al-Ithbāt named by al-Ashʿarī are Ḍirār, al-Kushānī and possibly Muḥammad ibn-Ḥarb. Since al-Kushānī was a follower of an-Najjār, and an-Najjār's views are similar to those ascribed to the Ahl al-Ithbāt,[123] he should probably be reckoned among them along with another follower Burghūth, and likewise the related group of Khārijites round Muḥammad ibn-Ḥarb and Yaḥyā ibn-Abī-Kāmil.

While Ahl al-Ithbāt was a name these people were perhaps ready to apply to themselves, their opponents (as in the quotation above) called them Mujbira, a name also employed by Ibn-Qutayba with the variant Jabriyya (less correctly Jabariyya).[124] The Sunnite al-Malaṭī (d. 987) says that 'one who calls another a *mujbir* is a Qadarite';[125] and this is confirmed by the fact that the Muʿtazilite al-Khayyāṭ has about a dozen references to Mujbira in *Kitāb al-Intisār*. The corresponding name for the doctrine is *jabr*, 'compulsion', or *ijbār*, 'compelling', which is used chiefly by Qadarites and Muʿtazilites, though a Māturīdite author is found accusing the Ashʿarites of *jabr*.[126] At a later date the Ashʿarites developed a theory that their doctrine—that of *kasb*, 'acquisition'—was a mean between *jabr* and *qadar*; and Jabriyya then became a convenient classificatory term for the purposes of heresiographers like al-Baghdādi and ash-Shahrastānī. These points make it clear that there never was a sect of Jabriyya. Jabriyya and Mujbira were nicknames applied by the Muʿtazila and their likes to those who may in anticipation be called middle-of-the-road Sunnites. As used by ash-Shahrastānī (who further distinguishes between 'pure' and 'moderate' Jabriyya, *khāliṣa*, *mutawassiṭa*) the term seems to refer only to spurious sects like the Jahmiyya (to be discussed in the next chapter). Where the term 'Qadarite' has been used in this book it is of course roughly in the Ashʿarite-Sunnite sense, and not in that of their opponents.

5

Faith and Community

The subjects to be discussed in this chapter are well indicated, at least in an Islamic context, by the title, but the connotations of the occidental word 'faith' (or *foi* or *Glaube*) have to be avoided. Moreover the starting-point for the consideration of these topics will be the sect of the Murji'a, and yet in the course of the study the sect will be found rather to melt away.

1
The application of the term 'Murji'a'
a) *The standard occidental view*

The treatment of the Murji'a in recent occidental books has tended to suggest that one was dealing with a single well-defined trend in Islamic thought. There might indeed be some development within it, but it was on the whole a unitary trend. An expression of this standard view is given by Arent Jan Wensinck in *The Muslim Creed.* He speaks of the Murji'ites as the 'extreme opponents' of the Khārijites, since they were prepared to accept temporal rulers even when their conduct was sinful in certain respects. They also held that works were irrelevant to faith, and this implied that faith had a degree of stability and was not impaired by sin.[1] A somewhat similar view was presented earlier by Duncan Black Macdonald.[2] Ignaz Goldziher was aware of the complexities introduced by some of the material in Ibn-Saʿd, but did not clearly formulate any alternative to the standard view.[3] It will presently become evident that this standard view, though not altogether false, is at best only a small part of the truth.

The complexity of the subject is further illustrated by the difficulties experienced by certain Muslim writers. One of the difficulties is that Abū-Ḥanīfa, from whom the Ḥanafite legal *madhhab* or rite takes its name, is sometimes called a Murji'ite. Since it is unthinkable that one of the Sunnite legal rites should be named after a heretic, various writers of a later date deny that he was a Murji'ite. Ash-Shahrastānī concedes that he might be called a Murji'ite of the Sunna; but his difficulties are made manifest by the fact that he had already subdivided the Murji'a into four: those of the Khawārij, those of the Qadariyya, those of the Jabriyya, and pure Murji'a.[4] If the problems are to be solved, the first task is to distinguish the ways in which different groups of writers use the term.

b) *The Ash'arite-Sunnite view*

Not unexpectedly the Muslim view closest to the occidental view is the Ash'arite version of the Sunnite view. This is because the leading heresiographers in later times were Ash'arites, and ash-Shahrastānī in particular has been influential with occidental scholars. It is necessary to specify the Ash'arite version, since on the points at issue in this chapter their fellow-theologians the Māturīdites, as followers of Abū-Ḥanīfa, sometimes differed from them, as also did the Ḥanbalites. Al-Ash'arī himself does not give any account of the views held in common by the Murji'ites. Ash-Shahrastānī distinguishes two meanings of the word *irjā'*, the verbal noun corresponding to the participle Murji'a: firstly, 'postponing' or 'putting after', and secondly, 'giving hope'. The first applies when the Murji'ites put works (*'amal*) after intention and assent (to doctrines—*'aqd*); and the second is found when they assert that 'where there is faith sin does no harm'. He goes on to state that *irjā'* can also mean postponing the decision about the grave sinner until the resurrection and putting 'Alī down from the first place (in succession to Muḥammad) to the fourth. Al-Baghdādī seems to think of *irjā'* as primarily the putting of works after 'faith'.[5]

c) *The Mu'tazilites*

A clear statement of the Mu'tazilite position is given by al-Khayyāṭ. It is linked with the Mu'tazilite conception of *al-manzila bayn al-manzilatayn*. Where the Khārijites say that the grave sinner is an unbeliever (*kāfir*), al-Ḥasan al-Baṣrī says he is a hypocrite (*munāfiq*) and the Murji'ites say he is a believer (*mu'min*), they say that he is neither the one nor the other, but is in an intermediate position.[6] This is perhaps a slightly unfair characterization of those who postponed judgement on grave sinners, since they did not assert that they were believers, but only that they were to be treated as believers in this world; but on the other hand many of those who postponed judgement, by also putting works after faith, did go on to hold that grave sinners were believers, and even that they would eventually reach heaven. Be that as it may, the point emphasized by the Muʿtazilites was that the persons they called Murji'ites made the grave sinner out to be a believer. Not too much weight need be given to the statement of ash-Shahrastānī, in defending Abū-Ḥanīfa from the charge of being a Murji'ite, that the Muʿtazila and the Khārijite sect of Waʿīdiyya gave this name to those who opposed them in their Qadarism; this does not tally with the early texts now accessible to us.

d) *The Shīʿa*

An important early Shīʿite (Imāmite) text is the book of sects ascribed to an-Nawbakhtī. In this there is a passage which states that the basic sects of the community are four : the Shīʿa, the Muʿtazila, the Murji'a and the Khawārij. This seems reasonable until one realizes that the Sunnites are not mentioned, and realizes further that the writer could not have considered himself a Sunnite. From this it follows that those normally called Sunnites must be included somewhere among the four groups mentioned. It is conceivable that men normally regarded as Sunnites but favourably disposed towards ʿAlī (such as Aḥmad ibn-Ḥanbal) might have been placed among the Shīʿa; but otherwise most Sunnites would seem to be included among the Murji'a. This inference is confirmed by another statement in the same book where the Murji'a are said to have four sub-sects : (1) the Jahmiyya, followers of Jahm ibn-Ṣafwān; (2) the Ghaylāniyya, followers of Ghaylān ibn-Marwān; (3) the Māṣiriyya, followers of ʿAmr ibn-Qays al-Māṣir, and including Abū-Ḥanīfa; (4) the Shukkāk or Batriyya, the Aṣ'ḥāb al-Ḥadīth, including Sufyān ath-Thawrī, Sharīk, Ibn-Abī-Laylā, ash-Shāfiʿī and Mālik ibn-Anas, and also known as the Ḥashwiyya. The writer had previously said that 'they are called the Murji'a because they associate with both the opposing sides and consider that all the people of the Qibla are believers through their public profession of faith, and they hope for pardon for them all'. [7]

From all this it would seem that for an-Nawbakhtī the distinctive characteristic of the Murji'ite is that he does not put ʿAlī above ʿUthmān. This is implied at one point by Ibn-Saʿd; of a certain Muḥārib (who died between 724 and 738) he reports that 'he belonged to the first Murji'a who "postponed" ʿAlī and ʿUthmān and did not bear witness to (their) faith or unbelief'.[8] The natural inference from this would be that anyone who places 'Alī above 'Uthmān belongs in the other camp. An example of this anti-Murji'ite position is Ibrāhīm an-Nakha'ī, of whom Ibn-Sa'd reported that he greatly disliked the Murji'a, and considered them worse than the Azraqites and the People of the Book; and further that he liked 'Alī better than 'Uthmān, but would not speak ill of 'Uthmān. His remark that he was neither a Saba'ite nor a Murji'ite, is thus seen to mean that he thought highly of 'Alī without attributing to him any supernatural powers and that, though he placed 'Uthmān lower, he neither condemned him (like the Khārijites) nor 'postponed' the decision about him.[9] Ibn-Sa'd does not appear to apply the name Shī'a to a position such as Ibrāhīm's, but he mentions six brothers in Kufa of whom two were Shī'ites (*yatashayya'ān*), two Murji'ites, while two held the views of the Khārijites;[10] and from this it might be supposed that these were the three groups into which the men of Kufa were divided.

It is not without significance that of eighteen persons described by Ibn-Sa'd as Murji'ites, eleven are from Kufa; of the others one was from Medina (al-Ḥasan ibn-Muḥammad ibn-al-Ḥanafiyya), one from Mecca, one from Basra, one from al-Madā'in and three from Khurasan.[11] From this it would seem that the Murji'a was specially connected with disputes which arose within the community of Muslims at Kufa. Kufa had always been a stronghold of men who were in some sense partisans of 'Alī, and so it would not be surprising if opposition to such partisanship also appeared at Kufa. One may also go further and wonder whether Ibn-Sa'd had in some sense Shī'ite sympathies. His senior colleague and friend al-Wāqidī (d. 823) had had among his teachers Sufyān ath-Thawrī, who was one of the leading anti-Murji'ites in Kufa (in the usual sense); and Ibn-Sa'd himself was a client of a member of the 'Abbāsid family.[12] Thus he himself may well have held views similar to those of Ibrāhīm an-Nakha'ī.

Ibn-Qutayba also may have sympathized with this position. He clearly distinguishes between Rāfiḍites and Shī'a; for him the Rāfiḍites are those who in some way reject the first three caliphs, while the Shī'a appear to be those who do not speak ill of these caliphs but who think more highly of 'Alī.[13] His list of the Shī'a, however, includes some of the men whom an-Nawbakhtī placed among the

Murji'a, namely, Sufyān ath-Thawrī and Sharīk. He also includes many respected names from among the scholars of Kufa, such as Ibrāhīm an-Nakhaʿī, al-Aʿmash and Wakīʿ, as well as Shuʿba from Basra.

e) *The Ḥanbalites*

It will be useful to mention an early Ḥanbalite criticism of the Murji'ites, since Ashʿarism grew out of the Ḥanbalite form of Sunnism (if the term may be applied in the ninth century). The criticisms occur in the appendix to the document called by Henri Laoust *ʿAqīda I*, which consists of material attributed to Aḥmad ibn-Ḥanbal himself and is certainly early. The theses to be condemned are : that faith is word (*qawl*) without works; that the faith of one believer is not superior in degree to that of another, and that the faith of men, angels and prophets is the same; that faith does not increase and decrease; and that there is no uncertainty about faith (that is, that it is incorrect to say, 'I am a believer, if God will').[14] It will be seen presently how these points emerge in the discussions.

f) *The Khārijites*

Aḥmad ibn-Ḥanbal also complained that he and his friends were called Murji'a by the Khārijites. It is easy to see how this comes about. The Khārijites held that ʿUthmān was a grave sinner, whereas it was a mark of Murji'ism to 'postpone' the decision about him and regard him practically as a believer.

2

Reconstruction of the development

After this review of the different ways in which the name of Murji'a was applied it is possible to attempt a reconstruction of the course of development to show how the different applications are connected with one another. The obvious starting-point is a verse of the Qur'ān which has not been mentioned so far.

a) *The Qur'ānic basis*

It is generally held by Muslim scholars—and the opinion seems to be justified—that the term Murji'a is derived from the Qur'ānic phrase, 'some are deferred for the command of God' (9.106/7). The word translated 'deferred' is either *murjawna* or *murja'ūna*, but the commentators (e.g. aṭ-Ṭabarī) hold that these are identical in meaning, and come from *arja'a*, 'to postpone, place later'. The verbal noun *irjā'* is used, at least from the time of Ibn-Saʿd, to mean 'the belief of the Murji'a'; but *irjā'* may also be the verbal noun from *arjā*, 'to cause to hope'. The verse in question is held to refer to three men who stayed away from the expedition to Tabūk in 631, and who were then 'sent to Coventry' by the Muslims on Muḥammad's orders. Though the men confessed that they were in the wrong, Muḥammad would not pardon them but said he must wait for a revelation of the command of God, that is, God's decision whether they were to be punished further or not. Verse 118/9 was later revealed and they were pardoned. There is no close parallel between the circumstances of 631 and those of later times, but the verse clearly expresses the idea that in some cases man should not judge a question of guilt or innocence but should leave the decision to God.

b) *The postponement of a decision about 'Alī and 'Uthmān*

It is most likely that the first application of the idea of *irjā'* was to the decision in respect of 'Uthmān and 'Alī. This is implied by the statement of Ibn-Sa'd quoted above to the effect that the first Murji'a 'postponed' the decision about the two men and did not say whether they were believers or unbelievers.[15] This presumably refers to the assignment of the man in question to heaven or hell. At a this-worldly level 'postponement' implies a rejection of the Khārijite thesis that 'Uthmān was an unbeliever and therefore excluded from the community. Some Khārijites had also for a time regarded 'Alī as an unbeliever and had fought against him. There is evidence of opposition between groups of Khārijites and Murji'ites at the time of the rising of Yazīd ibn-al-Muhallab (in 720).[16]

There is interesting contemporary evidence of this position in a poem by Thābit Quṭna (d. 728), who was put in charge of one of the regions of Khurasan by Yazīd ibn-al-Muhallab when he was governor there.[17] The poem is difficult to translate and interpret in places, but the following doctrinal assertions seem to be clear: (a) we postpone (decisions in) matters which are doubtful; (b) all Muslims are following Islam (*al-muslimūn 'alā l-islām kullu-hum*)—presumably meaning that all calling themselves Muslims are truly Muslims; (c) no sin amounts to *shirk* (idolatry) so long as men profess God's unity; (d) we shed (? Muslim) blood only in self-defence; (e) he who fears God in this world has the reward of his piety on the Last Day; (f) an affair decreed by God cannot be reversed, and what he decrees (*qaḍā*) is right (*rushd*); (g) every Khārijite errs in his view, even if he is earnest and God-fearing; (h) 'Alī and 'Uthmān are two servants of God who did not associate (any deity) with him; they will be rewarded according to their striving, which is known to God, but no verse is revealed (deciding their merits).

This material shows that the early Murji'a accepted both 'Alī and 'Uthmān as rightful rulers of the community, and refused to reject either on account of sin. They probably also refused to decide on the respective merits of the two men. In all this there is a concern for the unity of the community, and a refusal to accept the Khārijite theses that the grave sinner is by his sin excluded from the community. According to this poem a man ceases to be a Muslim only through *shirk*, idolatry, or, more exactly, the associating of other beings with God in the worship due to him alone. Assertion (f) appears to be directed against the Qadarites.

The political attitudes of the Murji'a are not altogether clear. A scholar of Kufa (d. 746) alleged that 'the Murji'a follow the religion of their kings', and the caliph al-Ma'mūn (813–33) is reported to have said something similar.[18] This is in line with their recognition of any caliph not guilty of *shirk*, and with assertion (d) about not shedding blood. On the other hand, some persons alleged to be Murji'ites took part in the rising of Ibn-al-Ash'ath (701–4).[19] Ghaylān ad-Dimashqī, who is reckoned a Murji'ite as well as a Qadarite, was suspected of plotting against the government; there were Murji'ites in arms at the time of the Muhallabid rising in 720, and al-Ḥārith ibn-Surayj, who led a rising on the north-eastern frontiers in the closing years of the Umayyads, did so on the basis of a Murji'ite doctrine.[20] Thus the Murji'a were not always out-and-out supporters of the Umayyads.

The 'postponement' of a judgement on 'Alī and 'Uthmān, when deliberately adopted by persons living more than half a century later, is itself the mark of a political attitude. In so far as it rejects the Khārijite claim that 'Uthmān was justly killed, it implies that the Umayyad dynasty, as heirs of 'Uthmān, are legitimate rulers. The relevance of its views on 'Alī up to about 740 are not so clear, except that they imply no support for the attempts of al-Ḥasan, al-Ḥusayn and others to gain the caliphate. When the 'Abbāsids began their bid for the caliphate on the basis that this was restricted to the clan of Hāshim and indeed to their own line, Murji'ite theory would oppose this. That is to say, they would not agree that the 'Abbāsid claim to the caliphate was superior to that of the Umayyads; but once the 'Abbāsids had gained control of the empire and eliminated the Umayyad family the Murji'ites would have no grounds for not accepting them. In general their chief concern was to preserve the unity of the community of Muslims.

c) *The 'postponement' of 'Alī to fourth place*

The point just discussed, though it has a particular reference, corresponds to ash-Shahrastānī's third way of applying *irjā'*, namely, to the postponing until the resurrection of the decision about the grave sinner. His fourth way was the putting of 'Alī down from the first place after Muḥammad to the fourth. As will be seen subsequently, the standard Sunnite view came to be that the chronological order of the first four caliphs was also the order of merit, but it is not clear how far this view was accepted in the first half of the eighth century. Most scholars in the general religious movement would have placed Abū-Bakr and 'Umar first and second, but perhaps some in Ibn-Qutayba's list of Shī'a would have made 'Alī first. The Zaydites (to be discussed later) held 'Alī to be first in order of merit, but asserted that he acquiesced in the 'imamate of the inferior' (*imāmat al-mafḍūl*), that is, Abū-Bakr and the others. In the first half of the eighth century the position of 'Uthmān was not clear, since it was sometimes linked with criticisms of the Umayyad dynasty. For this reason it seems unlikely that at this period *irjā'* had the connotation of reducing 'Alī to fourth place. That connotation or application was only meaningful after the later Sunnite view had been widely accepted.

d) *The regarding of the grave sinner as a believer*

The 'postponement' of the decision about the grave sinner naturally leads to the view that he is a believer. That he should be *treated* as a believer is the first consequence of the 'postponement'; but among the ancient Arabs there was a tendency to think in communal terms. That is to say, 'the believers' were thought of primarily as a social unit. The concept of 'belief' or 'faith' was, for those who thought in this way, secondary and derived from the concept of the social unit. 'Faith' or *īmān* was simply what made a man a member of this body of 'believers' or *mu'minīn*. In a similar way *irjā'* could indicate what made a man a member of the Murji'a, and *i'tizāl* what made him one of the Mu'tazila. Now for those who 'postponed' the decision the grave sinner was a member of the social unit; and they then had to face the problem of defining *īmān* so that it corresponded to that which made a man a member of this social unit. All this is in contrast to the modern European outlook which makes the concept of faith (or *foi* or *Glaube*) primary and from this basis proceeds to define the community. For this reason all European translations of *īmān* have misleading connotations, as will be seen when Muslim views are expounded more fully in the next section.

Since the grave sinner is to be a member of the community, 'works' must be excluded from *īmān*, and it therefore comes to be defined as intellectual assent to certain doctrines together with a public profession of this. The opponent has thus some justification for saying that 'works' are 'postponed' or 'put after' *īmān*. This was one of the applications of the term mentioned by ash-Shahrastānī. Another of his applications, the giving of hope, comes from the same line of thought by a slightly different route. It came to be widely held that everyone with *īmān*, in the sense of intellectual assent and public profession, had an assured hope of Paradise.

e) *The earliest Murji'ites*

The earliest Murji'ites were essentially men who wanted to preserve the unity of the Islamic community, and one source of *irjā'* seems to be opposition to the fissiparous tendencies of the Khārijites. Not surprisingly such men were criticized by the Khārijites as immoral, because they appeared to make light of grave sins. Yet the vast body of Muslims rejected the Khārijite view of the grave sinner. They held that he should be punished but not excluded from the community; and they did not exclude men from the community for minor differences in belief.

Any such account of the beginnings of Murji'ism, however, fails to explain the fact that a preponderant number of the men described as Murji'ites by Ibn-Sa'd or Ibn-Qutayba came from Kufa. [21] It is conceivable that our sources are biased, especially Ibn-Sa'd, or that the name was used more in Kufa than elsewhere. Yet at Basra there certainly was tension between Khārijites and those who held what might be called *irjā'*, and Mu'tazilite doctrine is presented as a middle way between these two groups. On the whole it seems most likely that the *irjā'* of Kufa was originally distinct from that of Basra and other places. In Kufa many men favoured 'Alī and this may have implied that they were liable to revolt against the Umayyads if a good opportunity presented itself. Other men would see this attitude as potentially divisive of the community and would work to maintain unity. They may have based their political position on the Qur'ānic verse with *murjawna*, and they would then be nicknamed Murji'ites in a pejorative sense. Nevertheless as opponents of the divisive tendencies of both Shīʿites and Khārijites all these early Murji'ites were forerunners of the Sunnites, and deserve to be honoured as such. The further problem of how some Murji'ism came to be regarded as heretical will be considered later.

3
Membership of the community
a) *The original basis of membership*

During the lifetime of Muḥammad there appear to have been two ways in which membership of the Islamic community was attained, one more applicable to groups and the other to individuals.[22] The first way is exemplified in the Qur'ān where *ṣalāt* and *zakāt* frequently occur together in contexts which suggest that these are the essential marks of membership of the community.[23] The performing of the *ṣalāt* or worship was normally a communal activity; and the collectors of *ṣadaqāt* mentioned in the accounts of Muḥammad's administration, who at this period were probably dealing with what is called *zakāt* in the Qur'ān, were sent to tribes or parts of tribes.[24] In the wars of the *Ridda* or Apostasy during the caliphate of Abū-Bakr it appears that the act by which a tribe publicly denounced its allegiance to the caliph in Medina was its refusal to send the customary money payments to him. It is virtually certain, then, that Muḥammad made a specific requirement of *ṣalāt* and *zakāt* from the tribes or groups who wanted to join his federation. There are indeed some later instances where the public performance of the worship by an individual apostate was taken as a proof that he had abandoned his apostasy; but this does not contradict the general principle that the performance of the *ṣalāt* was a communal obligation.

The more individualistic way of becoming a member of the Islamic community was by the repetition of the *shahāda* or confession of faith—'there is no deity but God, Muḥammad is the messenger of God'. This is attested in Tradition. A pagan Arab, whose name was on the list of persons proscribed at the conquest of Mecca, managed to avoid death by making his way secretly into Muḥammad's presence and then, before he could be arrested, repeating the confession of faith.[25] The precise wording of the whole confession is not found in the Qur'ān, though it may be said to be implied.[26] The first half, however, occurs many times (including variants), but not as a formula to be repeated; and it may well be that in Muḥammad's lifetime only this first half was used, since in most cases there would also be some act or gesture of personal loyalty. The need for the whole formula was perhaps only felt towards the year 700 when many *dhimmīs*, who had believed in God but not in Muḥammad's messengership, wanted to become Muslims; and this is all that the material in Tradition can be said to demonstrate, though it may contain some genuine reminiscences of the practice before 632.

In later times only a small proportion of Muslims were converts from something else, since the majority were born into Islam; and so there is more discussion of how a man loses the status of *mu'min* or *muslim* than of how he gains it. The latter was mainly by public profession of faith. The loss of status had serious legal consequences, and was therefore discussed by the jurists. They distinguished *takfīr* and *tabdī'*. The latter was the declaration that a man was a *mubtadi'*, guilty of *bid'a*, literally 'innovation' but tantamount to 'heresy'. The former was the declaration that a man was a *kāfir*, 'unbeliever', guilty of *kufr*, 'unbelief'. There was a tendency among theologians and others to make such charges far too readily against opponents, and al-Ghazālī wrote a short book to show when a charge of *kufr* was justified.[27] The point to notice here is that *kufr* is roughly the opposite of *īmān*, and that both corresponded more to the second way of becoming a Muslim than to the first.

b) *The distinction between* īmān *and* islām

Just as *īmān* was commonly understood to be that which made a man a *mu'min*, so *islām* could be that which made a man a *muslim*. It has sometimes been thought by occidental scholars that there was a difference of degree between the *mu'min* and the *muslim*. There was certainly some distinction between the two, but careful examination shows that it was not one of degree.

We may look more closely at a statement of the view by A.J. Wensinck.[28] He claims that there is a Tradition which 'seeks to state that there is a difference between faith and acceptance of the official religion; that faith, though expressing itself in rites and duties, lies deeper than these'. This seems to incorporate alien European connotations of the word 'faith'. The Tradition is one in which Muḥammad, in reply to questions, gives three definitions : *īmān* is believing in (*taṣdīq*—counting true) God, his angels, his book, his meeting, his apostles and the final resurrection; *islām* is serving God without associating anything with him, performing the ordered *ṣalāt*, paying over the obligatory *zakāt*, and fasting during Ramaḍān; *iḥsān* (acting uprightly) is serving God as if he were before one's eyes.[29] It is true that in this Tradition *islām* is a matter of 'rites and duties', but *īmān* appears to be mainly intellectual assent to certain doctrines. The same is the true conclusion from a saying of Muḥammad's which Wensinck quotes from Aḥmad ibn-Ḥanbal: '*islām* is external (*'alāniyatan*), *īmān* in the heart';[30] according to the ideas of the ancient Arabs the heart was the seat of understanding. In both these Traditions there is a distinction between *īmān* and *islām*, but it is not, as Wensinck seems to suggest, between depth of conviction or inner experience and a mere outward and formal observance.

Other material of about the same date leads to rather different conclusions. The Medinan scholar az-Zuhrī (d. 742) is reported to have said that *islām* refers to word (*kalima*) and *īmān* to action (*'amal*).[31] It is likely that 'word' here refers to the confession of faith, for elsewhere one finds *islām* defined as repeating the confession of faith.[32] It would be tempting on the basis of such views to hold that the grave sinner is a *muslim* but not a *mu'min*. There are numerous discussions in Islamic theological literature of the distinction between *islām* and *īmān*;[33] and some might seem to come close to what has just been suggested. Ultimately, however, no one form of the distinction is supported by the consensus of the theologians, nor does the Qur'ān give any grounds for holding that *īmān* is either higher or lower than *islām*. The theologians seem to be chiefly concerned with showing how the main assertions about these matters in Qur'ān and Traditions can be squared with their own particular views.

Perhaps the most important piece of evidence from the Qur'ān is the fact that in it the commonest name for Muḥammad's followers is *mu'minūn*; according to a count based on Flügel's *Concordance* this word occurs 179 times as against 37 occurrences of *muslimūn*. As late as 634 'Umar adopted the caliphal title of *amīr al-mu'minīn*, 'commander (or prince) of the believers'. On the other hand, there is a passage (49.14f.) which seems to place *islām* on a lower level than *īmān*:

> The nomads say, *āmannā* (we have believed). Say: You have not believed (*lam tu'minū*); but say, *aslamnā* (we have professed Islam), seeing that *īmān* has not yet entered into your hearts. ... (15) The *mu'minūn* are those who *āmanū* in God

> and his messenger, not afterwards doubting, and strove with goods and persons in the way of God . . .

The commentators notice that *īmān* here includes activity; and some (like aṭ-Ṭabarī) make a contrast by interpreting *aslamnā* of the outward confession of faith (as in the translation given). Others, however, realize that such a distinction is not in accordance with the general usage of the Qur'ān, and therefore interpret *aslamnā* as meaning *istaslamnā* which should probably be translated 'we have sought peace by submission'. [34] One of the following verses (49.17), probably not part of the same revelation, seems to use *īmān* and *islām* interchangeably:

> They claim credit (mention as a good deed deserving reward) from you because they *aslamū*. Say (to them) : Do not claim credit from me for your *islām*; rather God claims credit from you for guiding you to *īmān*.

There are, of course, other ways of understanding this verse; but sufficient has been said to show that there is no clear evidence in the Qur'ān for a distinction of level or degree such as was suggested by Wensinck. [35]

The conclusion of this discussion, then, must be that, while *īmān* and *islām* differ somewhat in meaning, the distinction is not fixed and rigid, but varies from time to time. In the theological views to be considered next it will be found that *īmān* comes close to 'acceptance of the official religion'.

c) *Murji'ite and Ḥanafite views of* īmān

It is convenient at this point to look at the views about *īmān* brought together by al-Ashʿarī in his section on the Murji'a. [36] We shall leave till later the question of why they are regarded as heretical. Meanwhile we notice the curious fact that many of these Murji'ites are nonentities, who appear only in heresiographers' accounts of the Murji'ites, while there is the outstanding exception of Abū-Ḥanīfa who cannot be considered a heretic. [37] A further point is that it is difficult to find discussions of the same questions in the writings of the heresiographers, whereas they are taken up by Ḥanafite, Ḥanbalite and Ashʿarite theologians. Let us therefore grasp the nettle boldly. Let us place Abū-Ḥanīfa and the Ḥanafites in the centre of our examination of the views about *īmān*, and dismiss the charge of heresy against him as proceeding from *odium theologicum* and not to be taken too seriously.

The report given of Abū-Ḥanīfa (d. 767) by al-Ash'arī states that he held that *īmān* was the knowledge (*ma'rifa*) of God together with the acknowledgement of him and the knowledge of the Messenger (Muḥammad) together with the acknowledgement of the revelation he brought; and this was to be in general and without interpretation (*tafsīr*), as illustrated by an example. Further—a point to be considered later—he held that *īmān* is indivisible and does not increase or decrease.[38] This report is found to be roughly confirmed by Ḥanafite documents of the eighth century and later.

The oldest is that called *Al-fiqh al-akbar I* by Wensinck. It may represent the actual views of Abū-Ḥanīfa, and cannot be much later than his lifetime. Article 5 states the basic principle of *irjā'* : 'we give back to God (the decision about) the affair of 'Uthmān and 'Alī'. Article 1 is a rejection of the main Khārijite doctrine : 'we do not declare anyone an unbeliever (*nukaffiru*) through sin, and we do not exclude anyone from *īmān*'.[39] This is not a definition of *īmān*, but it implies that acts are not a part of *īmān*. Article 9 is to the effect that : 'whoever says "I do not know whether God is in heaven or on earth" is an unbeliever'. This is not unlike the illustrations given in al-Ash'arī's report of 'interpretation' ; Abū-Ḥanīfa is said to have been asked about the man who said, 'God has enjoined pilgrimage to the Ka'ba, but I do not know whether he meant this Ka'ba in this place or some other', and to have replied, 'he is a *mu'min*'. The similarity of form between this report and article 9 tends to confirm that the report is genuine, while they differ in that article 9 does not deal with a question of 'interpretation'. Together the report and *Al-fiqh al-akbar I* seem to give us genuine views about the position of Abū-Ḥanīfa.

Next in order of development appears to be the *Creed* of aṭ-Ṭaḥāwī, who lived mainly in Egypt and died in 933.[40] This may be later chronologically than the *Waṣiyya* (to be considered next), but its conservative character means that it represents an earlier stage in the development. Article 10 of this creed repeats article 1 of the previous one : 'we do not because of sin consider as an unbeliever any of the people of the Qibla, so long as he does not consider it lawful'. Article 11 goes on to give an account of *īmān* similar to that of Abū-Ḥanīfa : it is 'confession (*iqrār*) with the tongue and counting true (*taṣdīq*) with the heart'. On the other hand, there is nothing in this creed about 'the affair of 'Uthmān and 'Alī' except that (§24)

'Uthmān is recognized as third of the rightly-guided caliphs and 'Alī as the fourth. Though *īmān* is said to be one, there is no mention of it increasing and decreasing.

The creed known as the *Waṣiyya* or Testament of Abū-Ḥanīfa is close to his views at many points, but in its extant form contains clauses which belong to a period later than the discussions inaugurated by the great Mu'tazilites on such matters as the analysis of human action and the createdness of the Qur'ān, and so can hardly be earlier than 850.[41] Some of the articles contain a brief proof, usually from the Qur'ān, of the doctrine asserted. Article 4 states the basic anti-Khārijite position : 'sinners (*'āṣūn*) of the community of Muḥammad are all believers, not unbelievers'. Article 1 has the same wording as article 11 of aṭ-Ṭaḥāwī : '*īmān* is confession with the tongue and counting true with the heart'. With regard to the caliphs it is not merely stated in article 10 that they are acknowledged in order, but also that the chronological order is the order of merit ; and this implies that 'Uthmān is superior to 'Alī.

Another Ḥanafite document is that called *Al-fiqh al-akbar II* by Wensinck, who dates it in the tenth century.[42] Wensinck's arguments about the date are vitiated by the fact that he is unaware of the contrast between Ash'arite and Ḥanafite doctrines ; his remark that 'it would appear that we do not possess sufficient data to ascribe it to himself' (*sc.* al-Ash'arī) is misleading because there are several points in the creed which show that it is *not* by al-Ash'arī.[43] The distinction (§2) between essential attributes and active attributes suggests a date in the late tenth century. The superiority of 'Uthmān to 'Alī is accepted (§10). The article on *īmān* (§18) is short, as if the issues involved had ceased to be live ones. The definition of *īmān* is abbreviated to 'confessing and counting true' ; it does not increase nor decrease ; the believers are equal in *īmān* and in *tawḥīd* (assertion of divine unity) ; *islām* is submission (*taslīm*—*sc.* to God) and the following (or obeying) of God's commands ; *īmān* and *islām* are linguistically distinct but inseparable and complementary.

The other aspect of Abū-Ḥanīfa's view, as reported by al-Ash'arī, was that '*īmān* is not divisible into parts and does not increase or decrease and that men are not superior to one another in respect of it'. This view is presumably derived from the idea that *īmān* is that which makes a man a member of the community, and that there is no halfway house between being a member and not being a member.

The point is not mentioned in *Al-fiqh al-akbar I*, and it is not made explicitly by aṭ-Ṭaḥāwī, though he states that the believers are one, even when the practice of one man is superior to that of another. The *Waṣiyya* and *Al-fiqh al-akbar II* explicitly state that *īmān* does not increase or decrease, but the latter allows that men may differ in respect of practice or activity. Thus later Ḥanafites are seen to follow closely the position ascribed to Abū-Ḥanīfa.

The other views on *īmān* mentioned by al-Ashʿarī in his account of the Murji'a are mostly slight deviations from Abū-Ḥanīfa's position and probably belong to the first half of the ninth century. Some of the persons named are said to have been disciples of the Muʿtazilite an-Naẓẓām (d. 835–45).[44] One of the questions discussed was the extent of the knowledge (*maʿrifa*) required for *īmān*. Abū-Ḥanīfa had said it was knowledge of God and of the Messenger; but one man wanted to reduce it to knowledge of God only, while others extended it to knowledge of all prophets and of religious duties. Most held that confession (*iqrār*) was an essential part of *īmān*, but some omitted it. Some, including Abū-Ḥanīfa himself, seem to have insisted that the knowledge of God had to be accompanied by appropriate feelings such as humility and love, but there was probably little discussion on this point and the later tendency was to omit any mention of feelings. There was also an interesting variation from the doctrine that *īmān* neither increases nor decreases, namely that it increases but does not decrease.[45] This is presumably based in part on the occurrence in the Qur'ān (in some half-dozen verses) of phrases like *zāda-hum īmānan*, 'he increased them in *īmān*'; but it was doubtless dropped because from the Ḥanafite standpoint at least it does not lead to any coherent view.

From the material here presented briefly the conclusion stands out that in the discussions about *īmān* the dominant influence was that of Abū-Ḥanīfa and the Ḥanafite tradition, and that the other persons mentioned as Murji'ites were completely insignificant.

d) *The critique of the Ḥanafites*

The earliest critique of the Ḥanafites was perhaps that of the Muʿtazilites. As noted above (p. 120), they objected to calling the grave sinner a believer because they maintained that he was in an 'intermediate position'. In accordance with this attitude they reject the definition of *īmān* as knowledge (or inner assent) and outward confession, and hold instead that *īmān* is the performance of all religious duties, obligatory and supererogatory, though in many cases the omission of a duty does not constitute *kufr* or 'unbelief'. An-Naẓẓām expressed a similar view negatively by saying that *īmān* is the avoidance of that in respect of which there is a threat (*wa'īd—sc.* of punishment), with the proviso that this might be either according to man's view or according to God's. Al-Ash'arī's report shows the various subtleties which were introduced into the discussion of this matter; but the opposition to the Ḥanafite view was clear.[46]

The critique of the Ḥanafites by the Ḥanbalites has also been mentioned previously (p. 123). The points already made may be illustrated from another Ḥanbalite writer, Ibn-Baṭṭa (d. 997). He first defines *īmān* as the counting true (*taṣdīq*) of all that God has said, commanded, enjoined and forbidden in his revelations to the messengers; and then in a jingle which adds a member to that of the Ḥanafites (as found, for example, in article 11 of aṭ-Ṭaḥāwī's creed) he says that this *taṣdīq* is *qawl bi-l-lisān wa-taṣdīq bi-l-jinān wa-'amal bi-l-arkān*, 'speaking with the tongue, counting true (or assenting) with the heart and acting (or practising) the duties'. He next contradicts the Ḥanafite doctrine that *īmān* is one by asserting that it increases by good acts and words and decreases by disobedience or sin.[47]

It is not surprising that al-Ash'arī, as a professed follower of Aḥmad ibn-Ḥanbal, adopted a similar position. He states it succinctly in his creed: '*īmān* is speaking and acting; it increases and decreases'.[48] The brief discussion of *īmān* in *Kitāb al-luma'* is directed against the Mu'tazilite doctrine of the intermediate position; it includes the statement that a man is a *mu'min* in respect of his *īmān*, though he may at the same time be a sinner in respect of a sin.[49] On these questions al-Ash'arī is not followed exactly by his disciples. Al-Baghdādī even reports al-Ash'arī's view as being that *īmān* is the counting true (*taṣdīq*) of God and his messengers, without any mention of acts, although he argues that it increases and decreases.[50] Later Ash'arites like al-Ghazālī (d. 1111) and al-Ījī (d. 1355) show little interest in these questions about *īmān*, though they deny the Khārijite doctrine of the grave sinner.[51] On the other hand, the Mālikite jurist Ibn-Abī-Zayd al-Qayrawānī (d. 996) in his creed follows Aḥmad ibn-Ḥanbal closely in the doctrine of *īmān*.

There is thus within Sunnite Islam a strong body of opinion which is definitely opposed to the Ḥanafite views on certain matters concerning *īmān*. Some of the later Ash'arites, indeed, favour the exclusion of *ʿamal* or action from the definition of *īmān* and so move closer towards the Ḥanafites, but on the question of its increase and decrease, if they discuss the point, they keep their own view. The Ḥanbalites show little change. Despite the criticisms, however, the Ḥanafites stand firm, and later creeds still define *īmān* as *taṣdīq* and *iqrār*, and assert that it neither increases nor decreases.[52] These creeds, of course, are centuries after the 'formative period' of Islamic thought which is being studied in this volume, but they are a significant part of the context of Abū-Ḥanīfa's doctrine of *īmān*.

4

The problem of 'moral anxiety'

a) *The apparent trend towards moral laxity*

Among the more pious members of the general religious movement during the Umayyad period there was undoubtedly a deep moral earnestness. Al-Ḥasan al-Baṣrī is an example of this, but there were many others. Moral earnestness, however, coupled with a high moral ideal, is always in danger of leading to a sense of failure or guilt or, more generally, anxiety. When a man has a high ideal, he will almost inevitably fall short of it; and he will then come to feel that he is an unsatisfactory person and will lose confidence in himself. In a Muslim this will naturally take the form of wondering whether he will attain to Paradise or whether he will spend eternity in Hell. If a man entertains these thoughts frequently, he will tend towards a constant state of anxiety, and this will reduce his ability to deal with the fundamental problems of life. Thus a corrective is required for undue moral earnestness.

Such a corrective appears to have been given to the Islamic world by the scholar Muqātil ibn-Sulaymān (d. 767), who lived mostly in Basra and Baghdad and was highly thought of as a commentator on the Qur'ān.[53] The assertion for which he became famous was that 'where there is *īmān*, sin does no harm'; that is to say, where a man has not forfeited his membership of the community through *shirk*, he will not be eternally punished for sin. To many scholars this view seemed to be an encouragement of moral laxity. It was explicitly repudiated in various creeds, such as that of aṭ-Ṭaḥāwī (§10): 'we do not say, "where there is *īmān*, sin does not harm the doer"; we hope for Paradise for the believers who do good, but we are not certain of it'. (It is perhaps relevant that Muqātil was not a Ḥanafite but belonged to the sect of the Zaydiyya.)

Despite the moral earnestness of many scholars, however, or perhaps just because of it, it came to be widely held that every Muslim would ultimately gain Paradise, provided he had not committed the one unforgivable sin of *shirk*. This exception was clearly stated in the Qur'ān : 'God does not forgive the associating (of any being) with him (*an yushraka bi-hi*—in worship), but he forgives what is short of that' (4.48/51, 116). Even the earnest preacher al-Ḥasan al-Baṣrī held that the man who affirms the *shahāda* at his death will go to Paradise.[54] By the time of aṭ-Ṭaḥāwī the point had been greatly elaborated, for he states (§13) that 'those who commit grave sins are in Hell, but not eternally, provided that at their deaths they were monotheists (*muwaḥḥidūn*)'. Then, after quoting the verse just mentioned, he continues : 'if he wills, he in his justice punishes them in Hell to the measure of their offence, then in his mercy and at the intercession of intercessors from among the people obeying him he removes them from Hell and raises them to his Paradise'. In *Al-fiqh al-akbar II* (§14), after a repudiation of Muqātil's assertion, there is a statement of the future prospects of those who have committed sins (other than *shirk* and *kufr*) but have died as believers ; the outcome is similar to that in aṭ-Ṭaḥāwī's creed—there is some hope for them of attaining Paradise, but it depends on God's will.

These assertions about the ultimate destiny of the grave sinner of the community are in accordance with the Ḥanafite definitions of *īmān*. By defining it as inner assent and outward confession, without any *'amal* or performance of duties, they make it easy for a man to remain a member of the community, and so to have a hope of Paradise (and in this way their *irjā'* is 'the giving of hope'). In this way they help to allay the moral anxiety caused by undue moral earnestness. On the other hand, they retain the element of fear, since the grave sinner may still suffer some unpleasant punishment. In practice such beliefs have often led to a relatively high level of morality in Muslim lands ; but in theory they may be criticized as retaining the negative motive of fear instead of replacing it (as is done in other systems) by the positive motive of devotion to a noble cause or inspiring leader.

Somewhat similar views are found among the Ash'arites. Al-Ash'arī himself holds that it is not inevitable that grave sinners of the community should go to Hell since, if he wills, God may forgive them ; and he also regards it as certain that some grave sinners will be brought out of Hell at the intercession of the Messenger of God.[55] Al-Baghdādī and al-Ghazālī had similar views on these points; and so also had the Ḥanbalites.[56] Since the earlier reports suggest that the Ḥanafites were the first to propound such ideas, it may well be that in this matter they converted other groups to their views.

b) *The intercession of the Messenger*

The intercession (*shafāʿa*) of Muḥammad for members of his community has already been mentioned incidentally and may be treated briefly. The idea of intercession occurs in the Qur'ān. Apparently some of Muḥammad's contemporaries believed that their idols would intercede for them, probably with the supreme God on the Last Day. The Qur'ān denies that this is so, but allows that intercession may take place by God's permission.[57] It is nowhere explicitly stated in the Qur'ān that Muḥammad has the right of intercession on the Last Day, though there are some verses which have been interpreted to mean this. A number of Traditions spoke of the intercession of Muḥammad, however, and it came to be a generally accepted article of belief. The earliest occurrence is probably that in *Waṣiyyat Abī-Ḥanīfa* (§25).

Wensinck suggested that the Sunnite community's adoption of the idea of intercession might be 'due to the need for something to counterbalance predestination, as well as the influence of Christian ideas'. This suggestion has little to commend it. For one thing the idea is present in the Qur'ān that God gives permission to angels and others to make intercession on the Last Day. Again, if something is needed to balance predestination, it is because a man may be predestined to have either *kufr* or *īmān*, and so to spend eternity in either Hell or Paradise. The root of the anxiety is thus the possibility that a man may be eternally in Hell and that nothing he can now do will prevent this. Where moral earnestness was dominant, as among the Khārijites and Muʿtazilites, it was held that God was bound to punish sinners eternally. Thus the doctrine of Muḥammad's intercession for sinners of his community served the purpose of relieving the despair caused by excessive moral earnestness.

c) *Certainty about one's status*

Another point of difference between Ḥanafites on the one hand and Ḥanbalites and some Ashʿarites on the other is that known as the question of *istithnā'* or 'making exception'. The Ḥanbalites and other morally earnest scholars, basing their ideas on the conception of *īmān* as determined by God, held that a man was not entitled to say 'I am a believer' but only 'I am a believer, if God will.'[58] A man may sincerely think that at the present moment he is giving full assent to the doctrines comprised under *īmān*, and yet there may be imperfections in his assent of which he is unaware. The practice is said to have begun fairly early among pious scholars, and Ibn-Baṭṭa gives a list. Those who criticized the practice called such persons Shukkāk or 'doubters';[59] and it is easy to see that the practice, if insisted on for ordinary people, would lead to an increase of moral anxiety. The believers in the practice were aware of this criticism, and tried to meet it. Ibn-Baṭṭa said it was a making exception which implied certainty (*istithnā' 'alā l-yaqīn*), and that the person employing the phrase should know this and should not suppose that it was an exception arising from doubt.[60]

All this was opposed by the Ḥanafites. The *Waṣiyya* (§3) puts the matter positively: 'the believer is really a believer and the unbeliever is really an unbeliever'. An explicit rejection of *istithnā'* is found in later Ḥanafites, such as the two called an-Nasafī.[61] The close connection in Ḥanafite thought between *īmān* and membership of the community meant that it was illogical to allow an appearance of doubt here; to say 'I am a member of the community, if God will' is as pointless for them as to say 'I am alive, if God will.' The matter is trivial, but it throws a little light on the conception of *īmān*. In this respect also Ḥanafite doctrine aimed at reducing the strain incurred by following an almost inaccessible ideal.

5

Murji'ism as a heresy

It has been seen that the term Murji'a can be used in many different ways. Indeed it can be applied to almost any member of the Islamic community except the Khārijites and the Shī'ites; and even some of those called Shī'a by Ibn-Qutayba are labelled Murji'a by an-Nawbakhtī. It is not meaningful to say that there was a sect of Murji'ites which was regarded as heretical by all Sunnites. Some of the men assigned to the Murji'a by heresiographers such as al-Baghdādī and ash-Shahrastānī would indeed be considered heretics by Ḥanbalites, Ash'arites and Ḥanafites alike; but these men are nonentities who played no significant part in the development of Islamic thought, certainly not a part commensurate with the attention paid to Murji'ism. Their views, too, differ only slightly from those of Abū-Ḥanīfa.

A more profitable approach is to put in the forefront the conception of *irjā'* or Murji'ism, whatever the sect-labels of the holders, and to ask how the various doctrinal emphases linked with this conception contributed to the development of Sunnism. The two matters in which an attitude of *irjā'* was first adopted are both matters in which this attitude came to be accepted by Sunnites in general. One was the rejection of the Khārijite doctrine that the grave sinner is excluded from the community, and the other the rejection of the proto-Shī'ite belief in the superiority of 'Alī.

The Khārijite doctrine of the exclusion of the grave sinner from the community was unworkable in practice. Since exclusion from the community meant that a man no longer had security for life and property, this doctrine was tantamount to saying that the punishment for every sin was death or exile; and this is unacceptable. Politically the doctrine justified military action against any ruler whom one declared guilty of a grave sin; and in particular it denied the legitimacy of Umayyad rule since that was based on the claim that the dynasty were the heirs and avengers of 'Uthmān, whom the Khārijites declared to be a sinner. Those who first adopted the attitude of *irjā'* towards 'Uthmān and others were men filled with zeal for the well-being of the community who considered that rebellion against constituted authority was in general wrong. On these matters Sunnism adopted the attitude of *irjā'*, rejecting the Khārijite doctrine and holding that no man lost the status of *mu'min* through any sin other than *shirk* or *kufr*. Sunnism also accepted the attitude of *irjā'* not merely towards 'Uthmān but also towards all sinners of the community. Examples of this have been given in the discussion of how grave sinners might be punished or forgiven. Something of the same attitude was even accepted by the Mu'tazila, as may be seen from a passage in al-Khayyāṭ.[62] The alleged founder of the Mu'tazila, Wāṣil, was said to have suspended judgement (*wuqūf*) in respect of 'Uthmān and his adversaries, and al-Khayyāṭ remarks: 'this was the way of the pious scholars, to suspend judgement in doubtful matters; and as in his (Wāṣil's) eyes 'Uthmān had committed crimes in the last six years, (the decision about) his case was difficult for him, and he postponed him (*arja'a-hu*) to the one who knows him (*sc.* God)'.

The second matter was prominent among those called Murji'a by the Shīʿa of Kufa. Their refusal to decide the question of ʿAlī and ʿUthmān implied a refusal to place ʿAlī above ʿUthmān, as the Shīʿa considered proper. This point also was adopted by later Sunnites. Indeed they went further and placed ʿUthmān *above* ʿAlī, as can be seen from al-Ashʿarī's creeds (§36/33), where the chronological order of the first four caliphs is said to be also the order of merit. Later Ḥanafite creeds, such as the *Waṣiyya* (§10) and *Al-fiqh al-akbar II* (§10), adopt a similar position.

In respect of the definition of *īmān* the original difference between the Ḥanafites and the Ḥanbalites seems to go back to the fact that the Ḥanafites thought of *īmān* merely as that which makes a man a member of the community whereas the Ḥanbalites included an element of moral idealism. In course of time, however, the two wings of Sunnism grew closer together. Ibn-Baṭṭa (d. 997), the Ḥanbalite writer, quotes with approval a saying ascribed to the Traditionists Sufyān ath-Thawrī (d. 777) and Ibn-al-Mubārak (d. 797): 'men in our eyes are believers (*mu'minūn*) in respect of inheritances and legal status; but we do not know how God considers them nor in what religion they will die'.[63] As a practical attitude this is almost identical with that of Abū-Ḥanīfa. It is also to be noted that al-Baghdādī is not so insistent as al-Ashʿarī that ʿ*amal* (action) is part of *īmān*, and does not mention it in giving al-Ashʿarī's definition, though it is prominent by implication in the third of the sections into which he divides 'our party' (*aṣ'ḥābu-nā*).[64] Here again, then, later Sunnites are close to Abū-Ḥanīfa, even when they express certain points differently.

Somewhat similar is the question of the eternal punishment of grave sins. The Khārijites held that the grave sinner would be eternally in Hell, and that this punishment was obligatory on God and so more or less automatic. The rejection of this view is given an extreme form when it is stated that, 'where there is *īmān* sin does no harm'; and this statement was generally rejected by Sunnism. The more moderate form of the rejection, however, was to hold that for the grave sinner of the community eternal punishment in Hell is not inevitable, since God may, if he will, forgive him at the intercession of the Messenger. Here, too, later Sunnites came close to adopting the early Ḥanafite position.

In various ways, then, ideas which grew out of the central conception of *irjā'* or 'postponing' played an important part in the development of Sunnism and came to be widely accepted. Occasionally some thinker or other adopted a formulation of a point which went to extremes and was adjudged heretical. The chief of these was probably the statement about 'sin doing no harm'. Most of the other assertions agreed to be heretical—and there were hardly any—were concerned with trifling matters. For the modern scholar, therefore, the problem comes to be why the Murji'ites are given so much prominence in the heresiographers and in other theological writings. The following account may be suggested as a likely explanation.

When al-Ashʿarī was writing there was as yet no clear conception of Sunnism. There were Ḥanafites and Ḥanbalites and perhaps other identifiable groups whose descendants would all come to be known as Sunnites; and opposed to some of these, at least, were the Muʿtazilites. There is no trace, however, of any awareness among the Ḥanafites and Ḥanbalites that they had anything in common. Al-Ashʿarī was at first a Muʿtazilite; and when he spoke of Abū-Ḥanīfa as a Murji'ite heretic he was expressing a Muʿtazilite judgement and not a Sunnite judgement.[65] Later as a professed follower of Aḥmad ibn-Ḥanbal he would not be averse to thus criticizing the leader of a rival legal school. By the eleventh century the other Sunnites had come closer to the Ḥanafites and there was some feeling of belonging together, so that al-Baghdādī and ash-Shahrastānī could no longer criticize Abū-Ḥanīfa as al-Ashʿarī had done. Both, however, as was seen in the Introduction, were interested in having seventy-two heretical sects. To help to make up this number they retained as Murji'ites the nonentities mentioned by al-Ashʿarī whom no one was now interested to defend. Jahm and Ghaylān were not nonentities, but they were already heretics on other grounds, while Bishr al-Marīsī had a bad reputation among his fellow-Ḥanafites. In this way the Murji'a obtained a definite place among the sects.

Finally it is to be noted that, when the pseudo-sect of the Murji'ites is thus excised from the body religious of Islam, it is possible to form a juster appreciation of the contribution of Abū-Ḥanīfa to the development of Islamic thought. He was at the centre of a wide movement which was mainly responsible for the formulation of important aspects of Sunnite doctrine. Some of those on the fringe of this movement might express views which had the appearance of being heretical; but Abū-Ḥanīfa himself was never a heretic. He was one of the great thinkers of the formative period of Islam, and his contributions were not confined to the matters discussed in this chapter. Something will be said later about his conception of *ra'y*.

6

The alleged sect of the Jahmiyya

The heresiographers describe a sect of Jahmiyya, and there are many arguments against them in theological treatises. There are even a number of 'Refutations of the Jahmiyya'. Yet when one looks closely at the material about the sect it is impossible to find the name of a single person who was a member of it apart from men who are normally reckoned to belong to some other sect, chiefly the Muʿtazila. There is thus a problem here which is an important part of the evaluation of the methods of the heresiographers. Before looking at these methods, however, it is necessary to examine the material briefly.

a) *Jahm ibn-Ṣafwān*

There is no doubt about the historicity of the man from whom the sect takes his name, Jahm ibn-Ṣafwān. He held subordinate offices, including that of secretary, under al-Ḥārith ibn-Surayj, a war-leader in eastern Khurasan, who appears frequently in the pages of aṭ-Ṭabarī's history. Al-Ḥārith, who summoned men to 'the Book of God and the Sunna of his Prophet', was an upholder of Persian rights, and had the support of the *dihqāns* and the Persian population generally. For a considerable part of the period from 734 to 746 he was fighting against the local Umayyad commanders. About 737, when hard pressed by the Umayyad armies, he entered into alliance with a Turkish prince, and later fought along with the Turks against the Muslims.[66] Jahm was captured and executed in 746, and al-Ḥārith was killed in battle shortly afterwards.

Not much can be said with certainty about the views of Jahm himself as distinct from the views ascribed to his sect. Both he and al-Ḥārith are spoken of as Murji'ites, which in this case probably means that they did not attach any special merit to the Prophet's family (in contrast to the Shīʿa) and did not refuse to associate with grave sinners (in contrast to the Khārijites). In general they considered that they were fighting for God and for true Islam, but it is not clear how they linked this with their advocacy of non-Arab rights. It is conceivable that a view ascribed to Jahm on the nature of *īmān* was intended to justify their alliance with Turks : '*īmān* is solely the knowledge of God in the heart, and if a man expresses Judaism or

Christianity or other kinds of *kufr* with his tongue and in his worship, while knowing God in his heart, he is a *muslim*'.[67] This fits exactly the situation in which we know Jahm to have been. When al-Ḥārith went over to the Turkish prince, one of the Muslim leaders spoke of him as 'the enemy of God', while another attacked him in a poem in which among other things he said that his (al-Ḥārith's) *irjā'* joined him to *shirk*.[68] For men who professed strong devotion to Islam it was a strange move, and may well be the point which made 'Jahmite' a term of abuse for later generations.

b) *The Jahmiyya as conceived by the Ḥanbalites*

When the earlier references to Jahm and the Jahmiyya are scrutinized it becomes clear that a great many of them are by Ḥanbalites or men of a similar outlook. Works entitled 'Refutation of the Jahmiyya' were produced by Aḥmad ibn-Ḥanbal himself,[69] by Abū-Sa'īd ad-Dārimī (d. 895),[70] and by several other Ḥanbalites.[71] A work directed in part against the Jahmiyya is ascribed to Ibn-Qutayba, whose standpoint was not far removed from that of the Ḥanbalites.[72] The Jahmiyya were likewise criticized in works of a more general character by Khushaysh,[73] al-Ash'arī (who claimed to follow Ibn-Ḥanbal),[74] and Ibn-Khuzayma.[75] Innumerable other references may be found to the use of the term 'Jahmite' by Ḥanbalites.

The chief point in Jahmite views which was criticized was the doctrine of the createdness of the Qur'ān. As the discussion increased in subtlety and came to embrace the question of man's speaking or utterance (*lafẓ*) or reciting (*qirā'a*) of the Qur'ān, Aḥmad ibn-Ḥanbal is reported to have said 'whoever supposes that the reciting of the Qur'ān is created is a Jahmite, and the Jahmite is an unbeliever'.[76] Another point that is frequently attacked is the Jahmite denial that God has a knowledge that is different from himself, and more generally a denial of the attributes of God.[77] The Jahmiyya are also said to have denied certain anthropomorphisms such as God's being on the throne and various points of eschatology.

It is also important to notice who are alleged to have been members of the Jahmiyya or to have had contacts with them. Only one person is said to have spoken of himself as a Jahmite, and he is the exception which proves the rule, for he made this remark only after he had ceased to be one; indeed he died in prison at Samarra in 843 for refusing to say that the Qur'ān was created, and is described as 'vehement in refuting the Jahmiyya'.[78] Aḥmad ibn-Ḥanbal asserted that some followers of Abū-Ḥanīfa and some of ʿAmr ibn-ʿUbayd (that is, some Ḥanafites and some Muʿtazilites) followed Jahm in his doctrine of God;[79] and the names of persons assigned to the sect fall into these two categories. (The categories overlap, since Muʿtazilites in theology might be Ḥanafites in law.) In a Ḥanbalite list of the followers of Jahm there occur two Ḥanafites: Bishr al-Marīsī and Burghūth; and four Muʿtazilites: al-Murdār, al-Aṣamm, Ibn-ʿUlayya and Ibn-Abī-Du'ād.[80] It has also been noted that there is a close similarity between views held by the Muʿtazilite Abū-l-Hudhayl and views attributed to the Jahmiyya and perhaps to Jahm himself.[81] Another Ḥanafite, known as al-Khaṣṣāf (d. 874), is said to have promoted Jahmites and renewed the 'empire' of Ibn-Abī-Du'ād.[82] It seems clear, then, that those attacked by Ḥanbalites for Jahmite views are either Muʿtazilites or Ḥanafites. There is no evidence of any link between them and the historical Jahm. The first person to spread 'the Jahmite doctrine' (*maqāla jahmiyya*) was (according to a Ḥanbalite) Bishr al-Marīsī the Ḥanafite; and he was singled out for attack by ad-Dārimī.[83]

c) *The Ḥanafites and the Jahmiyya*

It has just been noted that there were alleged Jahmites among the followers of Abū-Ḥanīfa. The most important was undoubtedly Bishr ibn-Ghiyāth al-Marīsī (d. 833), who is reckoned a Ḥanafite in law, having studied under Abū-Yūsuf. He is frequently said to have been the first to say openly that the Qur'ān was created, and this may well be so; though Jahm is said to have preceded him, this is unlikely, since the question was not being discussed in the lifetime of Jahm. The caliph Harūn ar-Rashīd (786–809) is said to have threatened to kill him for this, so that he went into hiding for about twenty years during his reign; but he had a warm welcome at the court of al-Ma'mūn (presumably between the latter's return to Baghdad in 819 and his death in 833) and was present at some of the discussions of the createdness of the Qur'ān which led to the acceptance of this as official doctrine.[84] The Ḥanafite biographer Ibn-Abī-l-Wafā' (d. 1373) says he was famous for having 'plunged into' rational theology (*ʿilm al-kalām*), and for this reason was criticized by Abū-Yūsuf and others.

This last point is important, since it helps to explain the appearance of opposition to the Jahmiyya among the Ḥanafites. Among those described as vehement in refuting the Jahmiyya were Ibrāhīm ibn-Ṭahmān (d. c. 780), a scholar in Khurasan, Nūḥ ibn-Abī-Maryam (d. 789), who was known as al-Jāmiʿ and was *qāḍī* of Merv under al-Manṣūr, and Ibrāhīm ibn-Yūsuf (d. c. 854).[85] The information of Ibn-Abī-l-Wafā' about the first two on this point comes from Aḥmad ibn-Ḥanbal himself, and in the third case from a later Ḥanbalite (who had his information through a grandson of the first man). It is sometimes explicitly stated, and otherwise can be inferred, that the main object of their vehemence was the doctrine of the createdness of the Qur'ān; but this may be due mainly to the special interest of the Ḥanbalite sources.

Finally it must be noticed that the Jahmiyya are criticized by name in *Al-fiqh al-akbar I* (§10) for their denial of the punishment of the tomb.[86] If this particular clause goes back to Abū-Ḥanīfa himself (d. 767), this fact, together with the dates of the first two men just mentioned, shows that the critique of the Jahmiyya had begun before Bishr al-Marīsī became active (which could not have been much before 790, if at all), and that it was not restricted to the doctrine of the created Qur'ān. The point of the article is not clear. A modern scholar would be inclined to regard it as a general attack on a rationalistic attempt to deny certain picturesque details of eschatology; but this view, though attractive, does not fully explain the bitterness of the attack on this particular point. An alternative suggestion would be that conservative Ḥanafites were interested in this point because it enabled them to say that, although the 'believers' were destined for Paradise, there would be a punishment of their sins.

d) *The Muʿtazilites and the Jahmiyya*

There are some important references to Jahm in *Kitāb al-intiṣār* by the Muʿtazilite al-Khayyāṭ, written in the second half of the ninth century. Though Jahm himself is spoken of, what is said applies chiefly to the later Jahmites. From al-Khayyāṭ's remarks and from other facts it may be inferred that up to his time the term Muʿtazila had been used for many persons who used rational methods in theology but who did not accept the full Muʿtazilite doctrine as it had come to be defined in the 'five principles'. Among the persons thus popularly reckoned among the Muʿtazila were Jahm himself and a group consisting of Ḍirār, Ḥafṣ al-Fard, an-Najjār, Sufyān ibn-Sakhtān and Burghūth.[87] In respect of the first two he quotes a poem by Bishr ibn-al-Muʿtamir asserting that they are followers of Jahm and far removed from the followers of ʿAmr (ibn-ʿUbayd), that is, the Muʿtazilites in the strict sense. The explanation of these references appears to be that when Bishr ibn-al-Muʿtamir and his contemporaries were labelled 'Jahmite', they tried to escape from being thus branded by carefully defining Muʿtazilism and then alleging that 'Jahmite' was only to be applied to persons outside this definition of Muʿtazilism.

e) *The methods of the heresiographers*

It is now time to present the conclusions to be derived from this examination of early statements about Jahm and the Jahmiyya. The only hypothesis which seems to cover all the facts is that 'Jahmite' was a purely vituperative term and that there never was any body of men who in fact were followers of Jahm or who professed to be such. The term presumably meant something like 'renegade' or 'quisling'. The earliest instances of its use are from some Ḥanafites in Khurasan (if we assume that the term was not introduced into the reports by Aḥmad ibn-Ḥanbal); and this could be explained by the fact that the eastern provinces were more familiar with the execrable conduct of al-Ḥārith ibn-Surayj and Jahm and more likely to appreciate the vituperative force of 'Jahmite'. Not merely are no immediate followers of Jahm known, but those alleged by the Muʿtazilites to be his followers, and even Bishr al-Marīsī, held very different views on many points.[88] Al-Ashʿarī, though following the Muʿtazilites in his heresiography, was constrained to distinguish the views of the Jahmiyya from those of Ḍirār and an-Najjār and their followers.[89]

The hypothesis also supplies an explanation of the history of the term. It was probably first used of persons who adopted certain rationalistic views in eschatology. When some of these persons, notably Bishr al-Marīsī, came to hold that the Qur'ān was created, the term 'Jahmite' was applied to this view also; and for some (the Ḥanbalites) this was its main use. The Muʿtazilites, believing in the createdness of the Qur'ān, were called Jahmites and objected to that. Instead of directly denying their connection with Jahm they insisted that 'Jahmite' was only correctly applied to men like Ḍirār. It is to be noted that Ḍirār and the others had made an important contribution in their time but had left no continuing school attached to their name which might defend them against the calumnies of the Muʿtazila. It was about this stage of the discussion that the heresiographers came on the scene. Khushaysh takes eight doctrines labelled as 'Jahmite' and speaks of each as 'a sect'; he then goes on to refute

'Jahm' on a score of particular points. It is noteworthy that this Ḥanbalite writer does not mention the determinism to which al-Ashʿarī's account gives greatest prominence. To al-Baghdādī and ash-Shahrastānī the Jahmiyya are of interest chiefly as an example of extreme determinism. Ash-Shahrastānī speaks of a group of sects as Jabriyya or determinists and subdivides this into pure determinists (the followers of Jahm and no others) and modified determinists (the followers of an-Najjār and Ḍirār), while claiming that the later Ashʿarite doctrine of *kasb* is not determinism at all.[90] It is doubtful if anyone ever held the pure determinism of the Jahmiyya as here described, but the concept is useful for contrasting with other views. In short, the heresiographers, taking over a popular vituperative term, appear to have created the sect of Jahmiyya to facilitate their classifications. (The existence of Jahmites at Tirmidh in the eleventh century is mysterious,[91] but there is insufficient information to hazard an explanation; it is unlikely, however, that any explanation would require a modification of the general view here adopted.)

Part Two

THE CENTURY OF STRUGGLE 750–850

The period from 750 to 850 is fittingly called 'the Century of Struggle'. The coming to power of the 'Abbāsid dynasty marked a radical change in the balance of power within the caliphate. In a vast and complex body such as the caliphate had now become there was an intricate network of party interests, sometimes conflicting and sometimes coinciding. The recovery of equilibrium was thus no simple matter; and for the whole of this century the caliphs had as a prominent aim the framing of a policy which would rally the majority of the inhabitants of the caliphate behind it. In an Islamic environment it was inevitable that this political struggle should have religious implications; and thus the student of the development of Islamic thought is bound to pay some attention to the politics of this century.

A.D.	*The first 'Abbāsid caliphs*	A.H.
750–754	Abū-l-'Abbās as-Saffāḥ	132–136
754–775	al-Manṣūr	136–158
775–785	al-Mahdī	158–169
785–786	al-Hādī	169–170
786–809	Hārūn ar-Rashīd	170–193
809–813	al-Amīn	193–198
813–833	al-Ma'mūn	198–218
833–842	al-Mu'taṣim	218–227
842–847	al-Wāthiq	227–232
847–861	al-Mutawakkil	232–247

Part Four

THE CENTURY OF STRUGGLE

6

The Establishment of the ʿAbbāsids

1

The theoretical basis of ʿAbbāsid rule

a) *The ʿAbbāsids and their opponents*

It was apparently about 718 that members of the ʿAbbāsid family began to make tentative plans for seizing power in the caliphate. This family took its name from Muḥammad's uncle al-ʿAbbās who had in fact opposed his nephew and remained a pagan until about the time of the conquest of Mecca in 630. His son ʿAbd-Allāh, the outstanding interpreter of the Qur'ān, played little part in politics, though at the beginning of ʿAlī's reign he gave him some support. ʿAbd-Allāh had a son ʿAlī (d. c. 736) with a reputation for piety, but the first plotters were this man's son and grandson, Muḥammad (d. 743) and Ibrāhīm (d. 748). There is nothing to show that these men had any profound belief in a charisma attaching to the clan of Hāshim, but they realized the strength of public sympathy towards the Hāshimites, and were ready to use it for their ends. They were even prepared to employ an extremist like Khidāsh (d. 736), it would seem,[1] though they had to disavow him in the end.

Propaganda for the ʿAbbāsids in Khurasan may have begun as early as 718, but it was intensified after Ibrāhīm ibn-Muḥammad took over the leadership of the ʿAbbāsids in 743 on the death of his father. He sent as emissaries to Khurasan first Abū-Salama about 744 and then a year later Abū-Muslim. Abū-Salama played an effective part in the movement in Khurasan, and was appointed governor of Kufa after its capture in 749, and 'vizier to the family of Muḥammad'. He was thought, however, to have wanted an ʿAlid instead of Abū-l-ʿAbbās as caliph, and a few months after the proclamation of the latter he was 'liquidated'.[2] Abū-Muslim managed to organize the change-over from general sympathy with the movement to active insurrection. From the time the black banners were raised in June 747 he seems to have been in charge of the military operations. These culminated in the total defeat of the Umayyad caliph Marwān II at the battle of the Greater Zab in 750. Soon afterwards Syria and Egypt were occupied, and Marwān and most of the Umayyad family put to death. ʿAbbāsid rule was thus established over most of the caliphate from Egypt eastwards.

After such a vast upheaval as this change of dynasty and the parallel transference of the seat of power from Damascus to Iraq it was naturally some time before peace was restored. Numerous risings are recorded during the next twenty years, and indeed for the next half-century. These may be mentioned briefly since they fill in a part of the background against which the ʿAbbāsids had to justify their claim to rule.

First may be mentioned a number of Khārijite risings.[3] A force in Oman (ʿUmān), led by al-Julandā, after some fighting with another body of Khārijites, was thought sufficiently menacing to warrant the sending of a combined land and sea expedition by the ʿAbbāsids; and this pacified the region for a time (752). Another Khārijite leader in the Jazīra (north-eastern Syria) proved very troublesome for over a year until his defeat in 755. The most serious Khārijite rising, however, was that of the North African Berbers belonging to the Ibāḍite sect under Abū-l-Khaṭṭāb al-Maʿāfirī. By 758 they had established themselves in Tripoli and Cairouan, and even after their defeat by an ʿAbbāsid army in 761 another of their leaders, Ibn-Rustam, founded an independent emirate at Tahert (Tiaret), which continued until 909. About the same time Berbers of the Ṣufrite sect established a small state at Tlemcen. The two groups joined to recapture Cairouan in 770, but lost it again after a disastrous defeat in 772. The chief importance of these Khārijite risings is that they prevented the ʿAbbāsids from extending their rule west of Tunisia, and so made possible the establishment of the Umayyad emirate in Spain. Theologically they had no influence in Iraq.

Nearer home at Medina there was the rising at the end of 762 of Muḥammad an-Nafs az-Zakiyya, 'the Pure Soul', coupled with that of his brother Ibrāhīm at Basra. Within two or three months both were defeated and killed by the ʿAbbāsid armies. Though they were ʿAlids (great-grandsons of al-Ḥasan), such support as they had was very mixed. In a speech in the mosque at Medina the Pure Soul is reported to have asserted that the descendants of the Emigrants and the Anṣār (the earliest Muslims) were best fitted to rule the believers; and in accordance with this descendants of the caliph 'Umar and of az-Zubayr are mentioned among those who followed them.[4] There is no insistence on the special charisma of the clan of Hāshim, but many of the insurgents are said to have been Zaydites, that is, supporters of a descendant of 'Alī who came forward publicly as imam with the sword (a body of opinion to be discussed further below). The insurgents also included among others the remnants of the party of the Mughīra, executed in 737, who had claimed to follow the Pure Soul.[5]

Another group of opponents which has to be mentioned is that which attributed a special charisma to Abū-Muslim. Presumably he had a quality of leadership which exercised great attraction over those in contact with him. When the caliph al-Manṣūr found him dangerous and in 755 had him killed, many in Khurasan and the east refused to believe him dead and attached messianic beliefs to his name. These are known as Abūmuslimiyya.[6] That they should have come into existence at all shows the mixture of views within the movement which brought the 'Abbāsids to power. Abū-Muslim is also mentioned in connection with other sects, notably the Rizāmiyya, or Ruzāmiyya, of Merv,[7] out of whom seem to have come al-Muqanna' and the Muqanna'iyya, who revolted there about 778.[8] The latter were alleged to be antinomian, to believe in transmigration, and to revive old Persian revolutionary doctrines and practices. They are thus of some interest to the student of religions but contributed nothing to the main stream of Islamic thought.

b) *The claim to 'legitimacy'*

At some point before the year 750 the 'Abbāsids claimed that the position of imam or head of 'the family' had been given to Muḥammad ibn-'Alī (a great-grandson of al-'Abbās) by Abū-Hāshim, the son of Muḥammad ibn-al-Ḥanafiyya. Muḥammad ibn-'Alī was the father of Ibrāhīm (leader of the 'Abbāsid movement from his father's death in 743 until his own in 748) and of the first two caliphs, as-Saffāḥ and al-Manṣūr. The claim implies that the head of the family after al-Ḥusayn was Muḥammad ibn-al-Ḥanafiyya and then Abū-Hāshim. It was seen in chapter 2 that there are independent grounds for thinking this was so.[9] It was also noted that the claim implies (1) that there is only one imam at any time, and (2) that the imamate is transmitted through appointment or designation by the previous imam. Even up to 750, however, it is unlikely that these principles were widely accepted. There was still much confusion, with many different men claiming to be imam. It would further appear that there was no general agreement among the 'Alids about who was head. When Abū-Salama was 'vizier to the house of Muḥammad' in Kufa in 749, and is said to have wanted to proclaim an 'Alid rather than an 'Abbāsid as caliph, there was no one 'Alid in authority to whom he could turn, and in fact he sent messages to several leading men.[10] This story also implies that the 'Abbāsid claim had not been made generally public, though it was presumably known and accepted by men like Abū-Muslim.

Once as-Saffāḥ had been proclaimed caliph, of course, the claim to have succeeded to the imamate through Abū-Hāshim must have been made public to some extent. Some of the sources, however, suggest that the main emphasis was on the fact that this was a member of the house of the Prophet;[11] and it should be remembered that it was normal among nomadic Arab tribes for the chief to be the best-qualified person from a certain family. From among 'the family' the chief opposition came from the Pure Soul, who asserted that no one had more Hāshimite blood than he; and against this assertion the claim through Abū-Hāshim would have some weight.[12] The 'Abbāsids seem to have encouraged people to refer to 'the family' as the Hāshimiyya or Hāshimiyyūn. Unfortunately Hāshimiyya could also be the followers of Abū-Hāshim. Two views are possible, however, of the relation of the two meanings of the term. Some writers have tended to think that the term was first used for the followers of Abū-Hāshim, and then later, with encouragement from the caliphs, applied to all members of the clan of Hāshim. Yet the alternative is attractive, namely, that the term was first used in the wider sense during the movement for the overthrow of the Umayyads, and that it was only after 750 that opponents of the régime tried to weaken its claim by narrowing the term to mean followers of the now relatively insignificant Abū-Hāshim. In so far as the 'Abbāsid caliphs were accepted as heads of the whole Hāshimite clan, they could be regarded as imams by persons of proto-Shī'ite sympathies. This may explain why Ibn-Qutayba includes reputable Traditionists in his list of Shī'a,[13] and perhaps why Aḥmad ibn-Ḥanbal tries to use the term of himself.[14] If the caliphs were imams of the Hāshimites, one could belong to the Shī'a without being Imāmite or anti-'Abbāsid. It was presumably the formulation of the doctrine of the twelve imams shortly after 874 which made it desirable to abandon the wider meanings of 'Shī'a'.

Under the caliph al-Mahdī (775–85) a different claim was put forward, namely, that the imam after Muḥammad was properly his uncle al-'Abbās, and that thereafter the imamate was handed on within the family of al-'Abbās.[15] If this report is correct, as it seems to be, it must indicate that an important body of opinion had been turning towards the 'Alids and away from the 'Abbāsids—or rather, had been insisting that the Hāshimite charisma was not equally spread through all the clan but was peculiarly present in the 'Alids alone. This may be partly a result of the efforts of Ja'far aṣ-Ṣādiq (d. 765), the sixth of the imams later recognized by the Imāmites, for he seems to have been active in scholarly matters, doubtless with a bearing on politics, though his activity did not arouse any suspicion among the 'Abbāsids. For the 'Abbāsids to claim that the imamate had come to them after having been in the hands of several 'Alids was to give a degree of recognition to the superior claim to charisma of the 'Alids. In particular it would seem to ordinary men that they were admitting the claim that on the death of the Prophet the man best fitted to rule the believers was 'Alī; and, as will be seen in the next section, this had become a party slogan in the caliphate.

Finally it may be noticed that the supporters of the 'Abbāsids, especially in Khurasan, are sometimes referred to as the Rāwandiyya. The name is said to be derived from one 'Abd-Allāh or Abū-Hurayra ar-Rāwandī,[16] but nothing is known about him. The Rāwandiyya are described as having developed out of a branch of the Kaysāniyya, and this roughly describes what seems to have happened, although the other Kaysāniyya have messianic hopes but no actual imam.[17] Al-Ash'arī describes the change from the Abū-Hāshim view to that of the direct designation of al-'Abbās; an-Nawbakhtī treats of the two claims separately so far as the Rāwandiyya are concerned, and specially associates the second claim with a sect of Hurayriyya, who are also the pure (*khullaṣ*) 'Abbāsiyya.[18] Both writers make the Abūmuslimiyya and Rizāmiyya (mentioned above) sub-sects of the Rāwandiyya; and an-Nawbakhtī mentions other extreme views among the Rāwandiyya, notably that al-Manṣūr was God and Abū-Muslim his prophet. When in 758 a party of the latter surrounded the palace in the temporary capital of al-Hāshimiyya, al-Manṣūr had them cut down by his troops.[19] From the standpoint of a study of the general development of Islamic thought the Rāwandiyya are not important, largely because they tended to adopt some 'extreme' views which were Persian rather than Islamic. They also, however, reflect the official 'Abbāsid attitudes, and these are central to this study.

2

History and contemporary politics

It is a notable feature of the medieval Islamic world that questions of contemporary politics are dealt with in terms of past history. The points that have just been discussed, namely the assertion that Abū-Hāshim transferred the imamate to Muḥammad ibn-'Alī and the assertion that the Prophet designated al-'Abbās to succeed him, are examples. They are both ways of stating that 'Abbāsid rule in the present is valid and legitimate. In other words it was normal for the Muslims at this period to define a contemporary political attitude by the precise view adopted on various historical matters in the past. That this is so may be taken as axiomatic. The problem is to discover what exactly the contemporary significance is.

a) *Attitudes in the later Umayyad period*

It will be helpful to begin by summarizing what has been stated in earlier chapters about the relation between political attitudes and historical assertions under the Umayyads. The focus of men's thinking on these matters was what was known as the question of 'Uthmān and 'Alī. Four main political attitudes may be distinguished, and it will then be seen that there corresponds to each a distinctive historical view.

1) At the one extreme are the partisan or whole-hearted supporters of the Umayyads. For these 'Uthmān had been truly caliph, and had been wrongly murdered; and the Umayyads were his heirs and successors. Such persons were often called 'Uthmānī,[20] and this indicates not merely that they insisted on the merits of 'Uthmān but also that they emphasized the demerits of 'Alī. In particular 'Alī was criticized for not punishing the murderers and for associating with them. Some of these partisans of the Umayyads seem to have denied that 'Alī had ever been caliph. In the latter part of the Umayyad period these historical views were coupled with full support of all Umayyad policies.

2) Others may be described as mild supporters of the Umayyads. They were not uncritical of Umayyad policies, but they held the Umayyads to be truly caliphs and considered that it was a duty of all Muslims to accept their rule. In this many were moved by a concern for the unity of the Islamic community. The position is indeed that often described as 'Murji'ite'. The historical standpoint corresponding to it is to hold that both 'Uthmān and 'Alī were truly caliphs, and to 'postpone' or leave to God the question whether either is a sinner and will go to Hell.[21]

3) Next come the mild critics of the régime, of whom Ibrāhīm an-Nakha'ī may be taken as an example.[22] In saying that he was neither a Saba'ite nor a Murji'ite, he probably meant that he did not ascribe to 'Alī any supernatural charisma or messianic quality but that he did not place 'Uthmān on a level with him. This seems to combine acceptance of the Umayyads with the suggestion that other and better rulers might be found.

4) A greater degree of criticism of the Umayyads seems to be involved in the position of the various groups which are brought under the general title of Kaysāniyya. After the death of Muḥammad ibn-al-Ḥanafiyya in 700 they held that he was still alive and would return as the Mahdī to set things right. In this doctrine it was further implied that 'Alī was the rightful imam after the Prophet and the best of the Muslims, and that he had designated Muḥammad ibn-al-Ḥanafiyya as his successor. The contemporary political attitude here is one of deep dissatisfaction with the Umayyads—they are inferior to other possible rulers; but there is no thought of taking action against them in the foreseeable future. It is an attitude not of acceptance but of resignation.

b) *The Rāfiḍites or Imāmites*

In the late eighth century and throughout the ninth century various men and groups are found called Rāfiḍites. This is a nickname given by opponents, whose meaning will be discussed presently. From about 900 there were men who were likewise nicknamed Rāfiḍites but who called themselves Imāmiyya and who regarded the previous Rāfiḍites as belonging to the Imāmiyya. The most satisfactory procedure is to examine the statements in early writers about those Rāfiḍites who died before about 870, that is, before the question of the twelfth imam arose. The most important early works are : *Kitāb al-intiṣār* by al-Khayyāṭ, the *Maqālāt* of al-Ash'arī, the *Fihrist* of

Ibn-an-Nadīm, *Murūj adh-dhahab* by al-Mas'ūdī and perhaps the *Fihrist* of Shaykh Ṭūsī (d. 1066). The last, though not itself early, contains lists of books from relatively early sources which supplement Ibn-an-Nadīm. Other late Shī'ite writers should be used only with great care, since they tend to rewrite history to bring it into line with Imāmite doctrine.

The first theological exposition of the doctrine of the imamate is said to have been given by 'Alī ibn-Mītham, who must have been roughly a contemporary of the Mu'tazilites Abū-l-Hudhayl and an-Naẓẓām, since he argued with them.[23] Other early theologians were Abū-Ja'far al-Aḥwal, nicknamed by opponents Shayṭān aṭ-Ṭāq, and Hishām ibn-Sālim al-Jawālīqī.[24] The man who attracted most attention, however, from later writers was Hishām ibn-al-Ḥakam.[25] This was doubtless because he discussed many of the questions with which the Mu'tazila were concerned, and indeed was the forerunner of an-Naẓẓām in respect of certain Greek philosophical conceptions.[26] He held, among other things, that Muḥammad had clearly indicated the individual who was to succeed him, even though most Muslims had not recognized him.[27] Al-Mas'ūdī gives a picture of the friendly relations between Mu'tazilites and Rāfiḍites in his charming description of the symposium on love arranged by the vizier Yaḥyā ibn-Khālid al-Barmakī.[28] Among the participants in this symposium are named Abū-l-Hudhayl, an-Naẓẓām, Bishr ibn-al-Mu'tamir, Thumāma and another Mu'tazilite as well as four 'Imāmites', including 'Alī ibn-Mītham and Hishām ibn-al-Ḥakam.

The political attitudes of these early Rāfiḍites are probably reflected in the statement ascribed by an-Nawbakhtī to 'Alī ibn-Mītham (Ibn-at-Tammār).[29] He held that 'Alī was deserving of the imamate, that he was the best of men (*afḍal an-nās*) after the Prophet, and that the community in associating with (*sc.* recognizing as caliphs) Abū-Bakr and 'Umar is in error, not sinfully but by leaving or abandoning the best; they dissociate from 'Uthmān and those who fought against 'Alī and consider them infidels. Two main points are found here (and are repeated by al-Ash'arī in his general account of the Rāfiḍites[30]) : the Prophet explicitly designated 'Alī to succeed him ; most of the Companions disobeyed the Prophet. The first of these points or something like it was held by all Shī'ites. It is to be noted, however, that at the time of 'Alī ibn-Mītham round about 800 the assertion is made about 'Alī alone, and there is no mention of a series of imams. Even when a friend of Hishām ibn-al-Ḥakam called as-Sakkāk writes a 'refutation of those who deny the necessity of the imamate by designation',[31] this should not be taken to imply that there was any general recognition of any particular series of imams. On the contrary it seems certain that there were nearly always several men struggling for recognition as leader of the 'Alids or of the Hāshimites. As was noted in the previous section, Abū-Salama in 749 sent messages to a number of leading 'Alids; and an-Nawbakhtī's account of the sects of the Shī'a shows a tangle of rival groups competing with one another (even if at times he projects later quarrels back into the past).

The primacy and superiority of 'Alī normally implied a rejection of the *shaykhayn*, that is, Abū-Bakr and 'Umar. The name Rāfiḍa or Rawāfiḍ comes from the verb *rafaḍa*, probably with the meaning 'desert', and so could be rendered 'deserters'. It is a nickname applied by opponents, and is used by al-Khayyāṭ, for example, when the Shī'ite work he is criticizing uses *shī'a*. The nickname was applied in at least five different ways:[32] e.g. it was given to those who 'deserted' Zayd ibn-'Alī who revolted in 740. Among non-Shī'ites, however, as al-Ash'arī states, the basic use was of the 'desertion' of Abū-Bakr and 'Umar. Whatever ground was averred, the application was always to those later known as Imāmites.

A more difficult question is: What did this mean in terms of contemporary politics? Al-Mas'ūdī's description of the symposium, along with many other facts, makes it clear that men like 'Alī ibn-Mītham, Hishām ibn-al-Ḥakam and as-Sakkāk were on friendly terms with the vizier of the time; and it follows that they could not have been plotting to overthrow the dynasty and replace it by an 'Alid dynasty. It also follows that, while their books on the imamate stated that the Prophet had designated 'Alī as his successor, they did not go on to state that Ja'far aṣ-Ṣādiq and Mūsā al-Kāẓim were rightful rulers of the Islamic world, even when they insisted on the necessity of the designation (*naṣṣ*) by an imam of his successor. The imprisonment of Mūsā al-Kāẓim by Hārūn ar-Rashīd suggests that something had begun to rouse the suspicions of the ruling institution; but there is nothing to show that writers of books on the imamate were in any way under a cloud. The friendship of these Rāfiḍites with the vizier may even be taken to show that they were not serious critics of the régime, and that the vizier had some sympathy with their view. At a later date Imāmism could be defended before al-Ma'mūn.[32a]

In these circumstances the most likely hypothesis is that these Rāfiḍites were arguing for a particular conception of the caliphate, namely, an absolutist one. The insistence on the 'designation' of the imam or caliph means that he has authority from above and not from below, not from any human electors, and certainly not from the *bayʿa* or act of allegiance of the ordinary people. In this connection it is significant that one of the points mentioned by al-Ashʿarī in his general account of the Rāfiḍites is that they altogether reject *ijtihād* or the independent judgement of the jurist in legal matters.[33] Presumably their view was that this important function must be reserved to the inspired imam, and could not be properly carried out by any ordinary man, no matter how extensive his knowledge of jurisprudence.

The hypothesis that the Rāfiḍites were chiefly concerned with upholding a form of absolutism has to meet the difficulty that disputes were going on about the identity of the rightful imam. While it is certain that Shīʿite writers often projected contemporary disputes into the distant past, it is clear that other disputes really happened at the time they were said to happen. Among the groups which were thought worthy of a distinctive name were the Fuṭ'ḥiyya (or Afṭaḥiyya), the Wāqifa (or Wāqifiyya) and the Qaṭʿiyya (or Qiṭṭiʿiyya). The name of the Fuṭ'ḥiyya is derived from the nickname al-Afṭaḥ (broad- or flat-footed) given to ʿAbd-Allāh, the eldest surviving son of Jaʿfar aṣ-Ṣādiq in 765. He died a few months after his father and had no son to succeed; so most of the associates of Jaʿfar recognized Mūsā al-Kāẓim as the next imam. This matter was probably of little moment in itself, but it raised a question of principle. If Jaʿfar was succeeded by al-Afṭaḥ and then by Mūsā, this meant that (apart from the exceptional case of al-Ḥasan and al-Ḥusayn) brother might succeed brother. In 818 ʿAlī ar-Riḍā could have been succeeded by either his brother Aḥmad or his son Muḥammad al-Jawād; in 874 al-Ḥasan al-ʿAskarī might have been succeeded by his brother Jaʿfar; so that in both cases the precedent was relevant.[34] This sect alone, then, gives evidence of genuine differences of opinion at least in 818 and 874, whatever happened in 765.

The Wāqifa and Qaṭʿiyya show a different type of dispute. The Wāqifa held that Mūsā al-Kāẓim would return some day and set everything right,[35] whereas the Qaṭ'iyya asserted 'decisively' that he was dead and that his son 'Alī ar-Riḍā had succeeded him.[36] This dispute has the appearance of one which really took place in the decade after the death of al-Kāẓim (probably in 799). Hishām ibn-al-Ḥakam, who probably died about 803 and certainly not later than 815, is reported to have been a Qaṭ'ī.[37] The insistence of the Wāqifa that there was no imam after al-Kāẓim might indicate a desire to produce a doctrine similar to that of the later Imāmites, but with seven instead of twelve imams; and it is noteworthy that Abū-Sahl an-Nawbakhtī, the chief exponent of later Imāmism, still thought it necessary to refute the doctrines of the Wāqifa as stated by aṭ-Ṭaṭarī (d. about 835).[38] In contrast the Qaṭ'iyya must be opponents of the messianism of the Wāqifa and so presumably, since they were not revolutionaries, supporters of the caliphate of Hārūn, though pressing for its interpretation in an absolutist sense. Since Hishām was a Qaṭ'ī, the position of the sect must have been defined before the events of 817 and 818, though later members made 'Alī ar-Riḍā the last imam.

These sects, then, are examples of some of the numerous disputes among the Hāshimites at this period. What were the disputes really about? Once again, it must be insisted, they cannot have been about the identity of the rightful ruler of the caliphate, for that would have led immediately to the death of any named individual in an 'Abbāsid prison. It might tentatively be suggested that the real question was who was head of the 'Alids. There seems to have been some continuing group-consciousness, for it was given official recognition early in the tenth century.[39] Round about 800 this would be mainly titular, but it would be the kind of position from which a wise statesman, by uniting those of 'Alid or Hāshimite sympathies, could have gained great political influence.

The second of the two basic points of Rāfiḍite doctrine was the accusation of unbelief against most of the Companions. This greatly worried men like Aḥmad ibn-Ḥanbal and Ibn-Qutayba.[40] The reason was doubtless that it went to the root of the 'religious institution' as a whole, for this was now based on the Traditions and these went back in the first place to the Companions. The first to insist systematically on chains of transmitters beginning with a Companion was ash-Shāfi'ī (d. 820), and it may be for this reason that ash-Shāfi'ī is much discussed by the jurists among the ninth-century

Rāfiḍites. This point, together with the rejection of *ijtihād*, the interpretative activity of ordinary jurists, suggests that the Rāfiḍites were trying to weaken the position of the ulema. In other words, the Rāfiḍites were not working for a revolution in the indefinite future but were part of the contemporary struggle which will be described later in this chapter.

c) *The Zaydites*

When one comes to consider the Zaydites, one's first impression is that it ought to be relatively easy to understand their historical position, since they were involved in many risings which are described in the history books. This first impression, however, is erroneous. To give an adequate account of the Zaydites is more difficult than to describe any other of the Islamic sects. All that will be done here is to select one aspect of Zaydism which is relevant to the topic of the relation between past history and contemporary politics.

In classifying sects as Zaydite the heresiographers take as the basic principle of Zaydism that the imamate is restricted to the descendants of Fāṭima (that is, to the Ḥasanids and Ḥusaynids) but that, if any such man with the requisite qualities of mind and character claims to be imam and takes to the sword in support of his claim, there is an obligation to follow him.[41] This principle is alleged to have been adopted by Zayd ibn-ʿAlī, a grandson of al-Ḥusayn, whose revolt against the Umayyads in 740 has already been described.[42] Other revolts which are spoken of as Zaydite in inspiration are those of Muḥammad ibn-ʿAbd-Allāh, the Pure Soul, in 762, of Muḥammad ibn-al-Qāsim in Khurasan in 834, and of Yaḥyā ibn-ʿUmar in Kufa in 864.[43]

In the present context the Zaydites with whom we are concerned are precisely those who were not involved in revolts, and more particularly the sub-sects of the Batriyya (or Butriyya) and the Sulaymāniyya (or Jarīriyya). The Batriyya derive their name from Kathīr (or Kuthayyir) an-Nawwā', who was nicknamed al-Abtar ('with tail docked');[44] but their most notable member was al-Ḥasan ibn-Ṣāliḥ ibn-Ḥayy (d. c. 783), who was widely recognized as a Traditionist.[45] The Batriyya held that ʿAlī was 'the best of men' (*afḍal an-nās*) after the Prophet, but that it was right to acknowledge Abū-Bakr and ʿUmar since ʿAlī had left the position to them. The distinction between the Batriyya and the Sulaymāniyya is not clear. The latter take their name from Sulaymān ibn-Jarīr, often called az-

Zaydī, about whom little is known. Though he himself is mentioned by an-Nawbakhtī, the sect is not named; but it is stated that some followers of Ja'far aṣ-Ṣādiq, impressed by certain arguments of the Batriyya and Sulaymān, gave up believing in the imamate of Ja'far and inclined to the views of Sulaymān.[46] Another of the rare statements about him is that some followers of his at 'Ānāt (south-east of Raqqa on the Euphrates) were converted to Mu'tazilism by Ja'far ibn-Mubashshir; since Ja'far died in 848, Sulaymān's activity must at latest have been somewhat earlier.[47]

The views of the Sulaymāniyya are very similar to those of the Batriyya, but the use of the phrase *imāmat al-mafḍūl* is specially connected with Sulaymān in writers from al-Ash'arī onwards. In this phrase *mafḍūl* has often been translated 'preferred' but this gives no adequate meaning, whereas there is ample warrant in the lexicons for the translation 'surpassed' or 'excelled' (*sc.* by others), not to mention a passage where al-Ash'arī speaks of the possibility of the imam being *mafḍūl* since there is among his subjects (*ra'iyya*) someone better (*khayr*) than he.[48] Similarly *tafḍīl 'Alī* means 'regarding 'Alī as *afḍal*, as excelling (all others)'. A convenient translation of the first phrase is 'the imamate of the inferior'. The basic point is that the imamate of Abū-Bakr and 'Umar is acknowledged, though they are admittedly inferior to 'Alī. Sulaymān is further reported to have held that Abū-Bakr and 'Umar did not do wrong in accepting the position of ruler, and that the community omitted something advantageous when it recognized them. In respect of 'Uthmān the Zaydites were not agreed, but many were inclined to recognize his caliphate for the first six years when he was widely held to have ruled well.[49]

Although Zaydism was closely linked with the support of rebel leaders of the house of 'Alī, not all Zaydites were revolutionaries. It is true that a Traditionist like al-Ḥasan ibn-Ṣāliḥ ibn-Ḥayy had to go into hiding from the agents of the caliph al-Mahdī; but this was probably because his daughter had married an 'Alid.[50] It is worth noticing in passing that he is the source of a report according to which Ja'far aṣ-Ṣādiq expressed a high regard for Abū-Bakr and 'Umar; this tends to suggest, of course, that Ja'far had Zaydite rather than Rāfiḍite sympathies.[51] Ibn-an-Nadīm asserts that most of the Traditionists were Zaydites; presumably he means at a relatively early period, since the only names he mentions, apart from al-Ḥasan ibn-Ṣāliḥ and his father are Sufyān ath-Thawrī (d. 778) and Sufyān ibn-ʿUyayna (d. 813).[52] Of these men al-Ḥasan and ath-Thawrī appear in Ibn-Qutayba's list of Shīʿa;[53] and doubtless others in the list were similar in outlook. In these cases Zaydism presumably meant little more than high regard for ʿAlī together with recognition for the first two caliphs. Another important piece of information in this connection is the statement of Ibn-Qutayba that al-Jāḥiẓ sometimes defended the ʿUthmāniyya against the Rāfiḍa and sometimes the Zaydiyya against the ʿUthmāniyya and Ahl-as-Sunna.[54] This evidence is not extensive, but even the ascription of Sufyān ibn-ʿUyayna and al-Jāḥiẓ to Zaydism is sufficient to show that there was a form of this doctrine which did not imply revolutionary activity.

The relation of the Zaydiyya to the Muʿtazila is a difficult question. There are undoubtedly many similarities. Among others we might notice that the Zaydite imam and scholar al-Qāsim ibn-Ibrāhīm ar-Rassī (d. 860) arranged his teaching under five heads which closely resemble the five principles of the Muʿtazila.[55] On the other hand Wilferd Madelung appears to be correct in holding that he differs in some fundamental ways from the Muʿtazilites, even though his writings paved the way for the acceptance of Muʿtazilite doctrine by the later Zaydites of the Yemen and other peripheral areas.[56] The latter are outside the purview of the present study, and al-Qāsim himself, though a fascinating figure from whose works much is to be learned, had no close contacts with contemporary thinkers in Iraq and is not mentioned by later writers within the main stream. For this reason little is said about him here.

Other facts are more puzzling. Thus the phrase 'imamate of the inferior', which in al-Ashʿarī and later writers is used almost exclusively of Sulaymān ibn-Jarīr and his followers, is applied by the slightly earlier Muʿtazilite an-Nāshi' not to Sulaymān but to Bishr ibn-al-Muʿtamir and the Muʿtazilites of Baghdad. Again there is a report in Ibn-an-Nadīm that the Rāfiḍite Shayṭān aṭ-Ṭāq wrote a refutation of the doctrine of the imamate of the inferior against the Muʿtazila, while al-Malaṭī makes the Muʿtazila of Baghdad a sect of the Zaydiyya. A late source is found saying that the pure Muʿtazilites or Wāṣiliyya first called themselves Zaydites.[57] It is clear that the sharp distinctions of later heresiographers were not present to contemporaries. In the early ninth century the term Muʿtazilite, which was afterwards restricted to those who accepted the 'five principles', was widely applied to many who engaged in the type of rational discussion known as Kalām, though it may originally have had a political reference (to withdrawing from both ʿUthmān and ʿAlī). Zaydite was primarily a political term, though both appellations were doubtless applied differently by different groups. The matter was further complicated, as will be seen presently, by the fact that something like Zaydite doctrine was implicit in the policies of al-Ma'mūn and his administration.

In the study of these matters the aim of the modern scholar is not to give a precise definition of the group names, since this varies, but to understand the relationship of individuals and their beliefs to one another and to the events of the times. Thus it is not specially enlightening to learn of the conversion of the people of ʿĀnāt from Zaydism to Muʿtazilism (as mentioned above), since we do not know what is implied in this bare statement; but we gain more insight if we can interpret the conversion as one from Sulaymān's view that the appointment of Abū-Bakr was based on mistaken *ijtihād* or *ta'wīl* to the view of the Muʿtazilites of Baghdad that the appointment was justified by a particular ground (*ʿilla*).[58] These points will be more fully appreciated after the policies of al-Ma'mūn and the views of individual Muʿtazilites have been discussed.

In general it may be concluded that non-revolutionary Zaydism is essentially a form of political compromise. It tries to get the support of Rāfiḍite opinion by agreeing that ʿAlī was best fitted for the caliphate in 632; but at the same time it tries to appease the critics of the Rāfiḍites by acknowledging that Abū-Bakr and ʿUmar were genuinely imams, even though it was an 'imamate of the inferior'. The latter point, at least in some forms, has the corollary that the great mass of the Companions were not in error. Like most compromises, however, this was not satisfactory. The Rāfiḍites retained their imam, but it was not allowed that he had his authority from above —probably the aspect in which they were most interested—for the Zaydites tended to hold that the imam should be appointed by a *shūrā* or council, or otherwise chosen by the community. The Traditionist critics, on the other side, were not assured that the revealed law was to be paramount in the Islamic state, since even an imam as conceived by the Zaydites, could presumably have overridden the interpretations of the jurists. The assertion that Zaydites restricted the imamate to descendants of Fāṭima is probably an inference by later writers from the persons of the leaders of revolts labelled 'Zaydite'. It is virtually certain that a non-revolutionary Zaydite like Sulaymān ibn-Jarīr supported the 'Abbāsids; he could argue that al-Ma'mūn was a member of the clan of Hāshim who had both publicly claimed the imamate and actively exercised it.

d) *The 'Uthmānites*

In an earlier chapter the use of the name 'Uthmānī up to 800 was described. Towards 850, however, the name reappears and is specially connected with al-Jāḥiẓ (d. 869). The latter's involvement with the 'Uthmāniyya is known from the statement of Ibn-Qutayba quoted above, from an account by al-Mas'ūdī of his works, *Kitāb al-'Uthmāniyya* and *Kitāb masā'il al-'Uthmāniyya*, and from the fact that the former work is extant. It is also known that a Mu'tazilite scholar, al-Iskāfī (d. 854/5), wrote a refutation of the *Kitāb al-'Uthmāniyya.*[59] Al-Iskāfī is said to have been a believer in the 'imamate of the inferior', but this presumably means that he held the general view of the Mu'tazilites of Baghdad; the statements that he was a Shī'ite can mean no more than some form of Zaydism. It would be interesting to know whether al-Jāḥiẓ wrote his defence of the 'Uthmāniyya against the Rāfiḍa before or after his defence of the Zaydiyya against the 'Uthmāniyya and Ahl-as-Sunna. The former must have been at latest a few years before the death of al-Iskāfī. The latter (if the report is true) could conceivably have been very much earlier, but is perhaps more likely (especially since it mentions Ahl-as-Sunna) to have been after al-Mutawakkil's change of policy when the Mu'tazilites fell from power and Sunnism was officially supported. A family of 'Uthmānite sympathies is known to have come to power only after the change of policy.[60]

The primary concern in the present context is to understand how statements about the first four caliphs were relevant to ninth-century politics. The *Kitāb al-'Uthmāniyya* is actually for the most part an argument for the superiority of Abū-Bakr to 'Alī.[61] It is implied that 'Uthmān was truly caliph, but the only point explicitly stated is that his selection by a council was a valid form of accession to the imamate. Thus the 'Uthmānites were primarily concerned to oppose the undue exaltation of 'Alī by the Rāfiḍites, and were not moved by any nostalgic longing for the return of the Umayyads, against whom al-Jāḥiẓ has some fierce criticisms.[62] For a time some of those who accepted the imamate of Abū-Bakr, 'Umar and 'Uthmān were inclined to hold that the order of merit was : Abū-Bakr, ʿUmar, ʿAlī, ʿUthmān ; but in the end, doubtless as a result of arguments such as those of al-Jāḥiẓ, the great majority of Muslims came to accept the view that the chronological order was also the order of merit.[63]

From this description it should be clear that the ʿUthmāniyya were not an obscure and heretical sect but were forerunners—or at least a section of the forerunners—of those who were coming to be known as Ahl-as-Sunna or Sunnites. Sunnite creeds contain an article making the chronological order of the first four caliphs also the order of merit.[64] Al-Jāḥiẓ remarks that the ʿUthmānites had many jurists and Traditionists, but that there were hardly any partisans of ʿAlī among the latter.[65] It is surprising to find al-Jāḥiẓ, a Muʿtazilite, among the Traditionists ; but by no means all the Muʿtazilites were of his opinion, for the five principles of Muʿtazilism did not necessitate any one political view. Most of the ʿUthmānites were men who believed that the Islamic state should be based on the principles revealed in the Qur'ān and the Traditions, and their insistence on the imamate of Abū-Bakr developed naturally as a reaction to the Rāfiḍite or Imāmite insistence on the superiority of ʿAlī. In the thought of such persons this superiority was linked with the superiority of the imams descended from ʿAlī and their immunity (*ʿiṣma*) from sin and error. Some went so far as to say that the imam could abrogate the Qur'ān ;[66] and even the more moderate held that the decisions of the imam were superior to all the methods of interpreting the Qur'ān approved by the Sunnites.[67] Thus the dispute whether Abū-Bakr or ʿAlī succeeded the Prophet was closely bound up with the dispute whether the Qur'ān and the Traditions, in their application to the life of the community, were to be interpreted by the generally accepted methods of the scholars or by the bare decision of the imam ; and this was a central question in the politics of the ninth century.

Once the imamate of Abū-Bakr had been affirmed it was difficult not to affirm also the imamates of ʿUmar and ʿUthmān, since to reject them would be to impugn the method of selection and play into the hands of the Imāmites. Another factor leading men to be ʿUthmānites was probably the strong tendency among Muslims to accept *de facto* rulers in the interests of maintaining the unity of the community.

e) *The admirers of Muʿāwiya*

This study of the discussions about ʿAlī, Abū-Bakr and ʿUthmān may be rounded off by a brief reference to the strange 'cult of Muʿāwiya' which was found in the ninth century.[68] The most illuminating item of information is the story from ʿAbd-Allāh, the son of Aḥmad ibn-Ḥanbal. When he was a boy his father took him to the mosque of ar-Ruṣāfa and he was puzzled to hear a man offering water 'for the love of Muʿāwiya'; his father explained that this was because the man hated ʿAlī. It is indeed clear from this and the other scraps of information that the voicing in public of admiration for Muʿāwiya was a way of expressing the most extreme opposition to the exaltation of ʿAlī. The cult of Muʿāwiya went beyond the views of the ʿUthmāniyya in that it seems to have implied that ʿAlī was never caliph at all. Such an assertion, if officially accepted, would of course have alienated much relatively moderate opinion; and this was something the caliphs could not afford to do. On at least two occasions the caliphs thought of having Muʿāwiya publicly cursed;[69] but this also would have led to loss of support. Scholarly criticism of Muʿāwiya as practised by al-Jāḥiẓ was in the long run more effective; and by the end of the ninth century there was wide agreement (apart from the Imāmites) that ʿAlī was caliph and fourth in order of merit.

Possibly connected with this cult was the belief in a kind of Mahdī or Messiah known as the Sufyānī (that is, a descendant of Muʿāwiya's father, Abū-Sufyān). The name was first given to a certain Umayyad insurgent defeated in 751, but later became the centre of an eschatological belief, especially among Syrian Muslims.[69a]

f) *Concluding remark*

Other historical questions besides those mentioned were discussed during the ninth century, such as the rights and wrongs of the battle of the Camel and the Arbitration. What has been said, however, is probably enough to show that all such arguments were really about contemporary politics. This was the form political arguments took at that time and place. There have, of course, been other times and places where history entered into current politics, but probably nowhere else have the historical discussions been so extensive and so apparently factual. This may have something to do with the Arab and Semitic preference for the concrete over the abstract; and in a sense the abstract principles were implicit in the concrete events.

The problem for the modern academic historian is that each party indulged in a large-scale rewriting of history in the interests of their own thesis. At some points they were limited by what the opponents or uncommitted third parties were prepared to admit. Yet it is amazing how much sheer invention eventually came to be accepted after it had been sufficiently often repeated. The assertion that 'Alī had been designated by Muḥammad as his successor was, in the eyes of non-Muslim historians, one such invention. What is not so clearly realized is that the Imāmites and other Shī'ites, besides repeating the basic assertion, gradually constructed a vast corpus of material to support it. Not all of this material is invention. Many, perhaps most, of the names are those of real men; but the accounts of their relationships to the Shī'ite imams, from the fourth to the eleventh, have been subtly modified to imply an acknowledgement of the imamate which is unhistorical. The modern scholar should approach the maze of Shī'ite material about the eighth and the ninth centuries only with great scepticism.

It is worth pointing out also that the political implications of a historical assertion may vary at different times. The assertion of the superiority of 'Alī meant something different in the Umayyad period from what it meant in the 'Abbāsid. Zaydite doctrines were the basis of a policy of compromise in Iraq in the ninth century, but later became the basis of the independence of a small state in the Yemen. Most fascinating are the transformations of Ismā'īlism from the Fāṭimids and the original Assassins to the modern followers of the Agha Khan.

3

The political struggle

a) *The self-assertion of the Persians*

A factor which came to have importance in the political struggle under the early 'Abbāsids was the self-assertion of the Persians. This also influenced the general development of Islamic thought in various ways; but in the period up to al-Ash'arī the Persian influences were mainly peripheral, and here a brief account will be sufficient.

While it is convenient to speak of 'the Persians', there was no common self-awareness comparable to nationalism as that is now understood. A measure of Persian self-awareness in an Islamic context may be said to have been produced by the *Shāhnāmeh* of Firdawsī at the end of the tenth century. Previously there had been a number of local traditions which had not coalesced, though the upper classes at least may have had some consciousness of their common attachment to the culture of the Sasanian empire. This culture was itself an amalgam. The Persian invaders of Iraq had imposed on the empire their language (Middle Persian or Pahlevi), but in return they had accepted many features of the ancient civilizations of the Tigris-Euphrates basin, and the Sasanian era was characterized by a spreading eastwards of the urban culture of Iraq. In many cases the inhabitants of Iraq are best described as 'persianized Aramaeans'. Among these Persians and 'persianized Aramaeans' there was a higher percentage of converts to Islam during the Umayyad period than in any other province, partly because the mobeds or clergy of the official religion had become too subservient to the ruling institution and had thereby lost the trust of the people.

Like other non-Arab Muslims the converts from the former Sasanian empire had to become 'clients' (*mawālī*) of Arab tribes, and resented this inferiority of status. Many gave their support to the movement which brought the ʿAbbāsids to power; and in due course the ʿAbbāsids satisfied the aspirations of the *mawālī* by ceasing to make any juridical distinction between Arab and non-Arab. At the same time many Persians and persianized Aramaeans received positions as 'secretaries' or civil servants. This was not just a reward for support, but because these men as the descendants of the Sasanian 'secretaries' were a trained body of administrators and the repository of the centuries-old art of ruling as it had been developed in this region of the world. Towards the end of the Umayyad period it was realized by those in authority that the old Arab system, by which the caliph like an Arab shaykh was only *primus inter pares* and was accessible to all, led to inefficiency in the administration of a large empire. The last Umayyad caliph, Marwān II (744–50), and his chief secretary are said to have studied histories of former Persian kings, presumably to learn about traditional methods of administration.[70] The ʿAbbāsids deliberately followed the Persians in using court ceremonial to emphasize the difference between the caliph and the ordinary man and to make access to the caliph more difficult. Many details of administration were copied from the Persians or developed in accordance with Persian principles. This new attitude of the ʿAbbāsids to the Persian tradition affected Islamic thought in three ways.

Firstly, the Persian tradition of government was brought into Arabic literature by collections of historical anecdotes and manuals of advice. The process began a few years after the ʿAbbāsids came to power through the activity of a 'secretary' of Persian origin, Ibn-al-Muqaffaʿ (d. 756 or later). Among other works he translated into Arabic a history of the Persian kings, a work on court ceremonial and a book of maxims of government.[71] Though only fragments of these have been preserved, much of their content seems to have been repeated by other writers such as Ibn-Qutayba, aṭ-Ṭabarī and al-Masʿūdī. The best-known work of Ibn-al-Muqaffaʿ is *Kalīla and Dimna*, a collection of Indian fables also known as the Fables of Bidpai and the Panchatantra. In this much practical wisdom is conveyed in the form of stories about animals. Although the work is originally Indian, in its Pahlevi form it had been influential in the Sasanian empire, and thus in a sense belongs to the Persian tradition. The books of Ibn-al-Muqaffaʿ led eventually to the appearance in Arabic and Persian of a special genre known as 'mirrors for princes' (Fürstenspiegel), of which several examples have been translated into English and other European languages.[72] It may also be noted that Persian history, including legendary history, was extensively incorporated in the world histories of aṭ-Ṭabarī and others, and thus gained a place in the Islamic historical tradition. This is in contrast to the neglect of Greek and Roman history apart from a small amount of mainly chronological material, and is doubtless to be explained by the fact that the great majority of Persians became Muslims at an early period.

Secondly, there appeared a form of heretical belief known as *zandaqa*; the individual guilty of this is a *zindīq*, in the plural *zanādiqa*. The word is vague and is perhaps best rendered 'irreligion'. In a statement by an early scholar of Kufa, Manṣūr ibn-al-Muʿtamir (d. 750), *zandaqa* appears to be 'rejection of the revealed law'.[73] This statement shows that men had begun to be worried about *zandaqa* before the advent of the ʿAbbāsids. The latter soon made it a capital offence; and it is probable that it was for *zandaqa* that Ibn-al-Muqaffaʿ was executed by al-Manṣūr, though the date is uncertain and may be as late as 772.[74] Ibn-al-Muqaffaʿ is named as the writer of a work which criticized Muḥammad, Islam and the Qur'ān from a Manichaean standpoint; of this there exists a refutation by the later Zaydite imam, al-Qāsim ibn-Ibrāhīm (785–860).[75] There were other executions about the same time and a little later, and from 782 to 786 under the caliph al-Mahdī there was systematic persecution of *zanādiqa*.[76] Many of those accused and sentenced belonged to the class of secretaries and were of Persian descent. Their conversion to Islam had presumably been without much conviction and mainly in order to keep their employment. One way of expressing their dissatisfaction with the new situation was to adopt Manichaean beliefs and ascetic practices. There were traditional Manichaean communities in the caliphate, but these were quiescent and were not affected by the persecution except where they gave support to the new adherents. It was against the latter that the accusations of *zandaqa* were made, since it was felt that the state was endangered by spoken or written criticisms of its basis, such as those in the book of Ibn-al-Muqaffaʿ. The existence of *zandaqa* of this type made it necessary for theologians to write refutations of it, but it does not receive much attention in the books of sects. This is doubtless because *zandaqa* as distinct from Manichaeanism was vague and fluid. At a later date it came to be defined legally as a form of heresy which endangered the state.[77] It seems probable too that as a result of the persecutions the dissatisfied secretaries turned from Manichaeanism to some form of Shīʿism (as will be mentioned presently).

Thirdly, there was the Shuʿūbite movement. This was primarily a literary movement whose productions contained criticisms of the Arabs and their contributions to culture and praise of the non-Arab peoples (*shuʿūb*) of the empire, especially the Persians. For the secretary class this was a safer way than *zandaqa* of giving vent to feelings of dissatisfaction with the existing situation. The importance of the Shuʿūbite movement in the history of Islamic thought is that it illustrates the negative aspect of the fundamental decision that was taken or reaffirmed during the early ʿAbbāsid period, namely, that the Islamic state was to be based on the revelation to Muḥammad (the Qur'ān and the Sunna) and that therefore the cultural language of the state must be Arabic. In a sense this decision was implicit in Umayyad practice, but the accession of the ʿAbbāsids gave an opportunity for reconsidering the matter. The secretary class of Iraq, as their power increased, found the dominance of Arabic irksome, and saw serious rivals in the ulema as bearers of the 'Arabic humanities'. It is not surprising, then, that one of the chief butts of their satire was the Qur'ān and Arabic literary style. The challenge presented by this criticism was the more formidable in that one of their number, Ibn-al-Muqaffa', was the foremost exponent of Arabic prose style in his time. The challenge was eventually met by men like al-Jāḥiẓ (d. 869) and Ibn-Qutayba (d. 889) who not merely refuted Shu'ūbite arguments but in doing so demonstrated that good literary style could be associated with defence of a traditional Arab and Islamic outlook.[78]

The profound significance of this matter is thrown into relief by contrasting the outcome of the Arab conquest of the Fertile Crescent with the Roman conquest of the lands of Greek culture. As Horace said, 'Captive Greece took her rude conqueror captive', meaning that the culture of the Roman empire became Greek, while the Greek language remained the vehicle of that culture, there being virtually no translations from Greek into Latin. The situation in the caliphate was very different. In literature the Arabs, when they burst out of Arabia, had nothing but the Qur'ān and a tradition of poetry and oratory; yet Arabic became the language, not merely of government and religion, but also of science, philosophy and belles-lettres. The traditional culture of the Fertile Crescent was in a sense accepted by the Arabs, but in being accepted it was transformed into a culture with its centre in the Qur'ān. Of this process the Shu'ūbite movement was a facet. As Sir Hamilton Gibb put it:

> The issue at stake was no superficial matter of literary modes and fashions, but the whole cultural orientation of the new Islamic society—whether it was to become a re-embodiment of the old Perso-Aramaean culture into which the Arabic and Islamic elements would be absorbed, or a culture in which the Perso-Aramaean contributions would be subordinated to the Arab tradition and the Islamic values.[79]

The final outcome owes much to those scholars who reproduced Persian material in Arabic and who by their philological studies made Arabic a fitting instrument for a great culture.

b) *The opposing groups of interests*

It is clear that during the first century of the 'Abbāsid caliphate a struggle was taking place between different groups or parties, but the identity of these is not clear. It is also clear that the matter is complex, since many groups were involved and there was a measure of fluidity in their relationships. Some aspects, however, have not yet been adequately studied, and so all that can be done here is to give some general indications. It seems most convenient to define the various groups in terms of their interests.

The political struggle on its intellectual side may be regarded as primarily a struggle between two groups of intellectuals, the secretaries or civil servants and the ulema or religious scholars. The ulema are here taken to be the leading men in what we have called the general religious movement. They were insistent that the life of the state and of society should be based on Islamic principles, that is, on the Qur'ān and the Sunna. Sunna means 'beaten path' and hence metaphorically 'normal practice'; but this may be understood in various ways. It may, for example, be the normal practice of the Prophet as that is reflected in the ongoing practices of the community. About 800 it came to be accepted that the Sunna was to be known through Traditions (*ḥadīth*), that is, anecdotes about Muḥammad. If the state was thus to be based on the Book and the Sunna, it was necessary that these should be authoritatively interpreted. Such interpretation was the function of the ulema and gave them a position of importance in the caliphate. This special position of the ulema was in part acknowledged by the 'Abbāsid caliphs, since the general religious movement had supported them during their struggle for power.

In the light of this situation it becomes clear that many of the heretical attitudes found among the secretaries were far from being doctrinaire and academic and were indeed aimed at the defence and improvement of their position in the caliphate. Their critique of the Qur'ān was indirectly an attack on the ulema, and so, though less obviously, was their critique of Arabic style. As regards the latter, it would have been difficult to maintain Qur'ān-interpretation as a rational discipline had there been no formal philological study of the Arabic language and no prose literature in Arabic. Once philology and literature are involved, however, the dispute touches a wider circle of interests. On the one side are those attached to the cultural forms associated with the Arabic language, and on the other side are those attached to Persian or Perso-Iraqi culture. These are wider groups than the ulema and the secretaries, but they are not to be simply identified with Arab and Persian nationalism. Apart from the fact that nationalism as now understood did not exist at this period, it has to be noted that men of Arab descent are found in the secretaries' camp, while there are men of Persian descent among the ulema.

The opposition of the two groups of intellectuals also moves into the field of political theory. It was suggested above that at least until about 870 the persons called Rāfiḍites were not revolutionaries plotting to overthrow the 'Abbāsids but advocates of an absolutist or autocratic form of government. This political attitude would obviously have been congenial to the secretaries, since an autocratic caliph would be able to overrule the interpretations of the ulema and consequently the secretaries as his officers would gain in influence at the expense of their rivals. Many others, of course, besides the secretaries shared this political attitude. It may be surmised that it appealed to men, like those from south-west Arabia, who because of their heritage, when they needed security in time of stress, looked to the guidance of an inspired or charismatic leader. [80] The contrasting political attitude, which looked for security to the collective wisdom of a charismatic community, was also widely held. This attitude was obviously congenial to the ulema, since the Qur'ān was regarded, or could be regarded, as a mark of the charismatic nature of the community; [81] and the ulema became the bearers of the wisdom of the community. This second attitude may be called 'constitutional'. [82]

These opposing groups of interests are probably also linked with economic interests and with the interests of social groups other than the secretaries and the ulema. Little study has been done in this field, however, and it does not seem that anything can usefully be added to what has already been said. Various relatively isolated facts are known, but their interpretation is uncertain. It is known, for example, that the most vociferous section of the populace of Baghdad supported the constitutionalists, but it is not clear why this should be so.

c) *Al-Ma'mūn's attempts at compromise*

Something of the struggle between the autocratic and constitutionalist blocs may be discerned in the first half-century of the 'Abbāsids. Al-Mahdī persecuted *zindīqs*, but also tried to conciliate 'Alids. [83] Under Hārūn ar-Rashīd the Barmakids had many close ties with Persians and Shu'ūbites, [84] and their policy tended to favour the autocratic bloc. After the fall of the Barmakids in 803 their successor al-Faḍl ibn-ar-Rabī' (son of the vizier of al-Manṣūr) appears to have stood for a policy nearer to that of the constitutionalists. [85] Under his influence ar-Rashīd is said to have imprisoned Bishr al-Marīsī for advocating the anti-constitutionalist doctrine of the createdness of the Qur'ān.[86] Al-Amīn retained al-Faḍl ibn-ar-Rabīʿ as vizier, and presumably pursued a similar policy. Iraq, which was the basis of al-Amīn's power, tended to be constitutionalist, whereas Khurasan, which was under his brother al-Ma'mūn, was more autocratic. All these statesmen, however, were sufficiently realistic to understand that they could not completely commit themselves to one of the blocs, and hence all their policies aim at finding a point of equilibrium, that is to say, a policy which would gain them the support of the majority of both blocs. The working out of this aim can be clearly seen in the reign of al-Ma'mūn, especially in connection with two important decisions, namely, the declaration that ʿAlī ar-Riḍā was heir apparent, and the institution of the Miḥna or inquisition.

It was in March 817, while still residing at Merv in Khurasan, that al-Ma'mūn designated ʿAlī ar-Riḍā as heir to the caliphate. ʿAlī was the son of the Ḥusaynid Mūsā al-Kāẓim (d. 799), seventh imam of the later Imāmites, and was himself their eighth imam. In 817 he can hardly have been recognized as leader by any politically significant body of men, though he was doubtless accepted as head of the Ḥusaynid family. He was not the sort of person who could have headed a revolt against the ʿAbbāsids. By designating him, however, al-Ma'mūn presumably expected to gain the support of most of those who hoped for the appearance of an inspired ʿAlid leader, or at least to prevent them actively siding with any such leader who rose in revolt against the ʿAbbāsids. Al-Ma'mūn's policy, however, had also a subtler side, as has been shown by Dominique Sourdel in his article, 'La politique religieuse du calife ʿabbaside al-Ma'mun'.[87] Sourdel notes repeatedly that the thinking of al-Ma'mūn approaches closely to that of the Zaydites, but does not further examine the nature of Zaydism at this period. It will thus be convenient to begin by considering more closely what might have been meant by Zaydism, on the assumption that this influenced the policies of al-Ma'mūn.

One essential Zaydite view was that, while ʿAlī was the 'most excellent' (*afḍal*) of the community after Muḥammad, he fully accepted the rule of Abū-Bakr and ʿUmar. The Rāfiḍites differed from this in that they did not acknowledge the caliphate of Abū-Bakr and ʿUmar, and laid more emphasis on the 'designation' (*naṣṣ*) of ʿAlī as Muḥammad's successor. Al-Ma'mūn was certainly aware of the differences, for he encouraged scholars to discuss them in his presence. His declarations that 'Alī was *afḍal* and superior to the other Companions of the Prophet must thus be taken as significant. In general he seems to have recognized Abū-Bakr and 'Umar, though one or two anecdotes have been preserved which suggest that sometimes he was critical of them.[88] It is also to be noted that in designating 'Alī ar-Riḍā as heir he asserted that he was *afḍal*. This might have been a preparation for the defence of 'Abbāsid rule as that of the most excellent of the clan of Hāshim. There was no statement of intention that 'Alī ar-Riḍā should be followed by his descendants, and it may be, as Sourdel suggests, that the idea was that in future the caliph should be the most excellent among the 'Alids and 'Abbāsids. Doubtless, too, the statement that someone was the most excellent implied that he was best able to rule and to make decisions for the community. Certainly al-Ma'mūn acted in various ways as if he had personal authority; and he was the first 'Abbāsid to use the title of 'imam' which was much on the lips of Zaydites and Rāfiḍites. In these ways he was trying to get the support of the autocratic bloc, while the acknowledgement of Abū-Bakr and 'Umar was a sop to the constitutionalists.

Zaydism also implied that the imam should actively assert his right to rule. Now al-Ma'mūn, when his brother deprived him of his right of succession, had put himself at the head of a rising and had been successful. Had he been a descendant of 'Alī and Fāṭima, he would without question have been a Zaydite imam. At this period, however, many points which were definitely formulated by later Shī'ite apologetic, were still fluid; and it is virtually certain that al-Ma'mūn was accepted as an active imam by many persons who could be described in a general way as Zaydites. It is noteworthy that an-Nawbakhtī says that on the proclamation of 'Alī ar-Riḍā as heir certain Zaydites accepted him as imam;[89] but too much cannot be made of this since an-Nawbakhtī's interpretation of his sources is influenced by his prejudices.

Fluidity also affected the relations between Zaydism and Mu'tazilism at this period, for the name of Mu'tazilite was still widely applied and its restriction to those holding the five principles was not yet effective (see chapter 8). The central Zaydite doctrines were those relevant to politics, but many Zaydites were interested in the intellectual defence and elaboration of doctrine, since there was a tendency for all forms of proto-Shī'ism to use rational considerations in contrast to the opponents' reliance on the scriptures. The Muʿtazilites Bishr ibn-al-Muʿtamir and Thumāma, who in 817 were witnesses of the document declaring ʿAlī ar-Riḍā heir, may well have been called Zaydites.[90] Some Zaydites, however, were anti-rationalist, and so cannot have been Muʿtazilites even in the widest sense. In the first half of the ninth century the essential difference between Muʿtazilites and Zaydites was perhaps connected with the doctrine of the createdness of the Qur'ān. On the other hand, we may be mistaken in looking for an essential difference. By 850 the compromise policies of al-Ma'mūn had been abandoned and there was no political group in Baghdad to whom the nickname 'Zaydite' was appropriate, while the Muʿtazila were constituting themselves into a definite theological school. It was probably also now known in Iraq that Zaydism had become the distinctive doctrine of an isolated peripheral group in the Yemen. At the centre of the caliphate Zaydism seems to have faded away.

The policy implicit in the designation of ʿAlī ar-Riḍā was thwarted by his death in 818 and by the fact that his son was still a child; but it was not altogether abandoned. In time, however, al-Ma'mūn was attracted by the possibility of compromise contained in the doctrine of the createdness of the Qur'ān which was held by the Muʿtazilites and others. This led to the Miḥna or Inquisition. Some examination in respect of the doctrine was made by al-Ma'mūn in 827, but the main application of the test apparently did not begin until 833, a few months before his death. About April 833 he instructed the governor in Baghdad to require from the *qāḍīs* and other prominent persons a public declaration of their assent to the doctrine that the Qur'ān was the created speech of God. Similar instructions were sent to other provincial governors, but the governors varied in their zeal in carrying out the instructions and not much had been done when the news came of the death of al-Ma'mūn in early August. In Baghdad there were several sessions before the governor. Some of those questioned agreed immediately. Some gave evasive answers, but eventually yielded under the threat of torture and death. Only a few, among whom was Aḥmad ibn-Ḥanbal, firmly refused to abandon their belief in the uncreatedness of the Qur'ān. These last were imprisoned and harshly treated, and as a result some of them died, though none seems to have been officially executed. The Inquisition continued spasmodically under the next two caliphs, but was brought to an end about 849, shortly after the commencement of the reign of al-Mutawakkil at a time when there was a general reversal of policy.[91]

The modern reader is at first amazed that it should have been thought necessary to establish an Inquisition in respect of a hair-splitting theological argument. The point at issue was whether the Qur'ān, which all agreed to be the speech of God, was created speech or uncreated speech. The view that it was uncreated speech probably originated in the concern of many scholars to assert that events occurred by the Qadar or determination of God. Part of their argument was that, since certain historical events are mentioned in the Qur'ān, these must have been eternally known by God and therefore predetermined for the apparent agent. The possibility was indeed entertained, but generally rejected, that God's knowledge was merely descriptive, that is, that God eternally knew what men would in fact freely choose at particular times. The obvious retort to this doctrine of uncreatedness, namely, that the Qur'ān had appeared in time, was parried by taking the Qur'ān as an expression of God's knowledge. Some upholders of human freedom therefore came to think that the best way of defending their position was to insist that the Qur'ān was created. They supported their view by quoting such verses as 43.3/2, 'we have made it an Arabic Qur'ān' and insisting that 'made' (*jaʿalnā*) was the same as 'created'.

In the circumstances of the time these opposing views had political implications. To say the Qur'ān was the created speech of God probably implied that he might have created it otherwise, just as he might create a man tall or short or of medium height. Uncreated speech, on the other hand, would somehow express the essence of God and so be unchangeable. This unchangeable character of the Qur'ān was part of the justification for making it the basis of the empire, and also increased the authority of the ulema as the authorized interpreters of it. A created Qur'ān had not the same prestige, and there could not be the same objection to its provisions being overruled by the decree of an inspired imam. Thus the doctrine of createdness enhanced the power of the caliph and the secretaries, that of uncreatedness the power of the ulema.

7

The Attraction of Reasoning

Rationalism or the use of reason in Islam tends to be associated in the minds of occidental scholars with the study of Greek philosophy in the Islamic world and its partial acceptance by theologians. This is a false impression, produced by the Arab habit of dividing men into categories, such as theologians and jurists, and by the comparative neglect of jurisprudence by occidental scholars. It seems likely that the appeal to the theologians of Greek philosophical concepts and methods was enhanced by the fact that they had already studied jurisprudence and there become familiar with rational forms of argument. In order to present a complete picture it is necessary to look briefly at the use of rational methods in early Islamic jurisprudence, even though the matter has not been fully studied and it is impossible to give an adequate account.

1
The beginnings of systematic reasoning

A feature of the Umayyad period was that many men in the chief Islamic cities were concerned to ensure that the life of the community should be governed by Qur'ānic and Islamic norms, or, as they usually phrased it, by 'the Book and the Sunna'. These men were the 'pious specialists' of Schacht or, as they were called above, 'the general religious movement'. When questions arose that were not covered explicitly by the Qur'ān or Muḥammad's practice, they generally adopted some particular view. This was said to be based on *ra'y*, 'opinion', that is, essentially 'sound and considered opinion', but the process was tantamount to individual reasoning. The formation of views on this basis was known as *ijtihād ar-ra'y*, 'the effort or exercise of opinion'. At first almost any type of rational argument came under this heading. Little attention was paid to the process by which the particular view was reached. Each of the 'ancient schools' in the main cities attained a measure of agreement among its members, and claimed that the totality of the particular views of this kind which they shared was in accordance with the Qur'ān and the Sunna of the Prophet; but by Sunna they meant in this usage what Joseph Schacht has called 'the idealized practice as recognized by representative scholars'.[1]

The use of reasoning in matters of law met with opposition, and this took the form of producing anecdotes about Muḥammad to show that he expressed some other view or that his practice was different. These anecdotes are the *ḥadīth* or Traditions. The exponents of the use of reasoning then came to be known as Aṣ'ḥāb (or Ahl) ar-ra'y and the opposing party as Aṣ'ḥāb (or Ahl) al-ḥadīth. As noted above, the Aṣ'ḥāb al-ḥadīth do not include all the persons engaged in transmitting Traditions. There was indeed fluidity in the use of both terms. The Aṣ'ḥāb ar-ra'y were sometimes—for example, by ash-Shahrastānī[2]—identified with Abū-Ḥanīfa and his followers; but in the early period we find, for instance, Ibn-Qutayba ascribing Mālik and Sufyān ath-Thawrī to this group.[3] Apart from the specific application of the names, extant texts show that there continued to be two very different approaches to questions of law, namely, one in which extensive use was made of rational arguments, and one in which little more was done than to quote Traditions. The two approaches are even more obvious in theology. On the rational side are the writings of the Ash'arites and the Māturīdites, and on the other side the work of a man like Ibn-Khuzayma (d. 924).

A measure of reconciliation between the two approaches was effected by ash-Shāfi'ī (d. 820). On the one hand, he gave a more precise meaning to the conception of the Sunna or 'standard practice' of the Prophet. Hitherto there had been many groups all claiming to follow the Sunna; but what they asserted to be the Sunna, though the assertion might have some basis in the facts, was usually an idealized or otherwise modified version of the facts. Consequently the alleged Sunna varied from group to group and from school to school. This disarray among the upholders of the Sunna had been criticized by the secretary Ibn-al-Muqaffa' during the reign of al-Manṣūr. He insisted that the alleged Sunna was a reflection of Umayyad practice, and urged the caliph to exercise his rights in this matter and to give an official revised version of the Sunna which all might be expected to accept.[4] Presumably the members of the general religious movement were aware of this critique, and attempted in various ways to make their legal reasoning more systematic.

What ash-Shāfiʿī did was to make it obligatory to prove any assertion about the Sunna of the Prophet by a properly attested Tradition. In this technical sense a Tradition was an anecdote about something seen or heard by a Companion of the Prophet and handed on by him through a named series of transmitters (the *isnād* or support). The use of these attested Traditions had been spreading before ash-Shāfiʿī, but after him it became universal. Obviously, once one school claimed that a particular view was supported by a Tradition, it was unsatisfactory for another school to support an alternative view by a bare assertion. Virtually all Muslims came to agree that the Sunna of the Prophet was known through the Traditions, though they might reject particular Traditions, usually on the ground that the *isnād* was unsatisfactory.

In the second place ash-Shāfiʿī elaborated a theory of methodology in law, according to which only certain types of reasoning were admissible. This was his doctrine of *uṣūl al-fiqh* or 'the roots or principles of jurisprudence'. These were four in number : the Book, the Sunna, Consensus (*ijmāʿ*) and Analogy (*qiyās*). In effect this meant that the only kind of reasoning permitted was analogical reasoning. This doctrine was widely accepted beyond the circle of the followers of ash-Shāfiʿī and with one modification became the 'classical' theory of the roots of jurisprudence. Where ash-Shāfiʿī had taken the Consensus to be that of the whole community, for the 'classical' theory that Consensus was that of the scholars. This discussion of the roots of jurisprudence affected the whole future course of Islamic thought, for jurisprudence was the central intellectual discipline in the Islamic world. Even the Muʿtazilite theologians who spent their time arguing about Greek scientific concepts had been trained in jurisprudence. In this way systematic reasoning in law prepared the way for reasoning in theology and other spheres.

2
The beginnings of Kalām

The Arabic word *kalām* normally means 'speech', as when the Qur'ān is called *kalām Allāh*, 'the speech of God' ; but it also has a technical meaning which may be rendered 'speculative or rational theology', with *mutakallim* as corresponding participle. This was doubtless at one time a nickname, perhaps suggesting people 'who are for ever talking'; but it came to be accepted as a neutral term. In later centuries there was little difference between the application of systematic reasoning to jurisprudence and to theology, but round about 800 this was not so, and some who approved of *ijtihād ar-ra'y* in law did not approve of Kalām. This was because Kalām, in addition to using rational arguments, introduced and discussed non-Qur'ānic concepts, mostly taken from Greek science and philosophy. Kalām was an interesting and exciting development, and it is important to examine the reasons for it.

When the Arabs conquered Iraq just before the middle of the seventh century, they came into contact with a living tradition of Hellenistic learning. In Iraq and neighbouring parts of the former Persian empire there were a number of Christian schools or colleges. The most important appears to have been that at Gondēshāpūr, where both medicine and religious disciplines were taught by Nestorian Christians. The curriculum included Greek medicine and philosophy, but the medium of instruction was Syriac, and the necessary Greek books had been translated into Syriac.[5] There were also non-Christian schools of Hellenistic learning, notably that of the so-called Ṣābi'ans in Ḥarrān. The Sasanian Persian empire had some familiarity with Indian thought, and some books had been translated into Pahlevi or middle Persian. It was supposed for a time that Aristotle had been translated from Persian into Arabic, but this view is now known to be without foundation.[6] The living intellectual tradition with which the Arabs came into contact in Iraq was thus composite. The Hellenistic element in its Syriac form was the dominant strand, but there were subordinate elements from India entering mainly through Pahlevi.

The precise form of the contact is to some extent a matter of conjecture. We must presume that there was some meeting between Arab governors and administrators and the heads of the various educational institutions. More important than this, however, was the number of conversions to Islam from the educated classes. By the latter part of the Umayyad period many of the leading Muslim scholars of Iraq were non-Arabs. These men, even if they had not themselves been at one of the schools, must have brought with them into Islam something of the Hellenistic intellectual outlook of the milieu in which they had been brought up. Such men were not committed to any one form of Greek philosophy, but selected whatever ideas were useful to them in their current controversies. By the middle of the ninth century a few men were becoming wholehearted devotees of some branch of Greek philosophy, but in so doing were cutting themselves off from the main stream of Islamic thought (see section 4 below).

The influence of Hellenism on Islamic thought is to be seen chiefly in Iraq, first of all in Basra and Kufa, and later in Baghdad. Perhaps people in Iraq, or certain groups, of them, were specially gifted for speculative thinking. Hellenistic learning had flourished in Egypt, but almost exclusively, it would seen, among men of Greek descent like Origen. The writing of the native Egyptians or Copts is concrete rather than abstract, apart from a few exceptions such as Athanasius. It is not surprising that the school of Alexandria, after being cut off from easy contact with the Byzantine empire by the Arab invasion, was (in 718) transferred to Antioch. There was some study of Islamic law in Egypt, but Egypt made virtually no contributions to theological discussion. In Syria during the Umayyad period there were some intellectual stirrings which found expression, for example, in the political theology of Ghaylān and the jurisprudence of al-Awzāʿī; but after 750 Islamic Syria did little for some centuries. There were distinguished scholars in Mecca and Medina, but the influence of Greek ideas on them was slight. The eastern regions of the caliphate had long been exposed to Hellenistic culture, and rationalizing Islamic theologians were active there, but little is known about the period before al-Māturīdī (d. 944).

The contacts between Muslims and non-Muslims led to polemical arguments, and these were a stimulus to rational thinking in Islamic theology. The doctrine of the corruption of the Qur'ān protected the ordinary man from the attacks of sophisticated Christians and others,[7] but the more educated Muslims did not shrink from discussion. Evidence of the existence of these discussions is to be found in the works of John of Damascus (d. 749), an Orthodox Christian theologian who had a secretarial post under the Umayyad caliphs,[8] of his disciple Theodore Abū-Qurra (d. c. 826),[9] and of the Nestorian Catholicus Timothy I (d. 823, aged 95). Among the works of the last is one which purports to be an account of a discussion between the Catholicus and the caliph al-Mahdī about the year 782.[10] The main purpose of these works is probably to reassure Christians, and the discussion form may be a literary device; but they certainly indicate the type of argument to which Muslim thinkers had to reply. The earliest extant work against the Christians appears to be that of 'Alī aṭ-Ṭabarī (d. 855),[11] but earlier writers such as Ḍirār[12] are reported to have written a 'Refutation of the Christians'.

There were also many arguments against Muslims of different views, whether near-outsiders like the Zanādiqa, or rival theologians from whom one diverged only on relatively minor points. There is ample evidence for such arguments in the lists of books preserved by Ibn-an-Nadīm, Shaykh Ṭūsī and others. There had been intra-Islamic arguments, of course, at least from the time of the murder of 'Uthmān; but these took place within an agreed framework of ideas, mainly derived from the Qur'ān. In arguing against Christians, however, and also to some extent against Zanādiqa, one could no longer base oneself on the Qur'ān; and it was at this point that Greek conceptions became useful. In this way polemics led to the growth of Kalām. Once Kalām had established itself it was naturally employed on suitable occasions in intra-Islamic debates.

While Greek ideas first entered Islam through various forms of contact with the living tradition of Hellenistic scholarship, the scene was later dominated by the translations of Greek works into Arabic. The translation of medical works is indeed said to have begun under the Umayyads.[13] The early 'Abbāsid caliphs were interested in Hellenistic and other foreign cultures and encouraged translators. It was al-Ma'mūn or his advisers, however, who realized the importance of Greek science and philosophy, and established a team of translators in the Bayt al-Ḥikma, which was also a library.[14] By the time of Ibn-an-Nadīm (d. c. 996) a great number of books of Greek philosophy and science had been translated, and many Muslims had written original works on similar topics, as can be seen from the seventh section of his *Fihrist* or *Catalogue* (pp. 238–303). During the nineteenth century several European authors studied the *Fihrist* carefully and compared it with extant manuscripts. The results of their labours were brought together by Moritz Steinschneider and published in several periodicals between 1889 and 1896.[15] Since then research has continued and many more manuscripts have come to light. The vastness of this work of translation can be gathered from the fact that Steinschneider's index contains the names of over eighty Greek authors of whom at least one work was translated, and that for men like Aristotle, Hippocrates, Galen and Euclid there are many items. This was part of the soil from which the movement of Kalām grew.

The advocates of Kalām were full of enthusiasm and there was an air of intellectual excitement. There were also opponents of Kalām, however, who were just as forceful in proclaiming their views. The Ḥanafite judge, Abū-Yūsuf (d. 798), said that to seek knowledge (or 'religion', *dīn*) by Kalām was a form of *zandaqa*.[16] Ibn-Qutayba in his book on 'The Divergence of Traditions' devotes the first chapter to Ahl al-Kalām, and tries to show that they disagree among themselves just as much as they allege that Traditionists do.[17] The opposition to Kalām continued through the centuries especially among the Ḥanbalites, and we find al-Ash'arī, for example, writing a defence of Kalām.[18]

3

Early exponents of Kalām

It is clear that Kalām as a discipline was well established by the caliphate of Hārūn ar-Rashīd (786–809), since we hear, for example, of discussions taking place in the salon of the Barmakids. To this period also belong the first men of whose views we can form an adequate idea. The name of *mutakallim* is indeed applied to men of an earlier date, but information about them is so scanty that it is impossible to tell how far they used Greek ideas and how far they confined themselves to the rational methods already applied in jurisprudence. The two outstanding early names are Hishām ibn-al-Ḥakam and Ḍirār ibn-'Amr, who seem to have been roughly contemporary.

a) *Hishām ibn-al-Ḥakam*

Hishām ibn-al-Ḥakam was born in Wāsiṭ as a client of the tribe of Kinda, but for long lived in Kufa where he was joint owner of a shop along with an Ibāḍite *mutakallim* 'Abd-Allāh ibn-Yazīd.[19] Here he must have had a prominent place in scholarly circles, since an-Naẓẓām the Mu'tazilite on one occasion came to Kufa, met Hishām, and was introduced to 'the books of the philosophers'.[20] Later Hishām went to Baghdad and became an associate of Yaḥyā al-Barmakī, entering into the philosophical and theological discussions of the scholars who gathered in the latter's salon.[21] Hārūn ar-Rashīd is said to have considered his views dangerous and to have ordered his arrest, whereupon he went into hiding and shortly afterwards died. The dates given for his death vary from 795 to 815. The arguments for the earliest date [22] are not entirely convincing; and, if the story of the order for his arrest is true, a more appropriate date would be shortly after the fall of the Barmakids in 803, since they were presumably sympathetic towards his views. There is certainly no record of any activity of his after the Barmakid period.

The most important fact about his education, apart from his having been in the intellectual atmosphere of Kufa, is that he came under the influence of Abū-Shākir ad-Dayṣānī. [23] This man, as the *nisba* indicates, was reckoned as belonging to the sect of the Dayṣāniyya, whose name is derived from Bardesanes, a second-century Christian heresiarch. [24] In a history of the development of Islamic thought it is not necessary to attempt to trace the processes by which this name came to be applied to men of Iraq in the eighth century. The significant fact is that in Iraq at this time there were men who 'professed Islam but secretly believed in *zandaqa*', though the list given by Ibn-an-Nadīm with this heading is 'very heterogeneous'. In particular there were groups entitled 'Manichaeans' (Mānawiyya, Manāniyya), 'Dayṣānites' and 'Marcionites' (Marqūniyya). From descriptions of their views in al-Ash'arī, al-Māturīdī, the *qāḍī* 'Abd-al-Jabbār [25] and others it is clear that they mingled dualistic speculations with Hellenistic ideas. The confrontation of sincere Muslim scholars with such a challenge not merely gave them an example of a kind of Kalām in action but forced them rapidly to acquire a degree of skill in it.

Only fragments have been preserved for us of Hishām's views on scientific-philosophical matters, and these mostly in connection with his influence on an-Naẓẓām. Thus Hishām held that bodies are infinitely divisible and that there is no such thing as an atom (*al-juz' alladhī lā yatajazza'*); and in this an-Naẓẓām followed him. [26] Hishām held certain views on the problems of *mudākhala* and *kumūn*, 'intermingling' and 'concealment', that is, the intermingling of two entities in one place, like heat and light, and the concealment of fire in wood before the wood is burnt; [27] and Josef van Ess in his monograph on Ḍirār has now shown that an-Naẓẓām's ideas on these matters were derived from Hishām as well as from Ḍirār. [28] It is perhaps just a coincidence that, while Hishām wrote a 'refutation of Aristotle on God's oneness (*tawḥīd*)', an-Naẓẓām is said to have orally refuted before Ja'far the Barmakid the various points in a book of Aristotle's. [29] Among Hishām's books is one entitled 'The Proof of the Origination of Things' (*K. ad-dalāla ʿalā ḥudūth al-ashyāʾ*), which is presumably philosophical.[30] He appears to have been one of the first to employ the term *maʿnā* (literally 'meaning') in a technical sense; from examples in the *Maqālāt* of al-Ashʿarī he appears to use it of inseparable aspects of a *jism* (which for him is something like 'substance'), such as movement, rest and acts, and even of 'body' and 'spirit' (*badan, ruḥ*).[31]

Hishām also discussed most of the topics of the intra-Islamic Kalām of the time, such as the attributes of God and whether the Qur'ān was created.[32] On the question of human acts and predestination he held a view similar to that of Ḍirār, which will be mentioned presently. He is said to have written a book on this subject, as well as refutations of Zanādiqa, Dualists and Aṣ'ḥāb aṭ-ṭabā'iʿ.[33] He was much criticized by Muslim scholars for his use of the word *jism*. As just noted, it was roughly equivalent to 'substance', since he applied it to every existent entity; but when he called God a *jism*, he was accused of 'corporealism' (*tajsīm*) and 'anthropomorphism' (*tashbīh*).[34]

Politically Hishām was a Rāfiḍite, and more particularly one of the Qaṭʿiyya.[35] The latter, as noted above, were a group of Rāfiḍites who on the disappearance of the imam Mūsā al-Kāẓim in prison decisively affirmed his death and acknowledged his son ʿAlī ar-Riḍā as imam (according to later Imāmite accounts); they are contrasted with the group of Wāqifa or 'undecided' who thought Mūsā was not dead and looked for his return. It seems likely that at this date Rāfiḍism was the expression of a belief in an autocratic or absolutist form of government, namely, one in which the caliph had supreme authority, in which this authority was seen as coming from above by 'designation' or 'testament' on the part of the predecessor, and in which the caliph was 'the most excellent' of the community. The Barmakids were probably sympathetic to this view. As a Qaṭʿī Hishām would be an opponent of the messianism of the Wāqifa and a supporter of the caliphate of Hārūn ar-Rashīd. He presumably also accepted the Rāfiḍite critique of the Companions, since he wrote against Zaydism and 'the imamate of the inferior'. It is curious that both Ibn-an-Nadīm and Shaykh Ṭūsī say of Hishām's contemporary 'Alī ibn-Mītham that he was the first to give theological expression to the doctrine of the imamate, or of Imāmism (*awwal man takallama fī madhhab al-imāma / al-imāmiyya*).[36] The evidence is insufficient to show whether this was because Hishām was younger, or because his views were less acceptable to later Imāmites or because his specialism was rather Kalām. His books against two fellow-Rāfiḍites, Abū-Ja'far al-Aḥwal and Hishām ibn-Sālim al-Jawālīqī, [37] may have been about philosophical rather than political questions.

b) *Ḍirār ibn-'Amr*

Perhaps the chief casualty of the Islamic style of heresiography has been Ḍirār ibn-'Amr, together with his followers. A full study has been made of him recently by Josef van Ess under the title 'Ḍirār b. 'Amr und die "Cahmīya" : Biographie einer vergessenen Schule'; [38] and this will be drawn on in what is said about Ḍirār. In particular it has become clear that he made an essential contribution to the development of Islamic thought, and probably did more than any other single thinker to make possible the flowering of the Mu'tazila in the first half of the ninth century. He is remembered in the books of sects for some of the unusual views he held, but few details have been preserved about his life. The later Mu'tazilites would not have him as one of theirs (though other men called him a Mu'tazilite) because he differed from them on the question of free will; and likewise the Ash'arites, though they accepted the conception of *kasb* or 'acquisition' which he seems to have invented, could not look on him as a forerunner because he held one or two views with which they disagreed. So he was passed over in relative silence. Because he was a pioneer in a transitional period, his contribution to the development of thought was enormous; but for heresiographers, chiefly interested in classification and the labelling of false doctrines, the only things to be mentioned with regard to him were the ideas rejected by later thinkers.

Ḍirār's *floruit* may be placed in the reign of Hārūn ar-Rashīd. He is supposed to have lived in the time of Wāṣil ibn-'Aṭā' (d. 749), [39] the alleged founder of the Mu'tazila, but this may simply be part of the later Mu'tazilite image (to be discussed in the next chapter). He is also, however, said to have been a pupil of Yazīd ibn-Abān ar-Raqāshī (d. 748), [40] who is reckoned to belong to the Khārijite sect of the Wa'īdiyya, who held that God must punish the evildoer eternally in Hell, and whose doctrine was in part taken over by the Mu'tazila. [41] It would seem, then, that Ḍirār was born not later than about 730. His full name is given as Abū-'Amr Ḍirār ibn-'Amr al-Ghaṭafānī al-Kūfī, which means that he is of the tribe of Ghaṭafān and was presumably born in Kufa. He seems to be mostly connected with Basra, however. Both Wāṣil and Yazīd ar-Raqāshī belonged to the circle of al-Ḥasan al-Baṣrī, while Ḍirār is reported to have been the leader of the discussions on Kalām in Basra before Abū-l-Hudhayl.[42] He must also have visited Baghdad, but it may have been for only a short period. While there he took part in discussions before Yaḥyā al-Barmakī with Sulaymān ibn-Jarīr, ʿAbd-Allāh ibn-Yazīd al-Ibāḍī, Hishām ibn-al-Ḥakam, the chief of the Zoroastrian clerics and the Rēsh Galūthā.[43] It was probably also at this period that he was accused of *zandaqa* before the *qāḍī* Saʿīd ibn-ʿAbd-ar-Raḥmān al-Jumaḥī (d. 790/2 ?) and declared to be an outlaw; but the sentence was apparently ineffective, probably because he was hidden by Yaḥyā al-Barmakī.[44] He is himself said to have been a *qāḍī*.

There are some reports about his relations with other scholars, and further points may be inferred from such evidence as book titles. One may accept the statement that he discussed with Hishām ibn-al-Ḥakam the respective merits of Abū-Bakr and ʿAlī, but it is not credible, as the late Shīʿite author of the statement also claims, that Ḍirār was convinced by Hishām, since he is the author of a refutation of the Rāfiḍites.[45] Though they differed in politics, there were many parallels between the thought of the two men. Another scholar who was roughly contemporary was the Muʿtazilite Muʿammar, who was concerned with the defence of Islam against the Indian Sumaniyya and the materialistic Dahriyya; Ḍirār wrote a book in criticism of him.[46] In certain political attitudes, however, Ḍirār agreed with both Muʿammar and the slightly later Abū-l-Hudhayl;[47] and this suggests a degree of association. The fact that Ḍirār did not write against Abū-l-Hudhayl and Bishr ibn-al-Muʿtamir, though these two men wrote against him, presumably indicates that they were his juniors by a number of years.[48] An-Naẓẓām speaks of Ḍirār rejecting the doctrine of *kumūn*, but this is not necessarily an-Naẓẓām's own doctrine, since at an earlier date some Manichaeans had held a doctrine of *kumūn*;[49] and so Ḍirār need not be dated later than an-Naẓẓām's publishing of his doctrine. The sources say he lived to be seventy or ninety, but it is not important to decide whether he died towards 800 or 820, since there is no evidence of any activity after the caliphate of Hārūn ar-Rashīd. Ḍirār is roughly in the same generation as Hishām ibn-al-Ḥakam and Muʿammar and a generation before Abū-l-Hudhayl and Bishr ibn-al-Muʿtamir; but it is impossible to be more precise.

One aspect of Ḍirār's political attitude was that, while in respect of the quarrel of ʿAlī and Muʿāwiya he thought the latter was in the wrong, in respect of the battle of the Camel he did not decide which side was in the wrong but associated with both separately.[50] This means that he avoided the extreme opposition to ʿAlī of those contemporaries who put Muʿāwiya above him, but did not give unlimited support to ʿAlī. This is a kind of compromise between the absolutists and constitutionalists of the late eighth century, and it is not surprising that Muʿammar and Abū-l-Hudhayl agreed with him in this, though the Muʿtazilite attitude came to be more precisely formulated. The titles of Ḍirār's books tend to confirm that he adopted a middle-of-the-way position. He wrote against the Zanādiqa (nos. 20 and perhaps 17, 18, 19), against the Rāfiḍites (no. 35), and against the revolutionary proto-Shīʿite sects of the Mughīriyya and the Manṣūriyya (no. 36). In the case of the two last the chief objection was to the assertion that there were prophets after Muḥammad; the danger was that charismatic leaders of this kind might fundamentally alter the basis of the state. The Mughīriyya had also held messianic views, while there had been a revival of the Manṣūriyya during the reign of al-Mahdī.[51]

On the other hand, Ḍirār did not support the 'constitutionalists'. He wrote various books against the Murji'a, the Ḥashwiyya and the Mushabbiha (nos. 25–31, 35), and these are the names he would naturally apply to certain of the 'constitutionalists' of his day. He was not far removed from them, however, since he himself is called a *mushabbih* by the Muʿtazilite al-Khayyāṭ.[52] His book (no. 11) on 'the intermediate position' (*al-manzila bayn al-manzilatayn*) is presumably a defence of the doctrine and thus a sign of his opposition to that body of 'constitutionalist' opinion which treated the grave sinner as a believer and so was felt by others to be morally lax.

While Ḍirār agreed with the later Muʿtazila in 'the intermediate position' and the use of rational arguments, he sided with the majority of the general religious movement in believing that all events, including human actions, were determined or controlled by God. This he expressed by means of the conception of 'acquisition' or 'appropriation' (*kasb, iktisāb*), which he was probably the first to use in this way. According to al-Ashʿarī

> The ground of the separation of Ḍirār ibn-ʿAmr from the Muʿtazila was his view that the acts of men are created and that a single act comes from two agents, of whom one, God, creates it, while the other, man, 'acquires' it (*iktasaba-hu*); and that God is the agent of the acts of men in reality, and that men are the agents of them in reality. [53]

The choice of the conception of 'acquiring' for this special purpose is doubtless due to its frequent occurrence in the Qur'ān in a metaphorical sense. [54] The original meaning according to Lane is firstly to collect (wealth or property) and then to gain, acquire, or earn (wealth and the like). Joseph Schacht suggested that the connecting link between the original meaning and the Qur'ānic usage is the commercial employment of the word in the meaning 'to engage, pledge, one's credit', or 'to be credited'. [55] Schacht seems to be correct in claiming the link with commerce, but his first meaning only really fits 52.21, while the second is passive where something active is required. Perhaps 'to acquire as credit or debit' would retain both the commercial reference and the activity. The terse statement in 2.286 could then be rendered as follows : 'to him (on the credit side) is what he has acquired (as credit), and against him (on the debit side) is what he has acquired (as debit)'—*la-hā mā kasabat, wa-ʿalay-hā mā ktasabat*; the reference is to *nafs*, 'person'. The picture is thus of a man through his actions 'collecting' credit and debit entries in a heavenly ledger. Though there is a distinction in this passage (as usually interpreted) between *kasb* and *iktisāb*, the distinction is not maintained elsewhere and the two are virtually synonymous.

The problem Ḍirār was trying to solve here was to reconcile God's omnipotence with his justice in punishing wrongdoers. It would be unjust to punish someone for an act for which he was not responsible. Ḍirār starts from the common Islamic doctrine that all outward events and so the whole course of history are determined by God. With much of this doctrine any modern scholar might agree ; for on reflection it is clear that human activity would be impossible without the continued operation of nature according to its laws, and natural operations, at least for Islamic theologians, are the creation of God. Most Muslims went further, however, and held that God determined human acts ; A cannot kill B unless God so wills. This leads to the question : if God determines A's act, how can A justly be punished ? The conception of *kasb* is a way of saying that a man is responsible for his acts, at least to the extent that he may justly be punished for them if they are wrong. Ḍirār thought of the act as proceeding from a 'power' (*istiṭāʿa*) which God created in the man. This was presumably something different from mere physical capacity, since it was a mark of the difference between voluntary and involuntary acts. The verb is used a number of times in the Qur'ān in the sense of 'to be able', but sometimes (e.g. 5.112) there is also the suggestion of 'complying with a desire';[56] and it was perhaps because of this suggestion that the Ashʿarites preferred *istiṭāʿa* to *qudra* and *quwwa*, though the two latter were used by the Muʿtazilites in a similar sense.[57]

The importance of the conception of *kasb* may be judged from the fact that it became one of the distinctive features of Ashʿarite theology. The examples of this technical usage of the root in the *Maqālāt* of al-Ashʿarī give some indications of the early development of the concept, and make it probable that Ḍirār was its originator.[58] In some cases the word *kasb* or its derivatives may have been introduced into the account by al-Ashʿarī or his immediate source, but mostly *kasb* seems to have been used by the theologians themselves. To begin with we find the conception used by Ḍirār's two contemporaries, Hishām ibn-al-Ḥakam and Muʿammar. For the latter there are only two slight references in which *kasb*, apparently 'voluntary action', is contrasted with 'creation'.[59] Hishām's theory is similar to Ḍirār's but he seems to prefer a different form of expression;

> Hishām ibn-al-Ḥakam held that men's acts are created by God; and also, according to Jaʿfar ibn-Ḥarb, that a man's acts are choice (*ikhtiyār*) for him in one respect and compulsion (*iḍṭirār*) in another respect—choice in that he wills and 'acquires' them (*arāda, iktasaba*), compulsion in that they proceed from him only when there comes into being the cause (*sabab*) inciting to them.[60]

By *sabab* Hishām probably meant what others called *istiṭāʿa*, though he took the latter in a wider sense to include various necessary conditions of an act.[61] While there is thus evidence for original thinking by Hishām on these matters, there is no evidence that he attached special importance to the conception of *kasb*.

The other men named by al-Ashʿarī as using the term *kasb* are all later. There were several from the groups influenced by Ḍirār, namely the Ahl al-Ithbāt,[62] Muḥammad ibn-ʿĪsā,[63] an-Najjār,[64]

Yaḥyā ibn-Abī-Kāmil,[65] and Aḥmad ibn-Salma al-Kūshānī.[66] Then there were several Muʿtazilites, who, if they themselves used the term, must have meant by it no more than 'voluntary action'. The Muʿtazilites in general denied that God could create or have power over any act which could be described as *kasb*, that is 'voluntary'.[67] Ash-Shaḥḥām, the leader of the Muʿtazilites of Basra between Abū-l-Hudhayl and al-Jubbā'ī, seems to have tried to reverse Ḍirār's theory by admitting that God and man might both be capable of an act—presumably a movement that could be either involuntary or voluntary—but if God produced it in the man it was compulsion, whereas if the man did so it was 'acquisition'.[68] Ash-Shaḥḥām is described as a disciple of Muʿammar, and is also the source of a report about Ḍirār.[69] His successor al-Jubbā'ī, however, rejected the technical use of *kasb* as improper.[70] It was used still by another Muʿtazilite, roughly contemporary, an-Nāshi' al-Akbar (d. 906). This man is perhaps a little closer to al-Ashʿarī in his views and may have known him personally, since al-Ashʿarī had discussions with his son.[71] Apart from the above persons who dealt with the question of human activity in general, the conception of *kasb* was applied by Ibn-Kullāb (d. 854) to man's utterance of the Qur'ān, perhaps following on Ḍirār himself.[72] Altogether the conception had played an important part in Islamic thought before it was taken over by al-Ashʿarī and the Ashʿarites.

The philosophical aspects of Ḍirār's teaching may be mentioned briefly, since they have been dealt with at length by Josef van Ess. Ḍirār's rejection of the doctrine of *kumūn*—the doctrine that substances have their potentialities present but concealed within them—was probably due, as van Ess suggests, to his desire to maintain God's supremacy over natural processes. If natural processes depended solely on the natures of the substances involved, he felt that they were removed from God's control. He therefore tended to a view which, though he rejected the conception of 'atom', could be regarded as 'atomism'. Thus Ḍirār held that the accidents (*aʿrāḍ*) which are other than bodies do not continue to exist for two times or moments (*zamānayn*);[73] by this he implies that they are created separately by God in each moment. Linked with this was his account of body in general and also of man as consisting of accidents joined together; it is difficult to know precisely the points he was emphasizing here, since the brief reports in al-Ashʿarī are coloured by later criticisms.[74]

He also speculated about God and asserted that he had a *māhiyya* or 'quiddity' (literally, 'what is it?', 'whatness'), which man cannot know in this world but will be able to apprehend on the day of resurrection by having a sixth sense created.[75] He further asserted, doubtless as part of this same line of thought, that God's names or attributes give us no positive information about him, but are to be interpreted negatively; to say he is knowing and powerful (*'ālim, qādir*) means he is not ignorant and impotent (*jāhil, 'ājiz*).[76] Ḍirār was far from being in any sense a dualist, but there were sufficient philosophical ideas to justify a charge of *zandaqa* in the eyes of a man like Abū-Yūsuf.

Finally, a word must be said about the relation of Ḍirār to the Jahmiyya although this has already been touched on in the discussion of that name; and it was noted that the Mu'tazilites, such as Bishr ibn-al-Mu'tamir, called him a follower of Jahm probably because of his determinism.[77] Other points relevant here are that Ḍirār wrote a 'Refutation of the Wāqifiyya, the Jahmiyya and the Ghaylāniyya', and that he denied the punishment of the tomb, the view ascribed to the Jahmiyya in *Al-fiqh al-akbar I*.[78] The latter point is probably to be connected with Ḍirār's adoption of 'the intermediate position' with its implication that the grave sinner went to Hell. The nicknaming of him a Ḥarūrite is probably a way of saying that he held this doctrine, and would be the work of someone who thought, like the Ḥanafites, that all believers ultimately went to Paradise.[79] It seems to be impossible to say more about this matter without further information about the 'anti-Jahmite' groups among the early Ḥanafites and about the precise points they criticized. With regard to the book against the Jahmiyya, one cannot be certain of its subject. The Wāqifiyya could be those who 'refrained from deciding' in respect of one of several questions; the most likely are perhaps those who were undecided about Traditions in respect of 'the promise and the threat', that is, the question of eternal punishment.[80] The combination of Jahmiyya and Ghaylāniyya would perhaps best fit their ideas about faith as 'second knowledge' and its indivisibility; the distinction between knowledge that was compulsory and knowledge by 'acquisition' (*iktisāb*), while not identical with Ḍirār's technical terms, might conceivably come from his criticism of the matter. While many of the details are thus obscure, it is clear that Ḍirār was near the centre of several lively circles of discussion.

c) *Bishr al-Marīsī*

While the question of the createdness of the Qur'ān does not seem to have become a live one while Ḍirār was active, the somewhat younger Bishr (ibn-Ghiyāth) al-Marīsī is credited with a prominent place in the publicizing of the doctrine that the Qur'ān was the created word of God. [81] Although Bishr must be counted as a theologian, no very distinctive views are recorded of him, and he seems to have become notorious chiefly because he was involved in the political application of theological doctrine. An attempt must therefore be made to look at his career in all its aspects.

He must have been born not later that 760, since he is said to have studied Traditions with Ḥammād ibn-Salama (d. 781 or 784). [82] For this he may have gone to Basra, but most of his early life is connected with Kufa. There he was born, the son of a Jewish goldsmith, it is said, and there he studied jurisprudence and Traditions with Abū-Yūsuf (d. 798), the distinguished Ḥanafite, and Traditions with Sufyān ibn-ʿUyayna (d. 813). It is not stated where he was initiated into Kalām, but he became outstanding in this discipline sufficiently early for the Traditionist of Basra, Ḥammād ibn-Zayd (d. 795), to pronounce him an infidel. [83] At some point, perhaps during the reign of Hārūn ar-Rashīd, he went to Baghdad, and there became familiar among others with ash-Shāfiʿī (d. 820). His mother is said to have begged ash-Shāfiʿī to persuade her son to abandon Kalām, but Bishr was adamant and urged the other to become a *mutakallim*. [84]

There are difficulties about the dating of this story, but, especially if it is taken in a political sense, it may well be true. Certainly Bishr's theological views were such as to make the government suspicious of him at various times. The first occasion was during the reign of ar-Rashīd. According to a report from the Ḥanbalite Ibn-al-Jawzī (d. 1200) ar-Rashīd threatened to put him cruelly to death because he held that the Qur'ān was created, and he then went into hiding for twenty years until after the death of ar-Rashīd in 809. [85] While the main point of this story is probably true, the figure of twenty years is likely to be an exaggeration, and during the reign of ar-Rashīd the specific charge about the Qur'ān is less likely than a general charge of being involved in Kalām. This latter charge, however, could hardly have been made when the Barmakids were in power, and there are therefore grounds for thinking that the whole incident was subsequent to the fall of the Barmakids in 803.

The second and third occasions have been brought to light by Josef van Ess.[86] When the troops of al-Ma'mūn entered Baghdad as conquerors in 813, there was a popular uprising directed, amongst others, against the *mutakallimūn*; and the general Harthama seems to have arrested Bishr and others in the hope of quietening the people. Again between 817 and 819, when al-Ma'mūn's uncle Ibrāhīm was at the head of a rebellion against him and controlled Baghdad for two years, Bishr was thrown into prison and narrowly escaped with his life. When al-Ma'mūn arrived in Baghdad, however, later in 819, Bishr was in high favour at court and presumably remained so until the death of al-Ma'mūn. An obscure story that al-Ma'mūn quarrelled with him and had him crucified must be a sheer invention.[87] The earliest and most likely date for Bishr's death is 833—others are 834 and 842—and it is unthinkable that al-Ma'mūn could have put him to death within a month or two of instituting the Miḥna based on the doctrine associated with Bishr; had he done so there would have been an outcry and we would have been bound to hear about it.

From all this it appears that Bishr al-Marīsī was a prominent supporter and intellectual defender of the general line of policy followed by the Barmakids and then later by al-Ma'mūn, which may be designated 'absolutist'. This is in contrast with the 'constitutionalist' policy of al-Faḍl ibn-ar-Rabīʿ, al-Amīn and Ibrāhīm. Van Ess goes so far as to suggest that Bishr was closer to al-Ma'mūn than the Muʿtazilites who are usually credited with having influenced him to adopt the policy of the Miḥna; for Ibn-Ṭayfūr describes al-Ma'mūn as a 'Ḍirārite', presumably meaning among other things that he rejected the Muʿtazilite doctrine of Qadar or free will, and Bishr is known to have been opposed to the Muʿtazilites in this point.[88] In the presence of al-Ma'mūn there were discussions between Bishr and both Abū-l-Hudhayl and Thumāma ibn-Ashras; and Bishr is the source of an account of a discussion between an Imāmite and a Zaydite, also before the caliph.[89] In Baghdad Bishr had his own *majlis* or salon for intellectual discussion.[90] All this makes it likely that the statement in relatively late sources that Bishr was the first to propound the doctrine of the created Qur'ān—which is probably not the case—is to be interpreted as a distortion of the fact that he was chiefly responsible for getting it accepted officially by al-Ma'mūn.

There is evidence in the history of Bishr and his environment for the existence of a deep cleavage within the following of Abū-Ḥanīfa.

His teacher Abū-Yūsuf is said to have criticized and attacked him for his attachment to Kalām.[91] The examination of his case under Ibrāhīm was conducted by a Ḥanafite judge, Qutayba b. Ziyād.[92] His denial of the punishment of the tomb[93] was regarded as 'Jahmite' by some Ḥanafites in accordance with *Al-fiqh al-akbar I*. There is a statement by Ibn-Taymiyya that at the end of the second century (A.D. 815) when the Greek books were translated the doctrine known as Jahmite was spread by Bishr al-Marīsī and his generation.[94] From a Ḥanbalite this may only mean that Bishr advocated the doctrine of the creation of the Qur'ān; but the statement could be based on an earlier Ḥanafite source which was criticizing Bishr's general involvement in Kalām. All this is an indication that among the Ḥanafites there was one important group with 'constitutionalist' sympathies which attacked a group of 'absolutists' and labelled them Jahmites. At first it was chiefly the rational methods of Kalām that were attacked—though among our scanty records there is no evidence that Bishr himself used Greek conceptions—but later this merged into an attack on the official doctrine of the Qur'ān. The matter is complex, however, since some of the 'constitutionalists' managed to retain high positions under al-Ma'mūn.[95]

The heresiographers have little to say about the actual doctrines held by Bishr. Perhaps his beliefs did not differ greatly from those of the majority of Ḥanafites. The chief points al-Ash'arī reports about him are that he defined *īmān* or 'faith' as *taṣdīq* or 'counting true' with both heart and tongue, and that he held that God would not keep sinners of the 'people of the Qibla' in Hell eternally; the latter point he supported by the verse, 'he who works a grain's weight of good shall see it' (99.7).[96] The two matters are connected, for the sinner who continues to 'count true' God's existence and Muḥammad's prophethood has still *īmān* and deserves a reward for this. In these two points Bishr is close to later Ḥanafite views even as reflected in a conservative document like the creed of aṭ-Ṭaḥāwī.[97] The only real heresy which al-Ash'arī and others noted here was an inference he made from his definition, namely, that to prostrate oneself to the sun or to an idol was not *kufr*, 'unbelief', but only a sign of it; for him the essential *kufr* was the denial or rejection of a verbal statement.[98] It is further to be learned from the *Refutation of Bishr al-Marīsī* by ad-Dārimī (d. 895) that he took part in an early stage of the discussions of the attributes of God and recognized four—will (*mashī'a*), knowledge (*'ilm*), power (*qudra*) and creativity (*takhlīq*)—presumably as alone theologically significant. The anthropomorphic attributes of God mentioned in the Qur'ān and in Traditions he interpreted away.[99] A brief report in al-Ash'arī foreshadows the later distinction between essential and active attributes (*ṣifāt adh-dhāt, ṣifāt al-fi'l*).[100]

Thus from the little we know about Bishr al-Marīsī we have tantalizing glimpses of a stage in the development of Kalām. What comes out most clearly is the close connection at this period between theology and politics.

d) *Ḥusayn an-Najjār*

Another early *mutakallim* distinct from the Mu'tazila was an-Najjār —Abū-'Abd-Allāh al-Ḥusayn ibn-Muḥammad. He was in some sense a pupil of Bishr al-Marīsī,[101] and was therefore presumably younger; but he may have died about the same time, if the story is true that his death followed defeat in a debate with the Mu'tazilite an-Naẓẓām (d. 836 ?).[102] A passage in al-Khayyāṭ would seem to imply that Abū-l-Hudhayl was at least familiar with his views; while the Mu'tazilites al-Murdār and al-Iskāfī (d. c. 854) wrote books against him.[103] He must thus have flourished in the later part of the reign of al-Ma'mūn.

There is a relatively full description of his views in al-Ash'arī, and this is worth quoting here as an example of the kind of position adopted by many of the anti-Mu'tazilite *mutakallimūn* of the first half of the ninth century.[104]

1) The works of men are created by God; men are the agents of them.

2) There is nothing in God's realm except what he wills; God is ceaselessly willing that what he knows will be in its time will be in its time, and that what he knows will not be will not be.

3) The power (*istiṭā'a*) may not precede the act; help (*'awn*) from God is originated in the time (*ḥāl*) of the act along with the act, and this is the power.

4) Two acts are not performed by a single power, but for each act there is a power originated when (the act) is originated; the power does not endure (beyond one 'time'); when it exists the act exists, and when it does not exist the act does not exist.

5) The power of (that is, producing) faith is succour, right direction, grace, favour, benefit and guidance (*tawfīq, tasdīd, faḍl, niʿma, iḥsān, hudā*); the power (producing) unbelief is error, abandonment, affliction, evil (*ḍalāl, khidhlān, balā', sharr*).

6) An (act of) obedience may exist in the time of the sin which is the omission of it in so far as it is not the sin which is the omission of it at that particular time, and in so far as the time is not the time for the sin which is its omission.

7) The believer is a believer and rightly guided, whom God succours and guides; the unbeliever is one abandoned, whom God has abandoned and led astray, on whose heart he has set a seal, whom he has not guided nor regarded; (God) has created his unbelief, and has not made him good (*aṣlaḥa*); if he were to regard him and make him good, he would be good (*ṣāliḥ*).

8) God may inflict pain on children in the future life, or he may show (unmerited) favour (*yatafaḍḍal*) to them and not inflict pain on them.

9) If God were to show favour (*laṭafa*) to all the unbelievers, they would believe; he is able to perform such favours (*alṭāf*) for them that, if he did perform them, they would believe.

10) God has imposed on the unbelievers (duties) which they are unable to fulfil, not because of any inherent weakness or incidental defect but because they leave them undone.

11) Man does not act in another, but performs acts only in himself, such as movements, rest, volitions, cognitions, unbelief, faith; man does not make pain nor perception nor vision; he makes nothing at all by way of 'generation' (*tawallud*).

12) God is ceaselessly generous in that avarice is denied of him, and ceaselessly speaking in the sense that he is ceaselessly not incapable of speech (*kalām*); the speech of God is originated and created.

13) In respect of the unity (of God) he held the doctrine of the Muʿtazila except with regard to the will and to generosity; he differed from them in respect of the Qadar, and held the doctrine of 'postponement' (*irjā'*).

14) God may change the eye into the heart and (?or) give

the eye the power of the heart, so that man sees God with his eye, that is, knows him with it; God cannot be seen with the eyes except in this way.

15) The man who dies dies at his term (*ajal*), and the man who is killed is killed at his term.

16) God gives sustenance (*yarzuq*) both of the lawful and the unlawful; sustenance (*rizq*) is of two kinds, sustenance of food and sustenance of property.

Despite the connection between an-Najjār and Bishr al-Marīsī the views described here are in most respects those of Ḍirār in a more developed form, as would be natural after the lapse of a generation.[105] Article 12 reflects Ḍirār's view of the negative character of our knowledge of God's attributes.[106] He avoids Ḍirār's innovation of a 'sixth sense' to 'see' God at the resurrection, but has the alternative suggestion (art. 14) that the eye may be given the power of knowing; he apparently continued to hold the conception of God's *māhiyya* or quiddity.[107] He also accepted the conception of *kasb*, though it does not occur explicitly in this account;[108] but he interpreted it in a more deterministic way, for example, by insisting that the 'power' to act exists only along with the act (arts. 3, 4), whereas it had probably not occurred to Ḍirār to ask what was the temporal relationship between the 'power' and the act. Several of the other articles are strongly deterministic (2, 7, 9, 15, 16). From other material an-Najjār is seen to have followed Ḍirār in many of his speculations about bodies and accidents, though without slavishly accepting all Ḍirār's views.[109]

e) *Other men of similar views*

The conclusion to which the researches of Josef van Ess point is that there was in some sense a 'school' comprising all those who had been influenced by Ḍirār.[110] This does not mean that all these men held identical views or even that they were agreed about all fundamentals. Though they differ on various points, there is a family likeness among them, derived from a common stock of ideas and a common interest in asking certain questions. Though an-Najjār studied under Bishr al-Marīsī and was a Murji'ite, this did not prevent him being deeply influenced by Ḍirār who wrote books against Murji'ites.

The group around Ḍirār, Bishr al-Marīsī and an-Najjār, however, came to be clearly marked off from the Muʿtazilites in the later restricted sense of those accepting the 'five principles'. Originally the term Muʿtazila had been used in a wide sense to include all who engaged in Kalām; and some later writers (for example, al-Pazdawī) continue to speak of Ḍirār as a Muʿtazilite. At some point, however, a break occurred. It was possibly when Abū-l-Hudhayl took over from Ḍirār the leadership of the discussions at Basra, and it seems to have been over the question whether human acts are determined by God or not. From this time onwards there was a relatively compact 'school' of Muʿtazilites, all holding, at least nominally, the 'five principles', and considering themselves different from the persons described in this chapter.

In this connection a nearly contemporary remark of Aḥmad ibn-Ḥanbal is to be noted; speaking of Jahm he said that 'he misled many people and found supporters among the companions of Abū-Ḥanīfa and 'Amr ibn-'Ubayd in Basra'.[111] The Muʿtazilites in the strict sense are nearly all the spiritual descendants of ʿAmr, while most of the *mutakallimūn* whom the Muʿtazilites rejected were somehow connected with Abū-Ḥanīfa. Ḍirār is said to have adopted from Abū-Ḥanīfa his conception of God's quiddity; and the conception of *kasb* or 'acquisition', of which Ḍirār is the first prominent exponent, is sometimes specially associated with Abū-Ḥanīfa (presumably meaning his followers), and the phrase 'subtler than the *kasb* of Abū-Ḥanīfa' replaces the phrase 'subtler than the *kasb* of al-Ashʿarī'.[112] Although there were deep rivalries between various groups of Ḥanafites, there seems also to have been something of a common outlook which marked them off from others.[113] The importance of the Ḥanafites will become clearer if we look briefly at some of the other associates of Ḍirār and Bishr al-Marīsī.

1) *Ḥafṣ al-Fard.* The closest associate and disciple of Ḍirār, Ḥafṣ al-Fard was at the same time a pupil of Abū-Yūsuf.[114] From Egypt where he was born he came as a young man to Basra and for a time followed the lectures of Abū-l-Hudhayl. There are difficulties about the dating of his contacts with Abū-Yūsuf (d. 798) and of his disputations with ash-Shāfiʿī; but there are so many gaps in our knowledge that the difficulties are not in principle insuperable. Abū-Yūsuf was latterly in Baghdad, though he is said to have visited Basra in 792 and 796; but Ḥafṣ may well have spent some time in Baghdad. Ash-Shāfiʿī was in Egypt from 814 to 820, and Ḥafṣ eventually returned to Egypt. Some contact between Ḍirār and Ḥafṣ is to be inferred from the latter's views. From the titles of books listed by Ibn-an-

Nadīm it is clear that after Ḍirār had ceased to be active Ḥafṣ became the spokesman for Ḍirārite views against Abū-l-Hudhayl. It was at this period and through such disputes that the Muʿtazilite school in the restricted sense marked itself off from the general body of *mutakallimūn*.

2) *Sufyān ibn-Sakhtān*. Ḍirār's views about God's quiddity, the sixth sense, and other matters were shared by Sufyān ibn-Sakhtān.[115] He is described as belonging to the Aṣ'ḥāb ar-Ra'y, which is virtually a name for the Ḥanafites. He also helped the Ḥanafite ʿĪsā ibn-Abān to write a book against ash-Shāfiʿī.[116]

3) *Burghūth*. Nothing is really known about the life of Muḥammad ibn-ʿĪsā, nicknamed Burghūth, 'flea', who is probably the same as Muḥammad ibn-ʿĪsā as-Sīrāfī.[117] He is said to have been a pupil of an-Najjār, but differed from him in his view of 'generated effects'. He agreed with Ḍirār in the doctrine of God's quiddity. He is said to have died six months after al-Iskāfī, that is, in 854 or 855.

4) *Aḥmad ibn-Salama al-Kūshānī*. This man was a follower of an-Najjār, who disputed with the Muʿtazilite aṣ-Ṣāliḥī, and was reckoned among the Ahl al-Ithbāt or Mujbira.[118]

5) *Ibn-ath-Thaljī*. (Muḥammad ibn-Shujāʿ) Ibn-ath-Thaljī (d. 880) was a Ḥanafite judge who had once discussed with Bishr al-Marīsī, but who afterwards claimed that he differed from him. This did not prevent him from being attacked by ad-Dārimī in his book against Bishr, presumably because he was reckoned among the Wāqifa or Wāqifiyya, who tried to avoid the question whether the Qur'ān was created or not, and also among the Lafẓiyya, who held that man's utterance of the Qur'ān was created.[119]

Besides these men there were one or two others who engaged in Kalām about the same period, but were not accepted as Muʿtazilites and are instead reckoned Khārijites. This latter affiliation need not mean any great separation from the men just described, since these are known to have been in contact with the Khārijites in question, while Ḍirār is on occasion called a Ḥarūrite and Burghūth a Khārijite.[120]

6) *ʿAbd-Allāh ibn-Yazīd*. This man, who belonged to the Ibāḍite subsect, was a business partner in Kufa of Hishām ibn-al-Ḥakam, and engaged in discussions with him and others.[121]

7) *Yaḥyā ibn-(Abī-)Kāmil*. Though latterly an Ibāḍite, Yaḥyā was

originally a pupil of Bishr al-Marīsī. He held many of the views of the Ahl al-Ithbāt, including the conception of *iktisāb*.[122]
8) *Muḥammad ibn-Ḥarb as-Ṣayrafī*. This man was also close to the Ahl al-Ithbāt, but was reckoned an Ibāḍite.[123]

The sketch in this chapter of the beginnings of Kalām is far from complete, but it shows the width of the movement. Though there was opposition, Kalām attracted a broad spectrum of the more educated Muslims, especially among the 'absolutists'; but it was not confined to these, and eventually became a feature of much Islamic theology of nearly every school. This is the background against which the achievement of the Muʿtazilites is to be understood.

4
Al-Kindī and the Falāsifa

Out of the soil of translations from Greek in which Kalām sprang up there came also a philosophical movement. From the Greek *philosophos* the Arabs formed a word *faylasūf*, of which the plural is *falāsifa*. The corresponding abstract noun is *falsafa*, 'philosophy'. Since the exponents of Arabic or Islamic philosophy at times had something of the character of a sect, I shall refer to them as the Falāsifa. This term will also help to express the fact that these men did not confine themselves to philosophy in the narrow modern sense, but were usually also experts in one or more of the sciences studied by the Greeks.

Through the great philosophers writing in Arabic, notably Avicenna or Ibn-Sīnā (d. 1037) and Averroes or Ibn-Rushd (d. 1198), Islamic civilization made a significant contribution to the development of philosophy in the Western world; and this might lead those unfamiliar with that civilization to suppose that the philosophical movement was a prominent part of the stream of Islamic thought. Yet this is far from being the case. The truth is rather that the Falāsifa were never part of the main stream but at most an unimportant side channel—that is, unimportant for the great majority of Muslims. Despite the separateness of the Falāsifa, however, the body of thought which they represented had a powerful influence on Islamic thought, especially at two points. It is this influence which in the present context is the centre of attention in looking at the earlier Falāsifa. Their work can be and has been studied from other standpoints, of course. It is important to know, for example, what precise elements of Greek thought were most influential and in what respects the Falāsifa showed originality. The only question to be considered here, however, is that of the relationship to the main stream of Islamic thought.

The first of the two points mentioned was the period dominated by ar-Rashīd and al-Ma'mūn when the Falāsifa or their predecessors, the translators, were disseminating Greek ideas among educated Muslims. As has already been explained, this was an important factor leading to the development of Kalām, and several Greek conceptions appeared in the thinking of the men described in the last section. If the first infusion of Greek conceptions is dated to the generation of Hishām ibn-al-Ḥakam and Ḍirār, together with the following generation, that of Abū-l-Hudhayl, then it becomes evident, from a study of theological writings, that no further Greek conceptions came into the main stream until the time of al-Ghazālī (d.1111). There may have been some minor additions by Mu'tazilites like al-Jubbā'ī and Abū-Hāshim round about 900, but nothing more. Speculative discussions among *mutakallimūn* up to 1100 continued to be concerned with the problems first raised about 800, except in so far as these had been extended by the development of Islamic theology or by fresh experiences within Islam (e.g. the appearance of a man like al-Ḥallāj). The second point at which the Falāsifa were influential was through al-Ghazālī and his disciples. Between the two periods the Greek tradition of science and philosophy was cultivated by men who were almost entirely cut off from the main stream of Sunnite thought.

One of the reasons for this separation of the Falāsifa from other religious thinkers (whether supporters or opponents of Kalām) was that the devout Muslim considered that all essential truth had been revealed by God. The most the devout thinker could do was to employ Greek conceptions and methods for the defence of revealed truth, and perhaps occasionally for its further explanation. He could not follow the argument wherever it leads. Consequently he looked on the Falāsifa with suspicion, for they were first and foremost believers in philosophy and science who then—but only in the second place—tried to reconcile revealed truth with philosophy.[124] This attitude was doubtless fostered by the deep-rooted Arab suspicion of everything non-Arab. The studies of the Falāsifa were always known as the 'foreign' sciences or disciplines in contrast to the Arabic and

Islamic sciences. To reduce the prejudice against Greek ideas it was claimed, among others by al-Kindī, that Yūnān, the supposed ancestor of the Greeks, was a brother of Qaḥṭān, the legendary forefather of the southern Arabs; but this claim was vigorously rejected by the more traditionally minded.[125]

Another reason for the separation of the Falāsifa was the form taken by education. Devout Muslims, because of the attitude just mentioned, were not prepared to attend the Christian colleges that existed in the lands they had conquered. To replace the higher learning of the Christians the Muslims gradually elaborated for themselves a whole series of intellectual disciplines. The method of propagating these disciplines was at first informal. An acknowledged scholar would take up a position beside a pillar in a mosque and would expound his speciality to the interested persons who gathered round him. As time passed this educational method became more formalized until by the eleventh century it produced the institution of the *madrasa*, a college of something like university status. Meanwhile the Christian colleges continued to teach the Greek sciences. Since medicine was one of these and was appreciated by the caliphs, we find that until 870 the ʿAbbāsids had a Christian as court physician. In some manner not altogether clear, however, a few Muslims (not of the most devout) began to gain some understanding of Greek science and philosophy. Among these were the translators, in so far as Muslim. Though after the time of al-Ma'mūn there was little contact between the *mutakallimūn* and the exponents of Greek thought, the latter were not completely cut off from intellectual circles in the Islamic world. They were usually welcome in the salons of the caliph and of provincial rulers, where they might meet poets and other writers. With Christian intellectuals too they often had good relationships because of their common interests.

It is convenient at this point to consider al-Kindī, designated (according to Ibn-an-Nadīm) *faylasūf al-ʿarab*, 'the philosopher of the Arabs', probably in the sense that he was the first outstanding scholar of the 'foreign sciences' among the Arabs and the Muslims generally.[126] Abū-Yūsuf Yaʿqūb ibn-Is'ḥāq al-Kindī was born about 800 in Kufa where his father was governor. It is known that he studied in Basra, but his teachers are nowhere mentioned. Later he was in Baghdad where he enjoyed the favour of the caliph al-Ma'mūn. Subsequently he became tutor to Aḥmad, the son of the caliph al-Muʿtaṣim (833–42). After the change of official policy about 849 al-Kindī was dismissed from the caliphal service. Through the machinations of rivals, the Banū-Mūsā,[127] al-Kindī's library was confiscated and given to them, but he eventually recovered it. He died about 868 (or shortly after 870).[128]

An annotated list of 270 works by al-Kindī is given by George Atiyeh, following mainly Ibn-an-Nadīm. This shows the wide range of his interests, for the fields touched on include philosophy, logic, ethics, mathematics, astronomy and meteorology. There are even one or two essays on medical points and on chemistry, as well as a critique of the alchemical theory of the transmutation of metals into gold. At the same time he was a believer in astrology and wrote a number of short treatises on particular points in it. In all this al-Kindī was essentially a popularizer who was making Greek learning available to readers of Arabic. He was by no means a slavish follower of other men, however, but shows various elements of originality. Richard Walzer sees al-Kindī as the first thinker to 'attempt to naturalize Greek philosophy in the Islamic world',[129] and this doubtless explains the attention paid to him by Ibn-an-Nadīm. He was perhaps the chief formative influence on the next generation of students of Greek thought, notably the philosopher and geographer as-Sarakhsī (d. 899)[130] and the astronomer Abū-Maʿshar (d. 886).[131]

There are many pointers to the conclusion that al-Kindī's outlook was close to that of the Muʿtazilites of his time. Since Muʿtazilite influence was prominent in the ruling circle from the time of al-Ma'mūn until the change of policy under al-Mutawakkil, the fact that al-Kindī was favoured by the caliphs and made tutor to al-Muʿtaṣim's son is an indication that his essential politico-religious position was not unlike that of the Muʿtazilites. Several of his works are dedicated to al-Muʿtaṣim or his son. Apart from these general considerations the titles of several of his books show that he was dealing with conceptions which were also dealt with by the Muʿtazilites; e.g. atom, *juz' lā yatajazza'* (Atiyeh, no. 186); essences of bodies, *jawāhir al-ajsām* (no. 187; cf. 193); nature or quiddity, *māhiyya* (or *mā'iyya*) (nos. 194, 197); power to act, *istiṭāʿa* (no. 181). He wrote about *tawḥīd*, the unity of God (nos. 185, 189), and had a controversy on this topic with Ibn-ar-Rāwandī (whose book was attacked by the Muʿtazilite al-Khayyāṭ in *Kitāb al-intiṣār*).

Still more significant are the views expressed in some of the extant works about the relationships between the revealed scripture and philosophy. He accepted revelation as a reality (cf. no. 179, *tathbīt ar-rusul*, affirmation of the messengers of God, *sc.* as recipients of revelation). In discussing the Qur'ānic verse (36.82), 'it is so with him that, if he wills a thing, he merely says to it "Be" and it is', al-Kindī insists that the speaking of the word is metaphorical and that the verse means 'he merely wills and what he wills comes into being along with his willing it'.[132] This is specially interesting because it shows al-Kindī agreeing with Bishr ibn-al-Muʿtamir, the Muʿtazilite of Baghdad, against Abū-l-Hudhayl; Bishr held that the willing was the creation of the thing whereas Abū-l-Hudhayl held that creation was willing and word (*inna l-khalq irāda wa-qawl*).[133] Al-Kindī also seems to have opposed Abū-l-Hudhayl in the latter's view that the created world comes to an end and to have agreed with other Muʿtazilites.[134]

It is clear from these facts that al-Kindī was at times moving in the same universe of discourse as the Mutakallimūn of his own and an earlier generation. His wide interests, however, led him far outside this universe of discourse where the Mutakallimūn were not prepared to follow him. Even the Muʿtazilites seem to have neglected him and never to have explicitly discussed his views, for there is no mention of him in the Muʿtazilite-based *Maqālāt* of al-Ashʿarī. On the other hand, the very full treatment of him by Ibn-an-Nadīm argues a degree of admiration for him. In contrast to this Ibn-an-Nadīm has a very inadequate account of the works of al-Fārābī, although he was writing about 988, nearly forty years after the death of al-Fārābī in 950. This is perhaps evidence for the growing separation of philosophy from the main stream of Islamic thought. Certainly the separation of the 'foreign sciences' from both Kalām and the more traditional religious thinking is a manifest fact after al-Kindī. There is nothing to suggest that even important philosophers like al-Fārābī and Muḥammad ibn-Zakariyyā' ar-Rāzī (d. 923 or 932) had any influence on their contemporaries or immediate successors. This is here taken to justify the exclusion of an account of these men from this study of the formative period of Islamic thought.

8

The Great Muʿtazilites

The school of rational and, in some senses, liberal theologians known collectively as the Muʿtazila attracted the attention of European scholars during the nineteenth century, because they seemed to be closer to the occidental outlook than the dominant Sunnite theology of later times. This interest was justified, though fuller study has made it clear that the Muʿtazila were less purely rational and less liberal than was originally supposed. It can now be seen that their contribution to the development of Islamic thought was of the highest importance, but the question must also be kept in mind why so many of their distinctive views were rejected by the main body of Sunnite Muslims.

1
The origins of Muʿtazilism
a) *Critique of the standard account*

The account of the origins of Muʿtazilism given by ash-Shahrastānī is widely accepted as the standard one, not least among occidental Islamists.[1] According to this account someone once asked al-Ḥasan al-Baṣrī whether they should regard the grave sinner as a believer or an unbeliever. While al-Ḥasan hesitated, Wāṣil ibn-ʿAṭāʾ, one of those in the circle, burst into the discussion with the assertion that the grave sinner was neither, but was in an intermediate position (*manzila bayn al-manzilatayn*) literally 'a position between the two positions'. He then withdrew to another pillar of the mosque, followed by a number of those in the circle, whereupon al-Ḥasan remarked 'Wāṣil has withdrawn (*iʿtazala*) from us.' From this remark came the name Muʿtazila.

There are many difficulties about this account, not least the existence of important variants. About a century before ash-Shahrastānī al-Baghdādī gave a version in which there were five different views about the grave sinner and Wāṣil's assertion was that he was in an intermediate position between unbelief and belief (*manzila bayn manzilatay al-kufr wa-l-īmān*).[2] There is no suggestion of a dramatic interruption, but al-Ḥasan expelled him and he 'withdrew' to another pillar, where he was joined by ʿAmr ibn-ʿUbayd. At this people said 'The two have withdrawn (*iʿtazalā*) from the view of the community.' This is still close to the standard account, though the decisive word is not spoken by al-Ḥasan and has a different application. As early as the ninth century al-Khayyāṭ has a somewhat similar version.[3] He is replying to the charge made by Ibn-ar-Rāwandī that Wāṣil by his doctrine of the intermediate position had departed from (*kharaja min*) the consensus of the community which had agreed that the grave sinner was either believer, unbeliever or 'hypocrite' (the last being the view of al-Ḥasan). In defence of Wāṣil al-Khayyāṭ insists that Wāṣil accepted the point on which the three groups were agreed, namely, that the grave sinner was 'wicked' (*fāsiq, fājir*), and avoided the matters on which they differed; and he gives arguments from the Qur'ān and Sunna for rejecting the other three views.

Other versions have a similar story, but the man who withdraws is not Wāṣil but ʿAmr ibn-ʿUbayd. About the same time as al-Khayyāṭ Ibn-Qutayba wrote of ʿAmr that 'he held the doctrine of Qadar and made propaganda for it; and he and his companions withdrew (*iʿtazala*) from al-Ḥasan and were called the Muʿtazila'.[4] In the following century Ibn-an-Nadīm told the story not of al-Ḥasan but of Qatāda : 'when al-Ḥasan died and Qatāda conducted his circle (*majlis*), ʿAmr together with a group withdrew from him, and Qatāda called them the Muʿtazila . . .'[5] What looks like an attempt to harmonize the two last versions is found in Ibn-Khallikān in the notice of Qatāda : ʿAmr and others withdrew from al-Ḥasan, but Qatāda, who was blind, went up to them and, on finding they were not al-Ḥasan's circle, made the remark from which the name was derived.[6] It is to be noted, however, that Ibn-Khallikān gives as his source Abū-ʿUbayda Maʿmar ibn-al-Muthannā (d. 824/9), a scholar of Basra, who had it from a distinguished philologist of the same city, Abū-ʿAmr ibn-al-ʿAlā' (d. 770/6). If these data are genuine, this would be the oldest account of all.

Besides these versions of the story of the name which place ʿAmr in the centre there are other reports which ascribe to him a position of leadership or suggest something of this sort. The most notable is the poem of Bishr ibn-al-Muʿtamir quoted by al-Khayyāṭ (and already mentioned in connection with Jahm), in which he says that Ḍirār and Ḥafṣ have Jahm for their imam and are quite distinct from the followers of ʿAmr.[7] If the standard account were correct, it is remarkable that Bishr should not mention Wāṣil as leader. Another fact is that, according to the index, there are only two references to the Muʿtazila in the whole of the *Ṭabaqāt* of Ibn-Saʿd, and one of these speaks of ʿAmr ibn-ʿUbayd as a Muʿtazilite,[8] whereas Wāṣil is not mentioned at all. Similarly Ibn-Qutayba (d. 889) has some information about ʿAmr and connects him with the Muʿtazila in one of his rare references to that sect, but has nothing about Wāṣil.[9] Even in the tenth century the Ḥanbalite Ibn-Baṭṭa (d. 997) in a list of heretical leaders mentions ʿAmr as well as several Muʿtazilites of the generation of Abū-l-Hudhayl, but never speaks of Wāṣil.[10]

The material so far examined shows a divergence of view on whether the leader was ʿAmr or Wāṣil. Yet other considerations, however, suggest that the originator of the sect in the form in which it became famous was neither of these men but Abū-l-Hudhayl and his generation. There is no evidence whatsoever that either Wāṣil or ʿAmr was at all versed in the Greek conceptions or methods of argument which were at the heart of the distinctive Muʿtazilite position. The only references to Wāṣil and ʿAmr in the *Maqālāt* of al-Ashʿarī are where they are said to hold a particular view about the verses of the Qur'ān called *muḥkamāt* and *mutashābihāt*; and where a minor poet says he dissociates himself from the Khārijites, especially the Ghazzāl and Ibn-Bāb (*sc.* Wāṣil and ʿAmr).[11] Even the Muʿtazilite al-Khayyāṭ has little more than this. The arguments for the intermediate position already mentioned may be from Wāṣil himself. He is also stated to have held that the resolve to kill a Companion of the Prophet is unbelief.[12] Two other statements about both Wāṣil and ʿAmr will be referred to presently—one about political attitudes and one historical. Together with Bishr's poem about ʿAmr, this is all al-Khayyāṭ has to tell us about the two men. Thus these early works by a Muʿtazilite and an ex-Muʿtazilite give no information to explain how either of the men could have been the initiator of a vigorous intellectual movement.

b) *A revised account*

The material so far considered yields the negative conclusion that the story of the giving of the name in all its forms is a later invention. The story is not for this reason valueless. Besides supporting a non-derogatory interpretation of the name, it indicates some connection with the disciples of al-Ḥasan al-Baṣrī. When the story is thus dismissed, the way is open to piece together the relatively certain items of information about the matter.

Most of the intellectual life of Basra in the early eighth century was centred in al-Ḥasan and his disciples. For a time after his death the scholars of his following remained on friendly terms with one another, even when their views diverged. The stories about ʿAmr-ibn-ʿUbayd mentioned above (108f.) show how he became the butt of attacks on Qadarite doctrine, but also indicate that the opposing groups still had some contact with one another. This state of affairs may have lasted forty years or longer after al-Ḥasan's death in 728, that is, until after the deaths of Wāṣil and ʿAmr in 748 and 761 respectively. If the term Muʿtazila was used at this period, the group to which it was applied was not sharply marked off from the rest of the scholars, as is shown by the fact that towards the end of the century Ḍirār could be called a Muʿtazilite. Nor could the five principles of Muʿtazilism have been formulated at this period except in a very embryonic way. The principle of *ʿadl*, '(God's) justice', was accepted in the form of the doctrine of Qadar. *Tawḥīd* was held in the sense of the assertion of the unity of God against Manichaean and other forms of dualism, but almost certainly not in the sense of asserting God's internal unity, since the discussion of attributes was probably not a serious question until the reign of al-Ma'mūn. The doctrine of the *manzila* was presumably held in some sense, and also the principle of 'the promise and the threat' (*al-waʿd wa-l-waʿīd*), or the insistence that God is bound to carry out his promises and threats of eternal reward and punishment. The fifth principle, *al-amr bi-l-maʿrūf wa-n-nahy ʿan al-munkar*, 'commanding the good and forbidding the evil', that is, joining in the use of force against injustice or participating in risings against unjust rulers, expresses an attitude which though frowned on by al-Ḥasan, had been commonly associated with Qadarism under the Umayyads. Its precise application doubtless varied from time to time, and men who agreed on the other four principles may well have disagreed on this. Thus at best the five

Mu'tazilite principles could have been held only in an elementary form, and those who held some of them did not necessarily hold all.

Wāṣil may well have been one of the scholars of Basra during his later life, but the information about him is scanty, and from this it is to be inferred that he was not so prominent as 'Amr, at least as a scholar. What is mentioned is that he was a distinguished orator and preacher, and that with great ingenuity he avoided words with the letter *r* so as to conceal the fact that he could not pronounce this letter properly. Most of the later reports about his theological views are to be received with suspicion and discounted. He doubtless held the Mu'tazilite principles in some such embryonic form as that just described, and was possibly the inventor of the phrase *al-manzila bayn al-manzilatayn*, and the elaborator of arguments for this conception along the lines given by al-Khayyāṭ. No early evidence, however, gives grounds for regarding him as acknowledged leader of a coterie of scholars in Basra. It is even doubtful if 'Amr was the submissive disciple of Wāṣil suggested by some stories; they are both said to have been born in 699, and among the books ascribed to Wāṣil is one on 'what came about between him and 'Amr ibn-'Ubayd'.[13] That Wāṣil was married to a sister of 'Amr shows no more than that the two men were acquainted.

The verse by an early poet, mentioned above, which speaks of Wāṣil and 'Amr as Khārijites has been noticed by various scholars from al-Baghdādī onwards, but has not received the attention it deserves.[14] It is worth quoting al-Baghdādī's comments:

> Wāṣil and 'Amr agreed with the Khawārij in holding that the punishment of the grave sinner in Hell was unending, although they also held that he was a *muwaḥḥid* (monotheist), not a *mushrik* nor a *kāfir* (polytheist, unbeliever); for this reason the Mu'tazila were called the effeminates (*makhānīth*) of the Khawārij, since the Khawārij, holding that sinners are eternally in Hell, call them unbelievers and fight them, whereas the Mu'tazila, holding that they are eternally in Hell, do not dare to call them unbelievers and do not dare to fight any sect of them, far less to fight all their opponents. For this reason Is'ḥāq ibn-Suwayd al-'Adawī assigned Wāṣil and 'Amr ibn-'Ubayd to the Khārijites, since they agreed with them in making the punishment of sinners eternal; and he said in one of his poems . . .

This passage shows that al-Baghdādī, far from denying the attribution of Wāṣil and ʿAmr to the Khārijites, tends to confirm it. Reflection shows too that the doctrine of the *manzila*, though from one standpoint a novelty, from another could be reckoned one of several attempts by the moderate Khārijites of Basra to justify their decision to live peacefully under a non-Khārijite ruler (as noted on p. 29 above). It would further appear that moderate Khārijites would not oppose any of the five Muʿtazilite principles in the embryonic form in which, it has been suggested, they were held by Wāṣil. In other words, while Wāṣil and ʿAmr had their distinctive position, it was not very different from that of several groups of moderate Khārijites, so that the two could easily be regarded as Khārijites. The difference between them and the Khārijites was probably not given prominence until, under Abū-l-Hudhayl, the Muʿtazila became leaders in the development of Kalām.

This kinship with Khārijism also helps to explain the verses about Wāṣil sending out emissaries. The verses and the corresponding list of names were a part of the basis of H. S. Nyberg's hypothesis that in the period before 750 the Muʿtazilites were propagandists for the ʿAbbāsids. The account given in this chapter of Wāṣil and ʿAmr and of the political attitudes of the earlier Muʿtazilites constitutes a strong reason for rejecting the hypothesis. With regard to the sending of emissaries it is to be noted that an Ibāḍite leader, Abū-ʿUbayda Muslim ibn-Abī-Karīma at-Tamīmī, who was active in Basra about the same time as Wāṣil or a little later, sent teams of emissaries to the Maghrib, the Yemen, Ḥaḍramawt, Oman and Khurasan. In the list of Wāṣil's emissaries (which is derived from Abū-l-Hudhayl) these are said to have gone to the Maghrib, Khurasan, the Yemen, the Jazīra (roughly northern Iraq and north-east Syria), Kufa and Armenia. It may then reasonably be supposed that both Ibāḍites and Wāṣilites preached what was primarily a religious message, though it came to have political implications. The verses just mentioned speak of Wāṣil's emissaries as zealous, devout men, skilled in oratory, and imply that their message was religious. A similarity between Wāṣilites and Ibāḍites is also made likely by the fact that for a time there was a group of Wāṣiliyya near Tahert (western Algeria), which was for a time the centre of an Ibāḍite state.

The conclusion to be drawn from all this is that in the lifetime of Wāṣil and ʿAmr there was no group of men called Muʿtazilites who even faintly resembled the Mu'tazilites of the caliphate of al-Ma'mūn. If they were called Mu'tazilites, the name had some pejorative sense and did not mean what it later came to mean. Further, though many of those who engaged in Kalām came to be called Mu'tazilites, Mu'tazilism even in its widest sense was never identical with the practice of Kalām or the use of Greek ideas. The basic change in the meaning of Mu'tazilite presumably came about when some of those to whom it had been given as a nickname found a good or neutral meaning for it and accepted it as applying to themselves. Next, doubtless after some time, this good meaning was more exactly defined by the enumeration of the five principles, and it was insisted that the only true Mu'tazilites were those who accepted all five principles. Yet another step was the claim that the founder of Mu'tazilism was Wāṣil. The most important evidence for these latter points is the passage where al-Khayyāṭ refutes the assumption of Ibn-ar-Rāwandī that Ḍirār and some men of similar views are Mu'tazilites.[15] Adherence to the five principles is clearly stated to be the criterion of Mu'tazilism. In the same passage, however, Bishr ibn-al-Mu'tamir is quoted speaking of himself as a follower of 'Amr, not Wāṣil, though elsewhere Ibn-ar-Rāwandī acknowledges Wāṣil as the 'root' (*aṣl*) of the Mu'tazila.[16] It seems unlikely that al-Khayyāṭ was the first to insist on the five principles as a criterion, but this insistence may not have occurred much before his time. On the other hand, it seems likely that Abū-l-Hudhayl may have claimed the link with Wāṣil, since he is the source of information about Wāṣil's emissaries.[17] Wāṣil may have been preferred because the attacks on him were less numerous and less virulent than those on 'Amr, or because his political attitude was considered more satisfactory.

c) *The meaning of the name*

If the standard story about the name is rejected as the primary account, various other possibilities are open. Ignaz Goldziher was firmly convinced that the beginnings of the movement were due to 'fromme, zum Teil weltflüchtige Leute, *mu'tazila*, d.h. sich Zurückziehende (Büsser)', or in other words solitary ascetics.[18] Goldziher was, of course, correct in holding that the word often referred to 'withdrawal' of an ascetic or monastic type and also that there had been a number of ascetics among the early Mu'tazilites; but this did not explain the political side of the movement nor the absence of any reference to asceticism among the five principles, while it is contrary to the strong probability that the original meaning was pejorative.

An effective critique of Goldziher was made by Carlo Nallino, and an alternative meaning suggested, namely, 'the signification of "neutral", of "not participating in either of the two contrary factions" (orthodox and Khārijite) in the serious politico-religious question of how to consider the *fāsiq*'.[19] There is ample evidence for this meaning of 'withdrawal' as 'remaining neutral, siding with neither party', but the idea of neutrality can be applied in different ways, and Nallino does not seem to have hit on the correct application. The original application is almost certainly that suggested in a passage of an-Nawbakhtī (which was not in print when Goldziher and Nallino wrote). According to an-Nawbakhtī there were after the death of ʿUthmān three parties; the first were the supporters of ʿAlī and the third his opponents, while the second was a party

> which withdrew (*iʿtazalat*) along with Saʿd ibn-Abī-Waqqāṣ, ʿAbd-Allāh ibn-ʿUmar, Muḥammad ibn-Maslama and Usāma ibn-Zayd; these withdrew from ʿAlī and held back from warring against him and warring with him after taking the oath of allegiance to him; they are called the *muʿtazila* and are the forerunners of the Muʿtazila to the end of time; they held that it is not lawful either to fight ʿAlī or to fight with him.[20]

This passage does not necessarily tell us anything about the use of the word *muʿtazila* in 656, since it is well known that the Shīʿites rewrote history in the light of later conditions. What this passage shows is that an-Nawbakhtī himself (and doubtless his immediate sources) regarded the Muʿtazila of the ninth century as in some sense neutral in respect of ʿAlī.

On this basis the view may be put forward with some confidence that the name of Muʿtazila was originally applied to those who were neutral in respect of ʿAlī, and that it was applied to them by proto-Shīʿites. This is in accordance with various other items of early material. Thus Ibn-ar-Rāwandī (*apud* al-Khayyāṭ) speaks of Ḍirār as a Muʿtazilite but not of the Rāfiḍite Hishām ibn-al-Ḥakam, though the two had a similar interest in Greek thought. When Ibn-Saʿd refers to ʿAmr ibn-ʿUbayd as a Muʿtazilite, this could be in respect of his refusal to decide whether ʿAlī or ʿUthmān was in the right. Again we find an-Nawbakhtī referring to ʿAmr, Ḍirār and Wāṣil (in that order) as 'roots' (*uṣūl*) of the Muʿtazila.[21]

Ibn-an-Nadīm, after stating that Qatāda called those who withdrew with 'Amr the Mu'tazila, gives a piece of information about 'Amr which may be authentic. 'Amr, he says, accepted the appellation and was pleased with it, remarking that 'withdrawal (*i'tizāl*) is a quality praised by God in his book'.[22] No passage from the Qur'ān is quoted, but the reference must be to the two passages where Abraham and the Men of the Cave withdrew from their opponents and from what they worship apart from God, and are then suitably rewarded.[23] It is likely that such a point was actually made, and it would be appropriate for men arguing against Manichaeans; but it did not catch on. The Mu'tazila certainly accepted the name, but they were content to give it the non-committal meaning of 'withdrawal' from the circle of al-Ḥasan or Qatāda. Mostly they were then content to regard 'Amr or Wāṣil as the founder of Mu'tazilism, but it is perhaps worth noting that Ibn-an-Nadīm quotes a report from Zurqān, an early historian of the Mu'tazila, to the effect that Abū-l-Hudhayl had told him that he had received 'the doctrine of justice and unity' (Mu'tazilism) from 'Uthmān aṭ-Ṭawīl and that the latter had told him that he had received it from Wāṣil who had had it from Abū-Hāshim ibn-Muḥammad ibn-al-Ḥanafiyya who had had it from his father Muḥammad ibn-al-Ḥanafiyya who had had it from 'Alī who had had it from the Messenger of God, to whom Gabriel had brought it from God.[24]

2

The schools of Basra and Baghdad

Whatever the precise facts may be about the period of gestation, it is clear that Mu'tazilism as an outstanding intellectual movement did not appear until about the reign of Hārūn ar-Rashīd. It was about this date that the schools of Basra and Baghdad took shape, under the leadership of Abū-l-Hudhayl and Bishr ibn-al-Mu'tamir respectively; and it was these men and others of their generation who made Mu'tazilism one of the great formative influences in the development of Islamic thought. The present section brings together most of the available biographical information about these men and their immediate successors, leaving the generation of al-Jubbā'ī and Abū-Hāshim to a later chapter.

a) *The school of Basra*

Pride of place must go to the Mu'tazilite school of Basra, whose roots can be traced at least to al-Ḥasan al-Baṣrī. One aspect of his teaching

The Muʿtazila : main lines of discipleship

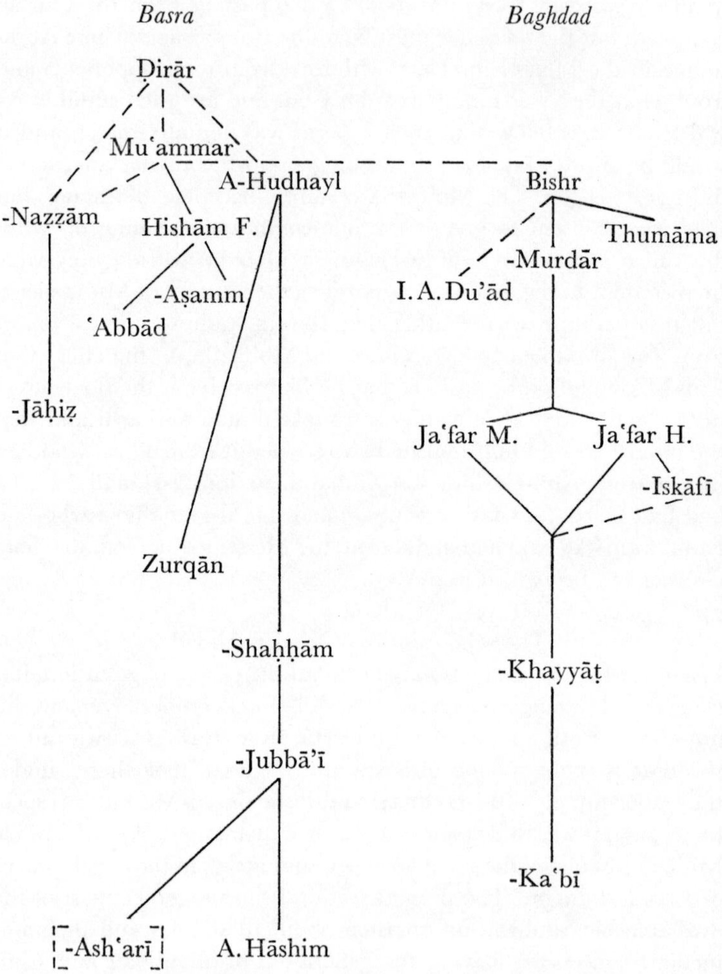

was kept alive by 'Amr ibn-'Ubayd and his associates. Then among the intellectuals of Basra there appeared the ferment of Greek ideas; and here, as described in the previous chapter, Ḍirār ibn-'Amr came to have the central place. Ḍirār was often called a Mu'tazilite, and might be entitled the chief 'professor of Kalām'; but Mu'tazilism proper (that is, as later understood) begins rather with his successor in this 'professorial chair', Abū-l-Hudhayl.

1) *Abu-l-Hudhayl.*[25] Abū-l-Hudhayl Muḥammad (or Ḥamdān) ibn-al-Hudhayl al-'Allāf al-'Abdī was born between 748 and 753 at Basra, and died at Baghdad between 840 and 850. He was a *mawlā* of the tribe of 'Abd-al-Qays. The death-date 842 has the early authority of al-Khayyāṭ (in ash-Shahrastānī); but it is also reported that he was infirm in his later years, and there is no evidence of any public activity after about 820. Most of his creative work was probably done before 800. None of his books have survived, but many of the titles are recorded, and from this it may be gathered that he argued against Magians and Dualists as well as against Jews and Christians. Several authors repeat the story of how he triumphed verbally over the *zindīq* Ṣāliḥ ibn-'Abd-al-Quddūs who was executed in 783. There is also a report of an argument with Hishām ibn-al-Ḥakam, and both men were present at the discussion on love in the salon of Yaḥyā the Barmakid.[26] This discussion must have taken place on a short visit to Baghdad, but he settled there permanently about 818 and was presented to al-Ma'mūn by Thumāma.

2) *An-Naẓẓām.*[27] Abū-Is'ḥāq Ibrāhīm ibn-Sayyār an-Naẓẓām was born and educated in Basra, but died in 836 (or 845) in Baghdad where he had been summoned by al-Ma'mūn about 818. He was probably a little younger than Abū-l-Hudhayl, whose disciple he is sometimes said to have been. He had studied under the great philologist Khalīl ibn-Aḥmad (d. 776/91) and been praised for his command of Arabic. Another philologist, Quṭrub (d. 821), had been his pupil, presumably in Kalām; and since Quṭrub was for a time the tutor of al-Amīn (b. 787; caliph 809–13), an-Naẓẓām must have been old enough to teach not later than 795 and so born about 760 or 765.[28] A similar date is to be inferred from the fact that he took part in Yaḥyā the Barmakid's discussion on love. He was more interested than Abū-l-Hudhayl in the scientific side of Greek philosophy, and in this seems to have been influenced by Hishām ibn-al-Ḥakam, whose lectures he is said to have attended. He probably also studied

with Ḍirār, but disagreed rather more with him. Among his books is one about his disagreement with Abū-l-Hudhay; others are against materialism (the Dahriyya) and dualism. His distinguished pupil al-Jāḥiẓ frequently refers to him.

3) *Muʿammar.*[29] Little is known about Muʿammar ibn-ʿAbbād as-Sulamī, and there are uncertainties about his full name.[30] He appears to have been born in Basra as a *mawlā* of the tribe of Sulaym. He is said to have died in 830, but he must have been very old, since he is also said to have been the teacher of Bishr ibn-al-Muʿtamir and Hishām al-Fuwaṭī, and was sufficiently prominent at an early date for Ḍirār to have written a refutation of his views. The story (in the *Munya*) that he was sent by ar-Rashīd to an Indian king to argue against his scholars seems to be legendary, but he met Indian physicians brought to Baghdad by the Barmakids and at some date (perhaps after the fall of the Barmakids) was imprisoned by ar-Rashīd. He is also said to have fled from Basra on being delated by other Muʿtazilites and to have died in Baghdad in hiding.

4) *Al-Aṣamm.* Not much has been recorded of the life of Abū-Bakr ʿAbd-ar-Raḥmān ibn-Kaysān. He is sometimes said to have died in 850, but the date 816/8 given by Ibn-an-Nadīm seems more likely in view of the fact that he had argued with Hishām ibn-al-Ḥakam.[31] The date also makes it doubtful whether he was a pupil of Hishām al-Fuwaṭī (as is stated by ash-Shahrastānī), but similarity in the problems discussed and in the forms of expression shows there was some connection between the two men, even if Hishām wrote a book refuting him.[32] Another argument for an early date is the fact that an-Naẓẓām commended to al-Jāḥiẓ his Qur'ān-commentary.[33]

5) *Hishām al-Fuwaṭī.*[34] Again little is known about the life of Hishām ibn-ʿAmr al-Fuwaṭī ash-Shaybānī; *fuwaṭī* is said to mean the seller of the garments called *fuwaṭ*.[35] He is sometimes said to have been a pupil of Abū-l-Hudhayl, sometimes of an-Naẓẓām; but he certainly wrote a book against Abū-l-Hudhayl. He eventually went to Baghdad and was accepted at court by al-Ma'mūn. He is thought to have died before 833. He had a pupil ʿAbbād ibn-Sulaymān (or Salmān) aṣ-Ṣaymarī, who argued with Ibn-Kullāb, and against whom Abū-Hāshim wrote a book.[36] There are full reports of his distinctive views.

6) *Al-Jāḥiẓ.*[37] Though his contributions to Muʿtazilism form a minor part of his literary output, brief mention must be made here

of Abū-ʿUthmān ʿAmr ibn-Baḥr, known as al-Jāḥiẓ, 'the goggle-eyed', who was born about 776 and died at the age of over ninety in December 869. He was of negro, probably Abyssinian, descent, but by his remarkable talents became 'the most genial writer of the age, if not of Arabic literature altogether'.[38] In contrast to the men just mentioned there is plentiful material about his life, while many volumes of his works have been preserved. He studied Arabic philology and poetry under the leading teachers in Basra, and was admitted to the Muʿtazilite discussions of Kalām, being regarded as a follower of an-Naẓẓām primarily. Though some of his writings were favourably noticed by al-Ma'mūn about 815, and though he was acquainted with some of the leading men in public life, he never had a permanent court appointment, but seems to have gained a livelihood from his writings. For a time he was attached to the vizier Ibn-az-Zayyāt (up to his fall in 847), and then for a few years he was patronized by the chief *qāḍī*, Aḥmad ibn-Abī-Du'ād and the latter's son Muḥammad. Though al-Baghdādī and ash-Shahrastānī make him the head of a separate sub-sect of the Muʿtazila, it was chiefly in the religio-political field that he had distinctive views.

7) *Ash-Shaḥḥām.*[39] Abū-Yaʿqūb Yūsuf ibn-ʿAbd-Allāh ash-Shaḥḥām was the youngest of the pupils of Abū-l-Hudhayl, and is also said to have been influenced by Muʿammar. He was given an official post by Ibn-Abī-Du'ād under the caliph al-Wāthiq. After the death of Abū-l-Hudhayl he came to be recognized as the head of the Muʿtazilite school in Basra, in which position he was succeeded by his pupil al-Jubbā'ī. No dates are mentioned for him, but if the report that he reached the age of eighty is correct, he must have lived from about 800 to 880. He is also said to have been accused of *zandaqa* during the regency of al-Muwaffaq (870–91).

b) *The school of Baghdad*

The distinctive feature of the Muʿtazilite school of Baghdad is that for most of the reign of al-Ma'mūn and for the whole of the reigns of his two successors, al-Wāthiq and al-Muʿtaṣim, the caliphs and their leading officials were men of Muʿtazilite sympathies, so that Muʿtazilism was an important factor in the determining of imperial policy. The clearest example of this is the policy of the Inquisition about the createdness of the Qur'ān. Shortly after al-Mutawakkil became caliph the Muʿtazilites lost their influence and never regained it.

1) *Bishr ibn-al-Muʿtamir.*[40] The founder of the school of Baghdad was Abū-Sahl Bishr ibn-al-Muʿtamir al-Hilālī. He was probably born in Kufa, but his parents must have moved to Baghdad soon after its foundation when he was still a child. The source of his Muʿtazilism is not clear, but he may have studied at Basra under Muʿammar. Among the men of whom he wrote refutations in verse—with whose works he must have been familiar—were Abū-l-Hudhayl, an-Naẓẓām, Ḍirār, Ḥafṣ al-Fard, Hishām ibn-al-Ḥakam, al-Aṣamm and the followers of Abū-Ḥanīfa. He first appears as a participant in the Barmakid symposium on love, along with Hishām ibn-al-Ḥakam, Abū-l-Hudhayl, an-Naẓẓām and others. It was presumably after the fall of the Barmakids that he was imprisoned by ar-Rashīd for alleged Rāfiḍite sympathies. It is doubtful if he was ever a Rāfiḍite in any strict sense, but he certainly took a favourable view of ʿAlī. It is therefore not surprising that he quickly found favour with al-Ma'mūn and in 817 appears at Merv among the signatories of the document declaring ʿAlī ar-Riḍā heir to the caliphate.[41] He presumably returned to Baghdad with al-Ma'mūn and spent his remaining years there, respected for his devout and ascetic manner of life.

2) *Thumāma.*[42] Abū-Maʿn Thumāma ibn-Ashras an-Numayrī is reckoned a disciple of Bishr ibn-al-Muʿtamir and is placed in the following *ṭabaqa* by Ibn-al-Murtaḍā; but he was probably very little younger than Bishr, for he took part along with him and others in the Barmakid symposium. He probably had most political power of all the Muʿtazilites. He apparently twice refused the vizierate from al-Ma'mūn, while continuing to have considerable influence over the caliph.[43] He is said to have deliberately sought the favour of ar-Rashīd and for a time he gained it; but he was also an admirer of Jaʿfar the Barmakid, and about the time of the fall of the Barmakids was imprisoned for an alleged criticism of the caliph.[44] He is next found in the court of al-Ma'mūn at Merv as a signatory of the same document as Bishr; and it was he who introduced Abū-l-Hudhayl to the caliph.[45] He was a master of witty argument which made his opponent look foolish, and he is quoted as the source of a number of good court stories.[46] His theological views, on the other hand, do not seem to deserve the attention given them by al-Baghdādī and ash-Shahrastānī. His date of death is most probably 828.

3) *Ibn-Abī-Du'ād.*[47] Abū-ʿAbd-Allāh Aḥmad ibn-Abī-Du'ād al-

Iyādī (b. 776, d. 854) was also primarily a political figure. He was greatly honoured at the court of al-Ma'mūn, and was appointed chief *qāḍī* by al-Mu'taṣim shortly after his accession in 833. In this post, which he retained until 851, he was responsible for the conduct of the Inquisition. His influence with the caliph was as great as that of the vizier, and he used it, among other things, to save men arbitrarily condemned to death. His dismissal in 851 was presumably linked with the change of policy which took place about that time.

4) *Al-Murdār.*[48] Abū-Mūsā 'Īsā ibn-Ṣubayḥ al-Murdār (d. 840) was a pupil of Bishr ibn-al-Mu'tamir. His views differed only slightly from those of Bishr and others of the school of Baghdad. Because of his asceticism he was called 'the monk of the Mu'tazila'. He tended to call those who differed from him infidels, and it was suggested teasingly to him that only he and three of his friends would be found in heaven. He wrote a book criticizing Abū-l-Hudhayl, but it is also said that on one occasion Abū-l-Hudhayl was present at his *majlis* and remarked that he had experienced nothing like it since as a youth he attended the *majlis* of their old shaykhs, the disciples of Wāṣil and 'Amr.

5) *Ja'far ibn-Ḥarb.*[49] Abū-l-Faḍl Ja'far ibn-Ḥarb (d. 850) came under the influence of al-Murdār and followed him in asceticism to the extent of giving away all his possessions. He is also said to have studied under Abū-l-Hudhayl and an-Naẓẓām, though it is not clear how this is to be interpreted, since he is critical of some of the views of an-Naẓẓām, and, if he was not born until 793 (as is stated by Sezgin), may not have met Abū-l-Hudhayl until the latter came to Baghdad about 818. He was at the court of al-Wāthiq but was persuaded to leave by Ibn-Abī-Du'ād who was afraid he might anger the caliph.

6) *Ja'far ibn-Mubashshir.*[50] Abū-Muḥammad Ja'far ibn-Mubashshir ath-Thaqafī al-Qaṣabī (d. 848) was similar in many ways to Ja'far ibn-Ḥarb, and the knowledge and asceticism of the Ja'farān ('the two Ja'fars') became proverbial. Their asceticism led them to refuse all gifts of money from the caliph and also appointments as *qāḍī*. Ja'far ibn-Mubashshir is credited with converting the people of 'Ānāt on the Euphrates from Zaydism to Mu'tazilism; but the interpretation of this fact will be further considered in the next section.[51] He was a pupil of al-Murdār and also influenced by an-Naẓẓām.

7) *Al-Iskāfī.*[52] A near-contemporary of the two Jaʿfars, often mentioned along with them, was Abū-Jaʿfar Muḥammad ibn-ʿAbd-Allāh al-Iskāfī (d. 854/5). He was a tailor and his family opposed his spending time in study, until Jaʿfar ibn-Ḥarb came to his rescue. He was admired by al-Muʿtaṣim.

The men of whom brief notes have just been given are the chief members of the Muʿtazila during its great creative period. The heresiographers al-Baghdādī and ash-Shahrastānī make most of them heads of sub-sects, but this is no more than a method of exposition and a device for reaching the number of seventy-two heretical sects (as explained in the Introduction). These sub-sects were never distinct groupings recognized by contemporaries, as may be seen, for example, from the book of al-Khayyāṭ. Geography made a certain separation between the schools of Basra and Baghdad, but even between these there was much coming and going. The sensible course is therefore to speak of these Muʿtazilite thinkers primarily as individuals. The table on p. 218 attempts to show the main lines of discipleship and influence.

3
Political attitudes

The relevance to contemporary politics of statements about ʿAlī, ʿUthmān and other early Muslims has already been discussed in a general way, but there is still room for an account of the views of individual Muʿtazilites, about whom we are relatively well informed. Most of the material has been easily accessible for forty years or more—some for much longer—but the recent publication of two works of an-Nāshiʾ al-Akbar has provided some useful additions.[53] A word about this author and his work will therefore not be out of place here.

Abū-l-ʿAbbās ʿAbd-Allāh ibn-Muḥammad al-Anbārī, sometimes called Ibn-Shirshīr, but best known as an-Nāshiʾ al-Akbar, died in 906 in Egypt whither he had gone, perhaps about 892, but he spent most of the earlier part of his life in Baghdad. The date of his birth is not known, but was presumably between about 830 and 845. He was educated as a 'secretary' and knew something of the Greek disciplines, though latterly he was critical of them. He shared in general the views of the Muʿtazilites of Baghdad, and is reckoned as one, but he had an eclectic tendency of which the others were critical.[54]

The first of the two works edited by Josef van Ess is the section on the imamate of a book which was probably entitled *Kitāb uṣūl an-niḥal*, 'the principles of the sects'. One curious fact noted by the editor is that among the Mu'tazilites no one is specifically mentioned who belongs to any generation later than that of Abū-l-Hudhayl (as reckoned by Ibn-al-Murtaḍā). Similarly, in his account of the Shī'ites, he mentions the imamate of 'Alī ar-Riḍā, but has not a word of the disputes which occurred after his death. On the other hand, among those he calls Ḥashwiyya he has references to Aḥmad ibn-Ḥanbal (d. 855) and al-Karābīsī (d. 862). Van Ess seems to be justified in holding that an-Nāshi' was using sources belonging to an earlier date than the period at which he was writing. It is interesting, however, to compare what an-Nāshi' says about the Mu'tazilites with the account of their 'political attitudes' given by al-Ash'arī in the *Maqālāt* (451–67). Al-Ash'arī is mostly dealing with the same names. The only Mu'tazilites of later date whom he mentions are 'Abbād, al-Jubbā'ī and Ibn-'Ulayya (a pupil of al-Aṣamm), all from the school of Basra. It is noteworthy that at one point he ascribes to 'Abbād, the pupil, a view which an-Nāshi' ascribes to Hishām al-Fuwaṭī, the teacher.[55] In neither is anything said about the political views of the school of Baghdad after Bishr ibn-al-Mu'tamir (and al-Murdār).[56] The simple explanation may be that the basic positions did not change, though there were many different arguments in support of them, such as those of al-Iskāfī against the 'Uthmānites.[57]

Whatever the explanation of the curious features in this book of an-Nāshi', it would seem that it contains early material of considerable importance.

a) *Individual thinkers*

The views of the schools of Basra and Baghdad were largely determined by those of Abū-l-Hudhayl and Bishr ibn-al-Mu'tamir respectively. Other men like an-Naẓẓām, Mu'ammar and al-Murdār are occasionally mentioned, but their variants are slight. Even al-Jāḥiẓ, about whose political views the material is plentiful,[58] is not greatly different from Abū-l-Hudhayl. The one man with a really distinctive view is al-Aṣamm. The exposition here will therefore be based on a study of his views and those of the founders of the two schools.

1) *Abū-l-Hudhayl*. Abū-l-Hudhayl was an opponent of Rāfiḍites such

as Hishām ibn-al-Ḥakam, who held that the imamate was conferred by designation (*naṣṣ*). The contrary view is commonly said to be that the imamate is conferred by the choice of the people (*ikhtiyār min al-umma*).[59] Those who take the latter view, especially among the Muʿtazilites, are divided by an-Nāshi' into those who hold that the choice should always fall on the best man (*afḍal*) and those who hold that an inferior (*mafḍūl*) may sometimes be chosen. The two views are described as *imāmat al-fāḍil* and *imāmat al mafḍūl*. To some extent this may be a schematization by an-Nāshi', but it corresponds to what is known otherwise. In accordance with this view Abū-l-Hudhayl is said to have regarded Abū-Bakr as *afḍal* in his time, and likewise ʿUmar, and also ʿUthmān during the first six years of his rule, while ʿAlī was *afḍal* at least at the date of his coming to power. These views were not peculiar to Abū-l-Hudhayl but seem to have been widely held in Basra; an-Naẓẓām shared them and also Abū-l-Hudhayl's precursor Ḍirār and his close associate Ḥafṣ.[60]

On the other hand, Abū-l-Hudhayl deliberately left certain questions undecided; he refused to say whether ʿUthmān was right or wrong during the last six years and whether ʿAlī or his opponents were in the right at the battle of the Camel.[61] This attitude of indecision was also widely adopted in Basra, but there were some divergences of view about the practical consequences. According to an-Nāshi' it had been inferred by Wāṣil and ʿAmr ibn-ʿUbayd that, since one did not know which party was right, but only that one was wrong, one might associate with each separately but not with both together; Ḍirār and Ḥafṣ, however, had preferred to hold aloof from the matter, associating with neither and dissociating from neither.[62] This does not altogether tally with the statement of al-Ashʿarī about Ḍirār, Abū-l-Hudhayl and Muʿammar; but the discrepancy does not greatly alter the general picture. There was a tendency in Basra to sit on the fence and avoid decisions, and it will be considered presently whether this was regarded as being implied by the adoption of the 'intermediate position'.

2) *Al-Aṣamm.* Various points have been reported about al-Aṣamm which it is difficult to fit into a consistent picture. Thus when al-Aṣhʿarī says that the rightness or wrongness of ʿAlī, Ṭalḥa and Muʿāwiya depended on their ultimate aim in fighting, this seems less definite than the statements of an-Nāshi'.[63] From al-Ashʿarī onwards al-Aṣamm becomes noted for the view that it is not necessary

to have an imam;[64] but an-Nāshi' does not mention him among those who denied the obligation to have an imam, though he speaks of him asserting that in turbulent times it is impossible in practice for anyone to function as an imam and that there may in fact be several imams.[65] The non-obligatory character of the imamate would thus seem to be an inference from some statement of al-Aṣamm and not something on which he vehemently insisted.

He is certainly one of the *as'ḥāb al-ikhtiyār*, and his views are close to those of the other Mu'tazilites of Basra. Like these he held that Abū-Bakr and 'Umar were *afḍal* when they became caliph, and likewise 'Uthmān, except that he said that on 'Umar's death 'Abd-ar-Raḥmān ibn-'Awf was *afḍal* but renounced the caliphate, and 'Uthmān was next in merit. On the other hand, al-Aṣamm was a more extreme opponent of the Rāfiḍites since he held that 'Alī was never imam. According to an-Nāshi' his reason was that there was no *shūrā* or council; but according to al-Ash'arī it was because there was no consensus about him, presumably of the Muslims as a whole.[66] An-Nāshi' classifies al-Aṣamm as holding 'the imamate of the *mafḍūl*', but this is an example of how the heresiographers' passion for logical classification leads them to obscure historical connections. All the other holders of 'the imamate of the *mafḍūl*'—chiefly the Mu'tazilites of Baghdad and some Zaydites—believed that 'Alī was *afḍal* when Abū-Bakr became caliph; but al-Aṣamm, like the Mu'tazilites of Baṣra, thought Abū-Bakr was *afḍal*. The reason for his being thus classified by an-Nāshi' was that he had somewhere said that a man's *faḍl* or 'merit' may vary from time to time, either increasing or decreasing, so that a man who was *afḍal* when chosen imam may decrease in *faḍl* and another increase, with the result that the imam is no longer *afḍal* but *mafḍūl*; in such circumstances, said al-Aṣamm, it would be wrong to change the imam, and so one is left with an imam who is in fact *mafḍūl*. Finally, in accordance with his denial of the imamate of 'Alī, he asserted that Mu'āwiya was right in all his dealings with 'Alī.[67]

3) *Bishr ibn-al-Mu'tamir*. As has just been noted, Bishr and the Mu'tazilites of Baghdad held 'the imamate of the *mafḍūl*' in the sense that, while considering 'Alī *afḍal* in 632, they nevertheless regarded Abū-Bakr as rightful imam, despite his being *mafḍūl*. They thus differed from the Rāfiḍites, for whom Abū-Bakr was never imam at all. They further held that the appointment of a *mafḍūl* as imam was

justified by some ground (*'illa*); and there appear to have been complicated discussions about the type of ground which might justify such an appointment. The preference of Bishr for 'Alī was also shown by his dissociating from 'Uthmān in the last six years, for this implied that those who killed 'Uthmān were justified and that 'Alī was right in not proceeding against them. Similarly 'Alī was in the right against Ṭalḥa and his party.[68] The emphasis laid by Bishr on the excellence or merit of the imam is perhaps to be balanced, if al-Ash'arī's report is correct, by his assertion that the two arbiters were wrong because they did not judge according to the Book. Not all the Mu'tazilites of Baghdad showed such a marked preference for 'Alī; some seem to have left undecided the question whether Abū-Bakr or 'Alī was *afḍal*.[69]

Of the three individual views described that of al-Aṣamm is most extreme in its opposition to 'Alī, and is doubtless linked with the cult of Mu'āwiya.[70] The other two views may be regarded as two attempts at compromise and reconciliation, aimed at creating as wide a unity as possible among the Muslims. One of the notable features of Abū-l-Hudhayl's view is that he leaves many questions undecided, and this looks like a policy of reducing tension within the community by removing minor causes of friction. The general idea is not dissimilar to that of the Murji'ites, but the application is different. Bishr, on the other hand, seems to have aimed at reconciliation by giving a measure of satisfaction to both sides. Thus he agreed with the Rāfiḍites in acknowledging 'Alī's merit and excellence, but joined their opponents in denying his charismatic qualities; and in his critique of the arbiters he seems to be siding with those who wanted the community to be based on inspired texts. In general the views ascribed to Bishr are close to those implicit in the policies of al-Ma'mūn, such as his designation of 'Alī ar-Riḍā as heir. This is not surprising since his disciples Thumāma and Ibn-Abī-Du'ād were in positions of power and had the ear of the caliph. As was indicated in chapter 6 (3, c), the reasons for the designation of 'Alī ar-Riḍā were similar to those for the institution of the Miḥna; but the doctrine of the createdness of the Qur'ān, though it was relevant to politics, will in this chapter be treated primarily from a theological standpoint.

b) *The three minor principles*

As has been mentioned several times, the name Mu'tazilite was eventually restricted to those who accepted 'the five principles'. These principles are mostly referred to briefly as (1) *tawḥīd*, 'unity'; (2) *'adl*, 'justice'; (3) *al-wa'd wa-l-wa'īd*, 'the promise and the threat'; (4) *al-asmā' wa-l-aḥkām*, 'names and judgements', or *al-manzila bayn al-manzilatayn*, 'the intermediate position'; (5) *al-amr bi-l-ma'rūf wa-n-nahy 'an al-munkar*, 'commanding the right and forbidding the wrong'.[71] The *Maqālāt* of al-Ash'arī makes it clear that most of the discussions in the ninth century were of matters arising out of the first two principles; and these will be dealt with in the following sections. The third principle, though mainly ethical, may be conveniently considered here along with the last two, which have important political implications. The last three are probably historically earlier.

1) *The promise and the threat.* Al-Mas'ūdī expands the third principle slightly: it means that 'God does not forgive the grave sinner except after repentance, and is truthful in his promise and his threat, not changing his words'. This principle expresses the moral earnestness which the Mu'tazilites had inherited from al-Ḥasan al-Baṣrī, and also expresses their opposition to the apparent moral laxity of the Murji'ites. The basic point was that where God in the Qur'ān had promised reward or threatened punishment, he was bound to carry this out. They tended to hold that the punishment of grave sinners was known by reason to be obligatory, and to insist that God must treat alike everyone in the same position. They all held that, once a man had been placed in hell, he would remain there eternally; in this they were implicitly denying the possibility of the sinner of the community being ultimately transferred from hell to paradise at the intercession of the Messenger.[72] The moral earnestness underlying these views is the presupposition of the political attitudes implicit in the other two principles.

2) *The intermediate position.* The story of Wāṣil or 'Amr declaring that the grave sinner was in an intermediate position and then withdrawing from al-Ḥasan's circle is probably apocryphal, but it may nevertheless express the relation of the political attitude of men like Wāṣil and 'Amir to the attitude of the Khārijites and the Murji'ites. It was impracticable to follow the strict Khārijite doctrine and expel from the community or execute every grave sinner, but to treat him as a believer, as the Murji'ites did, seemed to encourage moral laxity. It is difficult to see, however, how the doctrine of the intermediate position led to a different treatment of contemporary criminals from

that of the Murji'ites; the criminals were still punished. On the other hand, when it is remembered that in the Umayyad period—and Wāṣil and ʿAmr flourished under Umayyad rule—Khārijism and Murji'ism implied political attitudes, then the intermediate position may also be expected to lead to a political attitude. Roughly speaking, to hold that ʿUthmān was a grave sinner and so an unbeliever led to active opposition to the Umayyads, whereas to hold that the question of his status as believer was 'postponed' led to support of the Umayyads or at least acquiescence in their rule. It is likely, then, that the doctrine of the intermediate position was from the first applied to ʿUthmān and to the events immediately following his death.

These general considerations are confirmed by the few facts available. It is reported of Wāṣil that he refused to decide whether ʿAlī or his opponents were in the right at the battle of the Camel.[73] ʿAmr is sometimes said to have held the same view, sometimes a slightly different one; and it has been seen that Abū-l-Hudhayl left this and the question of ʿUthmān undecided. It appears that there is thus a close connection between the doctrine of the intermediate position and the device of leaving certain questions undecided. To say you do not know whether ʿUthmān was right or wrong in his last six years is to say you do not know whether he was a believer or an unbeliever, and this leads to the same practical attitude as saying he is in an intermediate position—you neither wholly identify yourself with him (and what he stands for) nor do you wholly dissociate yourself from him. The underlying aim is that Muslims should in some sense accept the whole past history of the Islamic state, and so avoid the situation in which some people identify themselves with one strand in it and others with another. It was a form of political compromise, but it was too negative to be satisfactory. It is not far removed in practice from the Murji'ite position, and it is not surprising that Ibn-al-Murtaḍā includes in his list of Muʿtazila some men who had leanings towards *irjā'*.[74]

The alternative name for this principle, rendered 'names and judgements', needs little explanation. The chief question at issue is whether a man is to have the 'name' of believer, unbeliever or wrongdoer (*fāsiq*). There is no good English translation for *aḥkām*, rendered 'judgements'. It means roughly the legal consequences of the judgement about the 'name'. 'Status' comes near to the meaning, but unfortunately cannot be used in the plural.[75]

3) *Commanding the right and forbidding the wrong.* This principle raises the question how far it is a duty to see that other people do what is right and do not do what is wrong. The general view of the Mu'tazila (and of others) was, as al-Ash'arī expressed it, 'that it is an obligation to command the right and forbid the wrong, where there is opportunity and ability, by tongue, hand and sword, as one may be able'.[76] To hold this principle, then, is to hold that armed revolt against an unjust ruler is justified where there is a chance of success. Moral exhortation is also a duty, at least where it is not likely to have an adverse effect. On the other hand, the principle may be said to imply that it is a duty to support a ruler who in fact commands right and forbids wrong; and this would presumably be taken to include support of the 'Abbāsids.

4

The principle of 'justice'

The principle of 'justice' (*'adl*), as one of the five Mu'tazilite principles, covers other matters but comes to stand primarily for the doctrine of Qadar or free will, because God would be unjust if he punished men for acts for which they were not responsible. The term Ahl al-'Adl or 'Adliyya is connected with this principle. In *Kitāb al-intiṣār* Ibn-ar-Rāwandī is quoted as saying that the Sakaniyya (Sakkākiyya ?), who hold Hishām ibn-al-Ḥakam's view of God's knowledge, are Mu'tazila because they are 'Adliyya; and it is in reply to this that al-Khayyāṭ insists that only those who hold all five principles are Mu'tazilites, the implication apparently being that the Sakaniyya hold *tashbīh* (anthropomorphism) instead of *tawḥīd* (unity).[77] At another point al-Khayyāṭ says that one of the Ahl at-Tawḥīd is either a *mujbir* or an *'adlī*;[78] he here mentions their divergent views about the purpose of creation, but these seem to be derivatives from the general positions of the Mujbira and Qadarites. An-Nāshi' al-Akbar's use of 'Adliyya seems to be, as van Ess suggests, for a subdivision of the Mu'tazila;[79] but since an-Nāshi' uses Mu'tazila in a wide sense, his 'Adliyya could in fact be the Mu'tazila in the restricted sense of al-Khayyāṭ. In later works 'Adliyya is occasionally found and is mainly used of the Mu'tazila by non-Mu'tazilites.[80] Before considering Mu'tazilite statements specifically about God's justice, it will be convenient to note certain other matters connected with this principle.

a) *The reinterpretation of predestinarian conceptions*

Nineteenth-century occidental scholars were attracted by the Muʿtazilites because their views seemed to be close to those of contemporary liberalism. For one thing they believed in free will, and for another they seemed to place reason above revelation. Had Muʿtazilite ideas become dominant in the Islamic world, the cleavage between Muslims and Christians might have been far less, it was felt. In the twentieth century, however, much more material became available and the results of further studies were published; and this led to a change of attitude. As H. S. Nyberg expressed it in 1929:

> Where previously one saw enlightened philosophers, who from disinterested love of truth spun out their paradoxes and built great systems, we have now to set theologians, forced of necessity to tackle the great spiritual problems of their time by the simple fact that, if they were to affirm their Islam in face of the environment, they could not pass them by; in brief, we have to do with strictly theologically-minded and practically active theologians and missionaries.[81]

In particular it has to be realized that the Muʿtazilites lived in an environment dominated by ideas such as those expressed in the predestinarian Traditions (chapter 4, 3c) and in the summary of the views of an-Najjār (pp. 199–201). This meant that there could be no question of simply rejecting or neglecting these ideas; a positive attitude had to be adopted, that is to say, the ideas had to be reinterpreted in a libertarian sense, at least wherever that seemed possible. One such idea was that of the *ajal* or predetermined term of a man's life. The problem was discussed of the man who was murdered. Some of the less intelligent Muʿtazilites wanted to say that this man's term was the date at which God knew he would have died if he had not been murdered; but the majority realized that this was unsatisfactory and held that, in whatever way a man died, he died at his term as previously known to God. Abū-l-Hudhayl, somewhat surprisingly, was so impressed by the inevitability of the date that he said of the murdered man that, if he had not been murdered on that date, he would have died in some other way.[82] That such a man should accept the conception of *ajal* in this way shows how deep-rooted it was; besides being part of the heritage from pre-Islamic Arabia it was supported by the Qur'ān. In respect of the *ajal* the view of an opponent like an-Najjār (p. 201, §15) seems very similar to that of the majority of the Mu'tazilites; but the Mu'tazilites' reference to God's knowledge removed the sheer determinism, since they interpreted it as knowledge of what men by their own activity would in fact do. Although God knew a man would not believe, he still made him able to believe.[83]

In respect of the associated conception of *rizq* or 'sustenance' the Mu'tazilites were chiefly concerned to avoid attributing evil to God. They therefore asserted that, if a man stole food and ate it, he was consuming another man's sustenance. A righteous God does not provide stolen goods as sustenance, but only lawful food and lawful property.[84] The contrary idea, that whatever serves to sustain a man is sustenance provided by God, was widely held—by an-Najjār (§16) for example—but the Mu'tazilites apparently felt that they did not need to take the conception of sustenance so seriously as that of the *ajal*.

Of the conceptions found in the Qur'ān one of the most difficult to interpret in a libertarian sense was that of God setting a seal on men's hearts which apparently prevented them understanding and responding to the prophetic message. One such passage runs:

> As for the unbelievers,
> it is the same for them whether you warn them or not,
> they will not believe.
> God has set a seal on their hearts and their hearing,
> and over their eyes is a covering;
> for them a great punishment![85]

The general idea underlying the interpretation of such passages was that God's sealing of men's hearts was something which followed on their unbelief and did not precede or cause it. Some held that it was the testimony and judgement that these men do not in fact believe and that it did not prevent them from believing. Others, while agreeing that the seal did not prevent a man from believing, adopted the more picturesque interpretation that it was the black mark placed on the heart of an unbeliever so that the angels may know that he is one of 'the enemies of God' and not one of his 'friends'.[86]

Similar treatment is given to the conceptions of guidance (*hudā*), leading astray (*iḍlāl*), succour (*tawfīq*), abandonment (*khidhlān*) and the like.[87] Various lines of thought can be distinguished. (1) Some of these acts of God may be interpreted as his naming or judging. This is particularly easy with negative acts like leading astray and abandoning. The verb *aḍalla* (with its noun *iḍlāl*) normally means 'he led astray' or 'he made to go astray', but the analogy of similar forms from other roots gives grounds of a sort for claiming that the word means 'he counted astray' or 'he made out to be astray'. On this interpretation, then, God simply declares that they are in fact astray. (2) God's guidance and succour may be said to come to men by his revealing his religion to them through prophets, by his summoning them to Islam, by his promises of Paradise and warnings of Hell, and in similar ways. (3) It is as a reward for their faith that God bestows favours on believers, strengthening them to obey or believe. Some thinkers held that he gives help and protection to the man he knows will benefit by it, as a kind of reward before the act. (4) Others considered that God gives his protection to all alike, but that it has a different effect on different people; the voluntary believer is helped and the unbeliever confirmed in his unbelief.

This account of Muʿtazilite views on such matters as the term of life and leading astray shows how the intellectual environment was still impregnated with predestinarian or deterministic ideas. The Qur'ān itself maintains a balance between God's omnipotence and man's responsibility, but the Muʿtazilites tend to neglect the former and overemphasize the latter. Indeed at times the Muʿtazilites seem to be interpreting the Qur'ān on the basis of ideas foreign to the thought-world of Arabic-speaking Muslims. It is not surprising that they failed to gain much popular support.

b) *The analysis of human actions*

From all that has been said so far about the doctrine of Qadar it will be clear that the terms in which Muslim thinkers discuss it are very different from those in which occidental philosophers discuss the problem of free will. At one point, however, the Muslims come close to the Kantian formula 'Ought implies Can'. This is where, from the fact that it would be unjust for God to punish men for acts for which they were not responsible, they deduce that, if God commands men, say, to believe, this implies that they are able to believe (or 'have the power' for it). The statement that 'they all deny that God imposes duties (*yukallifa*) on a man which he is not able (*yaqdiru*) for'[88] could be rephrased as '*taklīf* implies *qudra*', 'imposition of duty implies power'. Even 'the man God knows will not believe' is commanded to have faith and is able for it, while paralytics and those permanently lacking in power have no duties imposed on them.[89]

The conception of power present in this line of thought was at the centre of further developments. The opponents of the Mu'tazila were prepared to admit that an act came about through a power in a man, but they insisted that this power was created by God and was merely the power to do this particular act. Hishām ibn-al-Ḥakam listed five elements in the power (*istiṭā'a*) to act, such as soundness of body and the presence of an instrument, like hand or needle; but the essential element, the one which necessitates the act, is what he calls the 'cause' (*sabab*), and this apparently exists only at the time (*ḥāl*) of the act.[90] The Ahl al-Ithbāt are found using the phrases 'power of faith', 'power of unbelief' (*quwwat al-īmān, quwwat al-kufr*) in a way which suggests that this power necessitates faith or unbelief, as the case may be.[91] In order to parry these views of their opponents the Mu'tazilites had to elaborate the idea of power.

It may be noted in passing that three Arabic words are all being translated 'power' here, namely, *qudra, quwwa, istiṭā'a*. Though the latter is often rendered 'capacity', there does not seem to be any difference in al-Ash'arī's usage, since under the heading of *istiṭā'a* he brings passages with all three words.[92] Al-Ash'arī himself prefers *istiṭā'a* of men, probably because of its derivation from *ṭā'a*, 'obey', which makes it more appropriate for men and inapplicable to God, in whose case *qudra* is normally used.[93]

The general view of the Mu'tazilites on this point was that 'the power (*istiṭā'a*) is before the act and is power (*qudra*) over the act and over its opposite and does not make the act necessary (*ghayr mūjiba li-l-fi'l*)'.[94] In contrast to this the opponents held that the power is only 'with' the act (as an-Najjār, §3). This distinction probably arose out of a conception introduced by Abū-l-Hudhayl.

> Man is able (*qādir*) to act in the first, and he acts in the first, and the act occurs in the second; for the first moment (*waqt*) is the moment of *yaf'alu*, and the second moment is the moment of *fa'ala*.
>
> The moment is the division (*farq*) between actions and it extends through the interval from action to action; and with every moment there comes-into-being an act.[95]

The basis of this distinction is the common human experience of considering whether to do this or that, whether to do something or to leave it undone. For a time two or more possibilities are open to a man, then one of these is realized. The traditional Arab mentality found it difficult to apprehend a purely intellectual operation, and so Abū-l-Hudhayl expresses his distinction by two forms of the verb. These might be translated 'he will act' (or 'he is acting') and 'he has acted', but they only roughly correspond to our tenses, since the distinction between them is basically one between incomplete and completed action. The form *yaf'alu* (and still more the possible variant reading *yaf'ala*) has the suggestion of an act thought about but not carried out—either still in progress or not yet begun. The first moment is that of the internal aspect of the act, that is, the decision to do X and not Y, and the issue of commands to the body; the second moment is that of the execution of the act in the external or physical sphere. Ash-Shahrastānī understands the distinction in this way and says 'he distinguished between acts of the hearts and acts of the members'.[96]

An-Naẓẓām apparently tries to get rid of the ambiguity in *yaf'alu*, which does not make it clear whether the action has begun or not.

> Man is able in the first moment to act in the second moment. Before the second moment exists it is said that the act 'will be performed' (*yuf'alu*) in the second moment; when the second moment exists (it is said that) it 'has been performed' (*fu'ila*). That of which 'will be performed in the second' is predicated before the existence of the second is (the same as) that of which 'has been performed in the second' is predicated when the second moment has occurred.[97]

This view seems to imply that the essential act is the external act. On the other hand, in the discussions of 'the will as necessitating (*mūjiba*)' those who accepted the conception of moments are stated to have held that, where what is willed occurs immediately after the volition, the volition necessitates the object willed.[98] In this case the internal and external aspects are inseparably joined.

Among the Mu'tazilites there were further discussions of these matters and various refinements were added. Many analysed action into three moments, and some even into four.[99] In most cases it would seem that they were pushed into these elaborations by the arguments of opponents. Most Mu'tazilites seem to have accepted the view of an-Naẓẓām that man is able (or has power) in the first moment to act in the second moment. For those who hold that the power is a power of choosing, it is essential to assert that it is power in the first moment. Opponents, however, can take advantage of the ambiguities in 'power', and in the case of killing a man by shooting an arrow may suppose that the archer dies between releasing the arrow and its hitting the man. The victim is then killed by a dead man. Even Abū-l-Hudhayl himself was constrained to admit something of this kind.[100] This is not objectionable if one is thinking of the power of willing, but there was confusion between this and the physical power of executing what is willed. A passage in Ibn-Qutayba gives some indication of the ways in which the opponents tried to get the better of the Mu'tazilites by turning the ambiguities to their own advantage.[101]

It was probably at an early stage in the discussions of human activity that Bishr ibn-al-Mu'tamir introduced the conception of *tawallud* or *al-fi'l al-mutawallad*, which may be rendered 'generated or secondary effects'. Using this conception Bishr asserted that whatever is generated from a man's act is also his act.[102] This doctrine may be a counter-assertion to a doctrine of Mu'ammar's, under whom Bishr had probably studied. Mu'ammar had held that the accidents which inhere in a substance are the 'acts' of the substance in virtue of its 'nature' (*ṭabī'a*).[103] This means that when A flings a stone and hits B and the part hit swells, the flight of the stone is the 'act' of the stone, and the pain and swelling are the 'act' of B's body. In contrast to this Bishr held that all these generated effects are the act of A.

Bishr went to extremes in the application of his ideas. Among the examples he used were : the taste of *falūdhaj* (a sweetmeat) after the mixing of the ingredients, the pleasure from eating something, perception upon opening one's eyes, the breaking of a hand or foot upon a fall, and its sound condition upon the proper setting of the bones. Moreover, B's knowledge that A has struck him is A's act, B's perception of things after A has opened B's eyes is A's act, B's blindness when he has been blinded by A is A's act. Other Mu'tazilites accepted the conception of generated effects, but tried to avoid applying it to colours, pleasure, soundness of body and the like.[104] On the other hand, Abū-l-Hudhayl held that only those generated effects 'whose manner (*kayfiyya*) the agent knew' were included in his act—in other words, the foreseen consequences.[105]

The problems thus raised by Abū-l-Hudhayl and Bishr ibn-al-Mu'tamir continued to be discussed by the Mu'tazilites and their opponents for centuries. Though crudities were eliminated and much greater subtlety employed, the shape of the arguments was very much determined by the original formulations. Such advances as came about were due not to scientific curiosity but to zeal for overcoming the opponents in argument. Because the development was thus dialectical in character certain weaknesses in the analysis were never corrected, notably the absence of any clear idea of the intention of the agent. Abū-l-Hudhayl spoke of the foreseen consequences of an act, but did not ask how far they were desired. An-Naẓẓām had said that for a proper choice a man must have two 'ideas' or 'suggestions' before his mind (*khāṭirayn*), and this point was taken up by Ja'far ibn-Ḥarb, but after that it seems to have disappeared.[106] Al-Iskāfī went so far as to define 'generated effects' in such a way as to exclude whatever the agent had willed and intended; but there is no sign of this having led to a discussion of intention for its own sake, for the main topic of discussion here continued to be 'generated effects'.[107]

This apparently one-sided development is probably linked with the difficulty experienced by Arabs in observing the internal or mental aspects of human life. Certainly the emphasis is always on the external aspects. This can be seen even in the conception of responsibility inherited by modern Arabs from the past. If a taxi-driver injures a child with his taxi, he has to pay compensation, even if everyone agrees that it was entirely the child's fault—the child was injured and the taxi 'did it'. It is actually reported that, when a train killed a man asleep on the track, the verdict of the court was against the railway company. Responsibility is seen as external and physical and not in any way 'moral'. This is worth bearing in mind when considering the Mu'tazilite analysis of action.

c) *God and evil*

The principle of 'justice', besides asserting that God punishes men only for acts for which they are responsible, is taken to imply that in various other ways God cannot do evil.

Those Muslims who believed in the absolute omnipotence of God had necessarily to admit that he was responsible for all the evil in the world. They presumably believed, following the Qur'ān, that he was essentially good, and accepted his connection with evil as largely inexplicable. For the Mu'tazilites, on the other hand, much of the evil in the world was the responsibility of men; but there were a number of points at which God seemed to have some responsibility for evil, and these led to complex attempts by the Mu'tazilites to find some means by which they could avoid 'fixing evil upon God'. Take the case of a man who died from disease at an early age as an unbeliever and went to Hell; had he lived longer he might have become a believer and gone to Paradise; and thus his present evil condition is in some sense due to God. Bishr ibn-al-Mu'tamir seems to have tried to avoid such difficulties by asserting that, since God is omnipotent, he could always do something better than what he has done. Part of his argument for this view is his assertion that God has in store gifts or favours (*alṭāf*, sing. *luṭf*), such that, if he bestows this gift on an unbeliever, the man will believe and will merit the reward of faith. No example is given of what such a *luṭf* might be; it is presumably not to be identified with the Christian conception of grace, but might perhaps include such acts as extending a man's life to give an opportunity to believe. On the other hand, Ja'far ibn-Ḥarb seems to have understood it as some kind of inner strengthening, since he holds that, if a man believes after receiving a *luṭf*, his believing is less meritorious than it would have been without the *luṭf*.[108]

These views are connected with the discussions of 'the best' (*al-aṣlaḥ*) which will be mentioned presently. They also led to further considerations about the relation between God and evil, and in this matter 'Abbād ibn-Sulaymān of Basra is specially to be noted. He tried to explain the relation of God to evil by using a distinction apparently taken over from an earlier member of the school of Basra, Mu'ammar.[109] Just as a man has power over his wife's conception of a child, but has not himself power to conceive a child, so (thought Mu'ammar) God may have power over movement (causing men to move) although he himself does not have power to move, and likewise he may have power over evil (the evildoing of men) but not power to do evil. By using this distinction 'Abbād was able to maintain both that God does no evil in any respect and also that he is omnipotent.[110] He also indulged in what look like verbal quibbles to avoid saying in any sense that God made evil. While most other Mu'tazilites agreed that God made faith good and unbelief bad (presumably meaning that God was the source of these moral distinctions), 'Abbād denied this; and while the others said God made the unbeliever, but not as an unbeliever, 'Abbād refused to say God made the unbeliever, maintaining that 'unbeliever' is compounded of 'man' and 'unbelief' and that God made only the man.[111]

Of more general interest than this hair-splitting were the

discussions about whether God does what is best for men or not. Those who took the affirmative view were sometimes called Aṣ'ḥāb al-Aṣlaḥ, 'upholders of the best (or most fitting)'.[112] In contrast to Bishr ibn-al-Muʿtamir both Abū-l-Hudhayl and an-Naẓẓām held that it is not open to God to do anything better (*aṣlaḥ*) than what he has done, though it is open to him to act in alternative ways which are equally good; for the former these alternative goods are finite in number, for the latter infinite.[113] Perhaps the point of these views would be clearer if we translated *aṣlaḥ* 'perfect', since we feel there is something absolute about perfection, whereas there are different ways of being perfect. In respect of these matters Jaʿfar ibn-Ḥarb followed the tradition of Basra rather than that of Baghdad, but brought in his own special emphasis on the merit of doing things in one's own strength. By God's doing what is best for man he understood setting him in the highest mansion, which is the 'mansion of reward', where he is the subject of duties.[114] In other words, it is better for man to have duties imposed upon him, to be given power to perform these and then, if he does so, to be rewarded with Paradise, than to be created in Paradise by the unmerited grace (*tafaḍḍul*) of God.

In so far as the sufferings of children and of brute beasts could not be interpreted as punishment for sin (since children below a certain age were not subject to duties in Islamic law), and yet were attributable to God, this made it look as if God did evil and raised problems for the Muʿtazilites. Bishr ibn-al-Muʿtamir (or someone of similar views) had admitted that for children to suffer and then to receive an indemnity to compensate for their sufferings (such as admission to Paradise) was not so good as the experience of pleasure without pain; but God was not obliged to do what was best.[115] A suggestion attributed to Bishr was that, when God punished children, it was because when they grew up they would be unbelievers deserving of punishment;[116] though this is an unsatisfactory idea, it continued to find a place in the discussions. A common view in later times was that God allowed the children to suffer in order to warn adults, and then, since it would be unjust if he simply harmed them in this way, he indemnified them by giving them pleasure. This raised further problems, however, since, if the indemnity was entry into Paradise and was everlasting, and if Paradise was the reward merited by responsible acts of obedience, then they could not merit such an indemnity but could only receive it through God's generosity (*tafaḍ-ḍul*).[117] The inability of reason to explain the differences in the destinies of men was here beginning to emerge, and was later to become even more obvious.

Where animals suffered, the general Mu'tazilite view was that they ought to receive some sort of indemnity for their sufferings. They had had no duties imposed on them, and so could not be condemned to everlasting punishment. Some theologians held we could know only that they were indemnified, but not how it was done, nor whether in this life or elsewhere. Others ventured on suggestions, such as that grazing animals would be given everlasting enjoyment in Paradise in the best of pastures. Beasts of prey were more difficult; one suggestion was that they retaliate upon one another in the Stopping-place (*mawqif*), a form of 'intermediate state'. Most ingenious, however, was the idea of Ja'far ibn-Ḥarb and al-Iskāfī that the beasts of prey, after receiving their indemnity (either on earth or in the Stopping-place), are sent to Hell for the punishment of unbelievers and evildoers, though they themselves do not suffer there; doubtless this was to explain the mention of animals in Hell which would be unjust if it was intended as punishment.[118]

These questions about the suffering of children and animals are presented in a typically Islamic form, but they had been previously raised in Christian theology and elsewhere.[119] It was known to the Muslims, too, that to cause suffering to animals was forbidden in the religions of the Manichaeans and Brahmins.[120] The conception of *al-aṣlaḥ*, 'the best or most fitting', had also Christian and Hellenistic antecedents.[121] It is clear, then, that in these respects, as in more general metaphysical and scientific matters, the Mu'tazilites were taking over ideas which were already present in their intellectual environment; and it is interesting to try to trace these ideas backwards. It is more important, however, to observe how the Mu'tazilites bring them very naturally into a context of Islamic thought which has been largely determined by political events within the Islamic empire.

Finally it may be noted how the punishment of evildoers in Hell, though it is in accordance with justice, raises problems for those who believe that in no form can evil be attributed to God. Punishment in Hell, one naturally supposes, is harmful for men, and it is the result of the way in which God has created the world and of his condemnation of the evildoers. Al-Iskāfī apparently felt this difficulty, for he put forward the view that the punishment of Hell is really good and profitable and sound and compassionate; God is kind to his servants in that, while they are being punished, they are being withheld from unbelief. What he may have had in mind was that the punishment of some sinners in the next world warns and scares unbelievers in this world.[122] On such a view those who are treated as a warning to others appear to be unfairly treated compared with those who are warned, and the implication is that the whole universe is created for those who finally enter Paradise. Such a view is not indefensible, but it presages the failure of the attempt to propound a rational theodicy.

5
The principle of 'unity'

The principle of 'unity'—more exactly, of 'making (God) one' or 'asserting (God's) unity'—was at the centre of the Muʿtazilite position by the early ninth century and marked the Muʿtazilites off from others, such as certain Khārijites, who agreed with them in the principle of 'justice' (including the doctrine of Qadar). The chief matters which came under this principle were the denial of the hypostatic character of God's essential attributes, such as knowledge, power and speech, the denial of the eternity or uncreatedness of the Qur'ān as the speech of God, and the denial of any resemblance between God and his creation (the denial of anthropomorphism). Wensinck thought that their view about the Qur'ān 'was only a logical consequence of their denying eternal qualities as well as of their denying the eternal decree'. There is certainly a logical connection at this point, but historically it is more likely that the concrete discussions of the Qur'ān preceded the abstract discussions about the essential attributes. The question of the Qur'ān will therefore be discussed first.

a) *The createdness of the Qur'ān*

The first person to hold that the Qur'ān is created is said to have been Jaʿd ibn-Dirham, but little is known about this man. The earliest mention of him is in the *Radd ʿalā l-Jahmiyya* of ad-Dārimī (d. 895), where he is said to have been put to death as a kind of sacrifice by Khālid ibn-ʿAbd-Allāh al-Qasrī because he denied that Abraham was 'the Friend of God' and that God had addressed Moses.[123] This happened in 742 or 743, while Khālid was governor of Basra. The lateness of this report and the fact that ad-Dārimī was a Ḥanbalite make it probable that it is an attempt to discredit the upholders of the createdness of the Qur'ān by connecting them with a man with a bad reputation. The terms of the charge against him seem to be an inference from something he said. There is indeed a connection between the doctrine of createdness and God's not addressing Moses, since at a later period opponents argued that, if the words addressed to Moses from the bush were created, then it was not God but something created which addressed Moses. On the other hand, there is no obvious link between the doctrine of createdness and the remark about Abraham. It must therefore be concluded that the statement about al-Ja'd throws no light on the origin of the doctrine.

Nor is much help received from the view of Carl Heinrich Becker that Muslims began debating the createdness of the Qur'ān after Christians had argued with them about Christ as the Word of God. Since Christ is called the Word of God in the Qur'ān, the Christian could ask the Muslim to say whether he was created or uncreated; the first horn of the dilemma implies that God was for a time without a word, and the second that Christ is God.[124] Becker is probably right in thinking that Muslims got the idea of using the distinction of created and uncreated from the fact that it had been used against them by Christians; but the distinction was only incorporated into Islamic thinking when it was found that it fitted into an intra-Islamic argument (in much the same way as Greek conceptions were incorporated into essentially Islamic arguments by the early Mutakallimūn). Becker further argues that a passage in John of Damascus (d. 750) implies that the createdness of the Qur'ān was a heresy among the Muslims in his day. In this, however, he seems to be mistaken, for the crucial words are : 'such persons are counted heretics among the Saracens'; and it would be most natural to apply these to those who say God has no Word or Spirit—a view distinct from the view that the Qur'ān is created.[125] Since there is no clear evidence that the view of the createdness of the Qur'ān had even been propounded by 750, still less declared heretical, it would seem that, if Becker's interpretation is correct, the passage must be not by John himself but by someone writing at least a century later.

It is very probable that the intra-Islamic argument into which the distinction fitted was that about the doctrine of Qadar. In the Qur'ān there are many references to historical events; but there are also phrases suggesting that the Qur'ān has some sort of pre-existence on a heavenly 'table' (85.21f.), and that it is from this that it is 'sent down' on *Laylat al-qadr* (97.1). If these phrases were popularly taken to mean that the Qur'ān was pre-existent, even if not uncreated, there would be a presumption that the events were predetermined. There is some confirmation of this suggestion in the fact that 20.99 was used as an argument by al-Ma'mūn. It runs: 'thus we narrate to you accounts of what has gone before' (*mā qad sabaqa*); and the inference is drawn that the Qur'ān was produced *after* the happenings of which it is an account.[126]

In the *Maqālāt* al-Ash'arī has little to say about the Mu'tazilite views on the Qur'ān, though some idea of contemporary Mu'tazilite arguments may be gained from his counter-arguments in the *Ibāna* and the *Luma'*. An idea of the arguments used by the Mu'tazilites at an earlier period may be obtained from the letters of al-Ma'mūn preserved by aṭ-Ṭabarī in his *History*. One favourite line of argument is from verses which speak of God dealing with the Qur'ān in the same manner as he deals with creatures. The most quoted verse in this category is 43.3/2: 'we have made it (*ja'alnā-hu*) an Arabic Qur'ān'; and it is argued that *ja'alnā* (though it may be closer to 'render' than to 'make') implies 'create'. Again, from the fact that the Qur'ān is on the 'preserved table' (85.21f.) it is argued that it is finite or limited, and that finitude is only possible in the case of what has been created. A similar conclusion is drawn from 41.42: 'falsehood does not come to it from in front nor from behind'; for the possibility of having something in front or behind implies finitude.[127]

These verbal arguments, of course, are not suited to the type of summary which al-Ash'arī gives in the *Maqālāt*, and this may explain the paucity of references to discussions about the Qur'ān. The few references which he has[128] are to points where the enigmatic character of speech in general gave rise to speculative discussions. Was the Qur'ān a substance or an accident or neither? Can a man hear the Qur'ān which is the speech of God? Is the reciting different from the recited? And so on. Al-Ash'arī begins his main report by stating that 'the Mu'tazila, the Khawārij, most of the Zaydiyya and the Murji'a, and many of the Rawāfiḍ hold that the Qur'ān is the speech of God, and that it is created—it was not, then it was'. This tends to confirm the view that until about the time of Hārūn ar-Rashīd createdness had not been a subject of discussion, although, as it was known to have appeared in time, it was probably assumed that it was created. Some tried to say that it was temporal (*muḥdath*) but not created. The question of createdness had been raised by the time of Hishām ibn-al-Ḥakam, for he adopted the position that the Qur'ān was an attribute (*ṣifa—sc.* of God) and as such could not be characterized as either created or uncreated. Those who spoke of it as a 'body' probably meant merely 'self-subsistent entity', since the theological vocabulary had not been stabilized at this early period. Abū-l-Hudhayl asserted that God created the Qur'ān on the 'preserved table', so that it was an attribute (of the table), and that it also existed in three places, namely, where it was remembered, where it was written, and where it was recited and heard.[129] This was a recognition of the paradoxical character of any piece of literature. It was probably only after his time that this aspect led to the doctrines of the Lafẓiyya and the Wāqifiyya.[130]

b) *The attributes of God*

There is a logical connection between the doctrine of the createdness of the Qur'ān and the Mu'tazilite doctrine of the attributes of God; or perhaps the connection is rather between the views of those who opposed these two doctrines. For these opponents there was in some sense a multiplicity in the one God, whereas the Mu'tazilites insisted on his oneness in a more absolute sense.[131]

The difficulty was that, if one said that the Qur'ān is uncreated, one is apparently affirming the existence of two eternal beings, and this is a denial of monotheism. The point was apparently made at an early date, for ash-Shahrastānī ascribes to Wāṣil the assertion (which presupposes agreement on the impossibility of the existence of two eternal gods), that 'whoever affirms an eternal "form" (*ma'nā*) or attribute has affirmed two gods'.[132] Wāṣil himself cannot have used the word *ma'nā*, for its technical use developed some time after his death, so that the assertion must be a later summary; but ash-Shahrastānī also admits that it was only after study of the books of the philosophers that the doctrine was developed. The attribute of knowledge was important as a link, for what is in the Qur'ān belongs to God's knowledge.

Ash-Shahrastānī goes on to say that the Mu'tazilites reduced the attributes of God to knowledge and power, and these two are certainly most prominent in the discussions recorded by al-Ash'arī; but they seem to have talked about all possible attributes or names of God. Abū-l-Hudhayl held that God 'is knowing by a knowledge that is he, is powerful by a power that is he, and is living by a life which is he'; he also expressed this by saying that 'when I say that God is knowing, I affirm of him a knowledge which is God, I deny of him ignorance, and I indicate an object-of-knowledge (*maʿlūm*) which exists or will exist'.[133] Most Muʿtazilites appear to have felt that this view came too close to admitting that God had a knowledge which was in some sense a distinct entity. According to al-Ashʿarī not only most of the Muʿtazilites and the Khārijites, but also many Murji'ites and some Zaydites held that 'God is knowing, powerful and living by himself (*bi-nafsi-hi*), not by knowledge, power and life', and they allow the phrase 'God has knowledge' only in the sense that he is knowing.[134] An-Naẓẓām avoided the word 'knowledge', it would seem, for he held that 'the meaning of saying "knowing" is the affirmation of his essence (*dhāt*) and the denial of ignorance of him . . . the attributes belonging to the essence differ only in what is denied of God'. The negative aspect here was presumably influenced by Ḍirār, who held that the meaning of saying that God is knowing, powerful and living is that he is not ignorant, impotent and dead.[135]

After so many centuries it is difficult to know just why this question of the attributes generated so much heat. Why was it so important to deny that God had an attribute of knowledge? Was it because to admit it would mean admitting an attribute of speech and ultimately an uncreated Qur'ān? Or could it have been fear of confusion with the Christian doctrine of the Trinity? Ash-Shahrastānī has an interesting remark: 'Abū-l-Hudhayl's affirmation of these attributes as aspects of the essence is the same as the hypostases of the Christians.'[136] Or perhaps the Sunnite theologians came back to belief in the attributes because this was closer to the outlook of the ordinary Muslim. To insist on the bare unity of God was a tidy rational theory, but it did not do justice to the fullness of religious experience. The negative statements of Ḍirār and an-Naẓẓām are unsatisfactory to the ordinary worshipper, for the object of worship is thought of as unknowable or at least ineffable.

c) *The denial of anthropomorphism*

At this point the beginning of al-Ashʿarī's account of the Muʿtazila may be quoted:

> The Muʿtazila agree that God is one; there is no thing like him; he is hearing, seeing; he is not a body (*jism*, *shabaḥ*, *juththa*), not a form, not flesh and blood, not an individual

(*shakhṣ*), not substance nor attribute; he has no colour, taste, smell, feel, no heat, cold, moisture nor dryness, no length, breadth nor depth, no joining together nor separation, no movement, rest nor division; he has no sections nor parts, no limbs nor members; he is not subject to directions, left, right, in front of, behind, above, below; no place comprehends him, no time passes over him; inadmissible for him are contiguity, separateness and inherence in places; he is not characterized by any attribute of creatures indicating their originatedness, nor by finitude, nor extension, nor directional motion; he is not bounded; not begetting nor begotten; magnitudes do not comprehend him nor veils cover him; the senses do not attain him; he is not comparable with men and does not resemble creatures in any respect; infirmities and sufferings do not affect him; he is unlike whatever occurs to the mind or is pictured in the imagination; he is ceaselessly first, precedent, going before originated things, existent before created things; he is ceaselessly knowing, powerful, living, and will not cease to be so; eyes do not see him, sight does not attain him, imagination does not comprehend him; he is not heard by hearing; (he is) a thing, not as the things, knowing, powerful, living, not as (men are) knowing, powerful, living; he is eternal alone, and there is no eternal except him, no deity apart from him; he has no partner in his rule, no vizier (sharing) in his authority, no assistant in producing what he produced and creating what he created; he did not create creatures on a preceding model; to create a thing was no easier and no more difficult for him than to create another thing; he may not experience benefit or harm, joy or gladness, hurt or pain; he has no limit so as to be finite; he may not cease to exist nor become weak or lacking; he is too holy to be touched by women or to have a consort and children.[137]

This passage expresses very well the otherness and transcendence of God which has always been a prominent strand in Islamic thought. This has, of course, a Qur'ānic basis, and indeed some of the phrases in the passage translated are from the Qur'ān—'no thing like him' (42.11/9); 'sight does not attain him' (6.103). Those who differed from the Muʿtazilites in these points were accused of holding the false doctrines of *tashbīh*, 'anthropomorphism', and *tajsīm*, 'corporealism', and were called Mushabbiha and Mujassima. In many cases the persons to whom these nicknames were applied can be identified, so that there is no danger of supposing that these names represent sects. The term Mujassima was applied to men who held that God was a *jism*, 'body', and these included Hishām ibn-al-Ḥakam, Hishām al-Jawālīqī, Muqātil ibn-Sulaymān and others.[138] This was partly a dispute about terminology. Hishām ibn-al-Ḥakam, as an early Mutakallim, was feeling his way towards an adequate philosophical vocabulary in Arabic, and by *jism* meant not 'physical body' but 'existent', 'thing' (or 'entity'), 'self-subsistent' (*mawjūd, shay', qā'im bi-nafsi-hi*).[139] One cannot be certain that all the other persons mentioned by al-Ashʿarī in his account of the Mujassima understood *jism* in this way; some may have been thinking more naïvely.

The heart of the difficulty here was that the Qur'ān used anthropomorphic terms. No Muslim could deny that God had a hand, an eye and a face, because these were explicitly mentioned in the Qur'ān. And if a hand, why not a body? The accusation of *tashbīh* seems to have been levelled in the first place against those who took the Qur'ānic terms in a naïve fashion and made inferences from them. Most Sunnite theologians eventually adopted a sophisticated way of dealing with the Qur'ānic anthropomorphisms and vigorously rejected the Muʿtazilite position on this point. Thus it is chiefly earlier thinkers who are classified as Mushabbiha. The Muʿtazilite al-Khayyāṭ appears to include among them Muqātil ibn-Sulaymān, Dā'ūd al-Jawāribī, Ḍirār and Ḥafṣ al-Fard.[140] The Muʿtazilites themselves dealt with the anthropomorphisms by the method of *ta'wīl* or 'metaphorical interpretation'. More precisely this meant that they claimed they were justified in interpreting single words in a Qur'ānic text according to a secondary or metaphorical meaning found elsewhere in the Qur'ān or in pre-Islamic poetry. Thus in the phrase (38.75) about God 'creating with his hands' they said that hands meant 'grace' (*niʿma*), and justified this by a usage roughly parallel to our colloquial phrase 'I'll give you a hand'. Similarly *wajh*, usually 'face', was said to mean 'essence'. Verses which spoke of God being seen in the world to come were interpreted in the light of other verses where 'see' did not mean physical sight.[141]

In some ways this method of interpretation is artificial; but at least it keeps thinkers at the 'grass roots' of religious experience and away from an abstract academic discussion of the relations between attributes and essence.

6

The significance of the great Mu'tazilites

Whether Wāṣil and 'Amr ibn-'Ubayd can be considered Mu'tazilites or not, it is clear that their contribution to the development of Islamic thought was slight compared with that of 'the great Mu'tazilites', that is, the generation of Bishr ibn-al-Mu'tamir and Abū-l-Hudhayl and the following generation, with perhaps the addition of al-Jubbā'ī, Abū-Hāshim and al-Ka'bī. Even if we do not admire these men so much as did the nineteenth-century Islamists, yet we must admit that they made a contribution of profound importance to the growth of Islamic theology. Later Mu'tazilites may have exaggerated the uniqueness of these men and may have belittled the work of other early Mutakallimūn whom they were not prepared to accept as Mu'tazilites; and it has to be remembered that most of our information on such matters comes from Mu'tazilite or Mu'tazilite-influenced sources. What is to be said here, then, while mainly about 'the great Mu'tazilites', to some extent also applies to the other early Mutakallimūn.

Their outstanding service to Islamic thought was the assimilation of a large number of Greek ideas and methods of argument. One tends to think of these men as being intellectually fascinated by the Greeks and eagerly studying their books; but it may well be that it was the usefulness of Greek ideas for purposes of argument that first impressed them, and that this was brought home to them when an opponent used these ideas against them and they were unable to reply. It seems very likely that this was the way in which Christian influences come to be found in Islamic theology, for Muslims cannot have studied Christian books deeply. After certain ideas, say about the uncreatedness of the Word of God, had been used against them by a Christian in one context, they would use similar ideas against different opponents in another context.

The Greek ideas thus introduced by the Mu'tazilites came to dominate one great wing of Islamic theology, namely, rational or philosophical theology. This must be adjudged a good thing, even if latterly such theology became too rational and remote from ordinary life. Since the Mu'tazilites were regarded as heretics, however, by the Sunnites, their ideas and doctrines could not simply be taken over, but exercised an influence indirectly. An important role was played by al-Ashʿarī who, after being trained as a Muʿtazilite, was 'converted' to a form of Ḥanbalite view. There were other channels, however, by which Muʿtazilite ideas entered the main stream. Many of the theologians who argued against Muʿtazilism were forced in the course of the argument to adopt Muʿtazilite ideas to some extent. Thus the function of the Muʿtazilites was to take over all Greek ideas that seemed even remotely useful to Islamic doctrine. It was then left to other men to sift these ideas so as to discover which were genuinely assimilable. In the end a great many ideas were retained, though seldom in precisely the form in which the Muʿtazilites had presented them.

Part Three

THE TRIUMPH OF SUNNISM 850–945

The second ʿAbbāsid century could be characterized in various ways. It witnessed a sharp decline in the power of the ʿAbbāsid dynasty, and also the appearance of both semi-independent and completely independent states within the area of what had been the Islamic empire. From the standpoint of the present study, however, the outstanding feature of this period is the attainment by Sunnism of a position of dominance in Islamic society and the consolidation of this position. This leads in turn to a reorganization of Shīʿism with the result that for the first time Imāmite Shīʿism takes the form which subsequently became familiar. In a sense there is an emergence of polarity, but the Sunnite pole is much more important than the Shīʿite. By 945 the Sunnite framework of Islamic society is so well established that it easily maintains itself even under Shīʿite rulers.

9

The polarity of Sunnism and Shīʿism

The aim of the present chapter is twofold. First it tries to show how the social forces supporting Sunnism came to be accepted as dominant within the caliphate, how Sunnism came to be the 'established' religion in a way in which it had not been before, and how this led to a consolidation in various aspects of intellectual life. Though theology is central to this development it will be convenient to defer a consideration of it to chapter 10. Secondly it tries to show how the reshaping of Imāmism round about 900 increased the self-awareness of moderate Shīʿites, and perhaps contributed to the growing self-awareness of the Sunnites.

1

The political background

This period has not yet been adequately studied by the historians from the point of view most relevant to the present volume, and so the best that can be done here is to note the outstanding trends and offer a tentative interpretation of their significance.

The first matter to mention is the change of government policy that took place in the early years of the reign of al-Mutawakkil, that is, round about 850. This included the abandonment of the Muʿtazilite attempt at compromise and the ending of the Miḥna. Muʿtazilites still in office were gradually replaced. There were even some anti-ʿAlid measures such as the destruction of the tomb of Ḥusayn at Kerbela and the prohibition of pilgrimage to this spot. All this seems to indicate that the Muʿtazilite compromise had been found unworkable in practice, and that it had been decided to look for support mainly to what was described as the 'constitutionalist' bloc. Though the policy decision was taken early in the reign of al-Mutawakkil, the struggle was not ended then. The years of confusion between the assassination of al-Mutawakkil in 861 and the accession of al-Muʿtamid in 870 are probably to be regarded as a renewal of the old struggle. With the reign of al-Muʿtamid, however, the policy of relying on the 'constitutionalist' elements in the population seems to have proved successful, and from this time onwards even other elements in the population seem to have accepted the fact that state and society would be essentially 'Sunnite'. (The precise meaning of this term will be discussed in the next section.)

It is likely that the transference of the seat of government to the new city of Samarra by al-Muʿtaṣim in 836, and his introduction of Turkish officers into his personal guard, are also connected with the balance between the blocs. The populace of Baghdad was a strong force on the 'constitutionalist' side, and it may have been hoped that the move to Samarra would reduce their power. Perhaps it did, but, if so, this advantage came after a time to be outweighed by the disadvantage that the power of the Turkish troops was greatly increased. The restoration of Baghdad to the position of capital in 883[1] had presumably as its chief aim the reduction of the power of the Turks, but it was also in accordance with the new policy of relying on the support of the 'constitutionalist' elements.

The second important feature of the period was the way in which the control of events passed into the hands of military leaders or men with assured military support. At the centre of the caliphate it was Turkish generals who made and unmade caliphs. By 936, however, rivalries at the centre had so weakened the caliph that he handed over most of his functions to an outside military leader, Ibn-Rā'iq, with the title of *amīr al-umarā'*. In 945 a member of the Buwayhid family, Muʿizz-ad-Dawla, entered Baghdad at the head of his army and succeeded to the position of *amīr al-umarā'*. The Buwayhids were then for fully a hundred years the *de facto* rulers of Iraq and various eastern provinces. At an earlier date certain provincial governors had been recognized as semi-independent, and the caliph had authorized the succession of a son or other relative to the governorship. Such were the Ṭāhirids in Khurasan (821–73), the Ṣaffārids in Sistan from 867, and the Aghlabids in Tunisia, etc. (800–909). The chief way in which this provincial autonomy affected the development of Islamic thought was that it encouraged the extension of Islamic learning in the provincial capitals.

It is convenient to apply the term 'war-lord' to all the people just mentioned, both those who ruled at the centre and those who ruled in the provinces. The term indicates that their power was based on military force alone and had no distinctive ideational basis. The only idea behind it was that they had been appointed by the caliph. This applied even to the Buwayhids, who were Imāmite Shīʿites, for by 945 that form of belief had become an accepted variant within the Sunnite caliphate. The non-ideational basis of the rule of the war-lords mentioned was in strong contrast to the position of the Fāṭimids, who ruled in Tunisia from 909 and in Egypt from 969, for they, on the basis of Ismāʿīlite ideas, claimed to be the rightful rulers of the whole Islamic world. Of course, when a war-lord found two rival factions, as at Baghdad, he could ally himself with one; but the ideation of a Sunnite or near-Sunnite faction could only justify the rule of a war-lord in so far as he accepted the particular version of Sunnism. This meant that he accepted the Sharīʿa, became a servant, as it were, of the Sharīʿa, and renounced the possibility of making legal changes in those fields where the Sharīʿa was generally followed. The fact that the war-lords were in this respect subordinate to Sunnite ideation is not surprising when one notes that the Fāṭimids, and later in the Maghrib the Almohads, despite distinctive ideation, were unable to influence appreciably the structure of society. Their failure can perhaps be ascribed to a lack of intellectual vigour, of which a symptom was the inability to make converts among all classes of society.[2] On the other hand, an ideation is most likely to influence the whole life of society when, even if it originally was a reform programme for the whole empire, its function comes to be to mark off a small society from its neighbours. Such was the case with the Khārijism of the Rustamids (who ruled in western Algeria from 777 to 909) and with the Zaydism of the Yemen.

A third important feature of the period is that, accompanying the decline of the political power of the caliph, there was an increase in that aspect of his authority which might be called 'religious'. The caliphate indeed seems to have acquired some of the qualities which the Shīʿites ascribe to the imams. Thus, at a later date (about 1100) al-Ghazālī suggests that, if there were no imam-caliph, all administrative acts and all judicial acts, such as marriages, would be invalid.[3] This means that the caliphate is necessary for the validation of official acts based on the Sharīʿa. Though it is not until the end of the period being studied here that the caliph is altogether powerless politically, there are faint earlier indications that his 'religious' authority was growing; and this was happening despite the ease with which Turkish officers made and unmade caliphs.

Finally, it may be noted that, as the various events took place which together are being called 'the establishment of Sunnism', the success of this movement encouraged further steps in the same direction. The background of the whole was the insecurity arising from fighting between factions and from revolts in many areas. In so far as men felt that the establishment of Sunnism gave them security, they wanted to see further consolidation of the various aspects of Sunnism.

2

Aspects of Sunnite consolidation

During the second ʿAbbāsid century Sunnite Islam took a more definite form than it had had previously. It is convenient to look at some of the details before considering their significance.

a) *The formation of a canon of Tradition*

The word *sunna* has as its essential meaning 'standard practice' or 'normal and normative custom'. In pre-Islamic times one could speak of the *sunna* of a tribe. The Qur'ān speaks of *sunnat Allāh* and *sunnat al-awwalīn*, apparently meaning in both cases God's punishment of former erring peoples. [4] Thus *sunna* was a conception with deep roots in the Arab mentality. It was therefore natural for the early Muslims, in the years after 632, to look back to the *sunna* of the Prophet, and also a little later to the *sunna* of the four rightly-guided caliphs. Thus the word *sunna* could be used in several different ways. Though it now seems almost a contradiction in terms, there could be a Shīʿite *sunna*, namely, *sunnat ahl al-bayt*, 'the practice of the Prophet's family'. [5]

In the ancient schools of law—to follow the ideas of Joseph Schacht and others [6]—religious-minded men in each city criticized local legal practice in the light of Qur'ānic rules. In course of time they reached a measure of agreement on what was in accordance with Qur'ānic or Islamic principles. This constituted what Schacht calls 'the living tradition of the school', that is, of Medina or Kufa or some other city. On the one hand, this represented the consensus (*ijmāʿ*) of the scholars in that city, though it might differ from the views held in other cities. On the other hand, the living tradition was regarded as *sunna* or 'standard practice', and assumed to be continuous with the practice of the first Muslims. In so far as the scholars were critical of the Umayyad administrators—and they often were—the *sunna* was not actual practice, but an idealized practice. For long the continuity of the practice was simply assumed. Then in the later Umayyad period we find, for example, that Ḥammād ibn-Abī-Sulaymān (d. 738) of Kufa ascribed the views held in Kufa at this time to his own teacher, Ibrāhīm an-Nakhaʿī (d. c. 714). It was also claimed, however, that Ibrāhīm received these views from earlier scholars, called jointly 'the Companions of Ibn-Masʿūd'; and finally the views were ascribed to Ibn-Masʿūd himself, the chief of the Companions of Muḥammad who settled in Kufa. The last step in this process was to assert that the *sunna* was the *sunna* of the Prophet.

The phrase 'the *sunna* of the Prophet' had been much used in the past, especially by political leaders claiming a religious basis for their activity. Thus even the heretical al-Ḥārith ibn-Surayj (p. 143 above) summoned men to the Book of God and the *sunna* of the Prophet. Because the phrase was widely used it had ceased to have a very precise meaning, and stood for whatever any group or even individual considered to be true Islamic teaching. In the early ʿAbbāsid period this came to be changed by the work of an outstanding jurist, ash-Shāfiʿī (d. 820). Ash-Shāfiʿī was a member of the school of Medina, but he had also been impressed by the views of the group of men known as Ahl al-Ḥadīth. He saw that the Traditions could be used in the critique of unsatisfactory points in the teaching of the ancient schools and of the Aṣ'ḥāb ar-Ra'y. Of a particular practice, which an ancient school held to be 'the *sunna*', it could be said that it was contrary to something Muḥammad had done or said. When an ancient school claimed that a particular practice was 'the *sunna*' (even if it expanded this into 'the *sunna* of the Prophet'), it justified its claim usually by a general assertion that this was what had always been handed down in the school. On the other hand, the Tradition that Muḥammad had said or done something, was supported by a precise chain of transmitters (the *isnād*), each of whom had received the story from his predecessor.

Ash-Shāfiʿī was not the first jurist to concern himself with Traditions. Members of the ancient schools clearly had to meet their critics. A man who died in 813 is said to have remarked of three distinguished jurists that one, Sufyān ath-Thawrī (d. 772), excelled in Traditions but not in the *sunna*, another, al-Awzāʿī (d. 774), excelled in the *sunna* but not in Traditions, while the third, Mālik ibn-Anas (d. 795), excelled in both disciplines.[7] The same double skill was ascribed to the Ḥanafite Abū-Yūsuf (d. 799).[8] The mention of two disciplines, however, of which one is called 'the *sunna*', suggests that the two are not fully coordinated, and that there may be a *sunna* for which there is no evidence by way of a Tradition. The contribution of ash-Shāfiʿī to this question was twofold. He insisted that, if a particular practice was to be claimed as belonging to the *sunna* of the Prophet, it must be supported by evidence in the shape of a Tradition with an *isnād*; but he further insisted that men are bound to accept the *sunna* of the Prophet as they do the Book of God. This second point he inferred from various Qur'ānic verses where Muḥammad is said to have been sent by God to teach men the Book and Wisdom (*ḥikma*), arguing that Wisdom could only mean the *sunna* of the Messenger of God.[9] This identification of Muḥammad's practice with Wisdom gave 'the Sunna' a place parallel to that of the Book among the 'roots of law' (*uṣūl al-fiqh*). From this time onwards the older vague meanings disappear, and when 'the Sunna' is mentioned it normally means the standard practice of Muḥammad as evidenced by Traditions.

The study of Traditions was now accepted as one of the basic Islamic scholarly disciplines, and Traditions were much quoted in legal discussions. It came to be realized, however, that it was easy for an unscrupulous person to invent a Tradition and give it a false *isnād*; and this led to a critique of Traditions[10] and to outline biographical studies of the transmitters with a view to assessing their reliability. The critique was mainly but not exclusively directed towards the *isnād*. A detail may be mentioned here which seems to have escaped both Schacht and Coulson. It came to be realized that not all current practice could be justified by Traditions with an *isnād*, and so a new type of Tradition was invented, the *mutawātir* or 'widely-transmitted' Tradition. This was a Tradition for which no precise *isnād* could be given but which was so generally accepted that it was inconceivable that the number of people involved could have agreed on a forgery. In a sense this was a revival in a new dress of the conception of the 'living tradition'; and men began to argue whether this type of Tradition was superior or inferior to those transmitted by individuals or by a limited number of persons.[11]

By the middle of the ninth century thousands of Traditions with *isnād* were in circulation. There is much obscurity and dispute about the beginnings of the process of writing down Traditions. It is not necessary here to go into these beginnings, but merely to notice that in the half-century after ash-Shāfiʿī two scholars, building on the work of predecessors, produced what became standard collections of 'sound' or authentic Traditions. The books, both entitled *Al-jāmiʿ aṣ-ṣaḥīḥ*, 'the sound collection', and usually known as 'the two *Ṣaḥīḥs*', were by al-Bukhārī (d. 870) and Muslim (d. 875) respectively. Along with these two collections four others came to be regarded by scholars as specially reliable : those called *Sunan* by Ibn-Māja (d. 886), Abū-Dāwūd (d. 888) and an-Nasā'ī (d. 915), and the *Jāmiʿ* of at-Tirmidhī (d. 892). The four *Sunans*, as they are often called, and the two *Ṣaḥīḥs* are known to Muslim scholars as 'the six books'. Occidental writers refer to them as 'canonical', and this is roughly correct, except that this status is not conferred by any official decision or agreement but by the informal recognition implied in very widespread practice. There were many contrary views, of course. Even the two *Ṣaḥīḥs* were criticized in the tenth century, while the position of Ibn-Māja was uncertain as late as the fourteenth century. In the twelfth century the Almohad ruler Abū-Yūsuf Yaʿqūb had a law book compiled which was based on 'ten books'; Ibn-Māja was omitted and the *Muwaṭṭa'* of Mālik and several much later works included.

Early works not included in 'the six books' might still be highly regarded. Such was the collection of ad-Dārimī (Abū-Muḥammad ʿAbd-Allāh of Samarqand, d. 869), which, though called *Musnad*, was similar in structure to the four *Sunans*, that is, arranged in chapters according to the questions of law involved. Mostly the term *musnad* meant a collection of Traditions arranged in chapters according to the first transmitter of each Tradition. It was doubtless because of the arrangement that the *Musnad* of Aḥmad ibn-Ḥanbal (d. 855), despite the high respect in which he was held as a scholar of Traditions, was not included in 'the six books'. On the other hand, the *Muwaṭṭa'* of Mālik ibn-Anas (d. 795), though it contained many Traditions, was primarily a legal work, and on some points quoted opinions of distinguished jurists rather than Traditions. It thus belongs, as the date indeed indicates, to the period before the new conception of 'the Sunna' had been adopted.[12]

The important point to note is that the scholarly works of the period following ash-Shāfiʿī succeeded in giving a definite meaning to the conception of the Sunna. This now meant what was included in the corpus of Traditions vouched for by respectable scholars; and the respectability of scholars was measured by the assessments of a small number of recognized critics, such as Aḥmad ibn-Ḥanbal and Yaḥyā ibn-Maʿīn (d. 847). Some Traditions and some transmitters might still be disputed, but there was a wide area of agreement about 'the Sunna'. This contrasted with the position before ash-Shāfiʿī when the *sunna* recognized by most scholars in Medina was different from that recognized by most scholars in Kufa. Now it was in essentials the same corpus of Traditions which was recognized by practically everyone except those who separated themselves as Shī'ites from the main body.

b) *The establishment of the legal rites or schools*

The 'ancient schools' of law were geographically determined. In each city the majority was in agreement, but there was also a dissident minority. Gradually these geographical schools were transformed into 'personal schools' which regarded themselves as the disciples of an outstanding teacher.[13] Thus the majority of the scholars of Kufa came to regard themselves as followers of Abū-Ḥanīfa (d. 767), under the leadership of his disciples Abū-Yūsuf (d. 798) and ash-Shaybānī (d. 805). There was a rival group, however, which became the school of Sufyān ath-Thawrī (d. 778). In Medina and also in Egypt the majority became the followers of Mālik ibn-Anas. To the school of Medina ash-Shāfiʿī claimed to belong, but the new ideas in his writings led to a different position, and it was only natural that a 'personal school' attached to him should appear; a large part in the formation of the Shāfiʿite school was played by al-Muzanī (d. 878). The school of Syria, which had flourished when the Umayyads ruled from Damascus, became the personal school of al-Awzāʿī (d. 774) and gradually withered away.

Other schools had a personal basis from the beginning. Aḥmad ibn-Ḥanbal (d. 855) came to be named as the leader of the Ahl al-Ḥadīth, who emphasized the place of the Traditions in the basis of law and minimized the use of reasoning. Dāwūd ibn-Khalaf (d. 884) founded the Ẓāhirite school, in which reasoning was simplified and the emphasis placed on the *ẓāhir*, the obvious or literal meaning of a Qur'ānic verse or a Tradition. The great historian and Qur'ān-commentaror (Muḥammad ibn-Jarīr) aṭ-Ṭabarī (d. 923) founded a distinctive but short-lived school known as the Jarīrite. A number of other scholars propounded juristic theories with varying degrees of independence, but none gained an effective following. At a later date Ibn-Tūmart (d. 1130), the man out of whose preaching the Almohad empire arose, adopted a distinctive position in legal questions; but this system, although it had an official position within an empire, lacked the intellectual vigour among its adherents to enable it to survive the empire.

Though some schools are named after men who lived before ash-Shāfi'ī, they probably did not take definite shape as schools until after his time. The formation of personal schools may have been aided by the production of written works, especially in view of the practice of ascribing later works to the head of the school. Such an ascription was probably not intended to deceive but rather to indicate that the work in question contained the views of the head of the school as developed by his followers. The chief impulse to the formation of the schools, however, was probably ash-Shāfi'ī's doctrine of the 'roots of law'. The other schools were far from agreeing with ash-Shāfi'ī, but his work gave them a common conceptual and methodological framework within which they could discuss their disagreements and so circumscribe them. Rivalry between the schools continued, but the common discipline of *uṣūl al-fiqh* served to increase the degree of mutual recognition until by about the year 1300 this was virtually complete. By that date there remained only the four schools which still continue : the Ḥanafite, Ḥanbalite, Mālikite and Shāfi'ite. (The term 'school' has seemed appropriate in a discussion of the intellectual basis, though elsewhere in view of practical differences 'rite' is often preferable.)

c) *The Qur'ānic sciences*

In the field of Qur'ān-interpretation it would be difficult to maintain that there is any clearly-marked transition in the period from 850 to 945. It might perhaps be held in a general way that during this period *tafsīr* (as it is called in Arabic) attained a measure of stability, since some of the wilder suggestions of the previous centuries had been eliminated, while on many points there was broad agreement or at least only a narrow area of disagreement. To this agreement a discussion of methodological principles, of which there are a few traces, had probably contributed. The one solid fact is the appearance of the voluminous commentary of aṭ-Ṭabarī (who has just been mentioned). This quotes (with an *isnād*) all the more reputable interpretations of previous commentators before giving the author's own judicious conclusion. In a sense, then, this work of aṭ-Ṭabarī marks the close of an era, and prepares the way for the opening of another.

In the parallel discipline of *qirā'a*, the study of the text, however, the period under review saw a development comparable to the canonization of Tradition, namely, the widespread adoption as authoritative of 'the seven readings'. When the Qur'ān was first written down, it was in a *scriptio defectiva* which was more a mnemonic device than a system of writing. It did not indicate long or short vowels or doubled letters, and did not even distinguish clearly between certain consonants—those which are now written with a similar outline but distinguished by dots. These defects were gradually remedied, but it was only towards the end of the ninth century that the process of improving the script was completed. By the early tenth century it was possible to give practical expression to the general desire to secure uniformity in the reading of the Qur'ān. The scholar whose work proved effective was Ibn-Mujāhid (d. 935). He realized that it was now impossible to have complete agreement, since different cities had become attached to different readings in certain passages. He therefore propounded the view that there were seven sets of readings (*qirā'āt*) which were equally valid, basing himself on a Tradition which stated that Muḥammad had been taught to recite the Qur'ān according to seven *aḥruf*, and interpreting *aḥruf*, which is properly 'letters', as 'sets of readings'. The scholars whose sets of readings were thus chosen by Ibn-Mujāhid consisted of three men from Kufa and one each from Mecca, Medina, Damascus and Basra.

The restriction to seven sets of readings was not immediately accepted by all scholars, and some had a theory of ten and others of fourteen. Towards the end of Ibn-Mujāhid's life, however, his scheme received official approval through the action of the law-courts. One scholar was forced to renounce the view that he could adopt any reading of the consonantal outline which accorded with grammar and gave a reasonable sense; that is, he had to accept the vowels as now written. Another scholar was condemned for using the old readings of Ibn-Mas'ūd and Ubayy ibn-Ka'b, which were not included in the seven (nor indeed in the ten or fourteen).[14] Though the study of the Qur'ānic text was something of a specialism, the scholars who engaged in it were not isolated but moved in the same circles as the Qur'ān-commentators, the jurists, the philologists, the Traditionists and others. Thus the official acceptance by the courts of the view that uniformity in the Qur'ānic text was important was part of the process by which the main body of Muslims recognized as authoritative the results of the work of many scholars through more than two centuries. This and the other matters mentioned in this section are thereby marks of the establishment or consolidation of Sunnism.

d) *The contribution of the Ṣūfīs*

Since in this study the Ṣūfīs are receiving no special consideration, it will be convenient at this point to say a word about them. The main reason for not considering them separately is that there are Ṣūfīs in most of the strands of Islamic thought. Louis Massignon defined mysticism as 'l'experimentation *ab intrà* d'une religion dûment pratiquée', and went on to show the close parallelism between the development of Islamic theological dogma and the development of mysticism.[15] He held that the experiences of certain mystics had also contributed to the formation of the theological schools of the Faḍliyya, Bakriyya, Karrāmiyya and Sālimiyya, and what was virtually the school of the Ḥallājiyya. Of these the third will be mentioned in the next chapter, but the others can hardly be said to have made any significant contribution to the general course of Islamic thought in the period up to 945. The Sālimiyya, who followed a father and son, both called Ibn-Sālim (d. 909, 960) and both disciples of Sahl at-Tustarī (d. 896), had some influence at a later date.[16] Al-Ḥallāj (d. 922) was influential, perhaps chiefly in presenting new problems, but this was done more by his personality and achievements than by his dogmatic teaching.[17] Al-Faḍl ibn-'Īsā ar-Raqāshī was a popular preacher of the late Umayyad period whose views partook of Khārijism and Murji'ism;[18] while Bakr ibn-ukht-'Abd-al-Wāḥid (d. 793) was a minor figure among the early Mutakallimūn.[19]

In the period of about half a century round about the year 900 Ṣūfism seems to have undergone a process of concrescence or growing together, not unlike what was happening in the study of Tradition, in jurisprudence and in the Qur'ānic disciplines. Arthur Arberry has written of al-Junayd (d. 910):

> Whereas others before him and his contemporaries had by brilliant flashes of intuition grasped one or another of the

> spiritual heights now falling to their mastery, he, standing as it were upon the supreme mountain-peak of analytical thought, took within his ranging vision the whole landscape of mystical speculation stretching below him, and with an artist's eye brought it to comprehension and unity upon a single canvas . . . he sketches in profoundly subtle, deeply meditated language a consistent system of Islamic theosophy which has certainly not been improved upon and which formed the nucleus of all subsequent elaboration.

Louis Massignon gives a central place to al-Ḥallāj, but recognizes that he and al-Junayd had very similar views in essentials; and so, since al-Junayd was the teacher of al-Ḥallāj, his emphasis is perhaps not very different from that of Arberry.[20]

The centrality or climactic character of this period in the history of Ṣūfism may be further illustrated by a statement of the Persian historian of Ṣūfism al-Hujwīrī (d. about 1070). He writes : 'the whole body of aspirants to Ṣūfism is composed of twelve sects, two of which are condemned, while the remaining ten are approved'.[21] The founders of the approved sects are al-Muḥāsibī (d. 857), Ḥamdūn al-Qassār (d. 884), Abū-Yazīd al-Bisṭāmī (d. 875/7), al-Junayd (d. 910), an-Nūrī (d. 907), Sahl at-Tustarī (d. 896), al-Ḥakīm at-Tirmidhī (d. 893/8), al-Kharrāz (d. 892/9), Ibn-al-Khafīf (d. 981) and as-Sayyārī (d. 953). The condemned sects are the followers of Abū-Ḥulmān ad-Dimashqī (d. c. 950) and a section of those of al-Ḥallāj.[22] The dates of these men are noteworthy, for seven died between 875 and 910; one was a little earlier, al-Ḥallāj a little later; only three belong essentially to the tenth century.

The significance of this should not be exaggerated. Perhaps in the stage then reached by scholarship in general it was natural to codify and classify Ṣūfism in this way. The statement of al-Hujwīrī, however, further indicates a degree of acceptance or at least toleration of Ṣūfism among Sunnite scholars provided the individual did not commit himself to assertions which were heretical from the standpoint of dogma. While the particular contributions to theology of particular Ṣūfīs, as claimed by Massignon, are not impressive, it is likely that the existence of Ṣūfism as a tolerated aspect of Islamic life gave strong support to Sunnism in the process of 'establishing' itself. The existence of Ṣūfism and its toleration implied the validity, at least in certain cases, of the religious experience of individuals, and Sunnism was largely based on ordinary men (as distinct from the charismatic leaders of Shīʿism). Ṣūfism had to struggle, of course, with the prejudice in favour of *ʿilm*, the 'knowledge' transmitted from a few men of outstanding wisdom.[23]

3

The emergence of Sunnite self-awareness

a) *General considerations*

The problem to be discussed here is one which arises only after the concept of development has been taken seriously. For the traditional Muslim scholar there is no problem; Islam has always been Sunnite, Sunnite Islam has always existed. This is true, of course, in the sense that the elements of Sunnism always existed; but it is also true that other elements existed contrary to Sunnism, and that it had not become clear and explicit that the good Muslim chose the Sunnite elements and interpretations and rejected the others. For example, there were elements in the Qur'ānic text from which it might be inferred with a show of plausibility that the Qur'ān was created and others from which it might be similarly inferred that it was uncreated. For over a century, so far as we can tell, sound Muslim scholars made neither of the sets of inferences, though they accepted all the elements as part of the Qur'ānic text. It was only after the matter had been raised publicly and the inferences and other arguments explored in debate, that scholars and the community generally were in a position to decide to accept as 'true' the view that the Qur'ān was the uncreated speech of God.

The problem thus raised by the concept of development has various aspects. An important part of the task is to try to discover *when* the main body of Muslims *explicitly* accepted the various doctrines and practices which constitute Sunnite Islam. There is also the separate question of *when* Muslims began to think of themselves as Sunnites in contrast to Shīʿites, and why they came to use the term *sunnī*. This is the essential point when we speak of the emergence of Sunnite self-awareness, for that is closely bound up with the emergence of the polarity between Sunnism and Shīʿism. To gain light on these matters it is helpful first of all to ask two questions: (1) how far had the Sunnites common beliefs? and (2) how far did they accept one another as belonging together?

In respect of theological or dogmatic beliefs there was certainly a convergence (as will be seen in detail in the next chapter), but there was never complete agreement. Even a simple creed like *Al-fiqh al-akbar I* ascribed to Abū-Ḥanīfa was far from gaining universal assent; article 5, for example, which states that 'we leave the question of 'Uthmān and 'Alī to God', is distinctly Murji'ite in tone (though not heretical) and would have been rejected by other strands of opinion within the general religious movement.[24] On this particular question there came to be agreement, and this was one of the bases of Sunnism; but the agreement was to the effect that the order of excellence of the first four caliphs was the chronological order; in other words 'Uthmān was placed above 'Alī. As has been noted, however (e.g. p. 73), there was a time when many who accepted Abū-Bakr and 'Umar placed 'Alī above 'Uthmān. The fundamental question at issue was the extent to which ninth-century or tenth-century Muslims identified themselves with the past of the community. To make 'Alī third was a partial rejection of 'Uthmān, and this was intolerable to many among the main body of Muslims. By the later ninth century it had become clear that for the main body of Muslims the only satisfactory identity was an identity with the whole past history of Islam (or at least the whole of its early history) and that this implied the acceptance of 'Uthmān as best qualified to rule at the time he became caliph. Hence the article in the creeds accepting the first four caliphs in the chronological order.[25]

Other beliefs widely accepted among Sunnites by the late ninth century were the existence of the Sunna of the Prophet as defined by sound Traditions, the general scheme of 'the roots of law', the principles of Qur'ānic exegesis and many of the detailed interpretations and (in the tenth century) the sets of Qur'ānic readings. As indicated above, there were still points of dispute in all these fields, but the importance of these was slight compared with that of the wide agreements on general principles. In particular, by the late ninth century most of those in the general religious movement accepted the conception of a Tradition-based Sunna. This implied acceptance of the honesty of all the Companions; as *Al-fiqh al-akbar I* put it (§4): 'we do not dissociate from any of the Companions of the Messenger of God, nor do we associate with one rather than another'. This was directly opposed to the Shī'ite position, for the Shī'ites gave a special place to one of the Companions, 'Alī, and dissociated from all who had acknowledged Abū-Bakr as rightful caliph.

The points of belief, then, on which there was complete agreement among Sunnites were the acceptance of the general conception of the Sunna and the acceptance of the first four caliphs in chronological order. In contrast the Shīʿites thought that ʿAlī was the rightful successor to Muḥammad and that the Traditions in the 'six books' were of doubtful validity, if not clearly false. All Shīʿites except the Zaydites thought that the first three caliphs were usurpers.

To the question about the mutual tolerance of various Sunnite groups it is more difficult to give a clear answer. The recognition of men of divergent views was perhaps greatest in the field of Traditions, and rather less in the Qur'ānic disciplines. In jurisprudence there was common ground in the discussion of 'the roots of law', but it was apparently some centuries before there was complete mutual recognition of the schools of law. In theology there were still at least three groups in 945 : the rationalistic Ashʿarites and Māturīdites (Ḥanafites) and the anti-rationalistic Ḥanbalites; and these criticized one another harshly. Two centuries later al-Ghazālī (d. 1111) was still complaining (in his *Fayṣal at-tafriqa*) that theologians were much too ready to pronounce one another infidels. About the same time, however, al-Pazdawī (d. 1099) spoke of the *madhhab* of the Ahl as-Sunna wa-l-Jamāʿa as that of 'the jurists, the textual scholars, the Ṣūfiyya and the Aṣ'ḥāb al-Ḥadīth', and apparently accepted the claim of the Ashʿariyya and the Kullābiyya to belong to this group since he remarked that 'between "us" and them there is no difference except in a limited number of (secondary) matters'.[26]

On the other hand, it must be hailed as a great achievement that the Muslims were ready to accept certain differences within a common framework, first of all perhaps the seven *aḥruf* or *qirā'āt*, and later the legal schools. This convergence, together with the acceptance of limited variations and the gradual elimination of deviant sects, must be ascribed in part to the strong feeling for the unity of the community found in many Muslims. This feeling is probably indicated by the use of the word *jamāʿa* in the name 'Ahl as-Sunna wa-l-Jamāʿa'. It is perhaps also possible to trace the source of the feeling to a belief that the Islamic community is a charismatic community.[27] At an early period the Murji'ites were prominent exponents of the catholicizing and comprehensive tendency in Islam, of which article 7 of *Al-fiqh al-akbar I* seems to be an expression : 'difference in the community is a mercy' (*ikhtilāf al-umma raḥma*).

The convergence of belief and practice in Sunnite Islam owes little or nothing to governmental pressure. At the beginning of the 'Abbāsid period Ibn-al-Muqaffa' urged the caliph al-Manṣūr to work for agreement on legal principles between the various 'ancient schools'; and this may have had a slight effect. The Inquisition on the createdness of the Qur'ān begun by al-Ma'mūn was a not very successful attempt to attain doctrinal uniformity by 'official' means. In his account of the trial and condemnation of al-Ḥallāj Louis Massignon insists that in itself the *takfīr* or declaration of being an infidel did not lead to action by the 'secular arm'. Before the government acted there had to be a charge of *zandaqa*, a word whose meaning had been widened from 'Manichaean dualism' to 'doctrinal error threatening the security of the state'.[28] In the cases in 934 and 935 mentioned above when men were condemned for views about Qur'ānic textual matters, it was probably held by the authorities that this could lead to disturbances of public order (though of course it was not *zandaqa*).[29] In Sunnite Islam the 'secular arm'—caliph, sultan or subordinates—could never declare any doctrine official, since this was the prerogative of the ulema; al-Ma'mūn's Inquisition is to be connected with his Zaydite (Shī'ite) sympathies. On the other hand, a consensus of even the Sunnite ulema could seldom if ever be attained. Consequently there was no machinery for making a doctrine official or orthodox, so that in speaking of these matters we have to use such phrases as 'the view of the main body' (*sc.* of Sunnites) or sometimes 'the Sunnite view'; and we have always to remember that there may be variant views which are not heretical in any clear sense, for heresy too depends on consensus.

b) *The evidence of the names*

A common name for the Sunnites in later times was Ahl as-Sunna wa-l-Jamā'a. It is found in *Sharḥ al-fiqh al-akbar* probably by Abū-l-Layth as-Samarqandī (d. 983 or later); and Aḥmad ibn-Ḥanbal used it in the form Ahl as-Sunna wa-l-Jamā'a wa-l-Āthār.[30] There is at least one occurrence of Ahl as-Sunna in Ibn-Qutayba (d. 889);[31] though this occurs in a statement that al-Jāḥiẓ once argued for Zaydism against the 'Uthmānites and Ahl as-Sunna, the term probably comes from Ibn-Qutayba and not from al-Jāḥiẓ, but it is clear that the idea is not prominent in the thought of Ibn-Qutayba.

The most extensive early evidence is that from the *Maqālāt* of al-Ashʿarī. The creed given there is said to be that of Ahl al-Ḥadīth was-s-Sunna (290, in text; 298), while to Ahl as-Sunna wa-Aṣ'ḥāb al-Ḥadīth is ascribed the view (211) that God is not a *jism* (body, substance) and does not resemble *ashyā'* (things). The commonest term, however, is Ahl as-Sunna wa-l-Istiqāma, of which there are six occurrences, dealing with the beliefs that 'Uthmān acted rightly and had been wrongly killed, and consequently that he was the third of the four Rāshidūn, that there is a basin in Paradise from which Muḥammad will allow his community to drink, that he has the right of intercession (*shafāʿa*), that believers will not be eternally in Hell, and that Heaven and Hell already exist.[32] In one passage (473) the Ahl al-Istiqāma are said to affirm the questioning of the dead in the tomb by the angels Munkar and Nakīr, and in another (*Lumaʿ*, 76, §184) they are said to have held before Wāṣil a mediating view about the grave sinner. There is one reference (454) to Ahl al-Jamāʿa as holding that 'Uthmān was imam until killed and was killed wrongly, and one (471) to Ahl as-Sunna wa-l-Jamāʿa as holding that 'the Ten' Companions to whom Paradise was promised are certainly there. Finally it may be noted that the creed in the *Ibāna* is said to be that of Ahl al-Ḥaqq wa-s-Sunna.

Of the terms used here *jamāʿa* suggests an all-comprehensive community, and this is in fact the 'tendency' of the doctrines mentioned. *Istiqāma* doubtless refers to the 'straight path' of the Fātiḥa (v.6/5). *Ḥaqq* or 'truth' is, of course, ambiguous, since every sect claims that its doctrine is true. Al-Ashʿarī's phrase is repeated by al-Barbahārī (d. 940), and Ibn-Baṭṭa (d. 997) speaks of Ahl al-Ḥaqq.[33] In contrast to this an-Nāshi' speaks of the Muʿtazilites as Ahl al-Ḥaqq.[34]

It may be noted that the term Ahl al-Ḥadīth or Aṣ'ḥāb al-Ḥadīth sometimes has a meaning not unlike Ahl as-Sunna, but the precise connotation varies from writer to writer. For al-Khayyāṭ they are one of the five sects of the community along with the Shīʿa, the Khawārij, the Murji'a and the Muʿtazila; and he defends them against Ibn-ar-Rāwandī and insists that they accept all the Companions.[35] An-Nāshi' has an interesting account of their views on the imamate, in which he divides them into four groups: the Kufans, the followers of Ismāʿīl al-Jawzī, the followers of Walīd al-Karābīsī and the Basrans.[36] Al-Ashʿarī employs the term occasionally. The people to whom he applies it are fairly conservative, but some are apparently ready to discuss some questions bordering on Kalām, such as whether something known is known before it exists.[37] Ibn-Qutayba uses the term Ahl al-Ḥadīth in a fairly comprehensive sense, apparently meaning all or nearly all who transmit Traditions.[38] The use of the term Ahl al-Ḥadīth thus does not throw any light on the growth of Sunnite self-awareness, though it illustrates how the study of Traditions had become an accepted discipline. Similarly there is nothing to be learned from nicknames such as Ḥashwiyya[39] and Nābita,[40] applied to some or all of the Traditionists by Muʿtazilites and others.

Louis Massignon refers to a statement by al-Aṣmaʿī (d. 828/31), a grammarian of Basra, that the Ahl as-Sunna wa-l-Jamāʿa were founded by four men, Yūnus ibn-ʿUbayd al-Qaysī (d. 756), ʿAbd-Allāh ibn-ʿAwn ibn-Arṭabān (d. 768), Ayyūb as-Sikhtiyānī (d. 748) and Sulaymān at-Taymī (d. 760).[41] This is a group of scholars of Basra. When Ḥammād ibn-Zayd (d. 795) said 'our *fuqahā'* are Ayyūb, Ibn-ʿAwn and Yūnus', the man to whom he was speaking, Sufyān ath-Thawrī (d. 777) said 'ours are Ibn-Abī-Laylā (d. 765) and Ibn-Shubruma' (of about the same date), both scholars of Kufa.[42] This last is an expression of the rivalry between Basra and Kufa, and gives some ground for thinking that the statement of al-Aṣmaʿī is another expression of the same rivalry; but it is difficult to be certain without knowing the source of the statement.

The conclusion to be drawn from the general considerations advanced above and from this review of early instances of the names is that the facts which gave Sunnism an explicit form were present by the early tenth century. The policy of the rulers from al-Mutawakkil onwards sometimes contributed to the process of establishing Sunnism, but was not decisive. Yet even after the facts existed, that is, the wide measure of agreement in various fields, it was only gradually that men began to think of themselves as Sunnites. The name Ahl as-Sunna, by itself or in combination, is used from the ninth century, though the first instance noticed of the adjective *sunnī* is in Ibn-Baṭṭa (d. 997). In *Kitāb at-Tawḥīd* no distinctive name is used for al-Māturīdī's own party. Moreover it was only slowly over centuries that old rivalries died away, especially in questions of doctrine and dogma. Nevertheless there are good grounds for holding that it was the early tenth century which witnessed the essential part of the process of the polarization of Islam into Sunnite and Shīʿite. This point will appear more clearly when the Shīʿism of the period has also been examined.

4

The reshaping of Shīʿism

Shīʿism in the years after 850 presents the spectacle of a deeply divided movement. In 874, after the death of al-Ḥasan al-ʿAskarī, there were fourteen separate groups among his followers according to an-Nawbakhtī and twenty according to al-Masʿūdī.[43] In addition there were Ismāʿīlite and Zaydite groups. Half a century after the death of al-Ḥasan, however, nearly all the descendants of his followers and other moderate Shīʿites had been united in a single Imāmite sect. Through the Fāṭimid dynasty the Ismāʿīlites had obtained a state with its centre in Tunisia, and through the Carmathians (Qarāmiṭa) another with its centre at Bahrein. The Zaydites had strengthened the position they already held in the Yemen. In the study of these groups an important question to have in mind is whether they hoped to convert the whole Islamic world to their specific doctrines, or whether they had in practice abandoned any such hope and were content to be a small group marked off from the rest of the community of Muslims. This question is linked with the further question—specially important in the present study—of the extent to which they contributed to and influenced the main stream of Islamic thought.

a) *The Ismāʿīlites*

The Ismāʿīlites derive their name from the fact that they consider that 'the imam' after Jaʿfar aṣ-Ṣādiq (d. 765) was his son Ismāʿīl and not Mūsā al-Kāẓim, as the Imāmites say. They are sometimes called the Sabʿiyya or 'Seveners'. Since the movement was an underground one from about 765 until the end of the ninth century, there is much obscurity about its early history. It was probably revolutionary extremists with whom he had been associated who recognized Ismāʿīl, while the political moderates preferred Mūsā. As an underground movement Ismāʿīlism prospered through developing a hierarchic organization, or rather several such organizations about whose relationship to one another we have little information. In addition to the imam, who remained hidden while the movement was underground, there was a body of agents, each with the title of *dāʿī* or 'missioner', 'summoner', and under the supervision of a chief *dāʿī*. The agents, though often acting secretly, had certain contacts with persons outside the movement.

The first public success of the movement was about 894 when Abū-Saʿīd al-Ḥasan al-Jannābī, the *dāʿī* of the branch or sect known as the Carmathians, established a kind of republic in eastern Arabia with its centre at Bahrein. From Bahrein missioners carried Ismāʿīlite propaganda to various parts of the ʿAbbāsid caliphate, and in the disturbed condition prevalent often met with a good response. In the early years of the tenth century there was a Carmathian revolt in the Syrian desert, which was not suppressed without difficulty. In eastern Arabia the Carmathian state continued to flourish until at least the end of the eleventh century.

Shortly after the public appearance of the Carmathians an ultimately more significant success was gained in Tunisia by what was probably the main body of the movement. The work of the *dāʿīs* there had been so fruitful that it became possible for the hidden imam to show himself, in the person of ʿUbayd-Allāh with the title of al-Mahdī. The state thus founded in 909 quickly overthrew the semi-independent Aghlabid dynasty in Tunisia and the Khārijite Rustamid dynasty in western Algeria, as well as occupying Sicily. In 969 they conquered Egypt and transferred their capital to their new foundation, the city of Cairo. Under the Fāṭimids, as the Ismāʿīlite dynasty came to be called, Egypt prospered and was a centre of high culture. From the first appearance of al-Mahdī the Fāṭimids claimed to be the rightful rulers of the whole Islamic world, and at least until 1100 sent their *dāʿīs* throughout the lands acknowledging the ʿAbbāsid caliph. The message they proclaimed was not merely political but included also a theology, elaborated intellectually with great subtlety. It was not until the eleventh century, however, that the Sunnite theologians felt it necessary to reply to Fāṭimid intellectual arguments. For this reason, though Ismāʿīlism has an important place in any general history of Islamic thought, it need not be further mentioned in a study restricted to the formative period.[44]

b) *Zaydism on the periphery*

At an earlier point it was asserted that a form of Zaydism or something very like it was the doctrine followed by al-Ma'mūn and some of his chief officials. Perhaps it was to this period that Ibn-Qutayba's statement applies that al-Jāḥiẓ sometimes defended the Zaydiyya against the ʿUthmāniyya and the Ahl as-Sunna.[45] After the time of al-Jāḥiẓ little is heard in Iraq about the Zaydites, and the centre of interest in Zaydism shifts to two points on the periphery of the caliphate, to the region south of the Caspian Sea and to the Yemen, where small Zaydite states were created. The chief intellectual leader of the northern state was al-Uṭrūsh (d. 917).[46] Because of certain peculiarities in doctrine and practice the northern Zaydites were reckoned to belong to the sect of the Nāṣiriyya, from a name of honour given to al-Uṭrūsh, an-Nāṣir li-l-Ḥaqq. In the Yemen there was greater intellectual activity, the most important thinkers and writers being the imams, al-Qāsim ibn-Ibrāhīm ar-Rassī (d. 860) and his grandson known as al-Hādī ilā l-Ḥaqq (d. 911).[47] The Yemeni Zaydites are known from al-Qāsim as the Qāsimiyya. Their doctrines, as noted above, were close to those of the Muʿtazilites but not identical. What follows is chiefly about the Yemenis.

While the Zaydites thought of their doctrines as containing the truth for all Muslims, they made no missionary efforts comparable to those of the Fāṭimids. Once they had established themselves in their little states, they were content to remain in almost complete isolation from the rest of the Islamic world. Under these circumstances Zaydism came to have a twofold function. On the one hand it gave the state its justification—its conception of what it was and what it stood for; and on the other hand it marked it off from other states. At least in respect of this second function it differed from, say, the Zaydism of al-Jāḥiẓ, which was a doctrine for the whole Islamic world. Despite the high intellectual standard of Yemeni Zaydism it made virtually no contribution to the main stream of Islamic thought because of its isolation. Ash-Shahrastānī, for example, does not mention al-Qāsim ar-Rassī among the scholars of the Zaydites. Since al-Qāsim and his followers had no part in the formation of Islamic thought, and since he has been very fully written about by Wilferd Madelung,[48] no more need be said about him here.

The view of Zaydism adopted in the present study (especially in chapter 6) is relevant to the controversy about the authenticity and date of the *Corpus iuris* ascribed to Zayd ibn-ʿAlī (after whom Zaydism is named). The study of doctrine leads to the view that Zaydism has many different meanings, and that there is no necessary continuity with Zayd himself or between the different meanings and those who adopt them. In dealing with these matters it is always best as far as possible to speak of the views of individuals. These considerations affect the legal controversy in the following ways. Firstly, it is unlikely that there was much discussion of legal questions from a Zaydite standpoint until after a separate Zaydite state existed; though Muslims sometimes discussed legal matters *in vacuo*, it is certain that if the Zaydites in the circle of al-Ma'mūn, for example, had discussed legal matters, something of it would have been heard in the works of contemporary jurists. Secondly, if the Zaydite corpus contains genuine material from the eighth century (or earlier), it could not be linked with a close-knit Zaydite sect, since that did not exist, but must come from someone who participated in the general juristic discussions of his time and shared most of the views of his contemporaries. It will presently be seen that there is a certain parallel in the development of Imāmite law. To say more than this about the legal controversy would distract from the main aims of the present study.[49]

c) *The formation of Imāmism*

Later Shī'ite writers commonly refer to men like Hishām ibn-al-Ḥakam and his contemporaries as Imāmites, but it is not certain whether they used this name of themselves. As noted in chapter 6 their opponents mostly called them Rāfiḍites. In *Kitāb al-intiṣār* the name Ahl (or Aṣ'ḥāb) al-Imāma is used, both in the quotations from Ibn-ar-Rāwandī and in the replies of al-Khayyāṭ.[50] In the *Maqālāt* al-Ash'arī twice uses Imāmiyya, once Aṣ'ḥāb al-Imāma and twice the phrase 'those who *yaqūlūn bi-l-i'tizāl wa-l-imāma*'.[51] An-Nawbakhtī appears to use Imāmiyya three times, notably as the name of the twelfth group he describes of those existing after the death of the Eleventh Imam; at the end of his account he says: 'this is the way of the *imāma* and the clear, obligatory path, which the true Imāmite Shī'a does not cease to follow (*lam tazal at-tashayyu' 'alay-hi*)'.[52] Thus the name was in use by the year 900 or shortly afterwards.

The account of an-Nawbakhtī is specially valuable here, since it must date from before 922, the year of his death, and is the work of one who considered himself an Imāmite. It is not, of course, an exposition of Imāmite doctrine in its totality, but only of those points in which the Imāmites differed from other Shī'ite groups. It may be summarized as follows: (1) God has on earth a *ḥujja*, 'proof', from the sons of al-Ḥasan ibn-'Alī (the Eleventh Imam), and he is a *waṣī*, 'legatee', to his father; (2) the imamate may not fall to two brothers after al-Ḥasan and al-Ḥusayn; (3) the imamate is in the progeny of al-Ḥasan ibn-ʿAlī (XI); (4) if there were only two men on earth, one would be *ḥujja*, and if one died, the one left would be *ḥujja*; this applies so long as God's command and prohibition stand for his creatures; (5) the imamate may not be in the progeny of a man who died in the lifetime of his father, whose imamate was not established and who had no *ḥujja*; this excludes the Ismāʿīlite (*Mubāraki*) view that the imam after Jaʿfar aṣ-Ṣādiq (VI) was Muḥammad ibn-Ismāʿīl ibn-Jaʿfar; (6) the earth may not be without a *ḥujja*; we acknowledge the imamate and the death of (al-Ḥasan ibn-ʿAlī) and maintain that he has a descendant from his loins who is the imam after him and who will appear and publicly assert his imamate; it is for God to determine the times of appearing and remaining hidden, and it is wrong for men to investigate such matters; (7) it is not for any believer to choose an imam by rational consideration (*ra'y*) or choice (*ikhtiyār*); God appoints him for us; (8) there is justification for concealing the identity of the imam, and he will not be known until he appears.[53]

The impression one receives is that in the first half of the tenth century the Imāmite doctrine came to be widely accepted by moderate Shīʿites, so that most of the rival groups ceased to exist. This impression may be due mainly to lack of information, and the other groups may have continued longer. Certainly when the Buwayhids came to power in Baghdad in 945, it was Imāmism they encouraged. But whatever the date of the disappearance of the other groups, the work which led to the unification of non-revolutionary Shīʿism was mostly accomplished before 925. This is shown by the historical details collected by Louis Massignon.[54] On the death of the Eleventh Imam his *wakīl* or chief agent was Abū-Jaʿfar Muḥammad ibn-ʿUthmān al-ʿUmarī, but two or three other men disputed his claim to this position. According to the Sunnites his slave-girl Ṣaqīl gave birth posthumously to his male child, and for seven years claimed the Imam's property, until the courts finally gave it to his brother Jaʿfar. The uncertainty about a son is partly confirmed by the action of a Shīʿite dissident. The Shīʿites, on the other hand, assert that the Eleventh Imam had a son born on 25 July 870 called Muḥammad, who disappeared miraculously in 878. The date of the death of the Eleventh Imam is given as 1 January 874.[55]

According to a report quoted by Massignon the *wakīl* Muḥammad al-ʿUmarī had heard the Eleventh Imam say that the imam and the *ḥujja* after him would be his son Muḥammad, who would eventually reappear after an absence. He thus belonged to the Imāmite group, and before his death (apparently in 917) he decreed that Ibn-Rūḥ an-Nawbakhtī should be *wakīl* and intermediary between the imam and his followers. This man came from the powerful Nawbakht family, who were probably the chief influence in the formation of Imāmism at this period. The statesman who also gave Imāmism its intellectual formulation was Abū-Sahl Ismāʿīl ibn-ʿAlī an-Nawbakhtī (d. 923).[56] More philosophically minded was al-Ḥasan ibn-Mūsā an-Nawbakhtī (d. c. 922), the author of *Kitāb firaq ash-Shīʿa*.[57] On the other hand, it is puzzling to learn that in 893 yet another member of the family, with the nickname Shaylama, headed a plot against the ʿAbbāsid caliph in the name of an ʿAlid whom he refused to name, and as a result suffered death by burning.[58] Perhaps it was after this failure that the rest of the family adopted the more peaceful policy of the new Imāmites.

What was the practical significance of Imāmism as now constituted? How was it related to Sunnism and the ʿAbbāsid caliphate? The Imāmites of the tenth century claimed men like Hishām ibn-al-Ḥakam a century earlier as their fellow-Imāmites. In certain respects there was certainly continuity. Article 7 of an-Nawbakhtī's account, for example, asserting that men cannot appoint the imam but only God, repeats the insistence that the imam derives his authority from above and not from below. Again the new Imāmism, like the older Rāfiḍism, was not attempting to replace the ʿAbbāsid dynasty by an ʿAlid one in the foreseeable future. It may also be presumed to have taken the same critical view of the reliability of the majority of the Companions on whom the Sunnites based their Traditions. This matter is not mentioned by an-Nawbakhtī, but the slightly later evidence of Ibn-Bābawayh, known as ash-Shaykh aṣ-Ṣadūq (d. 991), in his *Risālat al-iʿtiqādāt*, probably represents the position at the beginning of the tenth century.[59] In chapter 45, dealing with Traditions, Ibn-Bābawayh says that the sources (or original transmitters) are of four kinds : hypocrites, those with inaccurate memories, those ignorant of matters of abrogation, and those free from these faults. Most of the Companions on whom the Sunnites rely are presumably in the first three categories; and it is made clear that fullest reliance is to be placed solely or mainly on reports from the imams.

While the tenth-century Imāmites thus continued the older attitude of hostility to the Sunnite ulema with their reliance on the Companions and on their own intellectual activity, there were also certain differences. Most noticeable is the adoption of the belief that the imam is in a state of hiddenness or occultation (*ghayba*, *khifā'*). This belief was not entirely new, for the Wāqifa (of the Shī'a), whose spokesman was aṭ-Ṭaṭarī (d. c. 835), had held a similar view of the Seventh Imam, Mūsā al-Kāẓim. Although twelve is a special number, there had previously been no idea that the imams would be limited to twelve. Thus an important part of the argument of Abū-Sahl an-Nawbakhtī was to prove that the series had indeed ended with the Twelfth Imam, Muḥammad the son of al-Ḥasan al-'Askarī. He achieved this by taking advantage of the fact that Muḥammad was alleged to have disappeared mysteriously, indeed miraculously. He also argued against various claims put forward on behalf of Ja'far, the brother of the Eleventh Imam, against the position of aṭ-Ṭaṭarī and against various other views. The intellectual arguments for the new Imāmite position and the political skill of those who adopted it eventually led to its becoming the form of doctrine to which nearly all moderate Shī'ites adhered.

It has also to be remembered that the political situation had greatly changed since the early ninth century. Al-Ma'mūn had wielded vast power; but his successors a century later were on the point of losing all their political power. Thus there would have been little point merely in trying to replace the 'Abbāsids by 'Alids; the desideratum was a different kind of ruler. It was now unrealistic to try to have the office of caliph interpreted in a more absolutist sense. So the Imāmites presumably acted in accordance with their principle of *taqiyya* or concealing one's true opinions, accepted the caliphs and sultans as *de facto* rulers in so far as they had power and then exerted whatever pressure they could on them. Belief in a hidden imam, even if this belief was expressed, was not a serious immediate threat to the régime, but in that it was the assertion of a social and political ideal it implied a criticism of actual circumstances. More serious than this criticism, however, was the fact that by their doctrines the Imāmites separated themselves from much of the Islamic community. The Sunnites aimed at being comprehensive by accepting the four rightly-guided caliphs and making the order of merit chronological. The Imāmites, on the other hand, by rejecting the first three caliphs and many Companions were refusing to identify themselves with the Islamic community as a whole and were regarding themselves as superior to the 'generality' (*'āmma*), as they called the Sunnites.[60] They were seemingly content to be a kind of permanent opposition. Since what marked them off from the Sunnites was also to a great extent their theological views (as can be seen from the creed of Ibn-Bābawayh), perhaps they might be regarded as coming near to the modern view of religion as essentially a private and not a communal matter.

While an-Nawbakhtī and others were elaborating the political and theological position of the Imāmites, another scholar al-Kulīnī (d. 939) was laying the foundations of Imāmite or Ithnā'asharite law in his book *Al-kāfī fī 'ilm ad-dīn* ('the sufficiency concerning the science of religion').[61] This is a collection of over 15,000 Traditions. Each is provided with an *isnād*, but for Shī'ites the essential name in an *isnād* is always that of an imam, even if the imam has heard the Tradition from an earlier scholar. It is noteworthy that the Imāmites should thus make use of Traditions (though of different ones from the Sunnites) and should make their own collections. This appears to be an adaptation to the central Imāmite position of a distinctively Sunnite practice, an indication of how Sunnite (or perhaps Arab) conceptions had a dominant position in Islamic thought. In some ways Imāmite law was not unlike an additional Sunnite rite or *madhhab*; but doctrine kept the Imāmites separate. Doubtless the success of Imāmism contributed to the growth of self-awareness among the Sunnites.

10

The Maturing of Sunnite Theology

1

Ninth-century Sunnite theologians

Most of what was written on early Islamic theology by occidentals up to the Second World War gives the impression that there was a rationalistic movement (the Muʿtazilites) and an anti-rationalistic party (men like Aḥmad ibn-Ḥanbal) but practically nothing else until al-Ashʿarī combined the doctrines of the latter with the methods of the former. The work that has appeared since 1945 has made clear how inaccurate this impression was. For one thing, as was seen in chapter 7, the rationalistic movement of Kalām was wider than the Muʿtazilite sect in the strict sense. For another thing, throughout the ninth century there were a number of upholders of a conservative doctrinal position who engaged in Kalām to some extent. Even an early Mutakallim like Ḍirār adopted a conservative position towards the doctrine of Qadar; and, as will be seen presently, there were other ninth-century Mutakallimūn who were still closer to standard Sunnism. The inaccurate impression probably came about through relying almost exclusively on Muʿtazilite and Ashʿarite sources and failing to realize that these were not concerned with the development of ideas. Actually al-Baghdādī in his *Uṣūl ad-dīn* had a section on the Mutakallimūn of Ahl as-Sunna and a short list (which was in fact quoted by Wensinck, though for another purpose) of early Mutakallimūn of Ahl al-Ḥadīth.[1]

The present chapter deals with those who were theologians in the sense of propounding views on questions of doctrine, and is not confined to rationalistic theologians or Mutakallimūn. It is indeed difficult to define Kalām exactly. One result of the long debate for and against the use of reasoning was that later theologians claim all sorts of persons as forerunners. Among the names included by al-Baghdādī in his account of the Mutakallimūn of Ahl as-Sunna are ʿAlī ibn-Abī-Ṭālib, ʿAbd-Allāh ibn-ʿUmar, ʿUmar ibn-ʿAbd-al-ʿAzīz, al-Ḥasan al Baṣrī, az-Zuhrī, ash-Shaʿbī and Jaʿfar aṣ-Ṣādiq. Abū-Ḥanīfa and ash-Shāfiʿī are included on the basis of certain of their books, those of ash-Shāfiʿī being one affirming the existence of prophethood against the Barāhima and one refuting 'the people of fancy'. The pages which follow will give a brief account of those who appear to be the most influential in their contributions to the formulation of Sunnite doctrine, regardless of whether they are described as Mutakallimūn or not. The aim is to give a balanced picture, not an exhaustive account. The latter is indeed impossible at present, for there is a vast amount of material which has not been examined from a developmental standpoint. The ninth century is here taken to include those who grew up in it and died before 950.

a) *The aftermath of the Miḥna*

It was apparently through the Miḥna or Inquisition and the question of the uncreatedness of the Qur'ān that many conservative theologians became reconciled to the use of Kalām. The men in al-Baghdādī's lists of early Sunnite Mutakallimūn are found to have been involved in discussions about the Qur'ān. This is not surprising, of course, since the Qur'ān must have been in the centre of theological discussions from about 825 until at least 875.

One of the earliest was ʿAbd-al-ʿAzīz al-Makkī (d. 849/54), who had heard Traditions from ash-Shāfiʿī among others.[2] He argued with Bishr al-Marīsī about the Qur'ān in the presence of al-Ma'mūn in 824, apparently with some success. He had made some study of the methods of Kalām, and was later presented as having vainly exhorted the Ahl al-Ḥadīth to become familiar with tools which would one day help them in their fight against their enemies.[3] Al-Makkī had a distinguished pupil al-Ḥusayn ibn-al-Faḍl al-Bajalī (Abū-ʿAlī), who continued the interest in Kalām. The date of his death is not recorded, doubtless because he had been persuaded to settle in Nishapur by ʿAbd-Allāh ibn-Ṭāhir (d. 844), the governor of Khurasan. He was specially renowned as a Qur'ānic commentator and exegete, and it was said that with him the scholarship of Iraq had gone to Khurasan. His political views were not unlike those of al-Ma'mūn, since he held that ʿAlī was superior but allowed the imamate of the inferior (*mafḍūl*).[4]

By the beginning of the reign of al-Mutawakkil many people were heartily sick of the endless hair-splitting discussions about the Qur'ān. Al-Mutawakkil was prevailed upon to forbid such discussions—*al-jidāl* (v.l. *al-kalām*) *fī l-Qur'ān*.[5] This attitude could be justified by reference to earlier scholars who through piety and scrupulosity adopted the view that such discussions were 'innovation'. One of the first men to take this view appears to have been al-Khuraybī ('Abd-Allāh ibn-Dāwūd; d. 828).[6] He was widely accepted as a Traditionist, yet at the same time held views similar to those of Abū-Ḥanīfa and the Aṣ'ḥāb ar-Ra'y. Contemporaries of al-Mutawakkil who supported his prohibition of discussion about the Qur'ān included Ya'qūb ibn-Shayba (d. 873/5)[7] and Is'ḥāq ibn-Abī-Isrā'īl (d. 859).[8] Both were given appointments by the caliph, as was also Bishr ibn-al-Walīd al-Kindī (d. 852), who under al-Ma'mūn and al-Mu'taṣim had refused to declare that the Qur'ān was created and had suffered somewhat, but who was now apparently ready to approve of the prohibition of discussion.[9] These men were sometimes known as the Wāqifa (*sc.* in respect of the Qur'ān) on account of their *waqf* (or *wuqūf*), 'suspension of judgement'.

The men just mentioned were primarily Traditionists and jurists. They are to be distinguished from another group sometimes also called Wāqifa,[10] but more accurately designated Lafẓiyya, who are interested rather in theology. The distinctive view of the Lafẓiyya was that, while the Qur'ān is uncreated, man's *lafẓ* or 'utterance' of it when he recites it is created.[11] Similar points may be made about a man's remembering the Qur'ān and still more clearly about his writing it, since the ink and paper must be created; but the *lafẓ* became the chief focus of attention. The question may have been suggested by the discussions of whether the words God addressed to Moses were his eternal speech, or it may have arisen spontaneously. In any case there is something paradoxical about the nature of speech or writing. When I read a letter from a friend, is my friend speaking to me and communicating with me? Does a long-dead author like al-Ash'arī communicate with me when I read his book? When I play a record of a speech by Sir Winston Churchill, do I hear him speaking? It was this paradox which the Lafẓiyya were exploiting to parry and defeat the arguments of the Mu'tazila and their like, and also to show other conservatives that the study of the Qur'ān and Traditions led to questions which could only be dealt with by using words and conceptions which did not occur in either.

Aḥmad ibn-Ḥanbal bitterly opposed the Lafẓiyya, whom he branded as 'Jahmites', even more pernicious than those who merely said the Qur'ān was created.[12] His venom was specially directed against the man whom he regarded as the fountain-head of the doctrine, al-Ḥusayn ibn-ʿAlī al-Karābīsī (d. 859/62).[13] Al-Karābīsī was a jurist, originally one of the Ahl ar-Ra'y, but latterly a disciple of ash-Shāfiʿī. His doctrine of the *lafẓ* of the Qur'ān shows that he was a Mutakallim at least to the extent of going beyond the range of questions explicitly mentioned in Qur'ān and Tradition. He played a part in the development of the critique of Traditions, and also wrote an account of heretical sects. He was thus, despite the nickname of 'Jahmite', not far from the central stream of Sunnite scholarship.

Much the same is true of al-Muḥāsibī (al-Ḥārith ibn-Asad; d. 857), except that his most influential works were in the mystical and ascetical field.[14] He was a jurist of the Shāfiʿite rite and a Traditionist, as well as a Mutakallim who wrote a *Refutation of the Muʿtazila.* He is sometimes said to have held the doctrine of the *lafẓ*, but in a passage in his *Kitāb ar-riʿāya* he dissociates himself from the doctrines of the created Qur'an, the *waqf* and the *lafẓ*.[15] Though he was bitterly attacked by Aḥmad ibn-Ḥanbal, this was for his general acceptance of the methods of Kalām, and there does not appear to be any specific mention of the *lafẓ*.[16] The bitterness of the attack was doubtless due to the fact that, apart from the 'Jahmite Kalām', which to Aḥmad was the source of all evil, al-Muḥāsibī's views were close to his own.

Rather different was another man, sometimes named as co-founder of the Lafẓiyya along with al-Karābīsī, (Muḥammad ibn-Shujāʿ) Ibn-ath-Thaljī (d. 869/79).[17] He was a Ḥanafite jurist and on good terms with various persons involved in the Miḥna, such as the chief judge Ibn-Abī-Du'ād and the governor of Baghdad from 821 to 850 Is'ḥāq ibn-Ibrāhīm al-Muṣʿabī. He was an active opponent of Aḥmad ibn-Ḥanbal. Though said to be inclined to Muʿtazilism, he did not go so far as to say that the Qur'ān was created but merely that it was *muḥdath*, 'originated in time,' that is, *kāna baʿd an lam yakun*, 'it existed after it did not exist'; because he avoided the word 'created' he is reckoned to the Wāqifa, but seems to be different from those mentioned above.[18] This is not inconsistent with his having held the doctrine of the *lafẓ*.

The great Traditionist al-Bukhārī (d. 870) became involved in serious arguments about the *lafẓ*. When, after settling in Nishapur, he was charged with holding this doctrine, he reluctantly replied that his view was that 'the Qur'ān is the speech of God uncreated, the acts of men are created, and inquisition (*imtiḥān*) is heresy'; by 'inquisition' he perhaps meant no more than further exploration of the subject.[19] This story has a ring of truth; it is formally sound and avoids entanglement in the paradoxes of speech, yet it gives an envious rival (as defenders of al-Bukhārī suggested) a slight ground for asserting that he held the doctrine of the Lafẓiyya. The charge of holding the doctrine of the *lafẓ* was also made, though not so publicly, against a distinguished Shāfiʿite jurist and Traditionist, Muḥammad ibn-Naṣr al-Marwazī (d. 906).[20] It may be significant that, while he had many other teachers, he had for a time studied with al-Bukhārī and had associated with al-Ḥārith al-Muḥāsibī. That men like al-Bukhārī and Muḥammad ibn-Naṣr should even have come near holding the doctrine of the *lafẓ* indicates that the necessity for some Kalām was beginning to be accepted by many Traditionists and jurists despite the last-ditch opposition of Aḥmad ibn-Ḥanbal.

One sees the point on which Aḥmad ibn-Ḥanbal insisted. When a man hears the Qur'ān recited, what he hears is 'the word of God'. Aḥmad quoted a Qur'ānic verse (9.6) which speaks of a man being granted protection 'so that he may hear the word of God'.[21] On the other hand, it is obvious that the reciting of the Qur'ān is a temporal human act and so, according to Ḥanbalite views, created; and the ink and paper of a written Qur'ān are created. There were numerous attempts to find a solution of these problems. Some unnamed Muʿtazilites distinguished between 'the reciting' (*al-qirā'a*) and 'what is recited' (*al-maqrū'*), making the first a human act and the second a divine act;[22] this fits in with the Muʿtazilite view that the Qur'ān is created, but the passive connotations of 'recited' rather conflict with the Sunnite idea that the Qur'ān is 'God speaking', and the distinction was not much used.

Among other Muʿtazilites who discussed the question the two Jaʿfars propounded an interesting view. They agreed that what is written, remembered and (when someone recites) heard is indeed the Qur'ān, and they justified this assertion by the ordinary use of language (as we might say of our record 'This *is* Sir Winston speaking on such an occasion'). They went on, however, to state that what is heard '*is* the Qur'ān' in the sense that it is a *ḥikāya*, 'imitation' or rather 'reproduction' of the Qur'ān and a *mithl*, perhaps 'likeness' of it.[23] Ibn-Kullāb (to be described presently), roughly a contemporary of the two Ja'fars, held a similar view, except that he said that the speech of God is a 'single meaning' (*ma'nā wāḥid*) subsisting in him, and that the sounds and letters are a 'copy' or 'trace' (*rasm*) of it and an 'expression' (*'ibāra*) of it.[24] The same point is made in the anonymous Ḥanafite document known as *Waṣiyyat Abī-Ḥanīfa*. This avoids all mention of the *lafẓ*, but admits that the pen, paper and writing are created. At the same time it maintains that the writing, letters, words and verses are a *dalāla*, an 'indication' or 'manifestation', of the Qur'ān to meet human needs.[25] This makes it probable that the *Waṣiyya* represents the opinions of Ḥanafite contemporaries of the men just mentioned. In contrast to this a rather later Ḥanafite document, *Al-fiqh al-akbar II*, does not mention anything like *ḥikāya* or *dalāla*, but allows without hesitation that 'our *lafẓ* of the Qur'ān is created, our writing of it is created, and our reciting of it is created, whereas the Qur'ān is not created'.[26]

This readiness to accept Kalām and the conclusions to which it leads was characteristic of only part of the Ḥanafite school. The contrast is clearly seen in the creed of aṭ-Ṭaḥāwī (d. 933). Like the Wāqifa he is not prepared to go beyond the terms used in Qur'ān and Tradition. So all he says (§9) is:

> We do not debate about the Qur'ān, but know that it is the speech of the Lord of the worlds; the Faithful Spirit brought it down and taught it to Muḥammad, the Prince of the first and the last. No speech of creatures equals the speech of God. We do not say (*sc.* we deny) it is created, and we do not oppose the body of the Muslims.[27]

Al-Ash'arī, despite his acceptance of Kalām, is reluctant to consider the question of the *lafẓ*—doubtless because of his admiration for Aḥmad ibn-Ḥanbal. In the creed in the *Ibāna* (§23) he merely says that the Qur'ān is the uncreated speech of God. In the creed in the *Maqālāt* (§22) he goes a little further, but still does not commit himself:

> They (Ahl al-Ḥadīth wa-s-Sunna) hold that the Qur'ān is the uncreated speech of God. As for the discussion (*kalām*)

> about the *waqf* (suspension of judgement) and the *lafẓ*, he who holds the *lafẓ* or the *waqf* is a heretic in their view. One does not say that the *lafẓ* of the Qur'ān is either created or uncreated.[28]

Despite this caution on the part of al-Ashʿarī himself his followers are found pursuing the line of thought introduced by Ibn-Kullāb and his like. Al-Bāqillānī (d. 1013) defined speech as 'a meaning (*maʿnā*) subsisting in the soul (*nafs*)', while for al-Juwaynī 'the affirmation of the speech subsisting in the soul' was a point on which he opposed the Muʿtazilites;[29] they also use such terms as *ʿibāra* and *dalāla*. Michel Allard regards this conception of the *kalām nafsī* as developing from al-Ashʿarī's insistence on the unity of the Qur'ān (a point in which he differed from the Ḥanbalites), and not as a new departure.[30]

b) *The Ḥanafites*

It is convenient to speak about the Ḥanafites as a distinct group or school although at first—probably until after 850—there was no clear line of demarcation. It was noted above (chapter 7, §1) that there was a similar vagueness about the term Ahl ar-Ra'y, which was also applied to the followers of Abū-Ḥanīfa. Of the earlier scholars to whom notices are given by Ibn-Abī-l-Wafā' in *Al-jawāhir al-muḍī'a fī ṭabaqāt al-Ḥanafiyya* some, though holding views akin to those of Abū-Ḥanifa, do not appear to have studied under him or his immediate disciples. It seems likely that, until the Shāfiʿite school took shape, most scholars of Iraq who used rational methods, even to a slight degree, were reckoned as Ḥanafites. Consequently there were differing and even opposed strands of thought among the Ḥanafites. Unfortunately the development of the Ḥanafite school has not been fully studied, and the biographical notices, though numerous, are tantalizingly inadequate. Thus all that can be done here is to give some brief indications.

The elaboration of Ḥanafite jurisprudence owed much to certain disciples of the master, chiefly Abū-Yūsuf (d. 798) and Muḥammad ibn-al-Ḥasan ash-Shaybānī (d. 805 or later), and to a lesser extent al-Lu'lu'ī (d. 819). Each of these men seems to have had his own disciples, but there was some 'cross-fertilization', and the lines of 'intellectual affiliation' are not clear. In any case attitudes to Kalām and the Miḥna—the matters of chief concern in the present context—did not coincide with group allegiance in jurisprudence. Thus

Bishr al-Marīsī incurred the anger of his master Abū-Yūsuf because he engaged in Kalām and believed in the createdness of the Qur'ān (p. 198 above). Because the Ḥanafites are upholders of *ra'y*, it is not surprising to find that many of them sided with the caliphal government in the Miḥna, even to the extent of taking an active part. It is more surprising to find some who vehemently opposed official doctrine. Among the latter were Bishr ibn-al-Walīd al-Kindī (d. 852), who has been mentioned above (p. 281), Abū Ḥassān az-Ziyādī (d. 856),[31] al-Ḥasan ibn-Ḥammād as-Sajjāda,[32] and Nu'aym ibn-Ḥammād (d. 842/3).[33] On the other hand, of the judges who administered the Miḥna the chief *qāḍī* Aḥmad ibn-Abī-Du'ād was reckoned a Ḥanafite,[34] as well as 'Abd-ar-Raḥmān ibn-Is'ḥāq,[35] Ibn-Abī-l-Layth,[36] Muḥammad ibn-Sammā'a,[37] 'Ubayd-Allāh ibn-Aḥmad,[38] al-Ḥasan ibn-'Alī ibn-al-Ja'd,[39] and 'Abd-Allāh ibn-Muḥammad al-Khalījī.[40] A grandson of Abū-Ḥanīfa, Ismā'īl ibn-Ḥammād, who was also a judge, accepted the doctrine of the created Qur'ān shortly before his death in 827.[41]

From the standpoint of present study the most interesting material about the Ḥanafites is in the credal statements mentioned in the previous subsection and in chapter 5. Aṭ-Ṭaḥāwī may be regarded as continuing the views of men like Bishr ibn-al-Walīd al-Kindī. The two anonymous creeds, on the other hand, come from circles more favourable to Kalām. The *Waṣiyya* appears to belong to the years round about 850, but with the evidence at present available it would be hazardous to guess at the name of its author. *Al-fiqh al-akbar II* is later in view of the changed emphasis in the article about the Qur'ān and the more developed doctrine of God's attributes. There are resemblances between certain articles and passages in al-Māturīdī's *Kitāb at-tawḥīd*,[42] but they are not exact parallels, and there are diffierences between this creed and other works ascribed to al-Māturīdī.

c) *Ibn-Kullāb and al-Qalānisī*

Possibly the most influential of the Mutakallimūn of the period of the Miḥna was Ibn-Kullāb ('Abd-Allāh ibn-Sa'īd), who died shortly after 854 and about whose exact name there is some dispute.[43] He is reckoned as a Shāfi'ite, though his teachers are not named. Al-Baghdādī says that 'Abd-al-'Azīz al-Makkī was his pupil,[44] but this seems doubtful, since the two were roughly contemporaries. He may, however, have been influenced by Ibn-Kullāb, since both are said to have argued against the Muʿtazilites at the court of al-Ma'mūn. In particular Ibn-Kullāb argued against ʿAbbād ibn-Sulaymān. It may be significant that al-Ashʿarī in the *Maqālāt* several times mentions Sulaymān ibn-Jarīr the Zaydite in close proximity to Ibn-Kullāb,[45] and that his associate al-Qalānisī approved of the distinctive Zaydite doctrine of the 'imamate of the inferior' (*mafḍul*).[46] Ibn-Kullāb's chief contribution to Kalām, however, was his elaboration of the doctrine of the attributes (*ṣifāt*) of God. He asserted that for each name such as 'powerful', 'knowing', 'eternal', there was an attribute of 'power', 'knowledge' or 'eternity'. Some of the reports use as an alternative to *ṣifa* the term *maʿnā* (which here might perhaps be rendered 'hypostatic quality'), but one cannot be certain that Ibn-Kullāb himself used this term. These attributes were 'not God and not other than God'. Among them he seems to have distinguished between 'active' and 'essential' attributes (*ṣifāt al-fiʿl; ṣifāt an-nafs* or *adh-dhāt*).[47] Ibn-Kullāb applied this view as widely as possible, though he was not prepared to say that God was 'existent' by 'existence' (*mawjūd, wujūd*). Others stopped short of saying God was 'enduring' by 'enduringness' (*bāqin, baqā'*), 'eternal' by 'eternity' and the like; but eventually there was wide agreement among Ashʿarites and others that there were seven 'essential' attributes; knowledge, power, will, life, speech, hearing, seeing. This aspect of Sunnite dogma may be regarded as largely due to Ibn-Kullāb.

In several passages al-Ashʿarī speaks of 'the associates of Ibn-Kullāb', but mentions no names. In the *Uṣūl* of al-Baghdādī, however, the name of al-Qalānisī (or Abū-l-ʿAbbās al-Qalānisī) is more often than not associated with that of Ibn-Kullāb as holding the same or very similar views.[48] Several men called al-Qalānisī are known, but it has been shown that the man whose views resembled those of Ibn-Kullāb must be Aḥmad ibn-ʿAbd-ar-Raḥmān ibn-Khālid, roughly a contemporary of al-Ashʿarī.[49] The man with whom we are concerned may even have been a little older than al-Ashʿarī, for it is reported that he was 'the imam of the Ahl as-Sunna' in the time of one Abū-ʿAlī ath-Thaqafī who died in 939.[50] He was sufficiently important for the later Ashʿarite Ibn-Fūrak (d. 1015) to write a book entitled 'The Difference between the two Shaykhs, al-Qalānisī and al-Ashʿarī'.[51] Al-Baghdādī speaks of him with great respect as 'our shaykh',[52] and even as apparently the leader of a group of Ash'arites—'al-Qalānisī and those of our associates who followed him'.[53]

These facts throw an interesting light on the intellectual history of al-Ash'arī and his school. They further illuminate two important statements about the 'conversion' of al-Ash'arī :

> . . . until it came to 'Abd-Allāh ibn-Sa'īd al-Kullābī, Abū-l-'Abbās al-Qalānisī and al-Ḥārith ibn-Asad al-Muḥāsibī; these were of the 'old school' (*jumlat as-salaf*), but they engaged in the science of Kalām and defended the doctrines of the old school by arguments from Kalām and proofs from fundamentals (*barāhīn uṣūliyya*). Thus they continued to write and teach until there occurred a dispute between Abū-l-Ḥasan al-Ash'arī and his teacher about the question of 'the good and the best' (*sc.* whether God does what is best for men, etc.); the two became enemies and al-Ash'arī joined this group and supported their view by the methods of Kalām, and that became a *madhhab* (? acceptable system of doctrine) for the Ahl as-Sunna wa-l-Jamā'a.[54]
>
> (Al-Ash'arī) was a Ḥanafite in (legal) *madhhab* and a Mu'tazilite in Kalām. He was the foster-son of Abū-'Alī al-Jubbā'ī, and the latter brought him up and taught him jurisprudence and Kalām. Afterwards he separated from Abū-'Alī because of something which occurred between them and was drawn to Ibn-Kullāb and his like, abandoning the principles of the Mu'tazila and adopting a *madhhab* for himself.[55]

It would thus appear that in the movement among the main body of Sunnites for the acceptance of Kalām a central place was taken by Ibn-Kullāb. Al-Muḥāsibī was possibly more influential than is indicated by the material here considered.[56] The views of these men were then continued in a group of which the leader was al-Qalānisī, and it was doubtless with this group that al-Ash'arī associated when he abandoned the Mu'tazilites. If one adopts the hypothesis that the first volume of the *Maqālāt* represents the author's views before his 'conversion', then he was already familiar with some of the doctrines of this group. A man of his intellectual stature, however, would not long be content with following others; and at various points he adopted views of his own. He must have remained on friendly terms, however, with the group of Sunnite Mutakallimūn and been regarded as one of them. It seems likely that it was as a result of the book of Ibn-Fūrak mentioned above that the Sunnite Mutakallimūn of Iraq came to regard themselves as the followers of al-Ashʿarī rather than of al-Qalānisī—al-Baghdādī, though he died some twenty years after Ibn-Fūrak, is thus still following an older pattern in regarding al-Qalānisī as one of their shaykhs. (Much of our information about al-Ashʿarī and the early Mutakallimūn seems to have come from a lost work of Ibn-Fūrak called *Ṭabaqāt al-mutakallimūn.*[57])

Among other scholars who may have belonged to this group are Dāwūd ibn-ʿAlī al-Iṣbahānī (d. 884), the founder of the Ẓāhirite legal rite,[58] and al-Junayd (d. 910), the important ṣūfī.[59] The latter, whatever his precise attitude to Kalām, certainly made no distinctive contributions in this field. Dāwūd ibn-ʿAlī devoted most of his writings to legal questions, but there is attributed to him a critique of Ibn-Kullāb's doctrine of the attributes. He objected to saying that God is hearing and seeing by a hypostatized 'hearing' and 'sight', because the Qur'ān only says God is 'hearing', 'seeing', and does not mention the other [60]

d) *Ibn-Karrām*

In the development of theology in the lands to the east of Iraq an important part was played by Ibn-Karrām (Abū-ʿAbd-Allāh Muḥammad).[61] (The correct spelling is possibly Karām or even Kirām, but the usual form is retained here.) He studied at Nishapur, Balkh, Merv and Herat, and then for five years at Mecca. About 844 he was in Jerusalem, where he built a *khānqāh* (monastery).[62] On returning to the east he conducted a preaching mission which gained him many disciples, but which was opposed by some rulers so that he spent eight years in prison (857 to 865). On his release he set out again for Jerusalem, where he died in 869. He had numerous followers in various regions, especially in those parts of Khurasan which looked to Nishapur as their intellectual capital. In this latter area the movement was a popular one, and by the second half of the tenth century had become a political force of some importance. In this period the Karrāmites play a part in several events mentioned in general histories. Karrāmite doctrine had official support from the sultan Maḥmūd of Ghazna (998–1030). By 1100 the Karrāmites had lost most of their political influence, but the sect continued to exist at least into the thirteenth century.

The material about the doctrines of the Karrāmites comes from opponents and is difficult to interpret. It is also difficult to know how much goes back to Ibn-Karrām himself, and how much was due to disciples at a later date. Massignon says that Karrāmism attracted Ḥanafites who were opposed to Muʿtazilite teaching,[63] and the Muʿtazilites and Ashʿarites regarded it as a form of *tajsīm* and *tashbīh* (corporealism, anthropomorphism). Ibn-Karrām certainly seems to have used *jism* of God in much the same way as Hishām ibn-al-Ḥakam (p. 188), and the Karrāmites are said to have been forced to keep to this term by their adherents from the ordinary people, though their scholars would have preferred *jawhar*. Long discussions are also recorded of the anthropomorphic terms in the Qur'ān, especially God's being seated on the throne, but the aim of the Karrāmites in these discussions is not clear. It was probably on points such as these that other Ḥanafites opposed the Karrāmites, e.g. Abū-Bakr as-Samarqandī (d. 881, but also said to be of the generation of al-Māturīdī).[64] It seems likely (as Allard suggests) that the Ḥanafite intellectual development which culminated in al-Māturīdī owed much to the opposition of the Karrāmites. Ibn-Karrām is not mentioned by name in *Kitāb at-tawḥīd*, but his doctrine of *īmān* is criticized.[65]

Despite concessions made to the conservatism of the ordinary man the Karrāmites dealt with some questions of Kalām. In particular, as part of the discussion of God's attributes, they wrestled with the problem of the relation of the temporal and the eternal. Where others distinguished between essential and active attributes and held that the latter were not eternal (since God could not properly be called creator, for example, until he had in fact created), the Karrāmites held that the active attributes also must be eternal. They argued that God had the name of 'creator' (*khāliq*) even when 'creation' (or 'creatures'—*khalq*) did not exist, and that this was in virtue of an attribute of 'creatorness' (or 'creativity'—*khāliqiyya*) which was 'power over creation' (*qudra ʿalā l-khalq*). They further insisted that the creation of any body required the origination or occurrence (*ḥudūth*) of several accidents (*aʿrāḍ*) in the essence of God, such as the willing of the origination of that originated-thing (*ḥādith*) and his saying to it 'Be'.[66] From the brief notices it is difficult to see all the implications of this theory, but it seems to have a measure of coherence.

One of the most interesting parts of Massignon's deeply perceptive account of Ibn-Karrām and his school is the new interpretation given by Ibn-Karrām to the terms *jabr*, *irjā'* and *shakk*.[67] It appears from Massignon's statements (since the original sources are hard to find) that Ibn-Karrām is rejecting the nicknames given to him and like-minded scholars—namely, Mujbira, Murji'a and Shukkāk (p. 139 above). *Jabr*, 'determinism', is defined as introducing grace (*istiṭā'a*) only at the moment of the act, which was the view eventually accepted by Sunnism. This was a kind of mean between the Mu'tazilite view that *jabr* is 'saying that God creates our acts and including evil in the divine *qadar*' and the view of the Ahl al-Ḥadīth that *jabr* is 'introducing grace *before* the act' (as the Mu'tazilites did). Ibn-Karrām himself held that beyond the formal acceptance of belief in God (which for him was *īmān*), there was a state of grace (*ṭuma'nīna*) which followed upon commitment to this belief. The heresy of *irjā'* was 'not taking account of the external accomplishment of an act', and also came between the views of the Mu'tazila and the Ahl al-Ḥadīth; this implied that Ibn-Karrām was not a Murji'ite, since he placed all the emphasis on the external profession of faith. *Shakk*, 'scepticism', he defined as 'making *istithnā'* in respect of one's own faith' (that is, saying, 'If God will, I am a believer') : and this is precisely what the Ḥanbalites did. These points show how there was a considerable area of agreement between the Karrāmites and the Ḥanafites, and some opposition between Karrāmites and Ḥanbalites. It was 'Uthmān ad-Dārimī (d. 895) who is said to have been responsible for the expulsion of Ibn-Karrām from Herat;[68] and he was a close associate of Aḥmad ibn-Ḥanbal.

While the Karrāmites cannot be said to have made a major contribution to the development of Islamic thought, they were an important strand, intertwined with others, in the intellectual life of the eastern caliphate.

e) *Aḥmad ibn-Ḥanbal and other opponents of Kalām*

To appreciate the full spectrum of Islamic thought in the ninth century we must also look at those who, though opposing Kalām, put forward formulations of theological doctrine. In general such persons belonged to the group called in the sources Ahl al-Ḥadīth. The best-known figure among them is Aḥmad ibn-Ḥanbal, who has already been referred to in several connections.

α) *Aḥmad ibn-Ḥanbal*, more fully Abū-ʿAbd-Allāh Aḥmad ibn-Muḥammad ibn-Ḥanbal ash-Shaybānī, was born in Baghdad in 780 and died there in 855.[69] He studied jurisprudence and Traditions in Baghdad, and also travelled to Kufa, Basra, the Hijaz, the Yemen and Syria. His insistence that the Qur'ān is the uncreated speech of God and his resistance to the official policy during the period of the Inquisition have already been mentioned. After the reversal of the policy of the Miḥna al-Mutawakkil tried to gain his support, but he seems to have been too old to play an active part in affairs. Although he rejected the rational methods of the Mutakallimūn and insisted on deriving religious doctrines and legal rules solely from the Qur'ān and the Traditions, he was clearly a man of powerful intellect capable of adopting a coherent view in matters of great complexity. Because he objected in principle to systematization his doctrinal views have come to us in various forms. To give some idea of his position there follows an abbreviated translation of the text called *ʿAqīda I* by Henri Laoust.[70]

1) *Īmān* is word and act and intention and holding to the Sunna. *Īmān* increases and decreases. There is *istithnā'* (saying 'I am a believer if God will') in respect of *īmān*, but the *istithnā'* is not doubt but only an old custom (*sunna māḍiya*) among scholars . . .

2) The Qadar (determination), the good of it and the evil of it, the little of it and the much of it, . . . is from God; . . . no one opposes God's will, nor transgresses his decree (*qaḍā'*), but all (men) come to what he has created them for. . . . This is justice from him. Adultery, theft, wine-drinking, murder, consuming unlawful wealth, idolatry and all sins are by God's determination and decree . . .

3) We do not bear witness of any of the people of the Qibla that he is in Hell for an evil he has done, unless there is a Tradition about that . . . : we do not bear witness of any that he is in Paradise for a good he has done unless there is a Tradition about that . . .

4) The caliphate is in Quraysh so long as there are two men (alive). . . . The Jihād is valid with the imams, whether they act justly or evilly. . . . The Friday worship, the (celebration of the) two Feasts, and the Pilgrimage (are observed) with the authorities (*sulṭān*), even if they are not upright, just and pious. Taxes (*ṣadaqāt*, *kharāj*, etc.) are paid to the commanders (*umarā'*), whether they deal justly or wickedly. . . . Those to whom God has entrusted your

affairs are to be followed . . . and not opposed by your sword. . . . To keep aloof (from both sides) in civil war (*fitna*) is an old custom whose observance is obligatory.

5) Hold back from the people of the Qibla, and do not call any of them an unbeliever on account of a sin . . . unless there is a Tradition about it.

6) The one-eyed Dajjāl will undoubtedly appear. . . . The punishment of the tomb is a reality . . . and the basin (*ḥawḍ*) of Muḥammad . . . and the bridge (*ṣirāt*) . . . and the balance (*mīzān*) . . . and the trumpet (*ṣūr*) . . . and the guarded tablet (*al-lawḥ al-maḥfūẓ*) . . . and the pen (*qalam*) . . .

7) The intercession (*shafāʿa*) on the day of resurrection is a reality. People (*qawm*) will intercede for others, and they will not come into Hell. Some will come out from Hell by intercession. Some will come out from Hell after entering it and spending in it what time God willed. . . . Some will be in it eternally, namely, the polytheists and those who deny and disbelieve in God.

8) Paradise and Hell and what they contain are already created. God created them, and created creatures for them. Neither they nor what is in them will ever disappear.

9) He created seven heavens . . . and seven earths . . . and the throne (*ʿarsh*) . . . and the sedile (*kursī*) . . .

10) The Qur'ān is the speech of God by which he speaks. It is not created. He who holds that the Qur'ān is created is a Jahmite and unbeliever. He who holds the Qur'ān is the speech of God and suspends judgement (*waqafa*) and does not say 'not created', is worse than the first. He who holds our utterance and reading of it are created, while the Qur'ān is the speech of God, is a Jahmite . . .

11) Vision is from God and is a reality. When the recipient sees something in a dream, which is not a jumble, and tells it to a scholar truthfully and the scholar interprets it by the correct principle without distortion, then the vision is a reality . . .

12) The good qualities (*maḥāsin*) of the Companions of the Messenger of God, all of them together, are to be mentioned, and their bad qualities are not to be mentioned . . .

13) The best (*khayr*) of the community after the Prophet is Abū-Bakr, then ʿUmar, then ʿUthmān, then ʿAlī. Some suspended judgement about ʿUthmān. . . . After these four the Companions of the Messenger of God are the best of the people. No one may mention

their evil qualities, nor accuse any of them of something shameful or some defect. He who does this must be punished by the government (*sulṭān*) . . .

14) He (? one) recognizes that the Arabs have rights and excellence and precedence (? in Islam), and he loves them . . . and does not follow the view of the Shuʿūbites . . .

15) He who forbids earnings and trading . . . is ignorant and in error . . .

16) Religion is only the book of God, the *āthār* (sayings or acts of pious men), the *sunan* (standard practices), and sound narratives from reliable men about recognized sound valid Traditions (*akhbār*), confirming one another . . . until that ends with the Messenger of God and his Companions and the Followers and the Followers of the Followers, and after them the recognized imams (*sc.* scholars) who are taken as exemplars, who hold to the Sunna and keep to the *āthār*, who do not recognize heresy and are not accused of falsehood or of divergence (from one another). They are not upholders of *qiyās* (analogical reasoning) and *ra'y*, for *qiyās* in religion is worthless, and *ra'y* is the same and worse. The upholders of *ra'y* and *qiyās* in religion are heretical and in error, except where there is an *athar* from any of the earlier reliable imams.

17) He who supposes that *taqlīd* (following an authority) is not approved and that his religion is not thus following anyone . . . only wants to invalidate the *athar* and to weaken knowledge and the Sunna, and to stand isolated in *ra'y* and Kalām and heresy and divergence (from others).

Several of these articles are the outcome of the major debates described in earlier chapters, and need no further comment, e.g. §1 (*īmān*), §2 (the Qadar), §3 (? question of *irjā'*), §5 (anti-Khārijite), §7 (intercession), §10 (the Qur'ān), §13 (order of excellence). Law-abidingness (§4) had long been a characteristic of the 'general religious movement' out of which the Ahl al-Ḥadīth grew; and so also had been acceptance of popular eschatological beliefs (§ 6). The article about Paradise and Hell (§8) is directed against certain 'Jahmite' views.[71] It is unusual in a creed to find an anti-Shuʿūbite article like §14. The excessive asceticism attacked in §15 is also mentioned by al-Ashʿarī.[72] The insistence on respect for all Companions (§§12, 13) is directed against forms of Shīʿism which help that most of the Companions disobeyed Muḥammad in not accepting ʿAlī as his successor; the reliability of the Companions was a necessary part of the structure of Tradition. It is noteworthy that Aḥmad ibn-Ḥanbal also gives a place to the recognized outstanding scholars of later generations by his references to *āthār* (sing. *athar*) in §§16, 17; the word here apparently means stories about Muslims other than Muḥammad,[73] so that the articles are emphasizing the emerging consensus of the Community as witnessed by the views of the leading ulema.

A specially important feature of this creed is its discussion of methodological questions in §§16, 17. The reasons for Aḥmad ibn-Ḥanbal's rejection of *qiyās* and *ra'y* are elucidated by Michel Allard's study of the reasons for the opposition to al-Ashʿarī by contemporary Ḥanbalites.[74] Reasoning in jurisprudence proceeds from a 'positive hierarchy of facts', namely, accepted rules and Traditions; but in theology there is no such hierarchy and the Mutakallim tends to argue from an analogy between God and created beings; thus from the fact that intelligently constructed human artefacts imply that the constructor has knowledge al-Ashʿarī argues to a similar relationship between the world and God's knowledge.[75] For the Ḥanbalites this procedure is *tashbīh*, 'anthropomorphism'. (They rebut the accusation of *tashbīh* made against themselves by holding that the anthropomorphic terms of the Qur'ān are to taken *bi lā kayf* or 'amodally'.) In short Ashʿarite Kalām is to be condemned on two counts: it falls into *tashbīh*; and it abandons the primacy of Qur'ān and Tradition, together with the body of accepted interpretations of these. On both counts the Ḥanbalites might be said to be defending objectivity against a growing subjectivity. In accordance with the attitude to Kalām there is no discussion in this creed of the many questions about the attributes of God which were exercising the Mutakallimūn (though there are some bare statements about what he knows and about his speech).[76] The question of the utterance (*lafẓ*, *qirā'a*) of the Qur'ān goes beyond the Qur'ānic terms in the direction of Kalām, but it does not involve *tashbīh*.

β) *Ibn-Qutayba* (Abū-Muḥammad ʿAbd-Allāh ibn-Muslim ibn-Qutayba ad-Dīnawarī), a man of letters even more than a theologian, was born at Kufa in 828 and died at Baghdad in 889.[77] From 851 to 870 he was *qāḍī* of Dīnawar in Kurdistan, but from 871 until his death he devoted himself to teaching. His views, which were close to those of Aḥmad ibn-Ḥanbal, were in favour with the government after the change of policy at the beginning of the reign of al-Mutawakkil. Yet he did not regard himself as a disciple of Aḥmad ibn-Ḥanbal, and was less rigid on the question of the *lafẓ* of the Qur'ān. He considered that he belonged to the Aṣ'ḥāb al-Ḥadīth, and that Aḥmad ibn-Ḥanbal was only one of at least a dozen distinguished scholars of this party.[78] He is thus interesting as representing the views of the group before the dominant position of Aḥmad ibn-Ḥanbal had been generally recognized.

At one point he gives a brief statement of the creed of the Aṣ'ḥāb al-Ḥadīth:[79]

All the Aṣ'ḥāb al-Ḥadīth agree that:

1) What God wills comes to be, and what he does not will does not come to be.
2) He is the creator of good and evil.
3) The Qur'ān is the speech of God not created.
4) God will be seen on the day of resurrection.
5) The two shaykhs (Abū-Bakr and 'Umar) have precedence.
6) They believe in the punishment of the tomb.

They do not differ in these principles. Whoever diverges from them in any of these (points), they repudiate, hate, regard as heretical and keep away from. They differ only in respect of the utterance of the Qur'ān, because of its obscurity. They all agree that:

7) The Qur'ān in every circumstance, recited, written, heard, remembered, is uncreated.

This is the consensus (*ijmā'*).

A longer though similar creed, but with a few variations, is found in a work called the *Waṣiyya* or 'Testament' ascribed to Ibn-Qutayba. The work is almost certainly not by him, but may be by his son or grandson. Besides the creed the work contains a ṣūfī homily, and there are even traces of ṣūfī ideas in the discussion of the creed.[80] Though not authentic, the work is evidence for the attitude of some of the Ahl al-Ḥadīth in the early tenth century.

Ibn-Qutayba was accused of being a Karrāmite by al-Bayhaqī (d. 1066), but an examination of his works gives ample ground for rejecting the accusation.[81] Thus a reference to *īmān* in his book on contradictory Traditions makes it clear that he did not restrict it to outward profession as did Ibn-Karrām.[82]

γ) *Other Ḥanbalites* in the period up to 950 include (Abū-Bakr Aḥmad ibn-Muḥammad) al-Khallāl (d. 923)[83] and (Abū-Muḥammad al-Ḥasan ibn-ʿAlī) al-Barbahārī (d. 941).[84] The distinctive feature of the creed of al-Khallāl as it is contained in his *Kitāb al-jāmiʿ* is that he pays special attention to the political aspect. Al-Barbahārī was a fiery personality and somewhat of a demagogue, whose influence was probably behind some of the civil disturbances in Baghdad at this time. His views are preserved in his *Kitāb as-sunna*, which is found in the *Ṭabaqāt* of Ibn-Abī-Yaʿlā, and are similar to those of his master.[85]

δ) The great historian and Qur'ān-commentator (Abū-Jaʿfar Muḥammad ibn-Jarīr ibn-Yazīd) *aṭ-Ṭabarī* (d. 923)[86] is not reckoned a Ḥanbalite, but in his creed he expressly follows Aḥmad ibn-Ḥanbal's view of the *lafẓ*.[87] On the other hand, he was bitterly opposed by some Ḥanbalites in the last year or so of his life, perhaps because in his commentary he had made some concessions to Muʿtazilite views. It is certain that some persons believed him to have sympathies with Shīʿism, but the accusation appears to be false,[88] though it was given verisimilitude by the existence of an Imāmite scholar of almost the same name, Abū-Jaʿfar Muḥammad ibn-Jarīr ibn-Rustam aṭ-Ṭabarī.[89]

ε) A view similar to that of aṭ-Ṭabarī was held by (Muḥammad ibn-Is'ḥāq) *ibn-Khuzayma* (d. 924), whose *Kitāb at-Tawḥīd* has been published.[90]

The scholars described in this chapter so far are all Sunnite theologians of the period up to 950. They illustrate the variety and lack of homogeneity in Sunnism at this period, and also the extent to which there were Sunnite Mutakallimūn before al-Ashʿarī.

2

The Silver Age of Muʿtazilism

The Golden Age of Muʿtazilism was the period of the great Muʿtazilites (studied in an earlier chapter) and the immediately following years when the government of the caliphate officially adopted at least some aspects of Muʿtazilite doctrine. In contrast to this the period up to the death of Abū-Hāshim in 933 is a Silver Age in which the zest and excitement of the previous period had been lost and thinkers, instead of exploring fresh fields, were seeking to introduce greater refinement into the answers to old questions. It will suffice to consider one or two of the leading Muʿtazilites of the period.

a) *Al-Jubbā'ī*

Abū-'Alī Muḥammad ibn-'Abd-al-Wahhāb al-Jubbā'ī was born at Jubbā in Khuzistan, and studied at Basra under the head of the Mu'tazila there, ash-Shaḥḥām,[91] who had succeeded his master Abū-l-Hudhayl. In turn al-Jubbā'ī succeeded ash-Shaḥḥām on the latter's death about 880 or 890. No work of al-Jubbā'ī has survived, but al-Ash'arī and other writers have reported on his views. He died in 915.[92]

One aspect of the thought of al-Jubbā'ī is a tendency towards the recovery of the primitive realization of God's omnipotence and inscrutability. God is not bound by human conceptions of justice and injustice, but only by what is involved in his own wisdom, namely, that his operations shall not be self-stultifying. So in al-Jubbā'ī's view God is not bound to do what is best (*aṣlaḥ*) for men in all respects but only in respect of religion ; in this he opposed those Mu'tazilites of Baghdad who held that God always does what is best for men.[93] He does what is best for them in religion because he has commanded them to have faith and his command would be stultified unless he did such things as sending prophets to them.

Connected with this is the conception of a 'favour' or 'grace' (*luṭf*, sometimes *laṭīfa*) which God may give to men. Al-Jubbā'ī believes that God has such 'graces', but a 'grace' would not be effective in the case of a man of whom God knew that he would never believe—presumably because in this case to bestow a 'grace' would contradict God's own knowledge. On the other hand, in the case of the man whom God knew to be capable of believing without 'grace', to bestow on him 'grace' would reduce his reward, since he would now believe without effort; yet al-Jubbā'ī thought that it was fitting for God to bestow 'grace' here and thereby make this man equal to one of whom it was known that he would never believe without 'grace'.[94] This line of thought appears to be connected with the story of 'the three brothers', which will be mentioned in the account of the conversion of al-Ash'arī. In other words al-Jubbā'ī is moving away from the older Mu'tazilite (and Khārijite) way of thinking, by which there was a fixed scheme of future rewards and punishments and, since all men had equal opportunities, a man's final destiny depended on the degree of his own moral effort. Al-Jubbā'ī saw that the details of God's dealings with men cannot be rationally explained. Self-consistence requires that God should do certain good things for men but beyond what he is in any sense obliged to do he shows much kindness to men. This is *tafaḍḍul* on his part—a conception to which al-Jubbā'ī gives prominence—that is, unmerited benevolence and generosity. This further implies a recognition of man's weakness and his inability fully to earn the reward of Paradise by his striving.

Among the fullest reports preserved by al-Ash'arī are those of al-Jubbā'ī's views on the attributes of God. Where Abū-l-Hudhayl had said 'God is knowing with a knowledge which is his essence', al-Jubbā'ī objected to the term 'knowledge' here and merely said that God is knowing by his essence. He dealt with the other essential attributes similarly. He accepted the distinction between essential attributes and active attributes (*ṣifāt adh-dhāt, ṣifāt al-fi'l* or *al-af'āl*), the latter being the attributes or names connected with God's temporal activity; and he tried to make the distinction more precise and give exact definitions of the two classes. When he considered the applicability or non-applicability to God of various names, he did not make occurrence in the Qur'ān a criterion but judged the question on rational and philological grounds. Thus he held that the word *'āqil*, 'intelligent' (from *'aql*, 'intelligence'), could not properly be used of God because the root suggested a hindrance or impediment, as in *'iqāl*, 'the tether of a camel', and God was not subject to hindrance or impediment.[95]

The general effect of this account of the attributes is the negative one of shutting man off from any real knowledge of God. Though the human mind takes each attribute or name as different from the others, it does not follow that there is any difference in God; and therefore all that the names tell us is that God is. This appears to be the interpretation of al-Jubbā'ī's assertion that 'the *waṣf* is the *ṣifa* and the *tasmiya* is the *ism*', that is, 'the describing is the "attribute" and the naming is the name'.[96] The discussion about what names may properly be applied to God is not about the reality of God but about the coherence of the human language applied to God. After noting the subtlety of the reasoning in this account and its non-recognition of the authority of the Qur'ān, Michel Allard remarks:

> The dominant impression received from reading the pages of al-Jubbā'ī consecrated to the problem of the divine attributes is that in these pages the writer is not addressing anyone, that he is not trying to convince but to demonstrate; the

> impression is unavoidable that the reality of both God and man has been so sterilized and desiccated that it has become fit material for all sorts of rational operations . . . there is something decadent in the pages preserved by al-Ashʿarī under the name of his master.[97]

b) *Abū-Hāshim*

Abū-Hāshim ʿAbd-as-Salām ibn-Muḥammad al-Jubbā'ī, the son of the man just described, succeeded his father as head of the Muʿtazilites of Basra and died in 933.[98] His date of birth is variously given as 861 and 890; but the latter would make him somewhat young to succeed his father in 915 and would make it impossible for him to have studied under al-Mubarrad, the great philologist of Basra, who died in 898, after spending his last few years in Baghdad. The followers of Abū-Hāshim are known as Bahshamiyya.

In most respects Abū-Hāshim's views were similar to those of his father. On the question of the differences in human destiny, however, he tended to revert towards the old rational scheme and to insist on man's ability to earn his salvation and on God's obligation to act according to (human) reason. In connection with the doctrine of the attributes of God he produced the chief novelty in Muʿtazilite thinking during the Silver Age, namely, the theory of the *aḥwāl* (sing. *ḥāl*), the 'modes' or 'states'. The term appears to be derived from grammatical usage. In such a sentence as 'Zayd came riding' (*jā'a Zaydun rākiban*) the word *rākiban* is in the accusative, and this is said to be because it expresses the *ḥāl*, that is, the state or condition or circumstances of the subject (or object) of the act while the act was taking place. In Abū-Hāshim's theory, when we say 'God is knowing', 'knowing' expresses the *ḥāl* or 'state' of God's essence distinct from that essence. The point of the theory appears to be that, just as we cannot say that 'riding' is existent or non-existent apart from Zayd so we cannot say 'knowing' is existent or non-existent apart from God. In other words the theory is avoiding the suggestion of the word *ṣifa* and of nouns such as 'knowledge' (*ʿilm*) that these have a quasi-substantive and partly independent existence within the being or essence of God. This conception of *aḥwāl* was in some respects accepted by certain later Ashʿarite theologians, notably al-Bāqillānī (d. 1013) and al-Juwaynī (d. 1085).

c) *Al-Kaʿbī*

Abū-l-Qāsim ʿAbd-Allāh ibn-Aḥmad al-Kaʿbī al-Balkhī (d. 929/31) is known sometimes as al-Kaʿbī and sometimes as Abū-l-Qāsim al-Balkhī, though the only name given to his followers is Kaʿbiyya.[99] He was a disciple of al-Khayyāṭ,[100] and succeeded him as head of the Muʿtazilites of Baghdad, though he spent the last years of his life in his native Balkh.

In general his views were along the lines of those of the Muʿtazilites of Baghdad. He held that God is bound to do what is best for men, at least in what he commands them. On the problem of the attributes he adopted a different position from either al-Jubbā'ī or Abū-Hāshim in that he tried to reduce the great variety of names of God to one or two basic ones. Thus he held that to say God is 'willing' only means that he is 'knowing' and 'creating', and to say that he is 'hearing' and 'seeing' only means that he is 'knowing', though with a restriction to what is audible and visible. At several points in his *Uṣūl* al-Baghdādī notes that al-Kaʿbī's views are similar to those of al-Ashʿarī.[101] Al-Ashʿarī himself in the *Maqālāt* seems to be most interested in al-Kaʿbī's atomistic tendencies, notably his assertion that accidents do not endure for two moments.[102]

The atomistic view of nature, of which al-Kaʿbī is the foremost representative among the Muʿtazilites, had a dominant place in Islamic thought at certain periods, not least among the Ashʿarites of the first few centuries. The idea of causal continuity in nature which was implicit in the Greek scientific and philosophical works absorbed by the Muslims, was soon excluded from Islamic formulations, though of course the Falāsifa continued to hold it. Perhaps the experience of the nomads in the deserts of Arabia, where the irregularity of nature can be more obvious than the regularity, predisposed the Arabs to treat events as isolated units, of which any one can be followed by any other. The releasing of the bowstring need not be followed by the flight of the arrow; the stone which is white in one moment may be black in the next moment. Each event or circumstance is seen as directly or immediately created by God, and his omnipotence means that he can do whatever he likes without anything resembling a stable policy. This view is doubtless to be linked with the idea that the strongest human ruler is the one with fullest power to carry out every momentary whim. The Islamic sultan, too, keeps most of the power in his own hands, and similarly the theologian, though he sometimes mentions the idea of *tafwīḍ*, or God's delegating responsibility to man and entrusting him with his own acts, never gives it a prominent place in his thought. Another factor contributing to Islamic atomism may be the Arab interest in language and grammatical science which argues a more developed perception of differences and of the relation of things to words than of relatedness and the causal relations between things.

d) *The transformation of the Muʿtazila*

The school of the Muʿtazilites arose out of the attempts to apply a limited number of Greek concepts and methods of argument to Islamic religious beliefs, that is, attempts to amalgamate the Greek rationalistic outlook with the basic religious thinking (mainly Qur'ānic) of ordinary men. This was indeed the aim of all Kalām, but for a time the Muʿtazilites made the running. In the reign of al-Ma'mūn it was realized that certain doctrines of the Muʿtazila were in close accordance with certain political aims of persons in the political institution, and for a time some Muʿtazilites were in positions of political power (as has been seen). This gave a fillip to Muʿtazilite theology, but as it developed it moved further away from the ordinary Muslim, leaving him to be represented by members of the general religious movement, chiefly those who may now be called Ahl al-Ḥadīth. The change of policy about 850 and the loss of political power by the Muʿtazilites was also an indication of their failure to gain wide popular support. At this point one might have expected the Muʿtazilites either to try to come closer to the ordinary man again or else to look for new Greek ideas; but they did neither. They left the first course to be followed by men like Ibn-Kullāb and al-Ashʿarī and the second by al-Fārābī and other Falāsifa.

After 850 the Muʿtazilites became more and more a small coterie of academic theologians cut off from the masses of the people and exercising little influence on the further course of Islamic thought. The men quoted and argued against by al-Ashʿarī are still quoted by his followers, but all later Muʿtazilites tend to be neglected by other Sunnite theologians. The chief exception is Abū-Hāshim, whose theory of *aḥwāl* aroused interest for a time. (The ultimate rejection of this concept is doubtless linked with the fact that it is derived from Arabic grammar and not from Greek science, and could not easily be harmonized with the further Greek ideas introduced into Sunnite theology by al-Ghazālī.) Even in the period of the decline of the Muʿtazilites there were still some first-class minds among them, notably the Qāḍī 'Abd-al-Jabbār (d. 1025), a

Shāfiʿite in law and a voluminous writer, many of whose works have recently been published.[103] The only Muʿtazilite who had much influence outside his own school and the Zaydites of the Yemen was az-Zamakhsharī (d. 1144) through his commentary on the Qur'ān, but his influence was due to his great philological learning and not to his Muʿtazilism.[104]

It is worth remembering that, while the Muʿtazilites were thus refusing to venture further afield, certain groups in the Islamic world were still actively engaged in the process of assimilating Greek science and philosophy. The following are among the more outstanding persons among the contemporaries of al-Jubbā'ī and Abū-Hāshim. Of those who were primarily translators there were Qusṭā ibn-Lūqā (probably d. c. 912), Is'ḥāq, son of the great Ḥunayn (d. 910/11), other pupils of Ḥunayn including his nephew Ḥubaysh, and Abū-Bishr Mattā (d. 940), who was also noted as a logician.[105] Those to be reckoned mainly mathematicians or astronomers include : Thābit ibn-Qurra the Ṣābian (d. 901) and his son Sinān (d. 942); the authority on Euclid an-Nayrizī (d. c. 921), who was known in Europe as Anaritius; the outstanding astronomer Abū-Maʿshar (in Latin Albumasar), who had originally been a Traditionist and who died at a great age in 886; and another distinguished astronomer al-Battānī or Albategnius (d. 929), who was a convert from the Ṣābian religion to Islam.[106] Ar-Rāzī (Muḥammad ibn-Zakarīyā) or Rhazes (d. 923/32) is best known for his contributions to medicine, but he was also interested in chemistry and was something of a philosopher.[107] The Spanish Muslim Ibn-Masarra (d. 931) was a philosopher on Empedoclean lines and also a mystic,[108] while a little later came one of the three greatest Islamic philosophers, al-Fārābī.[109]

3

The achievement of al-Ashʿarī

As European scholars in the nineteenth century gradually began to form some idea of the development of Islamic thought, they realized that the theology of al-Ashʿarī marked a turning-point. Up to his time there seemed to have been nothing but the wrangling of sects, whereas with him there came into being a rationalistic form of Sunnite theology which has persisted ever since. Yet as the writings of al-Ashʿarī became easily available and were perused, the puzzlement of the scholars increased. Arent Jan Wensinck, who greatly advanced the subject by calling attention in *The Muslim Creed* (1932) to three early Ḥanafite documents, was filled with surprise and dismay when he actually read the *Ibāna*. Its arguments, far from being rationalistic, seemed to him to be mainly quotations from Qur'ān and Tradition, and he exclaimed : 'Is this the al-Ash'arī whose spiritual descendants were cursed by the Ḥanbalites and who is detested by Ibn Ḥazm? Or is al-Ash'arī a man with two faces?'[110] Since these words were written the work of European and American scholars, notably Louis Gardet (in collaboration with G.-C. Anawati), Richard J. McCarthy and Michel Allard, has made it easier to appreciate Islamic theology in general and that of al-Ash'arī in particular. The careful and detailed study of Michel Allard on *Le problème des attributs divins dans la doctrine d'al-Ash'arī* . . . makes it unnecessary here to embark on a full treatment of his thought. The aim of the present section is therefore the limited one of showing how the view that he is a pivotal figure is to be understood and justified.

a) *His life, conversion and chief works*[111]

Abū-l-Ḥasan 'Alī ibn-Ismā'īl al-Ash'arī was born at Basra in 873. He was a descendant of Abū-Mūsā al-Ash'arī, one of the two arbiters after the battle of Ṣiffīn. He presumably spent some time in legal studies, like all young men of the time, and he is in fact claimed by both the Ḥanafites and Shāfi'ites.[112] The significant part of his education, however, was the study of Mu'tazilite theology under al-Jubbā'ī. He was a promising pupil, on occasion even taking the place of the master, and he might conceivably have succeeded him. About the age of forty, however, he was converted from Mu'tazilism to the doctrines of the Ahl al-Ḥadīth wa-s-Sunna, and for the rest of his life devoted himself to the defence of these doctrines and the critique of Mu'tazilism. He moved to Baghdad towards the end of his life and died there in 935.

There are several versions of the story of his conversion. These mostly link it with three dreams which came to him during the month of Ramaḍān and which presumably mark three stages in his crisis of faith. In each of the dreams the Prophet Muḥammad appeared to him. In the first (in one version) the Prophet commanded him to defend the doctrines related from himself (that is, in Traditions) and then in the second asked how he had been fulfilling this task. Other versions speak of him studying Traditions about the vision of God, about intercession, and about seeing the Prophet in dreams (since he doubted the reality of his experience). At some point al-Ashʿarī is usually said to have given up Kalām to devote himself entirely to Traditions and similar studies. The third dream indicated decisively the new theological line he was to follow, for the prophet angrily said he had commanded him to defend the doctrines related from himself, but had not commanded him to give up Kalām.[113] These stories would seem to be symbolically true, and may even have an element of factual truth.

It is impossible to have the same confidence with what may be called 'the story of the three brothers' (though the persons involved are not always so designated). The essential story is about three boys, of whom one became pious or believing, one became wicked or unbelieving, while one died as a boy. Now according to the view of some Muʿtazilites Paradise is reserved for those who earn or merit it by their good conduct; and so only the first of the three will be in Paradise. The exclusion of the third then appears to be unfair, since God caused him to die before he had an opportunity of becoming pious and believing. If the attempt is made to explain his early death by saying that God knew that, if he had lived, he would have become wicked, then the way is open for the retort that God in fairness should then have made the second die before he became wicked. This story is told in the form of a dialogue between al-Ashʿarī and al-Jubbā'ī, and is said to be the reason for the abandonment of the Muʿtazila.[114] One reason for doubting the story is that the precise Muʿtazilite view attacked is that of some of the Muʿtazilites of Baghdad, not that of al-Jubbā'ī. The latter might have been prepared to use the story against the school of Baghdad, since (as indicated above) he believed that God might act from *tafaḍḍul*, that is, show more kindness than men had merited. Another point is that the story is late in appearing. It is not mentioned by Ibn-ʿAsākir (d. 1176), but occurs in as-Subkī (d. 1370), who quotes from his teacher adh-Dhahabī (d. 1347). On the other hand, virtually the same story is used by al-Ghazālī (d. 1111) as a criticism of Muʿtazilite views, but without any suggestion that it had previously been used by al-Ashʿarī.[115]

Two other short anecdotes are not inconsistent with the story of the dreams. One tells how al-Ashʿarī often represented al-Jubbā'ī in public debates, and on one occasion was defeated in argument by an opponent and then changed his views.[116] One wonders whether the opponent was one of the school of Ibn-Kullāb and al-Qalānisī. The other anecdote is the account of how after his conversion he remained in seclusion for fifteen days and then publicly proclaimed his change of mind from the pulpit of the mosque, concluding with the words 'I divest myself of all I believed just as I divest myself of this cloak', and suited the action to the words.[117]

It is also in order to consider whether other factors in al-Ash'arī's circumstances may have contributed to his conversion. It seems probable that there was rivalry between the master's favourite pupil and the master's highly intelligent son Abū-Hāshim; but there is no evidence to support this presumption. Another possibility is that al-Ash'arī was worried at the unsettled political conditions of the times, with threats from the Qarmaṭian rebels not far from Basra and confusion at the centre of the caliphate. This possibility cannot be emphasized, however, for the exact date of the conversion must remain doubtful; the statement that it was about 912 (the Islamic year 300) seems to be a guess, perhaps made to support the claim that al-Ash'arī was the *mujaddid* or 'renewer of religion' to be expected at the beginning of the fourth century.[118] All such matters must remain conjectural. It is reasonably certain, however, that the Mu'tazilite school was turning in on itself and looking backwards to its past successes; and so it is likely that al-Ash'arī somehow became aware of this and found elsewhere more serious attempts to deal with the urgent problems of the day.

The most adequate discussion of the extant works of al-Ash'arī is that by Michel Allard, and it will suffice here to repeat his main conclusions.[119] The *Luma'* he accepts as authentic without qualification, following the conclusions of Richard McCarthy after he had edited and translated it in *The Theology of al-Ash'arī*. In the same way he accepts the much slighter defence of Kalām entitled *Risāla fī stiḥsān al-khawḍ fī 'ilm al-kalām*. With regard to the *Ibāna* the position is more complicated. Allard thinks it is authentic, but has been revised by al-Ash'arī himself, the aim being to meet criticisms of al-Ash'arī's new position made by al-Barbahārī and other Ḥanbalites. For the *Maqālāt* the view favoured by Allard is that it consists of three works originally distinct : (a) the *Maqālāt* proper, consisting of the first volume in Hellmut Ritter's edition, which is an objective account of the views of Islamic sects; (b) a book on 'The Fine

Points of Kalām', dealing with matters arising from Kalām but not strictly theological, and including the views of Christians, philosophers and other non-Muslims (ii. 301–482); and (c) a book on 'The Names and Attributes', where objective statements of views (as in the first part) are followed by brief but trenchant criticisms (ii. 483–611). He regards the first two parts as composed during al-Ash'arī's Mu'tazilite period and slightly modified after his conversion. The Ḥanbalite-type creed at the end of the first part (i. 290–7) might have been part of the original objective statement with no addition beyond the last words in which it is stated that he himself accepts these doctrines.

b) *His rational methods*

Wensinck's accusation against al-Ash'arī that his arguments consist chiefly of quotations from Qur'ān and Tradition is preceded by an examination of sections of the *Ibāna*, especially that dealing with the vision of God in Paradise.[120] Careful scrutiny of the text, however, shows that Wensinck's conclusion is unjustified. The charge of arguing by quotation could be fairly made against men like Khushaysh (d. 867), some of whose *Istiqāma* is contained in the *Tanbīh* of al-Malaṭī (d. 987), and Ibn-Khuzayma (d. 924), briefly mentioned above, whose *Tawḥīd* is extant. When al-Ash'arī is compared with these men, it is seen that, even when he is arguing from Qur'ānic verses, he is not simply quoting, but is building a considerable structure of rational argument round the verses. Thus in discussing the verse 'Faces that day are bright, Looking (*nāẓira*) to their Lord' (75.22f.) he rejects three metaphorical meanings, though they occur elsewhere in the Qur'ān, on grounds which are in a broad sense 'rational'. 'Looking to' here cannot mean 'considering', 'reflecting on', since that is inappropriate where faces are mentioned; it cannot mean 'expecting', since expectation has a negative aspect which is inconsistent with the bliss of Paradise; and it cannot mean 'looking with sympathy', since it is not proper for man to feel sympathy for God.

A similar method is to be observed in his refutation of the opponents' argument from the superficial meaning of 6.103, 'sight does not attain to him'. In this case he makes the general assertion that the Qur'ān does not contradict itself (*kitāb Allāh yuṣaddiq ba'ḍu-hu ba'ḍ*), and on this basis maintains that the verse must mean either that human sight does not attain to God in this world or the sight of infidels does not attain to God.[121] At a later stage various subtleties are introduced by both sides into the discussion of this verse, but there are no novelties of method. The assertion of the self-consistency of the Qur'ān, on the other hand, is seen by Allard (as noted above) as an important step forward.

Of the eight arguments on this question as enumerated by Wensinck only five are based on quotations. The sixth is a purely rational argument of which the core is this : 'whatever exists God may show to us ; but God exists, and so it is not impossible that he should show himself to us'. The seventh argument is somewhat similar in its basis : 'he who does not see himself, does not see things ; God sees things, and so he must see himself ; and so he must be able to show us himself'.[122] The eighth argument sets out from the agreement of Muslims that the life of Paradise is perfect bliss, and maintains that, since the greatest of delights is the vision of God, God will not withhold this. At the close of the paragraph there is a typical remark from Kalām to the effect that seeing does not affect the object seen but only the seeing subject. None of these three last arguments would be tolerated by the Ḥanbalites. They show clearly the element of novelty in al-Ashʿarī.

A comparison with the corresponding section of the *Lumaʿ* is instructive. The discussion of 'looking to their Lord' is repeated along identical lines, and there are brief discussions of some of the other Qur'ānic verses, such as 'sight does not attain to him'. In the forefront, however, there is placed a rational argument to show that the vision of God is possible from the standpoint of reason ; none of the factors occur which would make it impossible of God, such as involvement in temporality or similarity to creatures or injustice. At the end of the section there are replies to objections made by rationally-minded opponents : if God can be seen, then he may be touched, tasted and smelled ; whatever is seen is limited.[123] Curiously enough, the sixth, seventh and eighth arguments of the *Ibāna* are not repeated in the *Lumaʿ*. This may be because the whole treatment is rather shorter. This brief comparison, however, yields results which are in conformity with Allard's view of the relation of the two books. The *Lumaʿ* seems to be addressed to Muʿtazilites and other Mutakallimūn whereas the *Ibāna* has more of the type of argument which would be appreciated by Ḥanbalites.

Some of the surprise felt by Wensinck and other scholars at the way in which al-Ash'arī based his arguments on the Qur'ān was due to a failure to realize the extent to which the Mu'tazilites also based their arguments on the Qur'ān. For long European scholars had to derive their knowledge of the Mu'tazilites on works like the heresiography of ash-Shahrastānī which give a summary of sectarian views but without any detailed arguments. This together with admiration for the rationalistic outlook of the Mu'tazila led scholars to suppose that all their arguments were purely rational. This impression can now be corrected from actual Mu'tazilite texts and from quotations in works like al-Ash'arī's *Luma'* (where many of the objections which he meets must have been Mu'tazilite). Thus al-Ma'mūn's arguments about the createdness of the Qur'ān (which are presumably Mu'tazilite-inspired) are based on Qur'ānic verses, while al-Khayyāṭ's defence of the doctrine of the intermediate position consists in large part of quotations from the Qur'an.[124] Reflection shows that such references to the Qur'ān are only to be expected, since the text of the Qur'ān was the main piece of common ground between the Mu'tazilites and the other Muslims they were trying to convince. The absence of Mu'tazilite arguments from the Traditions is possibly due to the fact that the views of the school had taken shape at a period when Traditions were not widely accepted as a basis for argument;[124a] but in any case Traditions were probably less serviceable to the Mu'tazila than to a man like al-Ash'arī. It is perhaps significant that al-Ash'arī has no Traditions in the *Luma'*; but in the *Ibāna* to support the arguments from Kalām he has various Traditions and *āthār* concerning the uncreatedness of the Qur'ān and eschatological matters.

Perusal of the arguments from Qur'ānic verses shows the great ingenuity exercised in finding verses and phrases to support different points of view. It is worth while calling attention in this connection to an argument used by al-Ash'arī to show that, though God in his omnipotence wills the wicked acts of men, he is not wicked because of that. He refers to the verse (5.28/31f.) in which one son of Adam says to the other, 'If you stretch out your hand to kill me, I am not going to stretch out my hand to kill you; . . . I will that you should have the guilt of my sin and your sin, and should be an inmate of Hell.' Then he points out that in saying this the first brother, who wants to avoid the sin of himself committing murder, deliberately wills a course of action which includes his own murder (unless the second brother is restrained by the mention of God), and yet cannot be held guilty of murder. Similarly Joseph, after repeatedly refusing the solicitations of his master's wife, met her threats of imprisonment with the words, 'Prison is dearer to me than what they invite me to' (12.33). In this way Joseph wills his own imprisonment, which is a sin (on somebody's part) because of its injustice, but he is not in any sense sinful because of that. From this al-Ashʿarī concludes that God may will wickedness and folly without being wicked or foolish.[125]

The novelty here is the use of an analogy from the relation of human wills to elucidate the problem of the relation of divine omnipotence and human responsibility. This is a more promising line of thought than the use of material or physical analogies, and yet it does not seem to have been much used by later writers. The precise form of these arguments is doubtless al-Ashʿarī's own, but the general line of thought may have been suggested by Christian writers, since it is known that al-Ashʿarī had studied Christianity sufficiently to write two books expounding and criticizing it.[126] Thus there is a relevant passage in the *Apology* of the Nestorian Patriarch Timothy, recording a debate with the caliph al-Mahdī about 781. In replying to the objection that Jesus was either too weak to prevent his crucifixion or else willed it so that the Jews are not responsible, Timothy makes comparisons with the fall of Satan from heaven, the expulsion of Adam from Paradise and the killing by infidels of Muslims fighting in the way of God. He then goes on to argue that 'the fact that God had willed Satan to fall from heaven and Adam to go out from Paradise does not absolve Satan and Adam from blame and censure', and that the slayers of Muslim martyrs are blameworthy, even though they were fulfilling the desire of the victims, since they did not kill them in order to facilitate their entrance into heaven.[127] The Bible provides a somewhat similar example in the words spoken to David, 'You have killed Uriah the Hittite . . . with the sword of the children of Ammon.'[128]

The doctrines defended by al-Ashʿarī with his rational methods are roughly those of Aḥmad ibn-Ḥanbal. The chief difference is that al-Ashʿarī discussed the question of God's attributes which had been raised by the Muʿtazilites and adopted a definite position on it. Something will be said about this in the comparison of al-Ashʿarī's views with those of al-Māturīdī.

c) *His influence*

In an article published in 1953 Joseph Schacht raised the problem of the significance of al-Ash'arī and his importance in the eyes of his contemporaries and of the following generation.[129] One part of his thesis was that al-Ash'arī was far from being the first to defend conservative doctrines by Mu'tazilite methods. The point thus stated in very general terms is to be accepted; and in fact the first part of this chapter elaborates it by producing the names of the most distinguished of these predecessors, so far as they are known to us. Another point is that it was only at a later date that al-Ash'arī became the eponym of the theological school. This also may be accepted, in part at least, and may be expanded by further information. Al-Ash'arī was not alone but belonged to a group or school. In the *Luma'* he refers several times to 'our associates' (*aṣ'ḥābu-nā*), and he does so in a way which suggests that there was some divergence of view among them.[130] In the light of statements quoted above (p. 288) this must have been the group constituted by the followers of Ibn-Kullāb; and the point is confirmed by a statement of the geographer al-Maqdisī. Writing in the year 985 he speaks of the Kullābiyya as one of the theological sects (along with the Mu'tazila, the Najjāriyya and the Sālimiyya), but a little further on he says they have been absorbed into the Ash'ariyya (just as the Najjāriyya have been absorbed into the Jahmiyya).[131] During his lifetime al-Ash'arī was probably no more important in the group than al-Qalānisī. An important contribution to the predominance of the name of al-Ash'arī may have been made by Ibn-Fūrak (d. 1015), whose *Ṭabaqāt al-mutakallimīn* is the primary historical source for the life of al-Ash'arī and his first followers, and who also wrote a book comparing al-Ash'arī and al-Qalānisī.[132] The heresiographer al-Baghdādī (d. 1037) regards himself as a follower of al-Ash'arī, though he also speaks of al-Qalānisī as 'our shaykh'.

It is also clear now that the earlier European scholars had too little sympathy with the doctrines and methods of al-Ash'arī to understand fully what he was about and to grasp the distinctive qualities of his work. Thanks to the labours of their successors, we are able to form a juster appreciation of the intellectual stature of al-Ash'arī. There is no reason to doubt that he was chosen as eponym rather than Ibn-Kullāb or al-Qalānisī because it was chiefly in his writings that the members of the school were finding their inspiration. Three men in particular are named as his immediate pupils and the teachers of the following generation : Abū-Sahl aṣ-Ṣuʿlūkī of Nishapur (d. 979); Abū-l-Ḥasan al-Bāhilī of Basra; Abū-ʿAbd-Allāh ibn-Mujāhid of Basra and Baghdad (d. 980).[133] The three leading Ashʿarites of the next generation, al-Bāqillānī, Ibn-Fūrak and al-Isfarā'inī, were pupils of the second, while al-Bāqillānī also studied under the third and Ibn-Fūrak under the first.

From all this it may be concluded that the obscurity surrounding al-Ashʿarī and his immediate followers is not wholly impenetrable and does not justify a denial of the seminal importance of his thought.

4

The relation of al-Māturīdī to al-Ashʿarī

a) *The obscurity of al-Māturīdī*

Even less is known about the career and antecedents of al-Māturīdī[134] than about those of al-Ashʿarī. His *nisba* is from Māturīd or Māturīt, a small place on the outskirts of Samarqand, where he was born. He studied jurisprudence according to the Ḥanafite school in Samarqand, and Kalām would be a part of his studies. We know the name of his chief teacher and of the latter's chief teacher, and we have brief biographical notices of these and of several other Ḥanafite scholars of the period; but even these scanty materials have not yet been adequately studied, and all that we know is that schools of Ḥanafite jurisprudence somehow developed at many centres in the eastern half of the caliphate. Since al-Māturīdī died in 944, he must have been born about 870. One or two of his works have survived, the most popular being one of 'Interpretations (*Ta'wīlāt*) of the Qur'ān'. For the purposes of the present study the most important is the *Kitāb at-tawḥīd*, recently edited by Fathalla Kholeif. There also exist a number of manuscripts entitled 'Creed (*ʿAqīda*) of al-Māturīdī' but it will require some intensive study to decide whether these (some of which differ considerably from others) represent the views of the master himself, or are a later formulation of his views by his disciples.[135]

The obscurity continues in succeeding generations. It has been noticed that he has been passed over in silence in many books where some mention of him might have been expected, e.g. : the *Fihrist* of Ibn-an-Nadīm (written in 988), the description of the Ṣifātiyya by ash-Shahrastānī (d. 1153), the biographical dictionary of

Ibn-Khallikān (d. 1282), the account of Kalām by Ibn-Khaldūn (d. 1406) in his *Muqaddima*, and the dictionary of Qur'ān-commentators by as-Suyūṭī (d. 1505). On the other hand, there is a brief mention of a particular view held by him in the commentary by at-Taftazānī (d. 1389) on the creed of an-Nasafī. Soon after this appear claims that he is parallel to al-Ashʿarī. In *Miftāḥ as-saʿāda* Ṭāshköprīzāde (d. 1560) writes that 'at the head of the science of Kalām among the Ahl as-Sunna wa-l-Jamāʿa were two men, one a Ḥanafite and the other a Shāfiʿite', namely, al-Māturīdī and al-Ashʿarī. The idea of the parallelism of Māturīdites and Ashʿarites, and so of the eponyms, is found in *Ar-rawḍa al-bahiyya* written after 1713 by an obscure scholar Abū-ʿUdhba, who was apparently plagiarizing from Nūr-ad-dīn ash-Shīrāzī's commentary on a poem by as-Subkī (d. 1370) —the commentary was written about 1356 at the author's request.[136] There are doubtless many other references to al-Māturīdī in works of similar date to those mentioned, but the references quoted are sufficient to show that about the fourteenth century al-Māturīdī began to emerge from obscurity and to move right to the centre of the stage. How is this to be explained?

One reason for the original obscurity is that al-Māturīdī lived and worked in a province far distant from the centre of the caliphate. The scholars of Baghdad were not interested in what happened in Samarqand, though before the year 1000 the Māturīdite theologians were including in their works criticisms of the Ashʿarites, perhaps because of Ashʿarite schools at places like Nishapur. It is also probable that the Ḥanafites in general paid less attention than the Ashʿarites to the study of heresiography and to biographies of the leading members of their school. Despite the obscurity, however, it is a fact that with al-Māturīdī theology attained a high level and that it continued to be cultivated among the Ḥanafites in the eastern provinces, though they may not have called themselves followers of al-Māturīdī. The emergence from obscurity seems to have occurred after the Ḥanafites gained more importance in the central Islamic lands through the support of the Seljūqs and the Ottomans. One suspects that in the fourteenth century or earlier they deliberately began to look for an eponym of comparable rank to al-Ashʿarī.

It would seem that European ideas about the relation of al-Māturīdī to al-Ashʿarī have been distorted by these late statements and in particular by the book just mentioned, *Ar-rawḍa al-bahiyya fī-mā bayn al-Ashāʿira wa-l-Māturīdiyya*, which maintains that the two schools differ in thirteen points, seven of them verbal (*lafẓī*) and the remainder *maʿnawī*, perhaps 'genuine' or 'points of substance'. Before the work was published at Hyderabad in 1904 (1322) it was used by Wilhelm Spitta, who in 1876 produced a slightly inaccurate summary of the thirteen points.[137] This seems to have been used by Goldziher and other scholars until, and even after, the discovery of its plagiaristic character by Jean Spiro. In any case, though the thirteen points may show the relations of the two schools at the time when the list was made, they do not state correctly the views of the two eponyms. Now that we have a sufficiency of original texts published or readily available it should be possible to remove any distortions caused by this list.

The following sub-section is not intended as an exposition or critique of the thirteen points—most of which will in fact be neglected as dealing with minor matters or with questions raised at a later date—but as an attempt to state the main differences between the position of al-Ashʿarī and that of al-Māturīdī and other Ḥanafites of the tenth century. From what has just been said it is clear that the work of al-Māturīdī as an individual made little contribution to the formation of Islamic thought, at least in the heartlands where the main current ran. Though the Māturīdites were aware of the Ashʿarites, perhaps largely because of the school of Nishapur, the earliest Ashʿarite reference to al-Māturīdī so far noticed is that of at-Taftazānī in the fourteenth century. On the other hand, the Ashʿarites from al-Ashʿarī himself onwards were aware of the distinctive Ḥanafite position; and thus al-Māturīdī represents along with others a living strand near the centre of Islamic thought.

b) *The chief differences*

The chief differences between the Ashʿarite position and the Māturīdite-Ḥanafite position may be considered under four heads. Several of the points have been noted in previous chapters. The focus of attention is the thought of the two leaders during the first half of the tenth century, but at certain places it is helpful to look at other statements from the respective schools.

1) *Faith* (or *īmān*). In this respect there is a basic difference. For al-Ashʿarī and his followers, as for the Ḥanbalites, *īmān* consists in word and act, that is, in the formal profession of belief and in the fulfilment of the duties prescribed in the Sharīʿa. Since men vary in

the level of their performance of duties, this conception of *īmān* is accompanied by the doctrine that *īmān* increases and decreases. In contrast to this the Ḥanafite position is that *īmān* consists in word only, or, as they usually express it, belongs to the heart and the tongue; that is, *īmān* is inner assent or conviction accompanying the formal profession of belief.[138]

2) *The doctrine of the Qadar*. Al-Māturīdī here approaches to some extent the Muʿtazilite position, whereas al-Ashʿarī is strongly opposed to it. In his creeds al-Ashʿarī asserts that human acts are created by God and that man has no power to act before he in fact does so—a non-technical way of stating that 'the power is along with the act' (*al-istiṭāʿa maʿa l-fiʿl*), in contrast to the Muʿtazilite view that 'the power is before the act'.[139] Al-Māturīdī, on the contrary, emphasizes man's 'choice' (*ikhtiyār*), and agrees with the Muʿtazila in holding that man's power is for two opposite acts (*al-istiṭāʿa li-ḍiddayn*).[140] Other Ḥanafites were closer to al-Ashʿarī. The author of the *Waṣiyya* holds that human acts are created by God (§11) and that 'the power is along with the act' (§15). On the other hand, the author of *Al-fiqh al-akbar II* insists that *īmān* or *kufr* is the act of man and that God does not compel him to either, though he may aid him to the first or abandon him to the second (§6); God has written all that will happen, but this writing is descriptive (*bi-l-waṣf*) not determinative (§5). The related conception of *kasb* or 'acquisiton' plays a curious part. It was accepted by al-Ashʿarī, though he does not mention it in the creeds;[141] and it is also accepted in *Al-fiqh al-akbar II* (§6). Al-Māturīdī, however, regards *kasb* as a Muʿtazilite doctrine.[142] The views about the *istithnā'*—may a man say 'I am a believer', or must he add 'if God will'?—follow on those about *īmān* and *kufr*. Al-Māturīdī attacks the Ḥanbalite doctrine of the necessity of *istithnā'* in respect of *īmān*;[143] while some later Ashʿarites adopted the Ḥanbalite position, the master himself does not seem to have asserted it explicitly.[144]

3) *The punishment of sins*. Al-Māturīdī adopts a view in accordance with the old 'Murji'ite' views of Abū-Ḥanīfa; even grave sin does not remove a man from *īmān*, and where there is *īmān* a man cannot be eternally in Hell.[145] As noted above other Ḥanafites held similar views. The *Waṣiyya* (§25) asserts that by the intercession (*shafāʿa*) of the Prophet Muslims guilty of grave sins will belong to the people of Paradise; and the creed of aṭ-Ṭaḥāwī (§13) and *Al-fiqh al-akbar II*

(§14) express similar views, the latter even allowing that unrepentant Muslim sinners may go to Paradise. Al-Ashʿarī's position is not unlike this, but he is not prepared to assert that no *mu'min* will be eternally in Hell. He admits that some grave sinners who are Muslims will be removed from Hell at the intercession of the Prophet, but he emphasizes that the final decision is God's and that he may, if he will, punish some sinners—eternally, it would seem—in Hell.[146]

4) *God's active attributes*. Both al-Ashʿarī and al-Māturīdī hold that God has attributes (*ṣifāt*), such as knowledge, and that it is by this attribute of knowledge that he knows; in this they differ from the Muʿtazilites who say that it is by his essence that God knows.[147] They further accept the Muʿtazilite distinction between active and essential attributes (*ṣifāt al-fiʿl, adh-dhāt* or *fiʿliyya, dhātiyya*),[148] but, while al-Māturīdī said that all attributes are eternal,[149] al-Ashʿarī held, at least by implication, that the active attributes are not eternal. Since God cannot be 'creating' (*khāliq*) or 'providing' (*rāziq*) until creatures exist, 'most Ahl al-Kalām', he reports, do not allow one to say 'God has not ceased (or 'is eternally') creating';[150] and with this view he presumably concurs. At a later date we find al-Baghdādī explicitly asserting that active attributes are not eternal, though he does not mention Ḥanafites as opponents but only Karrāmites.[151] The Ashʿarites in general are criticized for this view in the Māturīdite work, *Sharḥ al-fiqh al-akbar*, on the grounds that it implies a difference between God's essence and attributes or a change in his attributes.[152]

This account shows that the differences between al-Ashʿarī and al-Māturīdī, though apparently slight, had profound implications, and that they were widely shared by the Ashʿarite and Ḥanafite schools respectively. In many ways al-Māturīdī follows the usual Ḥanafite line, but some points of his doctrine have been developed in contrast to his particular opponents in Central Asia, such as the Karrāmites. Al-Ashʿarī and his followers are similarly influenced by the intellectual environment of Baghdad.

5
The end of the formative period

By about 950 the formative period of Islamic thought had come to an end. This date is a convenient round number close to the death of al-Ashʿarī and other important thinkers and also to the attainment of power in Baghdad by the Buwayhid dynasty. These external events mark, not a cessation of intellectual development, but a change in its character. Fresh theological problems continued to appear, such as the question of the distinction between magic and evidentiary miracle (as treated by al-Bāqillānī) and the refutation of the critique of theology by al-Fārābī and Ibn-Sīnā (as undertaken by al-Ghazālī). These problems, however, did not lead to a revision of the central structure of Islamic dogma, as had happened with previous discussions. By the time of al-Ashʿarī the doctrines of the creed had assumed more or less their final form, not merely for the Sunnites but also for the Imāmite and Ismāʿīlite Shīʿites. At the same time, as has been seen, the legal rites or schools had taken definite shape, the canon of Tradition had been formed, and there had been agreement about the text of the Qur'ān. The stability of this whole Sunnite system and of the society founded on it is shown by the fact that it suffered virtually no disturbance during the period when supreme power was in the hands of the Imāmite Buwayhids.

In one important respect, of course, the formative process of Sunnite thought was incomplete. There was as yet no generally recognized name for 'Sunnites'; and there was still intense rivalry between certain legal and theological schools. More than two centuries later al-Ghazālī was still criticizing his fellow-theologians for denouncing opponents as 'infidels' because of some trifling difference of view. By 950, however, despite these continuing rivalries there was in actual practice a wide area of agreement. It was the matters falling within this area of agreement which gave stability to the intellectual structure. This wide agreement also coincided with a deep underlying loyalty to the community of Islam—a loyalty which seldom found explicit expression, but which must have been a potent factor making for unity and homogeneity. Of the continuing tensions in the heartlands, that between the Ashʿarites (or Kullābites) and the Ḥanbalites seems to have been the most creative. For the moment the Māturīdites and the Falāsifa were in backwaters, and it was only after some centuries that they made contributions to the main stream.

At times it may have appeared to the reader that the intellectual discussions recorded in this study were concerned with trivialities. Yet this appearance is misleading. The end product of the discussions was the formulation of a central body of doctrine or dogma, which has provided the basis for a great civilization throughout a further millennium. The formulation of dogma is not the source of the vitality of a society, but rather an analysis of a vitalizing renewal already experienced. Yet sound dogma makes possible the preservation of the vitality present in a community and its transmission to subsequent generations. As mankind seeks a new and more vital unity and harmony, it is to be hoped that this study of the formative period of Islamic thought may throw some light on the intellectual developments now to be expected on a world scale.

Abbreviations

A with name following	:	Abū
A.	:	Aḥmad
ʿA with name following	:	ʿAbd
ʿAA.	:	ʿAbd-Allāh
I with name following	:	Ibn
Ibr.	:	Ibrāhīm
Ism.	:	Ismāʿīl
Jf.	:	Jaʿfar
M.	:	Muḥammad
Sul.	:	Sulaymān
Ya.h	:	Yaḥyā
Yū.	:	Yūsuf
- after A or ʿA or I	:	article

Bibliographical abbreviations. (Cross-references to notes are in the form: n. 5/36; i.e. chapter 5, note 36.)

Abusaq
M. O. Abusaq, *The Politics of the Miḥna under al-Maʾmūn and his successors.*
(Edinburgh PH.D. thesis, 1971, to be published by Brill, Leiden; reference is by chapter and note)

AIUON
Annali dell'Istituto Universitario Orientale di Napoli

Allard, *Attributs*
Michel Allard, *Le problème des attributs divins dans la doctrine d'al-Ašʿarī et de ses premiers grands disciples*, Beirut 1965.

ANuʿaym, *Ḥilya*
Abū-Nuʿaym, *Ḥilyat al-Awliyāʾ*, 10 vols., Cairo 1932–8.

Ash. (or Ash., *Maq.*)
al-Ashʿarī, *Maqālāt al-Islāmiyyīn*, 2 vols. (continuous paging), ed. H. Ritter, Istanbul 1929–30.

Ash., *Ibāna*
al-Ashʿarī, *Kitāb al-ibāna ʿan uṣūl ad-diyāna*, Hyderabad, 1321/1903; Eng. tr. by W. C. Klein, *The Elucidation of Islām's Foundation*, New Haven 1940.

Ash., *Luma'*
al-Ash'arī, *Kitāb al-Luma'*, text and translation in McCarthy, *Theology*.

Ash., *Theology*
see McCarthy, *Theology*.

Bagh.
al-Baghādī, *Al-farq bayn al -firaq*, ed. M. Badr, Cairo 1328/1910.

Bagh. (Halkin)
al-Baghdādī, *Al-farq bayn al-firaq*, tr. by A. S. Halkin as *Moslem Schisms and Sects*, Part II, Tel Aviv 1935.

Bagh. (Seelye)
al-Baghdādī, *Al-farq bayn al-firaq*, tr. by Kate C. Seelye as *Moslem Schisms and Sects*, Part I, New York 1920, reprinted.

Bagh., *Uṣūl*
al-Baghdādī, *Uṣūl ad-dīn*, Istanbul 1928.

al-Balādhurī
— *Futūḥ al-buldān*, ed. M. J. de Goeje, Leiden 1863–6; Eng. tr. by Philip K. Hitti and F. C. Murgotten, *The Origins of the Islamic State*, New York 1916–24 (with the Leiden paging on margin)

Bukh.
al-Bukhārī, *Ṣaḥīḥ*, reference by *kitāb* and *bāb*, with paging in brackets of four-volume edition of L. Krehl and Th. W. Juynboll, Leiden 1862–1908.

Dozy, *Supplément*
R. Dozy, *Supplément aux dictionnaires arabes*,[2] two vols. Leiden 1927.

EI[1], *EI*[2]
The Encyclopaedia of Islam, first edition, Leiden 1913–42; second edition, Leiden and London 1960, continuing (reference is to article, since paging varies in different languages).

EI (*S*)
The Shorter Encyclopaedia of Islam, Leiden 1953.

Fihrist
Ibn-an-Nadīm, *Fihrist*, ed. G. Flügel, Leipzig 1870–1.

Fihrist (Arb.)
'New Material on the *Kitāb al-Fihrist* of Ibn al-Nadīm', in *Islamic Research Association Miscellany*, i (1948), London 1949, 19–45.

Fihrist (Fück)
J. Fück, 'Some hitherto unpublished texts on the Mu'tazilite movement from Ibn al-Nadīm's *Kitāb al-Fihrist*', *Muhammad Shafi Presentation Volume*, Lahore 1955, 51–76.

Fihrist (Houtsma)
fragments published in *Wiener Zeitschrift für die Kunde des Morgenlandes*, iv (1889), 217–35.

GAL (*S*)
C. Brockelmann, *Geschichte der arabischen Literatur*, two vols. (second ed.), and three Supplementbände, Leiden 1937–49.

Gibb, *Studies*
H. A. R. Gibb, *Studies on the Civilization of Islam*, ed. by Stanford J. Shaw and William R. Polk, London 1962 (reprints of articles).

Goldziher, *GS*
Ignaz Goldziher, *Gesammelte Schriften*, ed. Joseph De Somogyi, 5 vols., Hildesheim 1967–70.

Goldziher, *Koranauslegung*
— *Die Richtungen der islamischen Koranauslegung*, Leiden 1920.

Goldziher, *MS*
— *Muhammedanische Studien*, 2 vols., Halle 1889–90; Eng. tr. by S. M. Stern, *Muslim Studies*, London 1967–71.

Goldziher, *Vorlesungen*
— *Vorlesungen über dem Islam*, second edition, Heidelberg 1925.

Goldziher, *Ẓāhiriten*
— *Die Ẓâhiriten, ihr Lehrsystem und ihre Geschichte*, Leipzig 1884.

Graf, *GCAL*
Georg Graf, *Geschichte der christlichen arabischen Literatur*, 5 vols., Vatican City 1944–53.

I'Asākir, *Tabyīn*
Ibn-'Asākir, *Tabyīn kadhib al-muftarī* . . . , Damascus 1347/1928.

I Ath.
Ibn-al-Athīr, *Al-kāmil fī t-ta'rīkh*, Cairo 1348, etc. (reference to year)

I A Wafā'
Ibn-Abī-l-Wafā', *Al-Jawāhir al-muḍī'a*, two vols., Hyderabad, 1332/1913.

I A Ya'lā
Ibn-Abī-Ya'lā (also called Abū-l-Ḥusayn ibn-al-Farrā'), *Tabaqāt al-Ḥanābila*, two vols., Cairo 1952.

I Ḥanbal, *Musnad*
Aḥmad ibn-Ḥanbal, *Al-musnad*, 6 vols., Cairo 1313/1895.

I Ḥazm
Ibn-Ḥazm, *Kitāb al-fiṣal* . . . , 5 vols., Cairo 1345/1926.

I Hishām
Sīra, ed. F. Wüstenfeld, Göttingen 1859–60.

I Khall.
Ibn-Khallikān, *Wafāyāt al-A'yān*, translated by Baron MacGuckin de Slane, 4 vols., Paris 1842–71.

IQ, *Ḥad.*
Ibn-Qutayba, *Ta'wīl mukhtalif al-ḥadīth*, Cairo 1326/1908; French tr. by Gérard Lecomte, *Le traité des divergences du ḥadīṭ*, Damascus 1962 (paging of Arabic text on margin).

IQ, *Marf.*
Ibn-Qutayba, *Kitāb al-Maʿārif*, ed. F. Wüstenfeld as *Handbuch der Geschichte*, Göttingen 1850; also by Tharwat ʿOkāsha, Cairo 1969, with Wüstenfeld's paging marked, so that this alone is given.

IQ, *Shiʿr*
Ibn-Qutayba, *K. ash-shiʿr wa-sh-shuʿarā'*, ed. M. J. de Goeje, Leiden 1904.

IQ'bghā
Ibn-Quṭlubughā, *Tāj at-tarājim*, Baghdad 1962 (also ed. G. Flügel, Leipzig 1862) (reference is to number of article).

IS
Ibn-Saʿd, *Ṭabaqāt*, 9 vols., ed. E. Sachau, Leiden 1905, etc.

Isl.
Der Islam.

JAOS
Journal of the American Oriental Society.

JRAS
Journal of the Royal Asiatic Society.

Khaṭ, *TB*
al-Khaṭīb al-Baghdādī, *Ta'rīkh Baghdād*, 14 vols., Cairo 1931.

Khay.
al-Khayyāṭ, *K. al-intiṣār*, ed. H. S. Nyberg, Cairo 1925.

Lane
E. W. Lane, *An Arabic-English Lexicon*, London 1863–93.

Laoust, *Ibn-Taymiyya*
Henri Laoust, *Essai sur les doctrines sociales et politiques de Taḳī-d-dīn Aḥmad b. Taimīya . . .*, Cairo 1939.

Laoust, *Profession*
— *La profession de foi d'Ibn Baṭṭa*, Damascus 1958.

Laoust, *Schismes*
— *Les schismes dans l'Islam : introduction à une étude de la religion musulmane*, Paris 1965.

McCarthy, *Theology*
Richard J. McCarthy, *The Theology of al-Ashʿarī*, Beirut 1953.

Madelung, *Zaiditen*
W. Madelung, *Der Imām al-Qāsim ibn Ibrāhīm und die Glaubenslehre der Zaiditen*, Berlin 1965.

al-Malaṭī, *Tanbīh*
K. at-tanbīh wa-r-radd ʿalā ahl al-ahwā' wa-l-bidaʿ, ed. Sven Dedering, Leipzig 1936 (Bibliotheca Islamica, 9).

Masd.
al-Masʿūdī, *Murūj adh-dhahab*, ed. and tr. by C. Barbier de Meynard and Pavet de Courteille, 9 vols., Paris 1861–77.

Masd., *Tanbīh*
— *K. at-tanbīh wa-l-ishrāf*, ed. M. J. de Goeje, Leiden 1894.

Mass., *Essai*
Louis Massignon, *Essai sur les origines du lexique technique de la mystique musulmane*, second ed., Paris 1954.

Mass., *Passion*
— *La passion . . . d'al-Ḥallaj*, 2 vols. (continuous paging), Paris 1922.

MC
see Wensinck.

Mecca ; *Medina*
see Watt.

MSOS
Mitteilungen des Seminars für orientalischen Sprachen.

Mtrd., *Sharḥ*
Sharḥ al-fiqh al-akbar, sometimes ascribed to al-Māturīdī but probably by Abū-l-Layth as-Samarqandī (cf. Sezgin, i. 450) ; edition used is Hyderabad 1321 / 1903.

Mtrd., *Tawḥīd*
al-Māturīdī, *K. at-tawḥīd*, ed. Fathalla Kholeif, Beirut 1970.

Mufaḍḍalīyāt
Dīwān al-Mufaḍḍalīyāt, ed. and tr. by C. J. Lyall, Oxford 1918–21.

Munya
Ibn-al-Murtaḍā, *K. al-munya wa-l-amal*, selection entitled *Die Klassen der Muʿtaziliten*, ed. Susanna Diwald-Wilzer, Wiesbaden 1961.

MW
Muslim World.

Nāsh.
Josef van Ess, *Frühe muʿtazilitische Häresiographie* (zwei Werke des Nāšī' al-Akbar herausgegeben und engeleitet), Beirut 1971. (reff. to text by paragraph with 1 or 2, e.g. § 1 / 47 ; to Introduction by pages)

Nawb.
al-Ḥasan ibn-Mūsā an-Nawbakhtī, *K. firaq ash-shīʿa*, ed. H. Ritter, Leipzig 1931.

Paret, *Kommentar*
R. Paret, *Der Koran, Kommentar und Konkordanz*, Stuttgart 1971.

Pellat, *LWJ*
Charles Pellat (ed.), *The Life and Works of Jāḥiẓ*, tr. by D. M. Hawke, London 1969.

Pellat, *Milieu*
Charles Pellat, *Le milieu baṣrien et la formation de Gāḥiẓ*, Paris 1953.

REI
Revue des études islamiques.

RHR
Revue de l'histoire des religions.

RSO
Rivista degli studi orientali.

SA
Sa'd b. 'Abd-Allāh al-Ash'arī al-Qummī, *Kitāb al-maqālāt wa-l-firaq*, ed. Dr M.J. Mashkūr, Teheran 1963.

Sezgin
Fuat Sezgin, *Geschichte des arabischen Schrifttums*, vol. 1, Leiden 1967.

Shadhr.
Ibn-al-'Imād, *Shadharāt adh-dhahab*, 8 vols., Cairo 1350–1/1931–2.

Shahr.
ash-Shahrastānī, *Kitāb al-milal wa-n-niḥal*, ed. W. Cureton, London 1946; also 3 vols., Cairo 1368/1948.

Sourdel, *Vizirat*
Dominique Sourdel, *Le vizirat 'Abbāside de* 749 *à* 936, 2 vols.. Damascus 1959.

St. Isl.
Studia Islamica.

Subk.
as-Subkī, *Ṭabaqāt ash-Shāfi'iyya al-kubrā*, 6 vols., Cairo 1324/1906.

Ṭab.
aṭ-Ṭabarī, *Ta'rīkh*, ed. M.J. de Goeje, etc., Leiden 1879–1901.

Ṭab., *Tafsīr*
— *Jāmi' al-bayān fī tafsīr al-Qur'ān*, 30 (10) vols., Cairo 1321/1903.

Tadhk.
adh-Dhahabī, *Tadhkirāt al-ḥuffāẓ*, 4 vols., Hyderabad 1955–8.

Tahdh.
Ibn-Ḥajar, *Tahdhīb at-Tahdhīb*, 12 vols., Hyderabad 1325–7/1907–9.

Tritton
A.S. Tritton, *Muslim Theology*, London 1947.

Tusy
Shaykh Abū-Ja'far aṭ-Ṭūsī, *Fihrist kutub ash-shī'a*, ed. A. Sprenger, etc., Calcutta 1853–5 as *Tusy's List of Shy'ah Books*.

Watt, *Integration*
W. Montgomery Watt, *Islam and the Integration of Society*, London 1961.
Watt, *Mecca*
— *Muhammad at Mecca*, Oxford 1953.
Watt, *Medina*
— *Muhammad at Medina*, Oxford 1956.
Watt, *Philosophy and Theology*
— *Islamic Philosophy and Theology*, Edinburgh 1962.
Watt, 'Political Attitudes'
— 'The Political Attitudes of the Muʿtazilah', *JRAS*, 1963, 38–57.
Watt, *Political Thought*
— *Islamic Political Thought*, Edinburgh 1968.
Watt, *What is Islam?*
— *What is Islam?*, London and Beirut 1968.
Wellhausen, *Arab Kingdom*
Julius Wellhausen, *The Arab Kingdom and its Fall*, Eng. tr. by Margaret G. Weir, Calcutta 1927.
Wellhausen, *Oppositionsparteien*
— *Die religiös-politischen Oppositionsparteien im alten Islam*, Göttingen 1901.
Wensinck, *Concordance*
A. J. Wensinck, etc. (edd.), *Concordance et indices de la tradition musulmane*, seven vols., Leiden 1936–69.
Wensinck, *MC*
— *The Muslim Creed*, Cambridge, 1932 (the Arabic text used here for the Ḥanafite creeds is that of Hyderabad 1321/1903.
Yaʿqūbī, *Taʾrīkh*
al-Yaʿqūbī, *Taʾrīkh*, two vols., Beirut 1960.
Yqt., *Buld.*
Yāqūt, *Muʿjam al-buldān*, Leipzig 1866–73.
Yqt., *Irsh.*
— *Irshād al-arīb*, ed. D. S. Margoliouth, seven vols., London 1908–27.
ZA
Zeitschrift für Assyriologie.
ZDMG
Zeitschrift der deutschen morgenländischen Gesellschaft.

Notes

Introduction

1. 'Philologika III : Muhammedanische Häresiographen', *Isl.*, xviii (1929), 35–59. Other early writers : Wahb b. Jarīr, wrote about Azāriqa (Wellhausen, *Oppositionsparteien*, 26 ; from Ṭab., ii. 185f. and *Aghānī*, i. 11.28) ; Ḥ. b. Ziyād al-Lu'lu'ī (d. 819/204) (I Q'bghā, no. 55 ; cf. p. 285 below).
2. What appears to be essentially a variant text of the same work was edited by Dr M. J. Mashkūr in 1963 as *K. al-maqālāt wa-l-firaq* by Sa'd al-Ash'arī al-Qummī. The differences have not been examined here in detail.
3. These works are analysed in : Henri Laoust, 'La classification des sectes dans le *Farq* d'al-Baghdadi', *REI*, xxix (1961), 19–59 ; D. Sourdel, 'La classification des sectes islamiques dans le Kitāb Al-Milal d'Al-Šahrastānī', *St. Isl.*, xxxi (1970), 239–48.
4. 'Le dénombrement des sectes mohométanes', *RHR*, xxvi (1892), 129–37, and Goldziher, *GS*, ii. 406–14 ; cf. his *Vorlesungen*, 188f., 352 with further reff. See also Bagh. (Seelye), 2f., 21f. This Tradition and other questions raised in this Introduction are discussed in Watt, 'The Great Community and the Sects', in *Theology and Law in Islam* ed. by G. E. von Grunebaum, Wiesbaden 1971, 25–36, and 'The Study of the Development of the Islamic Sects', in *Acta Orientalia Neerlandica*, ed. P. W. Pestman, Leiden 1971, 82–91.
5. Cf. al-Pazdawi (d. 1099, Ḥanafite – see n. 9/26), 242.17 — the *madhhab* of Ahl as-Sunna wa-l-Jamā'a was that of 'the Messenger of God, his Companions, and after them the Followers and then the sound imams'.
6. *Fihrist* (Arb.), 31.

Chaper One

1. The important recent work of Laura Veccia Vaglieri is here followed ; cf. *EI*², art. "Alī b. Abī Ṭālib', with references

(to her basic articles in *AIUON*, iv (1952), 1–94; v 1953), 1–98. The complexity of the subject is well seen from the earlier treatment by Wellhausen, *Arab Kingdom*, 75–112.

2. Ṭab., i. 2954f.; further references: 2908, 2917, 2920, 2928, 2943f., 2986, 2991, 3017–21, 3034.
3. Meccan and Medinan opponents of ʿUthmān are mentioned in Ṭab., i. 2943, 2961, 2980f., 3004f., 3029f., 3048.
4. Al-Balādhurī, *Futūḥ al-Buldān*, Leiden 1866, 272–4; cf. 351; Abū-Yūsuf, *K. al-Kharāj*, Bulaq, (1885)/1302, 24–6.
5. Cf. list of governors, Ṭab., i. 3057f.
6. Cf. Masd., iv. 259–61.
7. Cf. R. A. Nicholson, *A Literary History of the Arabs*, Cambridge 1930, etc., 195.
8. Cf. M. Guidi, 'Sui Ḫārigiti', *RSO*, xxi (1946), 1–14, esp. 8.
9. This is based on L. Veccia Vaglieri, 'Sulla denominazione ḫawārig', *RSO*, xxvi (1951), 41–6. Of the four interpretations, the second is that of R. E. Brünnow, *Die Charidschiten unter den ersten Omayyaden*, Leiden 1884, and the fourth that of M. Guidi in *RSO*, xxi (cited in the previous note).
10. *RSO*, xxvi. 46, from al-Barrādī, cf. E. Sachau in *MSOS*, ii/2, 47–82, in dealing with ch. 27 of *Kashf al-Ghumma* (*GAL*, ii, 539).
11. Ṭab., i. 3372; quoted from *RSO*, xxvi. 43. As Veccia Vaglieri notes, *khārija* is the singular corresponding to *khawārij* (cf. Lane, s.v.). The authenticity is by no means certain. A similar usage by ʿUmar ibn-ʿAbd-al-ʿAzīz: IS, v. 264.5.
12. IS, vii/1.132; but T. Lewicki, *EI*², art. 'al-Ibāḍiyya', considers him the real organizer of the sect.
13. Masd., v. 442; Ash., 103, 119f.; Shahr., 95; *Fihrist*, 182; cf. Ritter, *Isl.*, xviii. 34ff. (no. 1).
14. Ash., 108, 120, 540; Shahr., 103; *Fihrist*, 182.
15. IS, v. 264.
16. E.g. v. 216.6; vi. 126.22, 204.9.
17. IQ, *Ḥad.*, 3.
18. Cf. *RSO*, xxvi. 43n.; cf. Masd., v. 318, 440.
19. Cf. *EI*(*S*), art. 'Ibāḍīya' (Lewicki), ad fin.; but not mentioned in art. 'al-Ibāḍiyya' in *EI*². Cf. *EI*², art. "ʿAbd-Allāh b. Wahb' (Gibb).
20. Ash., 86.
21. For a list and detailed references see Watt, 'Khārijite thought in the Umayyad period', *Isl.*, xxxvi (1961), 215–31, esp. 215–17. This article is drawn on largely in what follows.
22. Cf. Wellhausen, *Oppositionsparteien*, 27–41, for the events involving Ibn-al-Azraq and Najda; also *EI*², 'Azāriḳa' (R. Rubinacci).

23. Cf. Pellat, *Milieu*, 268f., 277f.
24. Masd., viii. 31 ; the leader of a Zenj revolt in 868 'held the view of the Azāriqa', esp. about killing women and children. Yqt., *Buld.*, i. 348 ; descendants of the routed army, between Ghazna and Kabul in modern Afghanistan.
25. Ash., 86–9 ; Bagh., 62–6 ; Shahr., 89–91 (i. 179–86).
26. Ash., 89–93 ; Bagh., 66–70 ; Shahr., 91–3 (i. 187–96).
27. Ash., 89.4.
28. A statement about not treating as sacred the life and property of certain people in the *dār at-taqiyya* is obscure (Ash. 91.2, *ahl al-maqām*) ; it is unlikely this could apply to *dhimmīs* as in Shahr., 92.1
29. Ash., 125.
30. Ash., 127.
31. Ash., 91.12 ; Bagh., 68.14 ; Shahr., 92.5. Cf. also Wellhausen, *Oppositionsparteien*, 31.
32. Cf. Wellhausen, op. cit., 41–54.
33. Ṭab., ii. 76, 91, 185–7, 390f. ; IAth, iii. 255f., 303f. Cf. Wellhausen, 27 ; Pellat, *Milieu*, 208f.
34. Ṭab., ii. 517.
35. Ibid.
36. Cf. *EI*², art. 'Abū Bayhas' (Houtsma).
37. Lane, s.v. *ṣufriyya*.
38. Ash., 95.11.
39. Cf. *EI*², art. 'Djābir b. Zayd' (R. Rubinacci).
40. E.g. *Tadhk.*, i. 72.
41. IS, vii/1.132 ; cf. ANuʿaym, *Ḥilya*, iii. 89.
42. Ash., 109, 120 ; IS, v. 216 ; *Tahdh.*, i. 267, spread views of Ṣufriyya in Maghrib.
43. *Tadhk.*, i. 95f.
44. Ash., 120 ; probably not an Ibāḍī as stated in Yqt., *Irsh.*, vii. 165.15. His name is Maʿmar b. al-Muthannā.
45. Ash. 120 mentions : ʿAA. b. Yazīd, M. b. Ḥarb, Ya. b. Kāmil, Saʿīd b. Hārūn (all Ibāḍīs), and al-Yamān b. Ribāb (Thaʿlabī, then Bayhasī) ; some of these and others are listed in *Fihrist*, 182f. Views reported in Ash., 106–9, etc. seem to arise from discussions with Muʿtazilites ; cf. book-titles in *Fihrist*.
46. E.g. Ash., 101, 111 ; cf. ii. 463f.
47. Ash., 111.8, 120.1.
48. Cf. *EI*(*S*), art. ''Ibāḍīya' (T. Lewicki) ; the spheres are *kitmān* and *ẓuhūr*, 'concealment' and 'open appearance'.
49. Shahr., 102 (i. 217).
50. Shahr., ibid. ; Bagh., 70 ; cf. Ash., 116, 119.
51. Ash., 102–12 ; Bagh., 82–7 ; Shahr., 100–2 (i. 212–16).
52. E.g. Ash., 104.14, 105.4.
53. Ash., 110.

54. 2.221/0; 5.5/7.
55. Ash., 110–15, term applied to opponents by Bayhasiyya; cf. Bagh. 87f., where it is said this Maymūn is not leader of Maymūniyya of ʿAjārida; Shahr., 93. The name Wāqifa is also used with a completely different reference; cf. pp. 160, 277, 281 below. Some of the Khārijite Wāqifa are called Ḍaḥḥākiyya, probably because they supported Ḍaḥḥāk b. Qays ash-Shaybānī who revolted in 745–6.
56. Ash., 112.1.
57. For the use of the terms cf. Wensinck, *MC*, 129–31 (*Waṣiyya*); cf. ibid. 55, Tradition on Qadar from Muslim (*Qadar*, 11), and similar Traditions under *Qadar* in al-Bukhārī and Muslim.
58. Ash., 97.8.
59. Ash., 91; Shahr., 92 (i. 191).
60. Ash., 113–19; Bagh., 87f.; Shahr., 93–5 (i. 196–201).
61. Ash., 93–100; Bagh., 72–82; Shahr., 95–100 (i. 201–12). His name was ʿAbd-al-Karīm.
62. Ash., 97.12 (ʿAjārida); 111.15, 112.1 (Ibāḍiyya).
63. Cf. L. Veccia Vaglieri, 'Le vicende de ḫarigismo in epoca abbaside', *RSO*, xxiv (1949), 31–44; T. Lewicki, art. 'Ibāḍiyya' in *EI*².
64. Bagh., 264f.
65. Ash., 95.
66. Ash., 103; Bagh., 263; Shahr., 102 (i. 216); cf. Goldziher, *MS*, i. 138f. ʿ*Ajam* may mean only 'non-Arab'.
67. Masd., i. 369f.; Yqt, *Buld.*, i. 815 (the two sects in alliance).
68. Cf. *Integration*, 102f., 142, 202–4, 217–19.
69. Cf. Elie Adib Salem, *Political Theory and Institutions of the Khawārij*, Baltimore, 1956, 56.

Chapter Two

1. 'Points de vue sur la "Révolution ʿabbāside" ', *Revue historique*, 1963, 295–338; my article, 'Shīʿism under the Umayyads', *JRAS*, 1960, 158–72, covered part of the ground and has been drawn on here.
2. Nawb., 27.13; 46.11; art. 'Hāshimiyya' (B. Lewis), *EI*², iii. 265. For Kumayt cf. *GAL*, i. 61 (*S*, 96), and IQ, *Shiʿr*, 369.
3. Ṭab., i. 3350f.
4. For historical details cf. Wellhausen, *Arab Kingdom*, 124 (Ḥujr), 146f. (Ḥusayn); also his *Oppositionsparteien*, 55ff.
5. Cf. Rudolf Veselý, 'Die Anṣār im ersten Bürgerkriege', *Archiv Orientální*, 26/1 (1958), 36–58.
6. Ṭab., ii. 136, 497, 559, 566, 599, 601.
7. Al-Barrādī, *K. al-Jawāhir*, 118, quoted from Veccia Vaglieri in *AIUON*, v (1953), 19–23; several men are not identifiable and have been omitted in the count.

8. *Isl.*, xxxvi (1961), 215–17; the ʿAdī mentioned in no. 2 is probably the *baṭn* of ar-Ribāb.
9. Tamīm : Azāriqa (other than leader), ʿAA. b. Ibāḍ, ABayhas, Ṣāliḥ b. Musarriḥ. Ḥanīfa : Ibn-al-Azraq, Najda and several of his followers. Shaybān : followers of Ṣāliḥ b. Musarriḥ, Shabīb b. Yazīd.
10. Al-Balādhurī, 253 (tr. i. 405).
11. Cf. Watt, *Medina*, 124, 343, 366 and references.
12. Cf. J. Ryckmans, *L'institution monarchique en Arabic avant l'Islam*, Louvain 1951, 329ff., etc.
13. Cf. H. Frankfort, *Kingship and the Gods*, Chicago 1948.
14. Ṭab., ii. 569f.
15. Ibid., 634, 649.
16. Ibid., 634. Cf. I. Friedlaender, 'The Heterodoxies of the Shiites in the presentation of Ibn Ḥazm', *JAOS*, xxviii (1907), 1–80; xxix (1909), 1–183; esp. xxix. 33f. Cf. also Nawb, 20f.
17. Cf. Friedlaender, op. cit. In Ash., 18–23, some small sects are reckoned sub-divisions of the Kaysāniyya; cf. Bagh., 27–38. In Shahr., 109f. (i. 236) al-Mukhtār is said to have become a Kaysānī. Other reff. : Ṭab., ii. 598ff., esp. 634, 636, 662, 671, 673, 702, 721; Masd., v. 180ff., 226f., 268, 475; vi. 58; vii. 117; I Ḥazm, iv. 94. 2, 179.20, 180.7, 182.7, 17, 184.10–12.
18. *Oppositionsparteien*, 87–95 (but note that he mistakenly regards the Sabā'iyya as the source of Shīʿite views, and does not realize that the Kaysāniyya are followers of al-Mukhtār).
19. Cf. Goldziher, *MS*, i. 106, quoting from *Al-ʿiqd al-farīd*, Boulac, ii. 334.
20. IS, v, vi, vii.
21. Cf. *JRAS*, 1960, 164 with references to IS, v. 208, 209, 220, 222, 228.
22. Cf. al-Balādhurī, 242f.
23. Nawb., 34. As noted by Friedlaender, *JAOS*, xxix. 90, there is a Persian version in al-Kashshī, *Maʿrifat ar-Rijāl* (Bombay 1317/1899), 196.
24. Nawb., 25 (Ḥamza of Karbiyya).
25. Nawb., 31.6.
26. Goldziher, *RHR*, xliii. 23; cf. *JAOS*, xxix. 80n.
27. Cf. A. Jeffery, *The Foreign Vocabulary of the Qur'ān*, Baroda 1938, 14–16.
28. Cf. Watt, *Medina*, 118, 128–32.
29. I Hishām, 191f., 235.
30. Watt, *Medina*, 344, nos. 2, 5 and perhaps 11.
31. Ash., 18–23; Bagh., 27–38; Shahr., 109–13; Nawb., 21f., 24–9, 37, 42. In a piece of presumably early material

(*Tadhk.*, i.81) a Kaysānī addressing ash-Sha'bi (d.722) seems to be interested chiefly in the attitude to 'Uthmān.

32. Cf. Cahen, op. cit. (n.2/1), 308.
33. IQ, *Shi'r*, 316–29; *Mufaḍḍalīyāt*, i.174,7; Friedlaender, *JAOS*, xxix, 38f.; IKhall., ii.529–35 ('Rāfiḍī'; no mention of messianism).
34. IḤazm, iv.171; 'Rawāfiḍ' are here believers in the 'hidden imām'. Cf. Friedlaender, *JAOS*, xxix.92.
35. Khashabiyya; cf. IQ, *Marf.*, 300 and H. Ritter, art. 'Kaisānīya' in *EI*[1]. The story probably does not give the true origin of the name.
36. Nawb., 25, and index.
37. Nawb., 26f., index.
38. IS, vi.192.
39. IQ, *Marf.*, 300.
40. Ash., 15.
41. IS, vi.157 (al-Aṣbagh b. Nubāta); the list is in *Marf.*, 301.
42. IS, vi.212f. ('Aṭiyya b. Sa'd al-'Awfī, d.111).
43. IS, v.391–5 (Ṭā'ūs).
44. IS, vi.188–99, esp. 192.
45. Ash., 23.
46. Nawb., 30, 25; cf. Bagh., 227f.; Shahr., 113f. (i.246f.); the Cureton edition reads incorrectly Banān. Also art. 'Bayān b. S.' (M.G.S.Hodgson) in *EI*[2]; Cahen, op. cit. (n.2/1), 315.
47. Ash., 6–9; Nawb., 52–5; etc.
48. IS, vi.240; cf. Bagh. (Halkin), 55n.; Goldziher, *MS*, ii. 112, 140.
49. Ash. 9f.; Nawb., 34; Bagh., 234f.; Shahr., 135f. (i.297–300).
50. Ash., 6, 22; Bagh., 233f., 235f.; Shahr., 112f. (=i.244f.); Wellhausen, *Arab Kingdom*, index; Nawb., 29, 31; IḤazm, iv.187f.; Tritton, 23n.
51. A summary of Imāmite accounts is given in the early chapters of D.M.Donaldson's *The Shī'ite Religion*, London 1933.
52. Ash., 23.7–9. Note the brevity of Nawb., 47.
53. Cf. Cahen, op. cit. (n.2/1), esp. 304f.
54. Shahr., 108 (i.234f.).
55. Ash., 5, 64.
56. Bagh., 114 foot (an-Naẓẓām), 230 (al-Mughīra b. Sa'īd), in 106 he writes 'our friends with most of the Shī'a hold . . .' where it would be inappropriate to suggest his school agreed with heretical Rāfiḍa. In *Uṣūl* (277.14; 278.6; 281.18) he uses Shī'a in the 'normal' sense.
57. Khay., see index; a partial exception is 164 top, but this may be either a taking up of his opponent's word or a reference to a group similar to those whom IQ calls Shī'a.

58. Laoust, *Profession*, 44n. The anecdote (ibid. 74f.) ascribing to 'Alī a definition of his *shī'a* as ascetics is doubtless another later attempt to claim the term.
59. Ibid. 74, n. 5
60. *Fihrist*, 175–7, etc. Masd., v. 80; etc.
61. *Fihrist*, 175; cf. IS, vi. 157—al-Aṣbagh b. Nubāta, *ṣāḥib shurat 'Alī* and one of his *aṣ'ḥāb*, was a *shī'ī*.
62. E.g. Nawb., 55, 15, 17. Cf. Bagh., 230; *shī'a* is used in a wide sense in the account of the views of al-Mughīra b. Sa'īd, and may well be the latter's own term and early evidence of this usage.
63. Khay., 139.
64. Laoust, *Profession*, 17n. (from al-Barbahārī); Mass., *Essai*, 173n. (from Ghulām Khalīl).
65. I Khall., ii. 12f.
66. *MS*, ii. 110f. IS uses the term occasionally for men in IQ's list (e.g. vi. 261, *mutashayyi'*; vii/2.22, 44, *yatashayya'*), but its presence or absence seems somewhat accidental.
67. Nawb., 37.11–14.
68. *ZA*, xxiii (1909), 296–327; xxiv (1910), 1–46.
69. Ash., 15, as fourteenth sect of the Ghāliya.
70. Nawb., 19f.
71. Al-Malaṭī, *Tanbīh*, 14f.
72. Nāsh., §1/33, p. 29 (only mention of Rushayd).
73. *Tahdh.*, vi. 16, quoted from Madelung, *Zaiditen*, 35.
74. I Kathīr, *Bidāya*, 40f., quoted from Laoust, *Schismes*, 58.

Chapter Three

1. *An Introduction to Islamic Law*, Oxford 1964, 27, 31. The account of jurisprudence here is based mainly on this work and on *A History of Islamic Law* by N. J. Coulson, Edinburgh 1964. Schacht's basic account of 'the Traditionists' is in *The Origins of Muhammadan Jurisprudence*, Oxford 1950, 253–7, etc.
2. Schacht, *Origins*, 253.
3. A list of early exegetes will be found in Theodor Nöldeke's *Geschichte des Qorāns*, second edition by Friedrich Schwally, etc., Leipzig 1909, etc., ii. 167–70; textual scholars are listed in iii. 162–9.
3a. Cf. n. 10/73.
4. Sezgin, i. 280; cf. Schacht, *Origins*, 37n.
5. Cf. *Mecca*, 180f.
6. *Tadhk.*, i. 101. Cf. also p. 84 below.
7. *Mecca*, 179–81.
8. *Tadhk.*, i. 144f.; *Tahdh*, xi. 89.
9. I Khall., ii. 581–3; cf. *Tadhk.*, i. 108–13; Schacht, *Origins*, 246f.; Sezgin, i. 280–3.

10. *Medina*, 352f.
11. Erling Ladewig Petersen, *'Alī and Mu'āwiya in early Arabic tradition*, Copenhagen 1964, 36f.
12. I Khall., loc. cit., etc.
13. Laoust, *Profession*, 31. Other reff. : IS, vii/2, 177f. ; *Tadhk.*, i. 98f. ; *Shadhr.*, i. 154. Cf. also p. 86 below.
14. *Tadhk.*, i. 178–83 ; I Khall., ii. 84–6. Other reff. in *EI*² art. 'al-Awzā'ī' by J. Schacht.
15. Cf. Wellhausen, *Arab Kingdom*, 232–48.
16. Wellhausen, 312–18 ; cf. I Khall., iv. 192–6.
17. *EI*², art. "Abdallāh b. 'Umar b. al-Khaṭṭāb' (L. Veccia Vaglieri), with further reff. Cf. Nawb., 5.2–8, quoted on p. 216 below.
18. IS, vi. 173 ; he is A'Amr 'Āmir b. Sharāhīl al-Ḥimyarī ash-Sha'bī. His ceasing to be a Shī'ite may be based on such reports as those in Laoust, *Profession*, 44, 69 (text 27, 42) where he opposes the Rāfida and the Khashabiyya ; the former is doubtful, since it is early for this use of *rafḍ*, but the latter seems probable, and presumably means absence of action and of belief in the return of the imam (cf. I Ḥazm, iv. 185 foot ; Friedlaender in *JAOS*, xxviii. 63 ; IQ, *Marf.*, 300 ; Tritton, *Muslim Theology*, 21n.
19. Goldziher, *MS*, ii. 200 ; I Khall., ii. 4–7.
20. *MS*, ii. 40.
21. Masd., v. 458f. ; cf. *MS*, l.c. Lane does not give the required meaning of *safsafa*, but it is justified by the last meaning of *safsāf*.
22. Laoust, *Profession*, 59 (text 34).
23. Studied by E. L. Petersen, *'Alī and Mu'āwiya* (n. 3/11), esp. 28–31. *Tulaqā'* on p. 29 here means not freedmen but those 'brought into Islam against their will' (Lane).
24. Ibid., 36–8.
25. Masd., v. 459.
26. M. b. Yū. al-Kindī, *Wulāt Miṣr*, Beirut 1959, 39.1, 42.2 ; references to other editions and other works in Veselý, op. cit. (n. 2/5), 43–9. Cf. Wellhausen, *Arab Kingdom*, 93n.
27. IS, vii/2.130.9 (Busr b. A Arṭā), 195.7 (Mu'āwiya b. Ḥudayj).
28. Masd. iv. 284, 295–7 ; *Aghānī*, Boulac, 1285, xv. 30.10 (27.24, Ka'b b. Mālik). Cf. Alfred von Kremer, *Geschichte des herrschenden Ideen des Islams*, Leipzig 1868, 355.
29. *Fihrist*, 90.5, 6. Cf. Goldziher, *MS*, ii. 119 ; IQ, *Marf.*, 172f.
30. Al-Balādhurī, 308.3 ; *MS*, ii. 120.
31. IS, vi. 192.15f.
32. Cf. remarks about A'A-Raḥmān ('AA b. Ḥabīb) (d. 73 in Kufa) and I'Aṭiyya in Bukh., *Jihād* (56), 195 (=ii. 268).

Also later remark of al-Aṣmaʿī (d. 813/216) that Basra is ʿUthmānī, Kufa ʿAlawī, Syria pro-Umayyad and Medina Sunnī (from *MS*, ii. 119n.).

33. *Tadhk.*, i. 129 (Yazīd b. AḤabīb, mufti of Egypt; d. 128).
34. *Tadhk.*, i. 143 (Mughīra b. Miqsam; d. 136, and not as in IAWafā').
35. IS, vii/2.24.23 (ʿAA b. ʿAwn; d. 151). An earlier scholar in Basra was ʿAA b. Shaqīq al-ʿUqaylī (IS, vii/1.91.23).
36. IS, vii/2.42.7 (Ḥammād b. Z.; d. 179), 44.19 (Yazīd b. Zurayʿ; d. 182), 45.5 (Bishr b. -Mufaḍḍal; d. 186). Cf. Petersen, op. cit. (n. 3/11), 112f.
37. Mass., *Essai*, 174–201 (this has been largely followed here); H. H. Schaeder, 'Ḥasan al-Baṣrī . . . ', *Isl.*, xiv (1925), 1–75 (deals with life; unfinished); Hellmut Ritter, 'Studien zur Geschichte der islamischen Frommigkeit: I. Ḥasan al-Baṣrī', *Isl.*, xxi (1933), 1–83; contains text of *Risāla*; do., art. in *EI²*, iii; J. Obermann, 'Political Theology in Early Islam: Ḥasan al-Baṣrī's Treatise on Qadar', *JAOS*, lv (1935), 138–62; Michael Schwarz, 'The Letter of al-Ḥasan al-Baṣrī', *Oriens*, xx (1967), 15–30. Also: IKhall., i. 370–3; *Tadhk.*, i. 71f.
38. IS, vii/1.4–6; Mass., *Essai*, 161f.
39. Goldziher, *MS*, ii. 32.
40. Schaeder, op. cit. (n. 3/37), 59.
41. IS, vii/1.103–6 (d. after 87); *Tadhk.* i. 64f. (d. 95).
42. Masd. v. 458f.; cf. p. 73 above. For his protest against Yazīd b. al-M. see Ṭab., ii. 1400.
43. IS, vii/1. 119. 7–13; cf. Ritter, *Isl.*, xxi. 61.
44. Masd., v. 459; cf. 75 above.
45. Ritter, 55f.
46. Quoted by Ritter, 52, from I-Jawzī.
47. Mass., *Passion*, 706–8; *Essai*, 186; Ritter, 43.
48. Mass., *Essai*, 188; Schaeder, *Isl.*, xiv. 71.
49. *Essai*, 181.
50. *Essai*, 180; criticized by Schaeder, 53f.

Chapter Four

1. What follows is based mainly on the study of the material by Dr ʿAwn al-Sharīf Qāsim of Khartoum in an Edinburgh doctoral thesis entitled 'Main Aspects of the Social and Political Content of Baṣrī Poetry until the end of the Umayyad Era'. I have presented the topic more fully in 'God's Caliph', in *Iran and Islam* (*Minorsky Memorial Volume*), ed. C. E. Bosworth (Edinburgh 1971), 565–74.
2. Cf. al-Farazdaq, *Dīwān*, ed. Beirut 1960, i. 25, 285, 62; ii. 210.
3. Al-Farazdaq, ii. 309. Goldziher was aware of the material

(*ZDMG*, lvii [1903], 394), but does not make much use of it, e.g. in his *Vorlesungen*, 91f.

4. Ibid., i. 24.
5. Jarīr, *Dīwān*, Beirut 1960, 380.
6. Al-Farazdaq, ii. 76.
7. Jarīr, 278.
8. Ibid., 21.
9. Wellhausen, *Arab Kingdom*, 238; *Tahdh.*, ii. 210f.
10. Jarīr, 355.
11. Al-Farazdaq, 1. 22, 47; ii. 312; Jarīr, 195; etc. The opponents considered themselves *mu'minūn* (Ṭab., ii. 1066).
12. Ibn-ʿAbd-Rabbihi, *Al-ʿIqd al-farīd*, ed. al-ʿUryān, Cairo 1940, v. 332f.
13. Ṭab., *Tafsīr*, ad loc. Cf. Watt, 'God's Caliph' (n. 4/1), 566.
14. Cf. 'God's Caliph', 571.
15. i. 10; cf. also p. 69 above and n. 3/6.
16. Al-Mubarrad, *Kāmil*, 573; quoted from Madelung, *Zaiditen*, 231; but it should be noted that the Marwānids sometimes claimed to have inherited the caliphate from ʿUthmān.
17. Text in Abū-Nuʿaym, *Ḥilyat al-awliyā'*, v. 346ff. Cf. J. van Ess, "Umar II and his Epistle against the Qadarīya', *Abr Nahrain*, xxi (1971), 19–26; also *EI*², art. 'Ḳadariyya'.
18. Either M. b. ʿAA. b. ʿUwaymir (or ʿUwaym or ʿUkaym) or M. b. Khālid; *Tahdh.*, and Ibn-ʿAsākir, *Ta'rīkh Dimashq* s.v. An earlier member of Juhayna called Maʿbad is mentioned in IS, i/2.24; cf. *Medina*, 355.
19. Mass., *Essai*, 176. Cf. p. 71 above.
20. As-Suyūṭī, *Lubb al-Lubāb*, s.v.
21. Cf. art. in *EI*² (C. Pellat); but the connection with al-Ḥārith ibn-Surayj is dubious.
22. *Fihrist*, 117; *Essai*, 177. *Ghaylāniyyāt* are mentioned in *Tadhk.*, i. 154, 319, 323, 392.
23. *Munya*, 25–7.
24. Laoust, *Profession*, 54; cf. van Ess, op. cit. (n. 3/17).
25. Josef van Ess, *Traditionistische Polemik gegen ʿAmr b. ʿUbaid*, Beirut 1967, Ar. text, §§20, 21; IS, v. 284.27 (to Mak'ḥūl).
26. *Munya*, 25–7.
27. In van Ess, loc. cit., §21, his death is said to have been witnessed by az-Zuhrī (d. 742); but there are difficulties about the *isnād*.
28. Van Ess, loc. cit.
29. Ṭab, ii. 1733 (quoted in Khay., 213f.); Ash., 513. For Maymūn and al-Awzāʿī cf. p. 71f above.
30. *Munya*, 121.3–8.
31. J. van Ess, 'Les Qadarites et la Gailānīya de Yazīd III',

St. Isl., xxxi (1970), 269–86; cf. Wellhausen, *Arab Kingdom*, 362–7. Other reff. in Ṭab. to politically active Qadarites about this period do not seem to raise new theological problems.

32. *EI*², art. 'al-Ḥārith b. S.' (M.J. Kister).
33. Nawb., 9; cf. Shahr., 106. Gh. may not have used the word *imāma*.
34. Ash., 136f. The story in *Tadhk.*, i. 147 probably refers to this.
35. Ash., 136f.; Bagh., 194 (Halkin, 7); Bagh., *Uṣūl*, 32, cf. 257.
36. IQ, *Marf.*, 244; an argument between Ghaylān and al-Awzāʿī is described by Ibn-Nubāta (d. 1366), *Sarḥ al-ʿUyūn*, quoted in Seale, *Muslim Theology* (n. 4/68), 17f.
37. IQ, *Ḥad.*, 102, §122, is aware that Traditions are accepted from some Qadarites.
38. See p. 97 below.
39. Cf. p. 28 above.
40. Ash., 93, 96, 97 mentions four sects of anti-Qadarite Khārijites; cf. Shahr., 96–100.
41. Cf. pp. 95–7 below.
42. Uppsala 1955. Cf. also: W. L. Schrameier, *Über den Fatalismus der vorislamischen Araber*, Bonn 1881; Th. Nöldeke, art. 'Arabs (Ancient)' in *Encyclopaedia of Religion and Ethics*, 1908, i. 659–73; W. Caskel, *Das Schicksal in der altarabischen Poesie*, Leipzig 1926.
43. Cf. *What is Islam?*, 26 and n. 6; also Ringgren, op. cit., 15, 29, 41.
44. Cf. Watt, *Mecca*, 62–72; *Prophet and Statesman*, 22–34.
45. Bukh., *Adab* (78), no. 101 (iv. 155); cf. *Tawḥīd* (97), no. 35 (iv. 478). Further references in Wensinck's *Concordance*.
46. Goldziher, *Ẓāhiriten*, 153f.
47. IQ, *Ḥad.*, 281–4 (§§249, 250).
48. Cf. Ringgren, *Arabian Fatalism*, 94–7; he found only some dubiously pre-Islamic examples of a written fate, ibid., 39, n. 5; 40, n. 11; 48 (Ṭarafa).
49. For details see Ringgren, 87–94.
50. Cf. Ringgren, 60.
51. Some details will be found in Watt, *What is Islam?*, 48–53.
52. Quoted in al-Malaṭī, *Tanbīh*, 126–35; the points translated are on pp. 126, 133, 134. For Khushaysh (not Khashīsh as Mass.) cf. Sezgin, i. 600; *Tadhk.*, ii. 551.
53. Cf. C. H. Becker, 'Christliche Polemik and islamische Dogmenbildung', *Islamstudien*, Leipzig 1924, i. 439 (reprinted from *ZA*, xxvi [1911], 175–95); also Ritter, *Isl.* xxi (1933), 58; van Ess, art. 'Ḳadariyya' in *EI*², ad fin.; Madelung, *Zaiditen*, 239.

54. Ash., 93–5; cf. n. 1/55.
55. Ash., 16; Nawb., 71; A. A. A. Fyzee, *A Shi'ite Creed*, London 1942 (I.R.A. series, 9), 100.
56. Laoust, *Profession*, ci, 105; cf. al-Kalābādhī, *Ta'arruf*, tr. A. J. Arberry ('The Doctrine of the Ṣūfīs'), Cambridge 1935, 55. These are doubtless based on sura 40. 44/7, *ufawwiḍu amrī ilā llāh.*
57. *Essai*, 194; *Passion*, 612, etc. based on aṭ-Ṭabarsī (d. 1153). The word is also used of Maymūn in Ash., 93, of Aṣ'ḥāb as-Su'āl in Shahr., 94, and in Fyzee, op. cit., 32.
58. IQ, *Had.*, 5 (§7).
59. Ash., 93, 96, 104, 116. Shahr., 94–7 is similar but has a sect of Aṭrafiyya and omits the followers of Ḥārith.
60. Ash., 115 and index; Wellhausen, *Arab Kingdom*, 230f.; Shahr., 94f.
61. Ash., 93. 12, 94f. (Shu'ayb), 96. 3, 11, 107f.; cf. p. 88 above.
62. *Ibāna*, 85 (tr. 125).
63. Ash., 37, 489. 9, 490. 10, etc.
64. Migne, *Patrologia Graeca*, 94. 1592; cf. Becker, op. cit. (n. 4/53), 440; Ritter, 58.
65. Ash., i. 126. 8.
66. Ash., ii. 549. 9; cf. also 477. 9 where it is said A Shimr was a Qadarī.
67. *Ibāna*, tr. 46 (Ahl al-Qadar), 47, 49, 74, 96, 107, 111, 113, 125, 128. *Luma'*, §§58, 116 (Ahl al-Qadar), 118, 120f.
68. Becker, op. cit. (n. 4/53); discussed by Jean-Jacques Waardenburg, *L'Islam dans le miroir de l'occident*, Paris 1963, 88–92, 250f.; also by Mass., *Essai*, 69n. Seale, *Muslim Theology, a Study of Origins with Reference to the Church Fathers*, London 1964.
69. *Essai*, 198f. (first edition, 1922, 176f.); cf. 175.
70. Ritter, op. cit. (n. 3/37).
71. *Marf.*, 225.
72. IS, vii/1. 122.2–9; cf. Ritter, 60.
73. I'Asākir, *Ta'rīkh Dimashq*, s.v. Ma'bad (quoted in Ritter, 60). For Yūnus see IQ, *Marf.*, 242f., and *Tadhk.*, i. 145f.
74. IS, vii/1.127.20–25; Ritter, 60.
75. Cf. Ritter, 26.
76. Shahr., 32.
77. Ritter, 75.6–76.2; cf. Schwarz, op. cit. (n. 3/37), 21.
78. Wensinck, *MC*, 51, says there are no Qadarite Traditions; but cf. Bukh., *Qadar* (82), bāb 8.
79. *Ris.*, 72.15–73.6 (Schwarz, 24). Other verses dealt with are: 39.19/20 in 73.6–11, quoting 40.6 and 10.33/4; 10.100 in 73.11–14; 11.105 in 74.20–75.6. Cf. Schwarz, 27–9.
80. *Ris.*, 76.3–9; Schwarz, 25.

81. *Ris.*, 77.4–19.
82. *Ris.*, 74.5–19; Schwarz, 22.
83. *Ris.*, 68.6–9; Schwarz, 16; cf. 22.
84. *Ris.*, 69.7–10; Schwarz, 18.
85. *Ris.*, 70.3f.; Schwarz, 20.
86. E.g. 41.40 ('do what you will') and 18.29/8 on p. 70.1; 32.17 on 70.15.
87. *Ris.*, 71.15–72.4; Schwarz, 23.
88. Schwarz, 30.
89. *Ris.*, 70.9.
90. *Ris.*, 74.1–4; Schwarz, 19.
91. *Munya*, 18, etc.
92. Cf. *What is Islam?*, 27–31.
93. IḤanbal, *Musnad*, v. 317; cf. ADāwūd, *Sunna*, 6.16 (quoted in *MC*, 108f.).
94. Bukh., *Qadar* (82), 1b (=iv. 251); cf. ibid., 1a; also *Tawḥīd* (97), 28 (=iv. 469); Muslim, *Qadar*, 3 (in *MC*, 54) and bab 1 generally; Ash., *Ibāna*, 66; etc. The 'drop', 'blood-clot', 'tissue' are the stages of the embryo mentioned in sura 23.14.
95. Second part of Bukh., *Qadar*, 1a; cf. ibid., 5; also Muslim, *Qadar*, 11 (in *MC*, 55).
96. ADāwūd, *Sunna*, 6.16 (abbreviated from *MC*, 107f.)
97. Bukh., *Qadar*, 11; *Tawḥīd*, 37a (=iv. 255, 485); also Ash., *Ibāna*, 85 (tr. 125).
98. Bukh., *Qadar*, 8.
99. Bukh., *Qadar*, 4e, quoting Sura 92.5ff. A similar but longer Tradition (Muslim, *Qadar*, 6) is translated in *MC*, 56.
100. Bukh., *Qadar*, 15.
101. *Romans*, 8.28.
102. Cf. van Ess, loc. cit. (n. 4/25), 43; but contrast IQ, *Ḥad.*, 11.
103. Cf. Sezgin, i. 592. For 'Amr see: Sezgin, i. 597; IQ, *Marf.*, 243; *Munya*, 35–41; Masd., vi. 208–12, 223; vii. 234–6; Khay., 67, 97f., 134; IS, vii/2.33; IKhall., ii. 393–6; Yqt., *Irsh.*, vi. 70; Mass., *Essai*, 168, 175, 177, 180, 184, 200.
104. Cf. n. 4/25.
105. Op. cit., 39–45.
106. *Marf.*, only 243 ('Amr); *Ḥad.*, only 76, 159. Cf. Gérard Lecomte, *Ibn Qutayba . . . l'homme, son œuvre, ses idées*, Damascus 1965, 320f.
107. Cf. *Ḥad.*, index to French translation.
108. The list is found in IQ, *Marf.*, 301 (Cairo 1960, 625). Where there are several death-rates a single one has been arbitrarily selected. The references also are a mere selection.
  1) Ma'bad al-Juhanī (703/84): see n. 18.

2) Naṣr b. ʿĀṣim (708/90): Sezgin, 4.24; IQ, *Marf.*, 264; *Fihrist*, 39, 23, 27; 41.12; IKhall., i.359; Pellat, *Milieu*, 77f.

3) ʿAṭāʾ b. Yasār (721/103): IS, v.129; IQ, *Marf.*, 233; *Fihrist*, 27.20; 37.13; *Tadhk.*, i.90; Mass., *Essai*, 176.

4) Khālid b. Miʿdān (721/103); IS, vii/2.162; *Fihrist*, 31.4; 37.22; *Tadhk.*, 93.

5) Wahb b. Munabbih (728/110): Sezgin, 305–7; IS, v.395; IQ, *Marf.*, 233; *Fihrist*, 22; *Tadhk.*, i.100; Yqt., *Irsh.*, vii.232; *Tahdh.*, xi, no.288.

6) Makʾḥūl (731/113): Sezgin, i.404; IS, vii/2.160; IQ, *Marf.*, 230; *Fihrist*, 227; *Tadhk.*, i.107; IKhall., iii.437–9; Mass., *Passion*, 190n.; above p. 87 (n.4/31).

7) Qatāda (735/117): Sezgin, 31; IS, vii/2.1–3; IQ, *Marf.*, 234f.; *Fihrist*, 34.3,4; 41.10; IKhall., ii.513f.; Yqt., *Irsh.*, vi.202f.; *Tadhk.* i.122–4.

8) Ghaylān (742/125); Sezgin, i.595; n.4/21–30.

9) ʿAwf b. Jamīla (—): *Tadhk.*, i.137 (no details).

10) (ʿAA) IANajīḥ (749/132): Sezgin, 29, 37; IS, v.355.

11) Thawr b. Zayd (752/135): *Tahdh.*, ii, no. 55 (probably error for Th. b. Yazīd, 18a below)

12) ʿAmr b. Fāʾid al-Uswārī (—): IQ, *Ḥad.*, 11, 37, 102; Mass., *Essai*, 168, 194; Pellat, *Milieu*, 110f.

13) al-Faḍl (b. ʿĪsā) ar-Raqāshī (—): *Fihrist*, 163; Ash., 118f., 513, 514; Nawb. 9; Shahr., 103, 106; IQ, *Ḥad.*, 99 foot; Mass., *Essai*, 167, 169, 171; Pellat, *Milieu*, 113.

14) ʿAmr b. ʿUbayd (761/144): see n.4/103.

15) ʿAbbād b. Manṣūr (762/145): IS, vii/2.31, 63.9; IQ, *Marf.*, 243; Pellat, *Milieu*, 289f.

16) Kahmas (766/144): IS, vii/2.31; Ash., 214; Shahr., 76f.; *Tadhk.*, i.174; Mass., *Essai*, 115, 167.

17) (M.) b. Isʾḥāq (767/150): Sezgin, i.288–90; *EI*², art. 'Ibn Isḥāḳ' (J.M.B. Jones).

18) Hishām ad-Dastuwāʾī (770/153); IS, vii/2.37; *Tadhk*, i.164; IQ, *Marf.*, 256; Mass., *Essai*, 163, 168. For the *nisba* cf. as-Suyūṭī, *Lubb*, s.v., followed by Dozy, *Supplement*; in Yqt., *Buld.*, s.v. the second vowel seems to be an editorial conjecture.

18a) Thawr b. Yazīd (770/153); IS, vii/2.170; IQ, *Marf.*, 253; *Fihrist*, 29.19; *Tadhk.*, i.175; *Tahdh.*, ii. no.57.

19) Saʿīd b. AʿArūba (773/156): Sezgin, i.91f.; IS, vii/2.33 (cf. 1, line 16); IQ, *Marf.*, 254; *Fihrist*, 226; *Tadhk.*, i.177; Pellat, *Milieu*, 88–90.

20) Ism. b. Muslim al-Makkī (—): IS, vii/2.34.

21) ʿUthmān b. Miqsam (776/160): IS, vii/2.41.

22) Ṣāliḥ al-Murrī (776/160); IS, vii/2.39; *Fihrist*,

183.23; Pellat, *Milieu*, 95, 107, 111; Mass., *Essai*, 133n., 167.
23) Hammām (or Humām) b. Yaḥyā (780/164): IS, vii/2.39; *Tahdh.*, xi, no. 108.
24) ʿUthmān (b. Khālid) aṭ-Ṭawīl (—); *Munya*, 42; Shahr., 33f., 40.
25) ʿA-Wārith (b. Saʿīd) at-Tannūrī (796/180): IQ, *Marf.*, 256; IS, vii/2.44; *Tadhk.*, i.257; *Tahdh.*, vi., no. 923; Mass., *Essai*, 168; van Ess, op. cit., 43–5.
26) Ghundar (809/194); IS vii/2.49.
27) Nūḥ b. Qays aṭ-Ṭāḥī (818/203); IS, vii/2.44; *Tahdh.*, x. 485; van Ess, 23, etc.
28) ʿAbbād b. Ṣuhayb (827/212); IS, vii/2.50.
29) Saʿīd b. Ibr. (—); probably Saʿd b. Ibr. (cf. *Munya*, 133).
30) Khālid al-ʿAbd: not identified.
31) Other early names from IS:
a) ʿAṭāʾ b. A Maymūna (748/131); vii/2.13.4.
b) Saʿīd b. Bashīr (786/170); vii/2.170.14.
c) Yazīd b. Abān ar-Raqāshī (748/131); vii/2. 13.9 (cf. Mass., *Essai*, 167; Pellat, *Milieu*, 95, 101.

109. Cf. Schacht, *Origins of Muhammadan Jurisprudence*, esp. 163–75.

110. Al-Aʿmash (AM. Sul. b. Mihrān); Sezgin, i. 9, 310f., 560; *Tadhk.*, i.154; IKhall., i.587–9. Zayd b. Wahb; *Tadhk.*, i. 66.

111. Selected references:
1) Manṣūr b. Muʿtamir (749/132); Sezgin, i. 404; IS, vi. 235; IQ, *Marf.*, 240; *Tadhk.*, i. 142.
2) Shuʿba (776/160); Sezgin, i. 92; IS, vii/2.38; IQ, *Marf.*, 251; *Tadhk.*, i. 193–7.
3) Dāwūd b. A Hind (757/140); Sezgin, i. 595 (argument with Ghaylān); IS, vii/2.20; IQ, *Marf.*, 243; *Tadhk.*, i. 146–8.
4) Maʿmar b. Rāshid (770/154); Sezgin, i. 290; IS, v. 397; IQ, *Marf.*, 253; *Tadhk.*, i. 190.
5) az-Zuhrī (742/124); see n. 3/9–12.
6) Hammām b. Munabbih (747/130); IS, v. 396; *Tadhk.*, i. 100 (in notice of Wahb).
7) Yūnus b. Yazīd al-Aylī (769/152); IS, vii/2.206; *Tadhk.*, i. 162.
8) al-Aʿraj (ʿA-Raḥmān b. Hurmuz) (735/117); IS, v. 209; IQ, *Marf.*, 236; *Tadhk.*, i. 97.
9) A-Zinād (ʿAA. b. Dhakwān) (747/130); Sezgin, i. 405; IQ, *Marf.*, 235; *Tadhk.*, i. 134.
10) A Ḥāzim (Salama) (757/140); Sezgin, i. 634; IQ, *Marf.*, 252; *Tadhk.*, i. 133.

11) A-Zubayr al-Makkī (745/128); *Tadhk.*, i. 126.

112. Cf. p. 105 above.

113. *RSO*, vii (1916–18), 461–6, 'Sul nome di "Qadariti"'; also in *Raccolta di Scritti*, ii, Rome, 1940, 176–80

114. I Khall., ii. 395; van Ess, op. cit. (n. 4/25), 37, and *Oriens*, 18–19 (1967). 127.

115. Ash., *Ibāna*, 73 (tr. 113); cf. *Luma'*, §§120, 121; IQ, *Ḥad.*, 97f.; Goldziher, *Korauanslegung*, 124; Madelung, *Zaiditen*, 76, 119.

116. *Ibāna*, l.c.

117. Ash., 93.7, 14; 116.2; 124.9.

118. Ash., 96.4; 97.2; cf. 93.13; 124.9.

119. Shahr., 96.10a; 97.2a, 12a, 2b.

120. Shahr., 96.3b; 97.2a.

121. Ash., 430 top; there are about twenty other instances in Ash., and one instance of the variant Muthbita (488.2).

122. *Ḥad.*, 37 foot, 158 foot, 159 top (Muthbita), 160 (§§40f., 165, 166, 166b); in §§165, 166 Lecomte translates 'ceux qui affirment l'existence des attributs', which is inappropriate. He follows Louis Gardet and M. M. Anawati, *Introduction à la Theologie Musulmane*, Paris 1948, 54n., but they merely suggest that this is the meaning in I'Asākir, *Tabyīn*, 163 (not 153). Van Ess (*Oriens*, xviii. 126f.) takes a similar view, but his reference to Ḍirār's negative position in Ash., 488.2 hardly implies an *affirmation* of attributes. There is no reason for denying that the phrase was used differently at different periods. Cf. Allard, *Attributs*, 78n., 135n. I Ḥanbal (IAYa'lā, i. 35.16) complained that the Qadariyya gave the name Mujbira to the Ahl as-Sunna wa-l-Ithbāt, presumably using the term in respect of the Qadar, since he was not interested in the question of attributes.

123. Ash., 383, 408, 540, 541, etc.

124. *Ḥad.*, 96f., §§109, 110.

125. *Tanbīh*, 144. That the correct vocalization is *mujbir* is shown by the occurrence of *ijbār*, e.g. Khay., 145, *Munya*, 93.4.

126. Mtrd., *Sharḥ*, 12. Other reff. will be found in my art. 'Djabriyya' in *EI*².

Chapter Five

1. *MC*, 38, 45; cf. also his article 'Murdji'a' in *EI*¹; Madelung (*Zaiditen*, 228–41) follows Wensinck on the whole and has useful additional material.

2. *Development of Muslim Theology, Jurisprudence and Constitutional Theory*, New York 1903, 122–7.

3. *Vorlesungen*, 79–81.

4. Shahr., 104f.; cf. Bagh., 190, where the last three classes (roughly) are distinguished.

5. Shahr., 103; Bagh., 190f.
6. Khay., 164–8.
7. Nawb., 15, 6f., etc. In Khay., 139 the Shī'ite I-Rāwandī mentions the four sects together with Aṣ'ḥāb al-ḥadīth.
8. IS, vi.214.
9. IS, vi.191f.
10. IS, vi.204.
11. References: vi.204, 205, 214, 232, 236(2), 252, 253, 263, 273; v.67, 362; vii/1.166; vii/2.66, 105, 106, 109.
12. IKhall., iii.61–4, 64f.
13. Lecomte, *Ibn Qutayba* (n.4/106), 315–18; cf. IQ, *Marf.*, 300f., mentioning subsects of the Rāfiḍa, then giving a list of the Shī'a.
14. *Profession*, 48n., summarizing IAYa'lā, i.31.23–32.4; for the following point cf. IAYa'lā, i.36.6.
15. IS, vi.214. The *irjā'* attributed to al-Ḥasan b. M. b. al-Ḥanafiyya (Madelung, *Zaiditen*, 228–30; cf. *Munya*, 17, 25) is an early expression of the attitude, but may not have gone beyond refusing to decide between 'Uthman, 'Alī, Ṭalḥa and az-Zubayr.
16. Wellhausen, *Arab Kingdom*, 317; Ṭab., ii.1399; etc.
17. IQ, *K. ash-Shi'r*, Leiden 1904, 400f. The poem is in *Aghānī*, xiii.52; and is discussed by G. van Vloten, 'Irdjā', *ZDMG*, xl (1891), 161–71, esp. 162f.; Wellhausen, loc. cit.; Tritton, *Muslim Theology*, 45.
18. Ruqaba b. Maṣqala in Laoust, *Profession*, 67; cf. Mass., *Essai*, 170, where he is a disciple of a man who died in 767/150.
19. E.g. Dharr b. 'AA (d.82; IS, vi.205; Shahr., 108; *Tahdh.*, iii.218); Sa'īd b. Jubayr (d.95; Murji'ite only in Shahr., 108; cf. IS, vii/1.166).
20. See section 5.
21. Early Murji'ites:
   1) Dharr b. 'AA. al-Hamdānī; Kufa, joined Ibn-al-Ash'ath, d. 701/82 (IS, vi.205; IQ, *Marf.*, 301).
   2) Sa'īd b. Jubayr; Kufa, joined I-Ash'ath, d. 713/95 (see n.5/19).
   3) Ṭalq b. Ḥabīb: Basra, d. 708–18/90–100 (IS, vii/1.166; IQ, *Marf.*, 301).
   4) al-Ḥasan b. M. b. al-Ḥanafiyya: Medina, d. c. 718/100 (IS, v.241; *Munya*, 17.5; 25.3–5).
   5) Ibr. b. Yazīd at-Taymī; Kufa, d. c. 718/100 (IS, vi.199f.; IQ, *Marf.*, 301; Mass., *Essai*, 170).
   6) Muḥārib b. Dithār; Kufa, d. 734/116 (IS, vi.214; IQ, *Marf.*, 301).
   7) 'Amr b. Murra; Kufa, d. c. 735/117 (IS, vi.220, not as Murji'ite; IQ, *Marf.*, 240, 301).

8) Ḥammād b. ASul.; Kufa, d. 737/120 (IS, vi.231f.; IQ, *Marf.*, 240, 301).
9) Khārija b. Muṣ'ab; Khurasan, d. 737/120 (?) (IS, vii/2.104; IQ, *Marf.*, 237, 301).
10) 'Amr ('Umar) b. Qays al-Māṣir; Kufa, d. c. 737/120 (IS, vi.236; IQ, *Marf.*, 301; Nawb., 7).
11) Mūsā b. AKathīr; Kufa, d. c. 737/120 (IS, vi.236).
Wilferd Madelung in 'Early Sunnite Doctrine concerning Faith as reflected in the *Kitāb al-īmān* of Abū-'Ubayd al-Qāsim b. Sallām (d. 224/839)' (*St. Isl.*, xxxii [1970]. 233–54) speaks of Murji'ism at Kufa (238f.) and notes as opponents there: al-A'mash, Sufyān ath-Thawrī, al-Ḥasan b. Ṣāliḥ b. Ḥayy and Wakī' b. al-Jarrāḥ. A'Ubayd was admired by A. b. Ḥanbal, though his views differed at certain points.

22. Cf. Watt, 'Conditions of Membership of the Islamic Community', *St. Isl.*, xxi (1964), 5–12.
23. E.g. 2.277; 4.162/160; also of the Jews in 2.43/40, 83/77.
24. Cf. *Medina*, 366–8.
25. *Medina*, 69., cf. Bukh., *Istitābat al-Murtaddīn* (88). 3 (iv.330); Wensinck, *MC*, 29f.
26. Cf. Wensinck, *MC*, 1–5.
27. *Fayṣal at-tafriqa bayn al-Islam wa-z-zandaqa.*
28. *MC*, 23.
29. Muslim, Īmān (1), 1.
30. *Musnad*, iii. 134 foot.
31. In Ṭab., *Tafsīr*, on 49.14; cf. al-Malaṭī, *Tanbīh*, 117.16; also AṬālib al-Makkī, *Qūt al-qulūb*, Cairo 1961/1381, ii.270.
32. Ash., 293; translated in McCarthy, *Theology*, 243, §25.
33. E.g. Laoust, *Profession*, 82 (cf. 77f.); al-Bāqillānī, *Tamhīd*, ed. McCarthy, Beirut, 1957, 346–8; al-Kalābādhī, *Ta'arruf* (tr. Arberry), Cambridge, 1935, ch. 17; AṬālib al-Makkī, *Qūt*, ii.250–82 (ch. 35); al-Ghazālī, *Iḥyā'*, book 2, section 4; Subk., i.41–70. The Tradition quoted is apparently discussed by al-Ḥakīm at-Tirmidhī (cf. p. 264) in a work entitled *Sharḥ qawli-hi mā l-īmān wa-l-islām wa-l-iḥsān.* Cf. also Wilfred Cantwell Smith in *Historians of the Middle East*, ed. B. Lewis and P. M. Holt, London 1962, 484–502.
34. E.g. Qatāda, ap. Ṭab.; this interpretation would be in line with the view of al-Ḥasan al-Baṣrī that the grave sinner was not a *mu'min* but a *munāfiq*. Az-Zamakhsharī, *Kashshāf* (ad loc.—iii. 127) defines *islām* as 'entering into peace and leaving a state of war'.
35. The above paragraph is based on the discussion of the topic in Watt, 'The Conception of *īmān* in Islamic Theology,' *Isl.*, xliii (1967), 1–10, esp. 8.
36. Ash., 132–54, esp. 132–41.

37. Murji'ites whose views are described by the heresiographers:
1) Jahm: see section 6 below.
2) A-Ḥusayn (M. b. Muslim) aṣ-Ṣāliḥī : (Ash., 132f., etc.; *Munya*, 72, argued with al-Khayyāṭ).
3) Ṣāliḥ b. 'Amr aṣ-Ṣāliḥī : (Shahr., 107; Bagh., *Farq*, 194f., 95f., 164—only 'aṣ-Ṣāliḥī', may be above).
4) Yūnus b. 'Awn as-Samarri(?) : (Ash., 133f.; *Farq*, 191; Shahr., 104, 106—'an-Numayrī'; Mass., *Passion*, 865).
5) AShimr : (Ash., 134f., 477, etc.; *Farq*, 193; Shahr., 105, 107, etc.).
6) AThawbān : (Ash., 135f.; *Farq*, 192; Shahr., 105f.).
7) an-Najjār : see pp. 199–201 below.
8) Ghaylān : see chapter 4 above.
9) Bishr (b. Ghiyāth) al-Marīsī : (Ash., 140, 143, 149; *Farq*, 192f.; Shahr., 106; EI^2, s.v.; also pp. 196–9 below).
10) M. b. Shabīb : (Ash., 134, etc.; *Farq*, 194; Shahr., 104, 106; Khay., 212n.).
11) AMu'ādh at-Tūmanī : (Ash., 139f., etc.; *Farq*, 192; Shahr., 107).
12) Ghassān al-Kūfī : (Ash., 139; *Farq*, 191f.; Shahr., 105).
13) M. b. Karrām : (Ash., 141, etc.; see also pp. 289–91 below).
14) Muways b. 'Imrān al-Baṣrī : (Shahr., 103, 105; Khay., 127, 211f.; *Munya*, 71).

38. Ash., 138f.

39. The text is incorporated in Mtrd., *Sharḥ*. Translated by Wensinck, *MC*, 103f. His numbering of the articles is adopted but not his translation.

40. The text was printed in Aleppo in 1344. The numbering of articles follows roughly the references in Wensinck, *MC*. There is a translation by E. E. Elder in *Macdonald Presentation Volume*, 1933, 107–27. Cf. Sezgin, i.441 (no. 7).

41. Cf. Sezgin, i.416f. (no. IV); the text used is that of Commentary (2), Hyderabad 1321. Translation in Wensinck, *MC*, 124–31.

42. Text printed along with *Sharḥ* by A-Muntahā al-Maghnīsāwī, Hyderabad 1321. Translation in *MC*, 188–97.

43. *MC*, 246. Apart from the differences in respect of *īmān*, the views about *lafẓ al-Qur'ān* differ.

44. Shahr., 18, 41; AShimr, IShabīb, Muways.

45. Ash., 136.2 (an-Najjār); 139.10 (report from Ghassān). Also Bagh., *Uṣūl*, 252.

46. Ash., 266–71.

47. Laoust, *Profession*, 77f.

48. Ash., 293.14 (§29 in McCarthy, *Theology*, 244f.; cf. §31 of creed from *Ibāna*).
49. McCarthy, *Theology*, §§180–5.
50. *Uṣūl*, 248, 252f.; cf. *Farq*, 343.
51. Al-Ghazālī, *Iḥyā*,' book 2, section 1 (translated by Macdonald, *The Development of Muslim Theology*, etc., 300–7). Al-Ījī, the so-called *'Aḍudiyya.*
52. E.g. Najm-ad-Dīn an-Nasafī (d. 1142), *'Aqā'id*, p. 3; A-Barakāt an-Nasafī (d. 1310), *'Umda*, p. 23 (both edited by W. Cureton as *Pillar of Faith of the Sunnites*, London 1843).
53. Sezgin, i. 36f.; Ash., 151–3, 209; I Khall., iii. 408–11; Shahr., 106; I Ḥazm, 205; *Fihrist*, 179 (of Zaydiyya); Mass., *Passion*, 666, 671, etc. (with a different interpretation of the saying about *īmān* and sin); Paul Nwyia, *Exégèse coranique et langage mystique*, Beirut 1970, 25–108, discusses the *Tafsīr* of Muqātil.
54. IS, vii/1.126.22.
55. Ash., 293f. (§§31, 32, 27); cf. *Ibāna*, §§28, 29 (numbering as in Ash., *Theology*, 235–54).
56. Bagh., *Farq*, 339; *Uṣūl*, 242. Laoust, *Profession*, 100; cf. below, 292f., §§3, 7.
57. Watt, *Bell's Introduction to the Qur'ān*, Edinburgh 1970, Index A, s.v. 'intercession'. Wensinck, *MC*, 61, 130, 180–2. The *isnāds* of the Traditions mentioned by Wensinck (182) might give a clearer idea of where and when the idea gained acceptance. Cf. also Fr. Kern, 'Murǵitische und antimurǵitische Tendenztraditionen . . .', *ZA*, xxvi (1912), 169–74; Watt, 'The "High God" in pre-Islamic Mecca', *Journal of Semitic Studies*, xvi (1971), 35–40, and *Actes du Ve Congrès International d'arabisants et d'islamisants*, Brussels 1971, 499–505.
58. Bagh., *Uṣūl*, 253; Laoust, *Profession*, 79f.; Mass., *Passion*, 585n.; *Essai*, 265, n. 4; Madelung, 'Early Sunnite Doctrine' (n. 5/21), 238–43.
59. I A Ya'lā, i. 35.14; Nawb., 7.3 (apparently also called Butriyya and Ḥashwiyya). Mtrd., *Sharḥ*, 10, speaks of Shakkākiyya in a similar sense. Cf. Kern in *ZA*, xxvi. 172.
60. *Profession*, 80; cf. *'Aqīda I*, §1 (p. 292 below).
61. See references in n. 52.
62. Khay., 97.
63. Laoust, *Profession*, 81.
64. *Uṣūl*, 248f.
65. Cf. Allard, *Attributs*, 58–72, and p. 306 below with n. 10/119.
66. Cf. art. 'al-Ḥārith b. Suraydj' (M. J. Kister), EI^2; also Wellhausen, *Arab Kingdom*, index; Ṭab., index; etc.

67. IḤazm, iii. 188; cf. Ash., 132, 279; Shahr., 61. IḤazm's attribution of the same view to al-Ash'arī gets some support from Bagh., *Uṣūl*, 248, but is contrary to the creeds in McCarthy, *Theology*. Some of the views ascribed to Jahm in Ash., 279f. may be genuine, but it is difficult to be certain.
68. Ṭab., ii. 1605, etc.; 1575, Van Vloten (*ZDMG*, xli, 167f.—cf. n. 5/17) translates the whole poem but does not seem to be aware of the flight to the Turks and interprets it of al-Ḥārith's Persian allies.
69. *Ar-radd 'alā z-zanādiqa wa-l-Jahmiyya*, Cairo, n.d. and *Dārülfünun Ilahiyat Fakültesi Mecmuasi*, v–vi (1927), 313–27. For IḤanbal's criticism of the Jahmiyya see IAYa'lā, 1. 32, 35, 62, etc.
70. Ed. G. Vitestam (with introduction and commentary), Lund and Leiden 1960.
71. *GALS*, i. 281 (p), 310 (3a); IRajab al-Baghdādī, *Histoire des Ḥanbalites*, Damascus 1951, i. 38, 40; *ZDMG*, liii (1899). 73; Sezgin, i. 133 (xii—al-Bukhārī), 598, etc.
72. *Al-Ikhtilāf fi-l-lafẓ wa-r-radd 'alā l-Jahmiyya wa-l-mushabbiha*, Cairo 1349 (1930).
73. In al-Malaṭī, *Tanbīh*, 75–110.
74. In *Ibāna* but not in *Luma'*.
75. *K. at-tawḥīd*.
76. IQutayba, *Ikhtilāf*, 54; cf. IAYa'lā, i. 142, top, foot
77. Laoust, *Ibn-Taymiyya*, 261; ad-Dārimī, 58–71; cf. Ash., *Ibāna*, 54–9 (tr., 94–9).
78. Nu'aym b. Ḥammād: *Tadhk.*, ii. 419; IAWafā', ii. 202, no. 630; I'Asākir, *Tabyīn*, 387f.; *GALS*, i. 257; Sezgin, 1. 104f.
79. *Radd* (n. 5/69), 315; cf. Madelung, *Zaiditen*, 242.
80. Laoust, *Profession*, 167f.
81. Salomon Pines, *Beiträge zur islamischen Atomenlehre*, Berlin 1936, 124–33.
82. *Fihrist*, 206; the notice in IAWafā', i. no. 161 omits the accusation concerning the Jahmiyya.
83. Ibn-Taymiyya, '*Aqīda Ḥamawiyya*, quoted by M. Schreiner, 'Beiträge zur Geschichte der theologischen Bewegungen im Islam', *ZDMG*, liii (1899), 72f.; lii (1898), 544. Ad-Dārimī, *Naqd 'alā l-Marīsī al-Jahmī*; cf. Sezgin, i. 601.
84. Sezgin, i. 616; *EI*[2] by Carra de Vaux, A. Nader and J. Schacht; Khay., 201f. (note); Walter M. Patton, *Aḥmed ibn Ḥanbal and the Miḥna*, Leiden 1897, 48f. (quoting Ibn-al-Jawzī); Yqt., *Irsh.*, vi. 383. 14, 19; IAWafā', i, no. 371, cf. no. 1146; etc.
85. IAWafā', i, nos. 24, 394, 61.

86. Mtrd., *Sharḥ*, 19ff., says the view is also that of the Qadariyya and Muʿtazila and makes no further reference to the Jahmiyya. For the punishment of the tomb, cf. Mass., *Passion*, 679f.
87. Khay., 126; 133f.; on p. 12 he denies a resemblance between Jahm and A-Hudhayl; but Ash., 163, shows that he overstates his case.
88. Madelung (*Zaiditen*, 242 foot) accepts this point but supposes there were other unnamed men who followed Jahm (not al-Jahm) more closely.
89. Ash., 279–85.
90. Shahr., 59–64 (i. 112–23).
91. Bagh., 200.

Chapter Six

1. Cf. Laoust, *Schismes*, 55f., and Cahen, 'Points de vue . . .', (n. 2/1), 295–338, esp. 324f.
2. *EI*², art. 'Abū Salama' (S. Moscati); Sourdel, *Vizirat*, 65–9.
3. Cf. Laoust, *Schismes*, 70–2; Ahmad Amīn, *Ḍuḥā l-islām*, iii (Cairo 1943), 337–40.
4. I Ath., v. 3 (year 145); Masd., vi. 188. Cf. Laoust, *Schismes*, 64–6.
5. Nawb., 52; cf. p. 51.
6. Nawb., 41f.; Ash., i. 21f.; Bagh., 242, also called Barkūkiyya, and perhaps Baslamiyya (Halkin).
7. Nawb., 42; Ash., 21; Bagh., 242 (and Halkin's notes); Shahr., 114 (i. 247).
8. Bagh., 243f. (Halkin, 75f.); Shahr., 115 (i. 248); Laoust, *Schismes*, 74.
9. 87ff., and n. 53.
10. Cf. Yaʿqūbī, *Ta'rīkh*, ii. 349 (beginning of reign of as-Saffāḥ).
11. Yaʿqūbī, ii. 350 (speech of Dā'ūd b. 'Alī).
12. Cf. *EI*², 'Hāshimiyya' (B. Lewis), quoting Ṭab., ii. 29ff., 209ff.
13. *Marf.*, 301; cf. Lecomte, *Ibn Qutayba*, 315–17.
14. Laoust, *Profession*, 44n.
15. Nawb., 43; SA, 65, Cf. Masd., vi. 55f. and Pellat, *LWJ*, 17.
16. Nawb., 46.17; Rēvand is near Nishapur. Nāsh., §1/47 (cf. p. 35) calls them Hurayriyya.
17. Ash., 21.9–13; Nawb., 32, 3–5. Cf. Masd., vi. 54.
18. Nawb., 43. 7–10.
19. Nawb., 46.15–47.9; cf. 30.1.
20. Cf. pp. 75f.
21. Cf. pp. 124–6.
22. Cf. pp. 49, 73

23. ʿAlī (b. Ism. b. Shuʿayb) b. Mītham, also known as Ibn-at-Tammār : *Fihrist*, 175.19–21 ; Tusy, 212 (no. 458) ; Nawb., 9 ; Khay., 99, argues with ʿAlī al-Aswārī, a pupil of A-Hudhayl.
24. AJf. M. b. an-Nuʿmān al-Aḥwal : *Fihrist*, 176.9–13 ; Tusy, 323, no. 698 ; Ash., 37f., 43–5, etc. ; Khay., 6.58 ; Nawb., 66. Hishām : Tusy, 356 ; Nawb., 66 ; Ash., 34, 41, 43–5, 349 ; Khay., 6, 57.
25. Ash., about forty references ; Nawb., 66 ; *Fihrist*, 175f. ; Tusy, 355, no. 771 ; Khay., frequent. Cf. pp. 186–9 below.
26. Josef van Ess, in *Isl.*, xliii (1967), 257.
27. Khay., 6.
28. Masd., vi. 369–76 ; 'Haytham' has been corrected to 'Mītham' ; ʿAlī b. Haytham was a Zaydī not an Imāmī (n. 6/32a).
29. Nawb., 9.
30. Ash., 16f.
31. Tusy, 292 (no. 634), M. b. Khalīl ; the note here spells out the name and derives it from *sikak* (probably 'dies' for coins) ; the forms 'Shakkāl' (*Fihrist*), 176 and 'Sakkāl' (Masd., v. 374) should be emended ; and possibly Sakaniyya (Khay., 126 : cf. ch. 8, n. 77) ; cf. Nyberg in Khay., 178.
32. Tritton, 20 ; Ash., 16. In Nāsh., §1/72, it is applied to the followers of Jaʿfar aṣ-Ṣādiq by Mughīra (cf. Nawb., 54) and Zayd b. ʿAlī.
32a. E.g. Yqt., *Irsh.*, v. 457 ; M. b. A-ʿAbbās -Ṭūsī defended Imāmism and ʿAlī b. Haytham Zaydism before al-Ma'mūn, Thumāma and Bishr al-Marīsī.
33. Ash., 17 ; cf. Nöldeke, *Isl.*, xiii (1923), 73f.
34. Nawb., 65f., etc. ; Shahr., 126 (i. 274) ; Tusy, 188 (no. 405), 235 (no. 509), 93f. (no. 191), 211 (no. 456).
35. Nawb., 68f., 80f. ; Ash., 28f. Cf. *St.Isl.*, xxxi (1970). 295f.
36. Nawb., 67 ; Ash., 17, 29 ; Khay., 136 ; Shahr., 17 ; Masd., v. 443. But al-Malaṭī, *Tanbīh*, 26. 11–15, distinguishes a greater and lesser Qaṭʿiyya, of whom the latter make ʿAlī ar-Riḍā the last imam.
37. Ash., 63.11 ; Masd., v. 443f. Tusy (355, no. 771) says he went to Baghdad in 199/814 and died shortly afterwards. This fits better than an earlier date his relation to A-Hudhayl and an-Naẓẓām. As a Qaṭʿī he must have been alive after the death of al-Kāẓim. Cf. van Ess in *Oriens*, xviii (1967), 115.
38. *Fihrist*, 177.1 ; cf. Tusy, 216f. (no. 470) ; a pupil (Tusy, no. 205) died in 877.
39. Cf. L. Massignon, *Opera Minora*, Beirut 1963, i. 263.

40. Laoust, *Profession*, 44n.; IQ, *Ḥad.*, 6, 295.
41. Shahr., 115 (i.249).
42. Cf. Laoust, *Schismes*, 34f.; also p. 52 above.
43. The men named were messianic figures for groups of Jārūdiyya (Ash., 67). Cf. *Schismes*, 64f., 101, 131; and for other Zaydite revolts, 93f., 100, 131–5.
44. Ash., 68; Nawb., 9, 12, 50f.; *Schismes*, 136. As-Suyūṭī, *Lubb al-Lubāb*, vocalizes as Batriyya, but the *nisba* could be formed from the plural *butr*, as with Fuṭ'ḥiyya from *afṭaḥ*; Nāsh., §1/68, says the name was given because they docked (*batarū*) 'Uthmān's last six years.
45. *Fihrist*, 178; IS, vi. 261; IQ, *Marf.*, 225.
46. Nawb., 55–7; cf. 9.
47. Khay., 89.
48. Ash., 461; 68; other suggestions: Mass. (*Passion*, 725) 'qualified'; Pellat (*St. Isl.*, xv [1961], 45, 52) 'preferred though not clearly superior'.
49. Ash., 454.
50. IS, vi. 261; IQ, *Marf.*, 255.
51. Laoust, *Profession*, 72 (Ar. 43).
52. *Fihrist*, 178.
53. *Marf.*, 301.
54. IQ, *Ḥad.*, 71 (Fr. tr. 65).
55. Madelung, *Zaiditen*, 104ff.
56. Ibid. 110f., etc.; 152.
57. Nāsh., §1/86, 94–8; al-Iskāfī is said to have held the doctrine; cf. Pellat, *Milieu*, 190. *Fihrist*, 176.12. Al-Malaṭī, *Tanbīh*, 27, naming the Ja'fars and al-Iskāfī; Mass., in *Isl.*, iii (1912), 409.
58. Nāsh., §1/69 (*ijtihād*), 98; Ash., 68.6 (*ta'wīl*).
59. Masd., vi. 56–8; cf. Sezgin, i. 620; Pellat, *Milieu*, 190. *K. al-'Uthmāniyya* (Cairo 1955), 281–343 has extracts from al-Iskāfī.
60. *EI*², art. 'Ibn Abi'l-Shawārib' (J. C. Vadet), ad init.
61. Pellat, *Milieu*, 190–2, summary of a section; also *LWJ*, 72–82, selections.
62. Pellat, *LWJ*, 84.
63. Cf. Pellat, 'L'imamat dans la doctrine de Gāḥiẓ', *St. Isl.*, xv (1961), 23–52, esp. 51.
64. Cf. Wensinck, *MC*, 127 (*Waṣiyya*), 192 (*Fiqh Akbar II*); McCarthy, *Theology*, 246f.
65. '*Uthmāniyya*, 176.
66. Ash., 611.
67. 'Allāma-i-Ḥillī, *Al-Bābu 'l-Ḥādī 'Ashar*, tr. W. McE. Miller, London 1928, esp. §§179, 183f.; this is much later, but there was presumably little development in Imāmite views on this point after the early tenth century.

68. What follows is based on Charles Pellat, 'Le culte de Muʿāwiya au IIIe siècle de l'Hégire', *St. Isl.*, vi (1956), 53–66. Cf. *Munya*, 56f. (al-Aṣamm).
69. Cf. Goldziher, *MS*, ii.46f.
69a. Wellhausen, *Arab Kingdom*, 555f.; H. Lammens, 'Le "Sofiāni", héros national des arabes syriens', in *Études sur le siècle des Omayyades*, Beirut 1930, 391–408. Also P.M. Holt, *The Mahdist State in the Sudan*², Oxford 1970, 25; van Ess, *Oriens*, 18/19.94; Sourdel, *REI*, 30.45.
70. Masd., vi.64; H.A.R. Gibb, art. "Abd al-Ḥamīd b. Yaḥyā' in *EI*². For the subsection cf. Watt, *Political Thought*, 78–82.
71. *GALS*, i.235, nos. 2, 3, 4; cf. F. Gabrieli, art. 'Ibn al-Muḳaffaʿ' in *EI*².
72. Cf. Watt, *Political Thought*, 81f. and notes.
73. Quoted in Laoust, *Profession*, 58; cf. *Schismes*, 72f. For other early cases cf. *Fihrist*, 338; Mass., *Passion*, 186.
74. Cf. D. Sourdel, 'La biographie d'Ibn al-Muqaffaʿ d'après les sources anciennes', *Arabica*, i (1954), 307–23.
75. Edited and translated by M. Guidi as *La lotta fra l'Islam e il Manicheismo*, Rome 1927.
76. Cf. I. Goldziher, 'Ṣāliḥ b. ʿAbd-al-Ḳuddūs und das Zindīḳthum während der Regierung des Chalifen al-Mahdī', *Transactions Congr. Or. London*, ii (1892), 104–29; *GS*, iii. 1–26. Also Georges Vajda, 'Les zindīqs en pays d'Islam au début de la periode ʿAbbāside', *RSO*, xvii (1938), 173–229. Watt, *Integration*, 119–22.
77. Mass., *Passion*, 188f.
78. Cf. Goldziher, *MS*, i. 147–216; H.A.R. Gibb, 'The Social Significance of the Shuʿūbīya', *Studia Orientalia Ioanni Pedersen . . . dicata*, Copenhagen 1953, 105–14 (= *Studies*, 62–73); Watt, *Integration*, 120–2.
79. *Studies*, 66
80. Cf. above pp. 54f. and *Integration*, 104–6, 168f., etc.
81. Cf. above 36f, and n. 1/68.
82. Cf. Watt, 'Political Attitudes', 43–6. For a similar distinction at a slightly later period, cf. Mass., *Passion*, i. 204.
83. D. Sourdel, 'La politique religieuse du calife ʿAbbaside al-Ma'mun', *REI*, xxx (1962), 27–48, esp. 28.
84. Sourdel, *Vizirat*, i. 175–80.
85. Watt, 'Political Attitudes', 45.
86. Sourdel, 'La politique . . . al-Ma'mun', 32.
87. See note 83. This appeared about the same time as Watt, 'Political Attitudes', which independently reached similar conclusions from the heresiographical side, whereas Sourdel was more concerned with political history. Cf. n. 6/32a; Zaydism is defended by al-Ma'mūn's secretary, presumably with the caliph's approval.

88. Sourdel, op. cit., 40f.
89. Nawb., 73.
90. Sourdel, op. cit., 31, 33. In the section in Ash., 451–67, on political attitudes, Bishr is specifically mentioned twice (453, 456), and on each occasion is in agreement with the Zaydites; in the incident in Yqt., *Irsh.*, v. 457 (n. 6/32a) Thumāma is not said to have opposed Zaydism.
91. Cf. Walter M. Patton, *Aḥmed ibn Ḥanbal and the Miḥna*, Leiden 1897.

Chapter Seven

1. *An Introduction to Islamic Law*, Oxford 1964, 47. The present section is based largely on this work and on Schacht's article 'Aṣḥāb al-ra'y' in *EI*². Cf. also N. J. Coulson, *A History of Islamic Law*, Edinburgh 1964, and *Conflicts and Tensions in Islamic Jurisprudence*, Chicago 1969.
2. Shahr., 161 (i. 365f.); but he makes both these and Aṣ'ḥāb al-ḥadīth subdivisions of the *mujtahidūn*.
3. *Marf.*, 249f.; cf. Goldziher, *Ẓāhiriten*, 3–10.
4. Schacht, *Introduction*, 55.
5. Cf. De Lacy O'Leary, *Arabic Thought and its Place in History*, London 1922, ch. 1; also his *How Greek Science passed to the Arabs*, London 1949; *EI*², art. 'Gondēshāpūr' (Aydin Sayili).
6. Cf. P. Kraus, 'Zu Ibn al-Muqaffaʿ', *RSO*, xiv (1933–4), 1–20.
7. Cf. *Integration*, 260–5; 'The Early Development of the Muslim Attitude to the Bible', *Transactions of the Glasgow University Oriental Society*, xvi (1967), 50–62.
8. Migne, *Patrologia Graeca*, xciv. 1585ff. and xcvi. 1335–48, discussions with a 'Saracen'.
9. Cf. Graf, *GCAL*, ii. 7–23.
10. Ed. and tr. by A. Mingana in *Woodbrooke Studies*, ii, Cambridge 1928. For a general account of Muslim polemics against Christians cf. Erdmann Fritsch, *Islam und Christentum im Mittelalter*, Breslau 1930.
11. *K. ad-dīn wa-d-dawla*, ed. A. Mingana, Manchester 1923. The *Risāla* of al-Hāshimī is probably later; cf. Graf, *GCAL*, ii. 135–45.
12. *Isl.*, xliv. 18, no. 30, from Ibn-an-Nadīm.
13. *GALS*, i. 106.
14. *EI*², s.v. (D. Sourdel); the library may have been established earlier.
15. Republished as a single volume, *Die arabische Ubersetzungen aus dem Griechischen*, Graz 1960. The translators are listed *GAL*, i. 219–29 and *GALS*, i. 362–71. There may also have been some translation from Pahlevi in this field. One

of the translators from Pahlevi, Abān al-Lāḥiqī (d. 815), wrote an Arabic poem on cosmology (*GALS*, i. 239).

16. *Tadhk*, i. 205 (*dīn*); cf. Sourdel, 'La Politique Religieuse d'al-Ma'mūn', 32n. (*'ilm*) quoting from Wakīʿ (n.6/83).
17. IQ, *Ḥād.*, §§23–96.
18. *Risāla fī stiḥsān al-khawḍ fī 'ilm al-kalām*, in *Theology*, 85–97 (Ar. text), 117–34 (translation).
19. Art. 'Hishām' in *EI*[2] (W. Madelung); Masd., v. 443f.
20. *Munya*, 44.8.
21. Masd., vi. 370–4; *Fihrist*, 175.
22. Van Ess in *Oriens*, xviii (1967), 115; Madelung in *EI*[2] and *Isl.*, xliii (1967), 46. Cf. p. 161 above, n. 37.
23. Khay., 40f.; *Fihrist*, 338.8; G. Vajda, 'Le témoinage d'al-Māturīdī sur la doctrine des Manichéens, des Dayṣānites et des Marcionites', *Arabica*, xiii (1966); 1–38, 113–28, esp. 114, 127; id., *RSO*, xvii (1937), 181, 192; Massignon, *Opera Minora*, Beirut 1963, i. 627–39, 'Esquisse d'une bibliographie qarmate', esp. 628f., where name given as Maymūn b. al-Aswad; van Ess, *Isl.*, xliii. 258.
24. Cf. Armand Abel, art. 'Dayṣāniyya' in *EI*[2].
25. Cf. Vajda, in *Arabica* (see n. 23).
26. Ash., 59; Bagh., 50.
27. Ash., 60, 329.
28. *Isl.*, xliii. 256–61.
29. *Fihrist*, 175; van Ess in *Isl.*, xliii. 256 (quoting *Munya*, 50).
30. Tusy, 355, no. 771.
31. Ash., 369, 44, 331; cf. 59–61, 213, 336, 345.
32. Ash., 37f., 40; cf. also pp. 242–6 below.
33. *Fihrist*, 175; Tusy, 355.
34. Ash., 207–11; Shahr., 141; etc.
35. See above p. 161.
36. See p. 158, notes 23, 29.
37. See p. 158, note 24.
38. *Isl.*, xliii (1967), 241–79; xliv (1968), 1–70, 318–20.
39. *Farq*, 16; further reff. in *Isl.*, xliv. 7
40. Mass., *Essai*, 167. For his nephew al-Faḍl b. 'Isā cf. n. 4/108, no. 13.
41. Shahr., 4, 17; Aṣ'ḥāb al-Waʿīd 'of the Muʿtazila' in Ash., 274.7 and 276.4 appear to be the same.
42. Al-Malaṭī, *Tanbīh*, 30.
43. *Isl.*, xliv. 7.
44. *Isl.*, xliv. 6.
45. *Isl.*, xliv. 1, 19.
46. *Isl.*, xliv. 18; see also below p. 219
47. Ash., 457; but cf. *Isl.*, xliv. 2.
48. *Isl.*, xliii. 274.
49. *Isl.*, xliii. 245; xliv. 8.

50. Ash., 457.
51. Cf. pp. 50–2. The numbers refer to van Ess's list of books, *Isl.*, xliv. 16–21.
52. Khay., 133 foot.
53. Ash., 281.
54. Cf. P. Boneschi, 'Kasaba et iktasaba, leur acception figurée dans le Coran', *RSO*, xxx (1955), 17–53; also J. Schacht (see n. 55).
55. 'New Sources for the History of Muhammadan Theology', *St. Isl.*, i (1953), 23–42, esp. 29–33.
56. Cf. Lane, s.v. The idea of complying with a desire is implicit in the root and is not simply brought in to solve an exegetical difficulty; cf. Goldziher, *Koranauslegung*, 23.
57. Cf. Ash., 230–3, where *qudra* and *quwwa* (232.14) are used in passages where the heading has *istiṭāʿa*.
58. Cf. Watt, 'The Origin of the Islamic Doctrine of Acquisition', *JRAS*, 1943, 234–47. The usage in connection with knowledge, attributed to Ghaylān in Ash., 136, is not considered here. Ash. gives his own definition in 542.8f.
59. Ash., 406.4; 417.3.
60. Ash., 40.12–41.3.
61. Ash., 42.12–43.4.
62. Ash., 540f., 551, 554; cf. above 117f.
63. Ash., 553; cf. below. p. 203
64. Ash., 566; cf. below. pp. 199–201
65. Ash., 540; cf. below. pp. 203f.
66. Ash., 540; follower of an-Najjār, 541.
67. Ash., 550, of Baghdādiyyūn; cf. al-Jubbā'ī, 551.
68. Ash., 549f.
69. Khay., 53; *Munya*, 72.
70. Ash., 542; cf. below pp. 298ff.
71. Ash., 501, 539; for son an-Nāshi' al-Asghar (d. 975) cf. Yqt., *Irsh.*, v. 235–44, esp. 237.
72. Ash., 602, 605; van Ess (*Isl.*, xliii. 275) suggests that Ash., 594.4–13 refers to Ḍirār in view of *Ka-dhālika* in line 14.
73. Ash., 359f.
74. Ash., 281, 305f., 317, 328, 330, 345; Bagh., *Uṣūl*, 46f.
75. Ash., 216 (*mā huwa*), 282, 339; cf. 154.
76. Ash., 166, 174 (anonymous), 281, 487.
77. P. 146.
78. *Isl.*, xliv. 18 (no. 30); *Munya*, 72
79. Quoted by Madelung, *Zaiditen*, 243 from a nineteenth-century Shīʿite author.
80. Ash., 136f.; cf. 132.
81. *GALS*, i. 340; Sezgin, i. 616; Khay., 89, 180, 201f.; Ash., 140, 143, 149, 515; Bagh., *Farq*, 192f.; do., *Uṣūl*, 25, 256, 308; Shahr., 63, 106f.; Nawb., 13; IKhall.,

i. 260f.; *EI*², s.v. (Carra de Vaux, A.N. Nader, J. Schacht); van Ess in *Isl.*, xliv. 30–40 is much fuller than the *EI*² article.

82. I Khall., i. 260; for Ḥammād see IS, vii/2.29; *Tadhk.*, 197f.
83. Ad-Dārimī, *Ar-radd ʿalā l-Jahmiyya*, (cf. n. 5/70), 98; for Ḥ. b. Zayd, cf. IS, vii/2.42; *Tadhk.*, 228f.
84. Cf. *Isl.*, xliv. 31.
85. From a passage of al-Maqrīzī quoted in Patton, *Miḥna* (n. 6/91), 48f.
86. *Isl.*, xliv. 32f.
87. Al-Pazdawī, *K. uṣūl ad-dīn*, Cairo 1963, 54.
88. *Isl.*, xliv. 34f.
89. Yqt., *Irsh.*, v. 457; he also discussed with Jf. b. al-Mubashshir (Khay., 89).
90. Ibid., v. 383.
91. I A-Wafā', i. 164; other versions say because of the createdness of the Qur'ān, but this seems unlikely before 798.
92. *Isl.*, xliv. 33, 54f.; I A-Wafā', i. 413 (no. 1146).
93. *Isl.*, xliv. 39.
94. *Al-ʿaqīda al-Ḥamawiyya*, quoted by Martin Schreiner, 'Beiträge zur Geschichte der theologischen Bewegungen in Islam', *ZDMG*, liii (1899), 72f.; cf. lii. 544.
95. *Isl.*, xliv. 54f.
96. Ash., 140f., 149; cf. 143.
97. Cf. 137. above.
98. Ash., 141; Bagh., 193; Shahr., 107.
99. *Radd ʿalā Bishr* —, Cairo 1358/1939, quoted from *Isl.*, xliv. 36–9.
100. Ash., 515.
101. I A-Wafā', i. 164.
102. *Fihrist*, 179.
103. Khay., 9; *Fihrist* (Fück), 62.12; 67.3. Cf. *Isl.*, xliv. 59. In Ash., 415, he is the source of reports about matters discussed by A-Hudhayl, an-Naẓẓām, etc.
104. Ash., 283–5; remarks about Burghūth attached to art. 11 have been omitted (following Ritter's punctuation).
105. Cf. van Ess, *Isl.*, xliv. 57, and contrast Madelung, *Zaiditen*, 243.
106. Cf. Ash., 514, also of 'willing'; repetitions in 182, 507.
107. Khay., 133f.
108. Ash., 566.
109. Ash., 317f., 359f.
110. *Isl.*, xliv. 21–3, etc.
111. *Ar-radd ʿalā z-zanādiqa wa-l-Jahmiyya*, quoted from Morris S. Seale, *Muslim Theology, a Study of Origins with Reference to the Church Fathers*, London 1964, 98.

112. A. de Vlieger, *Kitāb al-qadr*, Leiden 1902, 171n.; cf. *Isl.*, xliv. 23.
113. Conclusions about the Ḥanafites complementary to those of van Ess are reached by M. O. Abu saq in an Edinburgh PH.D. thesis on 'The Politics of the Miḥna' (1971).
114. I A-Wafā', i. 223. I'Asākir, *Tabyīn*, 339–41, reasons for ash-Shāfi'ī's disapproval. General reff.: van Ess in *Isl.*, xliv. 24–30; *Fihrist*, 180; Ash., 216, 282, 317, 339, 370, 407, 515; Khay., 133f.
115. Khay., 133f.; Ash., 339; *Fihrist*, 205; van Ess in *Isl.*, xliv. 41f.
116. 'Īsā b. Abān was mainly a jurist; cf. *Fihrist*, 205 and van Ess, loc.cit.
117. 'Burghūth': Ash., 235, 238, 284, 330, 540; Khay., 133f.; *Munya*, 46; M. b. 'Īsā' (only): Ash., 552. 'M. b. 'Īsā as-Sīrāfī': Ash., 168, 488 (adds an-Naẓẓāmī); cf. *Munya*, 47 ('M. b. 'Īsā an-Naẓẓām'). A'AA as-Sīrāfī: Khay., 53. For a discussion of identities, see van Ess in *Isl.*, xliv. 60f.
118. Ash., 262, 540f.; *Fihrist*, 181.23; cf. *Isl.*, xliv. 60f.
119. Ash., 583, 586; I A-Wafā', ii. 60f.; *Isl.*, xliv. 40f; cf. p. 282 below and n. 10/17.
120. Cf. p. 195, n. 79 (Ḍirār); Shahr., 103 (i. 219).
121. Cf. p. 186, n. 19; Ash., 120; *Fihrist*, 182.21; Shahr., 103.
122. Ash., 108, 120, 540; *Fihrist*, 182.13; Shahr., 103.
123. Ash., 108, 120, 383; *Fihrist*, 182.18; Shahr., 103. Despite similar views he is not to be identified with M. b.'Īsā as-Sīrāfī (n. 117).
124. Cf. G. von Grunebaum, *Islam, Essays in the Nature and Growth of a Cultural Tradition* (American Anthropologist Comparative Studies of Cultures and Civilisations, 4), Menasha 1955, esp. 111–26.
125. Masd., ii. 244f.; the refutation is in verses by an-Nāshi' al-Akbar (cf. n. 71 above).
126. *GAL*, i. 230f. (*S.*, i. 372–4); Sezgin, *Fihrist*, esp. 255–61; Nicholas Rescher, *The Development of Arabic Logic*, Pittsburgh 1964, esp. 100–3 (Part II, pp. 83–255, 'Register of Arabic Logicians' is a useful compendium of biographical and bibliographical information, much of it relevant to other fields than logic); Richard Walzer, *Greek into Arabic*, Oxford 1962, esp. 12–15, 175–205; cf. also Michael E. Marmura and John M. Rist, 'Al-Kindi's Discussion of Divine Existence and Oneness', *Mediaeval Studies*, xxv (1963), 338–54. Recent study of al-Kindī is based on the publication of texts by Muḥammad 'Abd-al-Hādī Abū-Rīda: *Rasā'il al-Kindī al-falsafiyya*, Cairo 1950; vol. 2, Cairo 1953; the introduction to the original volume was also published separately as *Al-Kindī*

wa-falsafatu-hu (Cairo 1950). *Al-Kindi, the Philosopher of the Arabs*, by George N. Atiyeh (Rawalpindi 1966) is a full study with an annotated list of works.

127. Cf. Rescher, op. cit., 105f.
128. Muṣṭafā ʿAbd-ar-Rāziq in *Faylasūf al-ʿarab wa-l-muʿallim ath-thānī* (Cairo 1945) argues for late 252 (late 866) and is followed by Atiyeh.
129. *Greek into Arabic*, 175.
130. *GAL*, i.231f.; F. Rosenthal, *Aḥmad b. aṭ-Ṭayyib as-Sarakhsī*, New Haven 1943.
131. *GAL*, i.250f. (*S.*, i.394–6); *EI*², art. by J. M. Millás; Aldo Mieli, *La science arabe et son rôle dans l'évolution scientifique mondiale*, reimpression, Leiden 1966, 89. He was known in Latin as Albumasar.
132. *Rasāʾil*, ed. Abū-Rīda, i.375; cf. Walzer, *Greek into Arabic*, 182f. Relations with the Muʿtazila are discussed by Abū-Rīda in his introduction, 27–31, and by Walzer, op. cit., 176–87.
133. Ash., ii.510; cf. Walzer, 182f.
134. Cf. Abū-Rīda, 28–30.

Chapter Eight

1. Shahr., 33 (i.64); translation by A. K. Kazi and J. G. Flynn in *Abr-Nahrain*, viii (1968–9), 40.
2. Bagh., 98.
3. Khay., 164–8.
4. *Marf.*², 483.
5. *Fihrist* (Arb.), 30.
6. I Khall., ii.513; repeated in iii.644 (notice of Wāṣil), where it is also stated that Wāṣil was expelled by al-Ḥasan because of the *manzila*.
7. Khay., 134.
8. IS, vii/2.33; ib. 27 speaks of the Muʿtazila attacking Ibn-ʿAwn (a man criticized by ʿAmr in a well-known story, e.g. IQ, *Ḥad.*, 101).
9. *Marf.*, 243.
10. Laoust, *Profession*, 169.
11. Ash., i.222, 16; the term Khārijites is probably used of them because of their insistence that God fulfils his threats of punishments; cf. story about ʿAmr, ibid., 148n.
12. Khay., 170.
13. *Fihrist* (Houtsma), ad init.; etc. Cf. also *Munya*, 36.12–37.3.
14. Al-Jaḥiẓ, *Al-Bayān wa-t-Tabyīn*, i.37f.; quoted in *Munya*, 32n. Bagh., 98f.; see also Watt, 'Was Wāṣil a Khārijite?' in *Fritz Meier Festschrift*, 1973.
15. Khay., 133f.
16. Ibid., 170.

17. *Munya*, 32.5.
18. *Vorlesungen*, 94, 326 n.63; *Isl.*, vii (1918), 207–9 (*GS*, v.410–12). Massignon's 'voluntary solitude of the heart' (*Passion*, 708) seems to be rather different.
19. 'Sull'origine del nome dei Muʿtaziliti', *RSO*, vii (1916–19), 429–54, esp. 447.
20. Nawb., 5.2–8 (names abbreviated), referred to by H.S.Nyberg, art. 'Muʿtazila' in *EI*[1]. For an apparently contrary use of Muʿtazila, cf. van Ess, *Naẓẓām* (see n.8/27), 119–25.
21. Nawb., 11.16f.
22. *Fihrist* (Arb.), 30 foot.
23. 19.48/9f.; 18.16/15. Other usages: 2.222 (menstruation); 4.90/2f. (in warfare); 44.21/0 (Pharaoh told to withdraw).
24. *Fihrist* (Arb.), 31.
25. Khay., index; *Fihrist* (Houtsma), ad init.; do. (Arb.), 32; Bagh., 102–13; Shahr., 34–7 (i.66–71); *Munya*, 44–9; IKhall, ii.667–9; *EI*[2], art. by H.S.Nyberg; *GALS*, i.338; Tritton, 83–9.
26. Masd., vii.232; vi.369f.; cf. viii.301.
27. Khay., index; *Fihrist* (Houtsma), 220f.; do. (Arb.), 33; Bagh., 113–36; Shahr., 37–41 (i. 72–82); Masd., vi. 371f.; viii, 35, 301; *Munya*, 49–52; *EI*[1], art. by H.S. Nyberg; J. van Ess, 'Ḍirār' (ch.7, n.38), esp. §§1, 2; R.Paret, 'An-Naẓẓām als Experimentator', *Isl.*, xxv (1939), 228–33; *GALS*, i.339; Tritton, 89–95 (but the report that he died aged thirty-six must be mistaken); J. van Ess, *Das Kitāb an-Nakṭ des Naẓẓām* . . . , Göttingen, 1972, came to hand as this book was going to print.
28. Yqt., *Irsh.*, vii.105; *GAL*, i.101f.
29. Khay., index; *Fihrist* (Arb.), 33; Bagh., 136–41 (for identity cf. 141.9); Shahr. 46–8 (i.89–92); *Munya*, 54–6; Anwar G.Chejne, 'Muʿammar ibn ʿAbbād al-Sulamī, a leading Muʿtazilite of the eighth–ninth Centuries', *Muslim World*, li (1961), 311–20; Tritton, 100–3; Sezgin, i, 616. A concept worked out by him is discussed by Harry A.Wolfson in 'Muʿammar's Theory of *Maʿnā*', *Arabic and Islamic Studies in honour of Hamilton A.R.Gibb*, ed. G.Makdisi, Leiden 1965, 673–88.
30. Chejne, op. cit., 311f., where the identity with Maʿmar Abū-l-Ashʿath is half accepted; contrast van Ess in *Isl.*, xliv.45f. Tritton's vocalization of the name is not generally accepted.
31. *Fihrist* (Arb.), 33; *Munya*, 56f. He is almost certainly not the judge al-Aṣamm under al-Muʿtaṣim in al-Masʿūdī, *Tanbīh*, 356; cf. Tritton, 126f.

32. Shahr., 19, 51, 53; *EI*², art. Hishām al-Fuwaṭī (Ch. Pellat); the two men are the chief subject of Goldziher's article, 'Hellenistischer Einfluss auf muʿtazilitische Chalifats-Theorien', *Isl.*, vi (1916), 173–7 (=*GS*, v.318–22).
33. Goldziher, *Koranauslegung*, 111f.; cf. 108n., 113. Cf. *Fihrist*, 34.2, 15. The mysterious passage in *Fihrist*, 100.29 is discussed by van Ess, *Isl.*, xliv, 25f. (n. 30 above). Sezgin, i. 614f., makes al-Aṣamm older than Abū-l-Hudhayl, but gives no source for this; in *Munya* the two had an argument.
34. Khay., index; *Fihrist* (Arb.), 33; Shahr., 19, 50f.; Bagh., 145–51; Masd., *Tanbīh*, 395 foot; *EI*², art. by Ch. Pellat; Tritton, 113–15; cf. Goldziher; *Isl.*, vi. 173–7 (as n. 32 above).
35. Cf. as-Samʿānī, *Ansāb* (ap. Khay., 192); as-Suyūṭī, *Lubb al-lubāb*, s.v.
36. Khay., 90f., 203n.; *Fihrist* (Arb.), 34; Bagh., 147f., 261f.; Shahr., 51; *Munya*, 77; Tritton, 115–19; *EI*², art. (Watt).
37. Khay., index (as ʿAmr b. B.); Masd., iii. 22–5; vi. 55–8; vii. 222–8; viii. 33–6; etc.; *Fihrist* (Arb.), 35–45; Bagh., 160–3; Shahr., 52f.; *Munya*, 67–70; Yqt., *Irsh.*, vi. 56–80; Ch. Pellat, *Milieu*; id., *LWJ*; id. art. 'al-Djāḥiẓ' in *EI*²; *GAL*, i. 158–60 (*S.*, 239–47).
38. H. A. R. Gibb, *Arabic Literature*², Oxford 1963, 75.
39. Khay., 53, 191; Bagh., 163; Shahr., 18.37; *Munya*, 71f.; for the accusation of *zandaqa* cf. Mass., *Passion*, 192.
40. Khay., index; Masd., vi. 373; *Fihrist*, 162.12–21; do. (Arb.), 32; Bagh., 141–5; Shahr., 44f.; *Munya*, 52–4; *EI*², art. (A. N. Nader); Tritton, 95–8; Sezgin, i. 615.
41. Sourdel, *REI*, xxx (1962), 33.
42. Khay., index; IQ, *Ḥad.*, 60; Masd., vi. 373f.; *Fihrist* (Houtsma), 2f.; Bagh., 157–60; Shahr., 49f.; *Munya*, 54.7 (pupil of Bishr), 62–7; Sezgin, i. 615f.; Tritton, 98–100.
43. Sourdel, *Vizirat*, i. 220, 238f., 241; cf. Ṭab., iii. 1040, 1067.
44. Sourdel, i. 149 n. 8, 169 n. 3; Ṭab. iii. 651.
45. Sourdel, *REI*, xxx. 33, 42n.; cf. *Fihrist* (Houtsma), ad fin., speaks of AHudhayl as his *ustādh* for 30 years.
46. Masd., iii. 107; v. 81; vii. 10–22.
47. Khay., 149, 224f.; *Fihrist* (Houtsma), 3f.; *Munya*, 62.2, 125.16, 126.4 (48.10 is mistaken); Masd., index; IKhall., i. 61–74; *EI*², art. Zettersteen / Pellat; Sourdel, *Vizirat*, i. 245n., index.
48. Khay., index; *Fihrist* (Arb.), 33; Bagh., 102f.; Shahr., 48f.; *Munya*, 70f.
49. Khay., index; Masd., vii. 231; *Fihrist* (Arb.), 33; Bagh., 153–5; Shahr., 41, 49; *Munya*, 73–6; *EI*², art. 'Djaʿfar b. Ḥarb' (A. N. Nader); Sezgin, i. 619.

50. Khay., index; Masd., v. 443, vii. 231; *Fihrist* (Arb.), 33; Bagh., 153f.; Shahr., 41, 49; *Munya*, 76f.; *EI*², art. Dja'far b. Mubashshir (Nader/Schacht).
51. Khay., 89; cf. p. 163 above; p. 223 below.
52. Khay., index; Masd., vii. 231; *Fihrist* (Arb.), 33; Bagh., 155f.; Shahr., 41, 49, 51; *Munya*, 78, 123.9; *EI*², art. Sezgin, i. 619f.
53. See 'Nāsh.' in list of abbreviations.
54. His life and works are described in Nāsh., pp. 1–17; sources for his biography are listed on p. 1. He is quoted in Ash., 184f., 500f., 539. Cf. also *GAL*, i. 128 (*S.*, 188).
55. Ash., 458; Nāsh., §1/92—Ṭalḥa and az-Zubayr did not really make war on 'Alī.
56. The view of Jf. b. Mubashshir (Ash., 464) that they live in 'the sphere of evildoing' (*dār fisq*) is hardly an exception.
57. Printed as an appendix to *K. al-'Uthmāniyya* of al-Jāḥiẓ, Cairo 1955; cf. Sezgin, i. 620; Pellat in *St. Isl.*, xv (1961), 31n.
58. Cf. Charles Pellat, 'L'Imamat dans la doctrine de Gāḥiẓ', *St. Isl.*, xv (1961), 23–52.
59. Masd., vii. 234f.
60. Nāsh., §1/85, 87.
61. Nāsh., §1/88, 89; cf. Ash., 455, 457.
62. Nāsh., §1/90, 91; contrast Ash., 457.
63. Ash., 457.13–458.2; Nāsh., §1/102.
64. Ash., 460.10; cf. Goldziher, as in n. 32 above.
65. Nāsh., §1/82f., 104.
66. Nāsh., §1/101; Ash., 456.9–11.
67. Nāsh., §1/99–102.
68. Nāsh., §1/94–8; Ash. 453.7–10; 456.16f.
69. Nāsh., §1/98 ad init.
70. Cf. p. 168 above.
71. Khay., 126; Ash., 278; Masd., vi. 20–3; cf. Nāsh., p. 97.
72. Cf. Ash., 274–8; Shahr., 33 (i. 65).
73. Khay., 97f.; Nāsh., §1/89f.; Nawb., 11f.
74. Cf. *Munya*, 57.9; 58.10; 60.15; 71.8, 10; 72.16.
75. Ash., 266–70 mentions the points discussed under this head in the ninth century.
76. Ash. 278; cf. 451. The phrase comes from the Qur'ān; 3.104/0, 110/06, 114/0; 7.157/6; 9.(67/8), 71/2, 112/3; 22.41/2; 31.17/16.
77. Khay., 126; Sakaniyya, otherwise unknown, should probably be emended to Sakkākiyya, who are said to have held a similar view of God's knowledge to Hishām Ḥ. (Ash. 219.7; 490.13). Cf. n. 6/31.
78. Khay., 24f.
79. Nāsh., §2/107; cf. p. 93.

80. Mtrd., *Sharḥ*, 11; further references in Nāsh., p. 93.
81. *Orientalische Literatur-Zeitung*, xxxii (1929), 427, in a long review (pp. 425–41) of *La lotta tra l'Islam e il manicheismo* by Michelangelo Guidi, entitled 'Zum Kampf zwischen Islam und Manichäismus'.
82. Ash., 256f.; Shahr., 36.
83. Ash., 243.15.
84. Ash., 257.
85. 2.6/5f., *Khatama 'alā*; other words used are *ṭaba'a*, *aqfāl*; for a list of passages see Paret, *Kommentar*, ad loc.
86. Ash., 259.
87. See esp. Ash., 260–6, where most views are given anonymously.
88. Ash., 230.13f.
89. Ash., 243.15; 267.7.
90. Ash., 40f., 42f.
91. Ash., 259.9; 262.6; 263.6; 265.6.
92. Ash., 230.12; 231.14f.; 232.14f.; etc.
93. God's power not *istiṭā'a*—cf. al-Bāqillānī, *K. al-inṣāf fī-mā yajib i'tiqādu-hu*, ed. al-Kawtharī[2], Cairo 1963, I, §28.
94. Ash., 230.12f.
95. Ash., 233, 443; cf. Shahr., 35.
96. Shahr., 35.
97. Ash., 234.
98. Ash., 415–18.
99. Ash., 238f., 236, etc.
100. Ash., 232.
101. IQ, *Ḥad.*, 54f. (§46).
102. Ash., 401f.
103. Ash., 331f., 405f.; Shahr., 46; cf. van Ess, *Isl.*, xliii. 259, etc.
104. Ash., 401–15; cf. Khay., 194f. (Nyberg's note to p. 63).
105. Ash., 402f.
106. Ash., 427 foot, 239, 429, etc.
107. Ash., 409.
108. Ash., 246; cf. 573–7.
109. Ash., 554; cf. 548f. The distinction was also used by Burghūth (553) and ash-Shaḥḥām (199, 549f.).
110. Ash., 200.
111. Ash., 227f.; Shahr., 51; Bagh., 147.
112. Ash., 250.14; 575.16; cf. Bagh., *Uṣūl*, 151f.
113. Ash., 249, 576f.
114. Ash., 246f.; 248.11–15 is anonymous but very similar.
115. Ash., 253.11f.
116. Ash., 201.7.
117. Ash., 253f.
118. Ash., 254f.; cf. Bagh., *Uṣūl*, 236f.
119. Cf. G. H. Bousquet, 'Des animaux et de leur traitement

selon le Judaïsme, le Christianisme et l'Islam', *St. Isl.*, ix (1958), 31–48.

120. Cf. Khay., 155.14; R.A. Nicholson, *Studies in Islamic Poetry*, Cambridge 1921, 136 (al-Ma'arrī); P. Kraus, in *RSO*, xiv. 350.

121. J. Schacht, in *St. Isl.*, i (1953), 29.

122. Ash., 249, 537.

123. Ed. Vitestam (cf. n. 5/50), 4, 97, 100; *Fihrist*, 337f.; cf. art. 'Ibn Dirham' (G. Vajda) in *EI*² with further reff. For ad-Dārimī cf. Sezgin, i. 600; *Tadhk.*, ii. 621f.

124. 'Christliche Polemik und islamische Dogmenbildung', *ZA*, xxvi (1911), 175–95; reprinted in *Islamstudien*, Leipzig 1924, i. 432–49; esp. 188 (=443). Cf. pp. 98f. above.

125. Cf. Migne, *Patrologia Graeca*, xcvi. 1341f. The objection to this suggestion by Vanna Cremonesi, 'Un antico documento ibāḍita sul Corano creato', *Studi Magrebini*, i (1966), 133–78, esp. 135n., does not meet the precise point made. (Pp. 137–46 summarize the views of the Mu'tazila; the document, translated pp. 160–78, is by the Rustamid imam Abū-l-Yaqẓān Muḥammad, d. 894, and follows the views of al-Jubbā'ī.)

126. Tab., iii. 1113 foot; Walter M. Patton, *Aḥmed ibn Ḥanbal and the Miḥna*, Leiden 1897, 58. Cf. above p. 108, no. 3; also letter of 'Umar II and the remarks of van Ess in *Abr-Nahrain*, xii. 23.

127. Ṭab., iii. 1113, 1118f.; cf. Patton, op. cit., 58, 68.

128. Ash., 225f., 582–603.

129. Ash., 598.

130. See pp. 280–3 below. For a fuller discussion see Watt, 'Early Discussions about the Qur'ān', *Muslim World*, xl (1950), 27–40, 96–105 (§1 on the Jahmiyya requires some revision).

131. For different senses of *wāḥid* cf. Nāsh., §2/60.

132. Shahr., 31.

133. Ash., 165. For this section cf. R. M. Frank, 'The Divine Attributes according to the Teaching of Abūl Hudhayl al-'Allāf' (*Muséon*, lxxxii [1969], 451–506).

134. Ash., 164. Cf. Shahr., 55 foot, al-Jubbā'ī similar but had *li-dhāti-hi*.

135. Ash., 166f.; for Ḍirār cf. 283, etc., and van Ess, *Isl.*, xliii. 277.

136. Shahr., 34 foot.

137. Ash., 155f. : no attempt has been made to distinguish nearly synonymous terms.

138. Ash., 207–17; Shahr. uses it as a convenient classification, 4, 8, 20, 80, 84.

139. Ash., 304.11f.; cf. 44; also van Ess, *Isl.*, xliii.257.
140. Khay., 22, 50, 67, 69, 133f.
141. Ash., 195, 218, etc.

Chapter Nine

1. Sourdel, *Vizirat*, 320f.
2. Cf. Watt, 'The Decline of the Almohads; reflections on the viability of religious movement', *History of Religions*, iv (1964), 23–9.
3. *Iqtiṣād, quṭb* 4, *bāb* 3, *ṭaraf* 2. Cf. *Transactions of the Glasgow University Oriental Society*, xxi (1966), 21.
4. Cf. Paret, *Kommentar*, on 8.38.
5. Goldziher, *ZDMG*, xxxvi (1882), 279 (=*GS*, ii.121).
6. This account mainly follows Schacht, *Introduction to Islamic Law* (n.3/1), esp. 29–33, and Coulson, *History of Islamic Law* (cf. ibid.). Ahmad Hasan, *The Early Development of Islamic Jurisprudence*, Islamabad 1970, follows Schacht and Coulson to some extent but gives a more traditional emphasis.
7. From Goldziher, *MS*, ii.12.
8. Goldziher, l.c., quoting *Tadhk*, i.293.
9. *Islamic Jurisprudence: Shāfiʿī's* Risāla, translated by Majid Khadduri, Baltimore 1961, 110–12; cf. Coulson, 56.
10. Cf. art. '(al-) Djarḥ wa-l-taʿdīl' (James Robson) in *EI*².
11. Cf. Bagh., *Uṣūl*, 11–13; translated and commented on by Watt, *Islamic Quarterly*, vii (1962), 31–4.
12. For detailed references to matters in the last two paragraphs see Goldziher, *MS*, ii, ch.8; also Sezgin, i.53–84, 115f.; *EI*², art. 'Ḥadīth' (J. Robson).
13. The following account is based mainly on Schacht, *Introduction to Islamic Law*, 57–68, and Coulson, op. cit.
14. Cf. Watt, *Bell's Introduction to the Qur'ān*, Edinburgh 1970, 47–50, with further reff.
15. *Essai*, 110–13.
16. Goldziher, 'Die dogmatische Partei der Sālimijja', *ZDMG*, lxi (1907), 73–80 (=*GS*, v.76–83); Mass., *Essai*, 294–300; do., *Passion* 361f.
17. Mass., *Passion*, 535, n.1, etc. A statement of his beliefs about God is quoted by al-Kalābādhī, *The Doctrine of the Sufis*, tr. A.J. Arberry, Cambridge, 1935, 15f.
18. IQ, *Marf.*, 240, 301; Ash., 118f., 513f; Nawb., 9; Shahr., 103, 106; Pellat, *Milieu*, 113 with note explaining possibilities of confusion; Mass., *Essai*, 167, 169.
19. Khay., 144, 218 (note); Ash., 5.216, 259, 286f., 457; Nawb., 13; Mass., *Essai*, 219. (Bakriyya is also used of supporters of Abū-Bakr especially by Shīʿites but cf. al-Ghazālī, *Faḍā'iḥ al-Bāṭiniyya*, Cairo 1964, 174 foot.)

20. *Sufism, an account of the mystics of Islam*, London 1950, 57; Mass., *Essai*, 304. See also p. 289 below and n. 10/59.
21. *Kashf al-mahjūb*, translated by Reynold A. Nicholson, new edition, London 1936, 130.
22. For the last two cf. Mass., *Passion*, i. 362.
23. Cf. Franz Rosenthal, *Knowledge Triumphant*, Leiden 1970, esp. 70–96, and review by Watt in *BSOAS*, also Mass., *Passion*, 467, 537, 545, etc.
24. Wensinck, *MC*, 104; his assumption (109f.) that this expresses 'the attitude of orthodox Islam', is mistaken, though it may be said to show 'the catholic tendencies' of Murji'ism.
25. *Waṣiyya*, §10; *Al-fiqh al-akbar II*, §10; Ash., *Māq.*, §36; *Ibāna*, §33 (*ap. Theology*, 246f.).
26. Al-Pazdawī, *K. uṣūl ad-dīn*, ed. Hans Peter Linss, Cairo 1963, 242.10–16. Cf. IQ'bghā, no. 198; IA-Wafā', ii. 270; *GALS*, i. 637, brother.
27. See Watt, *Integration*, index.
28. *Passion*, 182–9.
29. Cf. IKhall., iii. 16–18 (Ibn-Shannabūdh).
30. Mtrd., *Sharḥ*, comment on art. 3; IAYa'lā, i. 31 (as title of *'Aqīda I*. Van Ess, *Die Erkenntnislehre des 'Aḍudaddīn al-Īcī*, Wiesbaden 1966, 48, thinks that about 1050 this name applied mainly to the Māturīdiyya; but about 1040 it is used in the mainly Ḥanbalite creed of the caliph al-Qādir (George Makdisi, *Ibn 'Aqīl et la résurgence de l'Islam traditionaliste au XIe siècle*, Damascus 1963, 308f.).
31. IQ, *Ḥad.*, 71; in a letter (Ṭab., lii. 1114) al-Ma'mūn criticizes men who *nasabū anfusa-hum ilā s-sunna* and claimed to be *ahl al-ḥaqq wa-d-dīn wa-l-jamā'a*.
32. Ash., i. 3; ii. 455, 473–5.
33. Laoust, *Profession*, 11n., 166 (text 90).
34. Nāsh., §2/60, 2/178; cf. p. 90.
35. Khay., 139, 143; cf. index.
36. Nāsh., §1/110–14.
37. Ash., 504.11 (assuming Ḥawādith, also in 399, are the same people); cf. 586; other reff., 5, 172, 211, 217, 290ff. (creed), 434, 451f., 602.
38. IQ *Ḥad.*, passim.
39. IQ, *Ḥad.*, 96 (name given by opponents); Khay., 74, 132; Nawb., 6f., 14f.; M.Th. Houtsma in *ZA*, xxvi (1911), 196–202; A.S. Halkin in *JAOS*, liv (1934), 1–28; art. 'Ḥashwiyya' in *EI*².
40. IQ, as in previous note; Khay., index; G. van Vloten, in *Actes du XIe Congrès international des Orientalistes*, iii. 99ff.; Houtsma in *ZA*, xxvi. 201f.; Massignon, *Essai*, 219; A.S. Tritton, in *JRAS*, 1932, 137, suggests emending

Fihrist, 179 to 'Nābitat al-Ḥashwiyya' (as Massignon); Ch. Pellat, 'La Nābita de Djahiz', *Annales de l'Institut d'Etudes Orientales de l'Université d'Alger*, x (1952), 302–25; cf. Pellat, *LWJ*, 82–6.

41. *Essai*, 168, without a reference; the four are mentioned as 'our friends' to 'Amr b. 'Ubayd, who criticizes them, in IQ, *Marf.*, 243(483); and *Ḥad.*, 101; van Ess, *Traditionistische Polemik*, §15.
42. IS, vii/2.15.
43. Nawb. 79ff.; Masd., viii. 40.
44. A useful general account of Ismā'īlism is given by Bernard Lewis in *The Assassins : A Radical Sect in Islam*, London 1967, ch. 2, with further bibliography on pp. 144f. Cf. also *EI*², art. 'Ismā'īliyya'.
45. Cf. n.6/54.
46. Cf. Sezgin, i. 567.
47. Cf. ibid., 561–6.
48. Madelung, *Zaiditen*; he has also written a number of articles on related topics.
49. Recent items in the controversy are: Madelung, *Zaiditen*, 54–7 and Sezgin, i. 552–6, with references to the earlier discussions.
50. Khay., 132, 134, 164, 172 (*aṣ'ḥāb*).
51. Ash., 31.9; 64.5; 31.10; 41.8; 42.4.
52. Nawb., 84; 90.5; 93.3.
53. Nawb., 90–3.
54. *Passion*, 144–50.
55. *EI*², art. 'Ḥasan al-'Askarī' (J. Eliash).
56. Mass., *Passion*, 146–50; *Fihrist*, 176f., 191 top, 238, 244; Tusy, 57f. (no. 109).
57. *Fihrist*, 177; Tusy, 98 (no. 208); Sezgin, i. 539; Masd., i. 156.
58. Mass., *Passion*, 145n., Masd., viii. 141f.; *Fihrist*, 127.
59. English translation by Asaf A. A. Fyzee, *A Shi'ite Creed* (Islamic Research Association Series, 9), London 1942; cf. *EI*², art. 'Ibn Bābawayh(i)' (Fyzee); *GALS*, i. 322(7) wrongly speaks of a translation in 1932, and is followed by Sezgin, i. 548.
60. Cf. Goldziher, *ZDMG*, xxxvi (1882), 279 (= *GS*, ii. 121).
61. Cf. Dwight M. Donaldson, *The Shi'ite Religion*, London 1933, 284–90; *GALS*, i. 320; Sezgin, i. 540–2; G. Vajda, 'Aperçu sur le *K. at-Tawḥīd* d'al-Kulīnī', *Acta Orientalia Hungarica*, xii (1961), 231–4.

Chapter Ten

1. Bagh., *Uṣūl*, 307–10, 254; Wensinck, *MC*, 136.
2. Also called al-Kinānī; *GALS*, i. 340; Sezgin, i. 617;

Subk., i. 265; van Ess, *Oriens*, xviii/xix. 101.
3. Khāṭ, *TB*, viii. 53 (from Abusaq, i. n. 47); I'Asākir, *Tabyīn*, 352–4.
4. Bagh., *Uṣūl*, 293, 304; other reff., 166, 249, 254, 295, 306, 309.
5. Ya'qūbī, *Ta'rīkh*, ii. 484 foot; cf. Abusaq, 4/n. 4.
6. IS, vii/2. 49; *Tahdh.*, v. 200; IA-Wafā', i. 275f.; *Tadhk.*, i. 337f; Abusaq, 7/n. 1–6.
7. *Tadhk.*, ii. 577; Abusaq, 7/n. 11–16.
8. *Tadhk.*, ii. 484–6; Abusaq, 7/n. 17–23.
9. IA-Wafā', i. 166f. (no. 374); Abusaq, 1/n. 52–62.
10. IAYa'lā, i. 32.
11. Ash., 602. 10.
12. IAYa'lā, i. 62; cf. 142 (top, foot).
13. IAYa'lā, i. 41, 75, 111, 120. General reff.: Ash., 95 (source of reports about Khawārij; cf. Shahr., 96), 457, 602; Bagh., 265; id., *Uṣūl*, 254, 308; *Fihrist*, 181 ('of Mujbira'; wrote book against 'Alī, also *K. al-mudallisīn*), 207 (critique of the last by aṭ-Ṭaḥāwī); Subk., i. 251–6; IKhall., i. 416f.; Sezgin, i. 599f.; Mass., *Passion*, 467 n., 592; van Ess, *Oriens*, xviii. 102, 109.
14. *Fihrist*, 184; Ash., 546; Bagh., *Uṣūl*, 189, 222, 254, 308, 341; Subk., ii. 37–42; Shahr., 20, 65; al-Ghazālī, *Munqidh*, Damascus 1939, 109f.; Sezgin, i. 639–42; Margaret Smith, *An Early Mystic of Baghdad*, London 1935; van Ess (see next note).
15. Van Ess, *Die Gedankenwelt des Ḥāriṯ al-Muḥāsibī*, Bonn 1961, 205f.; *K. ar-Ri'āya*, ed. M. Smith, London 1940, 244 top.
16. IAYa'lā, i. 62 foot.
17. *Fihrist*, 206f.; IA-Wafā', ii. 61; IQ'bghā, no. 161; *Tadhk.*, ii. 629 (only date of death as 266); Sezgin, i. 436. 'Thaljī' may have been deformed to 'Balkhī' in Ash., 582. 12 and 602. 5, and *Fihrist*, 206. 2; IA-Wafā' says 'Thaljī or Balkhī'; cf. p. 203 above and n. 7/119.
18. Ash., 583. 3; cf. 586. 11.
19. Subk., ii. 12 top. General reff.: Subk., ii. 2–19; *Tadhk.*, ii. 555–7; Sezgin, i. 115–34 with further reff.; *EI*², art. by James Robson.
20. Subk., i. 252—the charge; see Sezgin, i. 494 for further reff.
21. IAYa'lā, i. 75.
22. Ash., 602. 3.
23. Ash., 600.
24. Ash., 584f., 601f.
25. §9; Wensinck, *MC*, 127.
26. §3; *MC*, 189; for the distinctive emphases of this creed cf. Watt, *MW*, xl (1950), 98f.

27. *Bayān as-sunna wa-l-jamā'a*, Aleppo 1344 (1925), 7.
28. Ash., 292. 9–11; the numbering of the articles is that of McCarthy, *Theology*, 241.
29. *K. at-Tamhīd*, ed. McCarthy, Beirut 1957, 251. 5f.; *K. al-irshād*, ed. Luciani, Paris 1938, 60. 14 (Fr. tr. 102).
30. Allard, *Attributs*, 413–16; detailed discussions, 239, 310, 391f., 398. Cf. *Ibāna*, 71.4; tr. 60.8.
31. IA-Wafā', i. 197 (no. 479); Abusaq, 1/n. 52, 2/n. 2.
32. IA-Wafā', i. 191 (no. 444); Patton, *Miḥna* (n. 6/91), index.
33. IA-Wafā', ii. 202 (no. 630); for further reff. cf. n. 5/78.
34. IA-Wafā', i. 56f. (no. 72).
35. IA-Wafā', i. 299f. (no. 795); Patton, *Miḥna*, index (text from ANu'aym on p. 102 speaks not of this man but of Abū-'Abd-ar-Rahmān ash-Shāfi'ī, presumably Aḥmad b. Yaḥyā; cf. Khay., index).
36. Abusaq, 2/n. 9, 15.
37. IA-Wafā', ii. 58f. (no. 189); Sezgin, i. 435.
38. IA-Wafā', i. 337 (no. 920); Abusaq, 6/n. 43*.
39. IA-Wafā', i. 198 (no. 484).
40. IA-Wafā', i. 290 (no. 764).
41. IA-Wafā', i. 148f. (no. 329); Abusaq, 1/n. 8.
42. E.g. in *Tawḥīd*, 59, sura 4. 164/2 (God's speaking to Moses) is quoted as in §3 (*MC*, 189).
43. Subk., ii. 51f.; *Fihrist*, 180; Khay., 111; Ash., 169–73, 177–80, 298f., etc.; Sezgin, i. 599, 550; J. van Ess, 'Ibn Kullāb und die Miḥna', *Oriens*, xviii/xix (1967), 92–142; Allard, *Attributs*, 146–53
44. *Uṣūl*, 309.
45. Ash., 171, 514, 522, 547, 582.
46. Bagh., *Uṣūl*, 293.
47. Ash., 179, 517, 582.
48. Both mentioned: *Uṣūl*, 89, 90, 97, 109, 113, 123, 132, 222; IKullāb alone: ibid., 104, 146, 249; Qal. alone: ibid., 10, 29, 40, 45, 46, 67, 87, 111, 230f., 234, 256, 281, 293, 304. In lists: ibid, 254, 309f.
49. As I'Asākir, *Tabyīn*, 398. The point is fully discussed by J. van Ess in *Oriens*, xviii. 100. Tritton, 182, mistakenly follows as-Sayyid al-Murtaḍā, *It'ḥāf as-sāda* (Cairo 1311/1893), ii. 5f. in identifying this man with A. b. Ibr., a contemporary of Ibn-Fūrak (d. 1015). (This man's father witnessed the crucifixion of al-Ḥallāj—Mass., *Passion*, 305.)
50. Bagh., *Uṣūl*, 310; cf. van Ess, loc. cit. In Bagh., *Uṣūl*, 254, he is one of the *mutaqaddimūn*.
51. As-Sayyid al-Murtaḍā, op. cit., ii. 5 foot.
52. *Farq*, 145 top; *Uṣūl*, 230.

53. *Uṣūl*, 256, 281; cf. al-Pazdawī (n.9/26), 188, 'al-Qalānisī of the Ash'ariyya'.
54. Shahr., 65; cf. Allard, *Attributs*, 134. The ideas of chronology in Shahr. are inaccurate.
55. I A-Wafā, ii. 247f. (no. 55); cf. i. 353f. (no. 978). The source is Mas'ūd b. Shayba, *K. at-ta'līm* (cf. *GALS*, ii. 953. 58a), who may be following Shahr., 65 in part. The mention of *fiqh* may be a mistake—it is omitted in i. 354; and al-Jubbā'ī is said to have been a Mālikite—Mass., *Passion*, 246.
56. He is linked with I Kullāb and al-Qalānisī in Bagh., *Uṣūl*, 222.
57. Cf. *EI*², art. 'Ibn Fūrak'.
58. Bagh., *Uṣūl*, 308. 14.
59. Ibid., 309. 14; art. 'al-Djunayd' (A. J. Arberry) in *EI*². Ali Hassan Abdel-Kader, *The Life, Personality and Writings of al-Junayd*, London (Gibb Memorial Series, N.S. 22) 1962, 6f., gives anecdotes showing his opposition to Kalām (but these may only refer to certain views). Mass., *Essai*, 305, and *Passion*, 535, holds that Junayd condemned Kalām in al-Muḥāsibī, with whom he had associated, but notes some connection with I Kullāb (*Passion*, 37). See p. 263f. above.
60. I Ḥazm, ii. 140f.; cf. Goldziher, *Ẓāhiriten*, 135n.
61. Ash., 141, 143; Bagh., 202–14; Bagh., *Uṣūl*, 5, 29–31, 73, 77, 88, 93, 95f., 103, 106, 112, 118, 122, 143, 150f., 154, 167f., 176, 189f., 217f., 250f., 290, 298; Shahr., 79–85; Subk., ii. 53f. (in art. 'Uthmān ad-Dārimī); *EI*¹, art. 'Karrāmīya' (D. S. Margoliouth); Mass., *Essai*, 255–72, 318f.; Allard, *Attributs*, 321–6, etc.; C. E. Bosworth, *The Ghaznavids*, Edinburgh 1963, 185–9, etc.; do., 'The Rise of the Karāmiyyah in Khurasan', *MW*, 50 (1960), 5–14.
62. Mass., *Essai*, 157.
63. *Essai*, 266; most of the names he gives are not found in the *Ṭabaqāt al-ḥanafiyya*.
64. Cf. Sezgin, i. 600; etc.
65. *Tawḥīd*, 373.
66. Bagh., 206, 204; Bagh., *Uṣūl*, 122; cf. Mass., *Passion*, 611.
67. *Essai*, 265.
68. Subk., ii. 23.
69. Henri Laoust, art. 'Aḥmad b. Ḥanbal' in *EI*²; do., *Profession*, vii–xx; Patton, *Miḥna* (n.6/91); Allard, *Attributs*, 98–101; Sezgin, i. 502–9.
70. Cf. *Profession*, xv; text in I A Ya'lā, i. 24–31, omitting the critique of heretical sects, pp. 31–6.
71. Not yet created: Khushaysh ap. al-Malaṭī, *Tanbīh*, 76f., 104. Will come to an end: ibid., 76f., 106; Ash., 148f.,

163, 279, 474, 542. For A-Hudhayl's sympathy with this view, cf. Ash., 163; Shahr., 35 (fifth point).

72. Ash., 467f.
73. Cf. Goldziher, *MS*, ii. 26, n. 3 (Eng. tr., p. 36, n. 7 should read 'going back *not* to M., but to . . . ').
74. 'En quoi consiste l'opposition faite à al-Ash'arī par ses contemporains hanbalites?', *REI*, xxviii (1960), 93–105.
75. McCarthy, *Theology*, text p. 12 (§18).
76. The statements in '*Aqīda I* are conveniently collected by Allard, *Attributs*, 99–101.
77. *GAL*, i. 124–7 (*S.*, i. 184–7); Gérard Lecomte, *Ibn Qutayba, L'homme, son œuvre, ses idées*, Damascus 1965; do., art. 'Ibn Ḳutayba', in *EI*². Besides the works listed under the abbreviation 'IQ', he wrote *The Divergence about the Lafẓ and the Refutation of the Jahmiyya and Mushabbiha.*
78. IQ, *Ḥad.*, 19f. (§§27f.)
79. Ibid., 19 (§27).
80. Cf. G. Lecomte, 'La Waṣiyya (testament spirituel) attribuée à . . . b. Qutayba', *REI*, xxviii (1960), 73–92.
81. Lecomte, *Ibn Qutayba*, 333–6; cf. Mass., *Essai*, 318.
82. IQ, *Ḥad.*, 212 (§196).
83. Laoust, *Profession*, xxivf., and n. 52; Sezgin, i. 511f.
84. Laoust, *Profession*, xxviii–xli; Sezgin, i. 312.
85. Laoust (*Profession*, 84 n. 4.) interprets a sentence in IAYa'lā, ii. 30 as meaning that al-Barbahārī held that man's *lafẓ* is uncreated, but it seems preferable to take the sentence as meaning that he condemned the Wāqifa as well as the Lafẓiyya. Cf. the account of I Ḥanbal's views by aṭ-Ṭabarī in *REI*, xxxvi (1968), 198 (and 192).
86. *GAL*, i. 148f. (*S.*, i. 217f.); Sezgin, i. 323–8.
87. Dominique Sourdel, 'Une profession de foi de l'historien al-Ṭabarī', *REI*, xxxvi (1968), 177–99, esp. 198 (and 192.)
88. In an unpublished Edinburgh PH.D. thesis al-Ḥibr Yūsuf Nūr-ad-dā'im examines the main passages in the *Tafsīr* where Sunnite and Shī'ite views differed and shows that aṭ-Ṭabarī always opposes the Shī'ite interpretations. Though he accepted the Tradition of Ghadīr Khumm, he interpreted it differently.
89. Cf. Sezgin, i. 540; *Fihrist*, 235.4 wrongly ascribes *K. al-Mustarshid* to the historian.
90. Cf. Sezgin, i. 601. The suggestion that he was a Karrāmite is to be rejected (Mass., *Essai*, 318, contradicting 266).
91. Ash., 162, 199, 277, 415, 504ff., 549f.; Khay., 53, 191; Bagh., 163; Shahr., 18, 37; *Munya*, 71f. Probably lived 800/10 to 880/90; Tritton, 140f.; Mass., *Passion*, i. 192.

92. Ash., index; Bagh., 167–9; Shahr., 54–9; Tritton, 141–8; Mass., *Passion*, 246 (says Mālikī in *fiqh*); Allard, *Attributs*, 113–33; art. '(al-) Djubbā'ī', EI^2 (L. Gardet).
93. Ash., 247f., 575.
94. Based on the obscure passage, Shahr., 57, last five lines (= i. 108 foot), where there are textual difficulties.
95. Ash., 526; what is said about the attributes here is based on Allard (n. 10/92). Ash., 522–37 are almost exclusively about al-Jubbā'ī.
96. Ash., 529f., cf. Allard, 120–2, and Mass., *Passion*, 568.
97. *Attributs*, 132f.
98. Bagh., *Farq*, 169–89; Shahr., 55–9; do., *Nihāyat al-iqdām* (ed. Guillaume, London 1934), 131–49; al-Bāqillānī, *Tamhīd* (ed. Abū-Rīda and al-Khuḍayrī, Cairo 1947), 152–60; do. (ed. R. J. McCarthy, Beirut 1957), 198–212; *Munya*, 94–6; I Khall., ii. 132f. (says born in 861); Sezgin, i. 623 (gives birth in 890); EI^2, art. '(al-)Djubbā'ī'.
99. Ash., 230–2, 358, 557, 602; Bagh., *Farq*, 165–7; Shahr., 53f.; do., *Nihāyat al-iqdām*, index; Sezgin, i. 622f.; EI^2, art. 'al-Balkhī (Abū l-Ḳāsim)' (A. N. Nader; with several false references). He wrote a *K. al-maqālāt* which has been found in ms. but not yet published. In Ash., 582.12 and 602.5 there may be confusion between Balkhī and Thaljī (cf. n. 10/17).
100. A-Ḥusayn 'A-Raḥīm b. Muḥammad al-Khayyāṭ: Bagh., *Farq*, 163–5; Shahr., 53f.; Sezgin, i. 621. Another Mu'tazilite of about the same period was an-Nāshi' (cf. above p. 224 and n. 8/53, 54).
101. Bagh., *Uṣūl*, 42, 50, 87, 116, 231, 234.
102. Ash., 230, 232, 358 (always A-Qāsim -Balkhī).
103. Sezgin, i. 624–6, where other Mu'tazilites are also mentioned. Many were Ḥanafites in *fiqh*; cf. Makdisi, op. cit. (n. 9/29), 291–300.
104. *GAL*, i. 344–50 (*S.*, i. 507–13).
105. *GAL*, i. 222–8.
106. *GAL*, i. 241–53 (*S.*, i. 384–97).
107. *GAL*, i. 267–71 (*S.*, i. 417–21).
108. *GALS*, i. 378f.; art. 'Ibn Masarra' in EI^2 (R. Arnaldez).
109. *GAL*, i. 232–6 (*S.*, i. 375–7); cf. p. 208 above.
110. *MC*, 91.
111. *GAL*, i. 206–8 (*S.*, i. 345f.); Sezgin, i. 602–4; McCarthy, *Theology*; Allard, *Attributs*; George Makdisi, 'Ash'arī and the Ash'arites in Islamic Religious History', *St. Isl.*, xvii (1962), 37–80; xviii (1963), 19–39; I'Asākir, *Tabyīn*; Subk., ii. 245–301 (from 254 mostly about followers); I Khall., ii. 227f.
112. Cf. n. 10/55. Subk., ii. 248, denies he was a Mālikī, and

says he was a pupil of AIs'ḥāq al-Marwazī, but he has no notice of this man.

113. I'Asākir, *Tabyīn*, 40–3 (summarized in McCarthy, *Theology*, 152–5); Wilhelm Spitta, *Zur Geschichte Abu'l-Hasan al-As'ari's*, Leipzig 1876, 47–9. (The source of the version in *Tabyīn*, 42, is an associate of al-Bāqillānī, and this is about as early as any information about al-Ash'arī.)

114. Subk., ii. 250f.; Spitta, op. cit., 41ff.; I Khall., ii. 669f.; at-Taftazānī (d. 1389), *A Commentary on the Creed of Islam*, tr. E. E. Elder, New York 1950, 9.

115. *Iḥyā'*, Book 2 (*Risāla Qudsiyya*), *rukn* 3, *aṣl* 7; *Iqtiṣād* (ed. Çubukçu and Atay, Ankara 1962), 184f. The lateness of the sources was noted by Michael Schwarz in an Oxford D.Phil. thesis. Cf. also McCarthy, *Theology*, 156n.

116. I'Asākir, *Tabyīn*, 91; McCarthy, 155f.

117. I'Asākir, 39; McCarthy, 151. It is unlikely, however, that he had already completed books in refutation of Mu'tazilism.

118. I'Asākir, *Tabyīn*, 51–5; McCarthy, 157.

119. *Attributs*, 48–72. George Makdisi partly anticipates his dissection of the *Maqālāt* (*St. Isl.* xviii. 26–30), but reaches different conclusions in other respects.

120. *MC*, 88–91; Ash., *Ibāna*, 13–23 (tr. 56–65).

121. *Ibāna*, 17 (tr. 60).

122. *Ibāna*, 18f. (tr. 61f.)

123. McCarthy, *Theology*, §§68–81.

124. Khay., 164–8.

124a. In van Ess, *Naẓẓām* (n. 8/27), 118, an-Naẓẓām is described by al-Jāḥiẓ as one of the *ḥuffāẓ al-ḥadīth*.

125. *Ibāna*, 64f. (tr. 104).

126. I'Asākir, *Tabyīn*, 135; McCarthy, *Theology*, 227, nos. 84, 86.

127. The *Apology* is ed. and tr. by A. Mingana in *Woodbrooke Studies*, II (Cambridge 1928), 1–162; see esp. 43–6.

128. 2 *Samuel*, 12.9.

129. 'New Sources for the History of Muhammadan Theology', *Isl.*, i. (1953), 23–42, esp. 33–6.

130. McCarthy, *Theology*, Ar. text, 33.8, 13, 18; 46.3; 47.2, 11.

131. Al-Maqdisī (Muqaddasī), *Aḥsan at-taqāsīm*, Leiden 1885, 37; tr. G. S. A. Ranking and R. F. Azoo (Bibliotheca Indica, 137), Calcutta 1897 etc., 52, 54. The year 985 was that of the first draft, but this passage might belong to the revision some years later. Al-Pazdawī, op. cit. (n. 9/26), 242 (cf. 2 and index s.v.—Qaṭṭān) speaks as if Kullābiyya still existed in the later eleventh century.

132. I'Asākir, *Tabyīn*, 125, 398n.

133. Ibid., 177, 178, 183–8; cf. McCarthy, *Theology*, 429.

134. IA-Wafā', ii. 130f.; IQ'bghā, no. 173; *EI*[1], art. 'al-Māturīdī' (D.B. Macdonald); as-Sayyid al-Murtaḍā (d. 1791), *It'ḥāf as-sāda* (Cairo 1893), ii. 5–15; Sezgin, i. 604–6; *GALS*, i. 346; Vajda, at n. 7/23 above.
135. Cf. Sezgin. Thus Laleli 2411/12 (foll. 16–31) has a reference to 'Ashʿariyya' (fol. 19v.) which suggests a date not earlier than about A.D. 1000.
136. Cf. *GALS*, i. 346 foot, quoting J. Spiro, Proceedings of 13th *International Congress of Orientalists* (Leiden 1904), 292–5. Most of the other material is mentioned in Kholeif's introduction to Mtrd., *Tawḥīd*, 7*–9*. The problem is discussed by Louis Gardet in *St. Isl.*, xxxii (1970), 135–9.
137. Spitta, op. cit. (n. 10/113): repeated by Klein, introduction to translation of *Ibāna*, 37. Cf. Max Horten, *Die philosophische Systeme der spekulativen Theologen im Islam*, Bonn 1912, 531.
138. Cf. above 131–4; Mtrd., *Tawḥīd*, 373–9. Also Manfred Götz, 'Māturīdī und sein Kitāb Ta'wīlāt al-Qur'ān', *Isl.*, xli (1965), 27–70, esp. 57–63.
139. Arts. 17/18, 16/17 (from *Maqālāt/Ibāna* as numbered by McCarthy, *Theology*, 236–54); for Muʿtazila cf. 235 above.
140. *Tawḥīd*, 239, 263; cf. Götz, op. cit., 52–7. For the resemblance to the Muʿtazila cf. al-Pazdawī, *Uṣūl ad-dīn* (n. 9/26), 207, 210 (ref. from van Ess, *Erkenntnislehre* [n. 9/30], 327).
141. Ash., 542.8f., his own definition; cf. above 192–4.
142. *Tawḥīd*, 91; cf. 235, 369.
143. *Tawḥīd*, 388–92; it is implicitly denied in *Fiqh akbar*, §6. For the Ḥanbalites, etc., cf. above 138f.
144. Bagh., *Uṣūl*, 253; cf. McCarthy, *Theology*, 92 (§155); Louis Gardet, *Dieu et la destinée de l'homme*, Paris 1967, 388–390.
145. *Tawḥīd*, 325; cf. above 137f.
146. Creeds (as n. 10/139), §§32/29a, 27/29b, 31/28.
147. *Tawḥīd*, 220.5; 44–9. *Lumaʿ* (in *Theology*), §§18–26; etc.
148. Ash., 508; the attribution of this distinction to Jahm or the Jahmiyya (Laoust, *Ibn-Taymiyya*, 158) is doubtless a Ḥanbalite way of saying the same thing.
149. *Tawḥīd*, 47; Götz (n. 10/138), 49–51; cf. *Fiqh akbar II*, §§2, 16.
150. Ash., 545.
151. *Farq*, 327; cf. 207 and *Uṣūl*, 122. Cf. al-Bāqillānī, *Tamhīd* (n. 10/29), 263 top.
152. 21f.

Index

Ghundar, 111, 340 n. 108
Gibb, Sir Hamilton, 173
God
abandoning, 93, 200, 233–4, 315
and evil, 238–42
as creator, 290
attributes of: Abū-Hāshim, 300; active, 199, 287, 290, 299, 316; Aḥmad ibn-Ḥanbal, 310; al-Ash'arī, 310, 316; Ash'arite, 287; Bishr, 198–9; Ḍirār, 195; essential, 199, 242, 287, 290, 299, 316; eternal, 290, 316; Hishām, 188; hypostatic character of, 242; al-Jubbā'ī, 298–300; Karrāmites, 290; al-Māturīdī, 316; Mu'tazilites, 245–6, 316; an-Najjār, 201; negative character of man's knowledge of, 195, 201; seven essential, 287
concern with upright conduct, 91, 92
delegating responsibility to man, 301–2
doing the best for man, 239–40
eternity, 287
favour, 200, 233, 239, 298–9
fixing evil upon, 96, 97, 238–9
forgiveness, 92–3
generosity of, 241
goodness of, 90, 91, 233
grace, 298–9
gratitude to, 90
guiding, 90, 93, 200, 233, 234
hearing, 287, 289
help and succour, 93, 233, 234, 315
Ibn-Kullāb's doctrine, 287
imposing duties on man, 240
inscrutability, 298
justice, 98, 192, 212
knowledge, God's, 233, 242, 245–6, 287, 316
Last Judgement by, 90, 91, 92–3
leading astray, 90, 93, 102, 200, 233–4
life, 287
living by himself, 246
mercifulness, 92, 114
modes or states, 300
names properly applied to, 299
names, reducing the number of, 301
omnipotence, 90, 91, 106, 192, 298; and justice, 192–3; and man's responsibility, 234, 238–9
power, 242, 245, 287
seeing, 287, 289
speech, 242, 287
transcendence, 247,–8
unity, internal, 210
unity of, 200, 207, 212, 242–9
will, 287
worship of, 90
Goldziher, Ignaz, 2, 59, 64, 67, 119, 215–16, 314
Gondēshāpūr, school at, 183
government
central: weakness of, 254; working of, *see* administration
Ḥanbalite acceptance of, 292–3
al-Ḥasan's attitude to, 79–80
Khārijite(s): acceptance of other, 28–9; as rebels against, 16; justification for rebellion, 34; view of Qur'ānic principles as basis for, 20, 22, 28
manuals on, 171
Persian tradition in, 171
governorships
hereditary provincial, 254
'Uthmān's disposition of, 10
grace
and human acts, 291
al-Jubbā'ī's view, 298–9
state of, 291
grave sinner
as: a believer, 17, 80, 120, 121, 126, 133, 191, 210, 229; a hypocrite, 17, 24, 80, 120,